Psychotherapy
of
Schizophrenia

PSYCHOTHERAPY
of
SCHIZOPHRENIA

The Treatment of Choice

BERTRAM P. KARON, Ph.D.
GARY R. VANDENBOS, Ph.D.

Jason Aronson Inc.
Northvale, New Jersey
London

Library of Congress Cataloging in Publication Data

Karon, Bertram P.
  Psychotherapy of schizophrenia.

  Bibliography : p. 473
  Includes index.
  1. Schizophrenia. I. VandenBos, Gary R. II. Title.
[DNLM: 1. Psychotherapy. 2. Schizophrenia—Therapy.
WM 203 K185p]
RC514.K273   616.89'82   81-65785
ISBN 0-87668-444-4   AACR2

Manufactured in the United States of America.
Jason Aronson Inc. offers books and cassettes.
For information and catalog write to
Jason Aronson Inc.
230 Livingston Street
Northvale, N.J. 07647

To several people who have been important to us and our work whose untimely deaths prevented them from seeing the completion of this work,

        Edward S. Karon,
        Stanley G. Ratner,
        Thomas D. Tierney,
        Paul M. VandenBos.

Contents

Preface

The statement that psychotherapy is the treatment of choice for schizophrenic patients raises two broad questions, the first concerning the empirical basis for such a statement, and the second concerning how such psychotherapy should be carried out. The answer to the first question lies in the clinical observations of the many human beings who were once schizophrenic and have been successfully treated by psychotherapists of various theoretical schools and in the more rigorously controlled empirical data of the Michigan State Psychotherapy Project. The answer to the second question lies in an extended discussion of theory and therapeutic procedure.

What one person or a few people know is of little value. Some versions of psychoanalytic therapy are not helpful to schizophrenic patients, and others are. We have been urged repeatedly by colleagues to compile an extended description of our view of schizophrenia and the appropriate treatment, along with the data that validate its effectiveness. This book is the result.

We have attempted to write this book in nonsexist language, as we are aware that both patients and therapists may be of either gender. We have achieved this goal imperfectly. We find the language style of chapters 1 through 5 and 10 to be acceptable and closest to our intent. We hope the language usage in the other sections will not offend or prove too cumbersome for female readers.

Acknowledgments

The senior author would like to acknowledge the people who helped form his ideas. While they are, of course, not responsible for the flaws in this volume, their ideas greatly influenced the book: Edward S. Karon, Ph.D., who first taught me that psychoanalytic therapy used flexibly is a powerful tool for alleviating human suffering; Silvan S. Tomkins, Ph.D., who insisted on the necessity for a broad scholarly knowledge of both traditional and innovative theories and relevant data, while encouraging the development of my independent views; Richard Sterba, M.D., who renewed and developed much further my understanding of psychoanalysis as a humane and intellectually exciting basis for effective clinical work; as well as Jack Rosberg, M.A. and Maxim F. Young, Ph.D., two colleagues whose innumerable hours of discussion, argument, and encouragement were invaluable, and my other principal clinical teachers—S. Roy Heath, Ph.D., Irving E. Alexander, Ph.D., Channing Lipson, M.D., and Viggo Jensen, M.D.

The junior author would like to express his appreciation to the individuals who helped to shape his clinical perspective and career. At Michigan State University, Bill L. Kell, Ph.D., Donald Grummon, Ph.D., Gershen Kaufman, Ph.D., and Griffith Freed, Ph.D. provided significant instruction, supervision, and support in addition to numerous and extensive discussions of theory and technique with Bert Karon. At the University of Detroit, Max Hutt, M.D., Robert O'Neil, Ph.D., Edward Wallon, Ph.D., and Etta Saxe, Ph.D. provided valuable clinical instruction and supervision. At the Howell-Area Community Mental Health Center, the supervision of Melvin Weinberg, Ph.D., Richard Zipper, M.S.W., Ph.D., Beverly Anderson, M.D., Herbert Silverman, Ph.D., Marvin Hyman, Ph.D., and Ann Andrews, M.S.W., were valuable and meaningful, as were my frequent clinical discussions with two important colleagues—Larry Newburg, M.A. and Patricia Hughes, M.S.W.

Both of us would like to express our appreciation to the following members of the Michigan State Psychotherapy Project reported in chapter 10: Paul J. O'Grady, Ph.D., Thomas D. Tierney, M.D., Leon Berman, M.D., Stanley Schonbuch, Ph.D., James Crowder, Ph.D., Howard Porter, Ph.D., Mohommed Ali Shami, M.D., Cheryl Lessin, M.A., Diane B. Humanansky, M.D., Edward Lessin, Ph.D., George Kates, Ph.D., Victor Pacheco, M.D., Andrew Pasternak, M.D., Susan Van Slambrouck, Ph.D., Alvin Robbins, M.D., Ross Carter, Ph.D., Frank Long, Ph.D., Charles Glatt, Ph.D., Erma Alperson, Ph.D., Gerritt DeYoung, Ph.D., Michael Miller, Ph.D., Janet Bullock, M.A., Christopher Pino, M.A., and Inta Silins, B.S.

We would also like to thank Kenneth Pitts, M.D., and the staff of the Detroit Psychiatric Institute, particularly Jacob Wertz, M.D., Bruce Danto, M.D., Richard Ruzumna, M.D., and Bernard Chodorkoff, Ph.D., M.D. for their cooperation. In addition, we appreciate the cooperation and assistance of Calvin H. Chen, M.D. and Eugene S. Martinovsky, M.D. of Northville State Hospital, and Alexander P. DuKay, M.D. and Joseph Mann, M.D. of Ypsilanti State Hospital in following our control patients.

We also express our appreciation to the National Institute of Mental Health, whose grant (MH 08790) provided the bulk of the support for the Michigan State Psychotherapy Project reported in chapter 10, and to Michigan State University for several grants which supported data analyses and some of the writing.

Finally, we wish to express our appreciation to Ms. Kathy Sharp, Ms. Carla Waltz, Ms. Anne Hatch, Ms. Mary Scott, and Ms. Betty Simon for their assistance in the preparation of this manuscript.

Psychotherapy
of
Schizophrenia

1

Lessons

The patient sat cross-legged in the middle of his bed; his arms were folded. He was making a clicking noise with his tongue. When I touched him gently on the shoulder, he fell off the bed as if he were made of stone, and he was still rigid when he hit the floor. Whenever I approached him, he would get up and run to the farthest corner, saying, "Don't hit me! Don't hit me! Don't hit me!"

"I won't hit you. I promise you I won't hit you," I replied.

"Not you, *him*," he said, pointing to the center of the room.

This was my first schizophrenic patient, and from this patient I learned that fifteen years of terrible, chronic disability could be remedied by psychotherapy.

The man sat there, rigid, tied to a chair. He had to be fed. A bottle had been put in place to collect his urine. He was catatonic and had been catatonic continuously for 5 years, but he would on occasion erupt into motion, yelling one word ("You!" or "Room!" or "Dear!") and swinging—at thin air, at anyone who was present, or at himself. It did not matter to him, but since he was very muscular it mattered to his victim. He suffered from urinary and fecal incontinence, and he defecated only once every 6 weeks. His

1

digestive processes were slowed, his skin bruised easily, and it healed slowly. He had been disturbed most of his life, but the symptoms had not always been as severe as they were now. He had been treated unsuccessfully at some of the best treatment centers in the United States.

What I learned from this patient was that even the most withdrawn of schizophrenic patients can be reached if the therapist is persistent and knowledgeable. Even though, in this case, the treatment at times reached heroic proportions—10 hours a day for 10 days with two therapists, before this patient uttered a single intelligible word—it was possible (though possibly not economically feasible on a large scale) to treat this patient successfully by psychotherapy.

The patient was an incarcerated delinquent adolescent male.

"I get these nightmares," he said. "I keep getting the same dream over and over every night, my stepmother beating me with a stick. I wake up and it keeps on going. I still get the nightmare. She keeps on beating me after I wake up. What I want to know is, if I run away from here and kill her, will the dream stop?"

From this patient, I learned how quickly acute schizophrenic patients can remit and function nonpsychotically if they have not been previously subjected to mishandling. After a week of treatment (five sessions), this individual was no longer psychotic.

The man bowed from the waist as he had in each of his earlier sessions. I asked him why he was bowing. "I don't bow," he said. I imitated his bow.

"That's not bowing," he said.

"What is it?"

"Balancing."

"Balancing what?"

"Emotions."

"What emotions?"

"Fear and loneliness."

This man described the dilemma of living schizophrenic—feeling lonely and moving toward people, then feeling scared and moving away from them. These patients are so overwhelmed that they can only try to resolve the problem symbolically in a realm (his bodily motions) seemingly far removed from the critical problem.

He was one of the patients in a rigorously designed controlled experiment comparing psychotherapy with currently available treatment, namely medication. The project taught me that even a small amount of meaningful psychotherapy (an average of seventy sessions) is more effective than medication in the long run and surprisingly enough, it is less costly.

This book represents an attempt to share what all of these people have taught the authors throughout their careers. Not everything is known about schizophrenia, any more than is known about human beings in general, but we do know enough about it to treat with success people who are labeled schizophrenic. The treatment of choice is clearly psychotherapy, by a knowledgeable and persevering therapist.

The Schizophrenic Patient

Patients are frightened, confused, usually lonely, and often angry human beings. They know they are different from other human beings, and that their experiences have been different from others. They notice that other people frequently do not react kindly toward them because of these differences.

They do not understand what is happening to them or what has caused it. Nor do they know what to expect of the future. In general, they do not expect anything very good. They try to understand what is happening to them, and because their experiences are unusual, their explanations are apt to be unusual. Probably they have learned that the professionals do not agree with each other, and professionals, as well as the popular culture, may have led them to believe they suffer from a genetic-physiologic "disease" that is incurable and with which they must therefore live forever. Treatment, they may have been told, must be perpetual and will at best ameliorate their symptoms. They must not expect too much.

Yet the genetic and physiologic evidence is at best questionable: at most, these are contributing, not causative factors. The outcome of treatment with psychotherapy can be as successful and as long-lasting for schizophrenic patients as it is for neurotic patients, but the journey may be longer and it may take more time to traverse.

The Patient's Family

The patient's family members are often as victimized as the patient. They too are confused and frightened by the disorder. There seems to be no logical connection between anything they know and the severe disturbance their child is now suffering. They struggle with fear and anger and misery and guilt. They ask themselves what they have done wrong and how could this happen? They have been good parents, they think.

It is generally believed in our society that the development of children is to a large extent the result of what their parents do. Consequently, when a child develops emotional problems, the parents begin to torture themselves with self-doubt and guilt. They may seize on genetic and physiologic explanations to assuage their self-reproaches, but the tactic is usually only partially successful. Unfortunately, it may prevent them from seeking psychotherapy for their child. Or they may seek help from a therapist on whom they project their punishing superegos. They perceive him or her as condemning them for having destroyed their child, whether or not such a view is held.

Schizophrenia is a complex disorder; its causes in any one individual are equally complex. For any human being, the most important human influences *are* one's parents, and this is as true for schizophrenic individuals as for normal human beings. For most schizophrenic patients there is a relationship between their childhood, especially their relations with their parents, and their later disturbance. But the parents of schizophrenic individuals are not criminals. They are victims.

Most parents of schizophrenic patients are decent people who would not knowingly hurt their children. Insofar as there is a parental factor in the psychology of schizophrenia, it is, in general, of unconscious origin; that is, the parents have a symptom, over which they have no control since they have no conscious awareness of it. The nature of this symptom has not been well known. We have termed it *pathogenesis*, because it has the effect of making the child vulnerable to severe emotional disorders. A considerable amount of work has gone into delineating this concept, demonstrating that it is measurable, and its nature and effects have been studied.

The parents of schizophrenic offspring are not culpable human beings, but people who could have been helped by appropriate counseling or psychotherapy if enough had been known about their symptoms. Unfortunately, no such help has been available. It is our hope that further exploration will lead to the availability of such preventive intervention. Our experience leads us to believe that most parents of schizophrenic patients would have made use of appropriate help in order to prevent the later suffering of their children *if* their problem had been discovered.

The Therapist

It is one of the anomalies of psychotherapy in our society that the best trained and most experienced psychotherapists, the fully trained psychoanalysts, typically treat neurotic patients possessing social and economic resources sufficient to receive treatment three to five times per week, while the least trained and most inexperienced therapists are apt to be assigned the most severely disturbed psychotic patients, who often have little by way of social or economic resources. The latter type of therapists are expected to carry out the treatment in very restricted periods of time, so it is no wonder that they so frequently feel overwhelmed.

The inexperienced therapist becomes aware of a conflicting mass of scientific literature which presents many contradictory theories, none of which are entirely convincing. Most of these theories do not recommend psychotherapy with such patients. Genetics and physiology have been frequently presented in such rationalizations. Even in the psychoanalytic literature supposedly good reasons are advanced for not attempting psychoanalysis with schizophrenic patients, who are "narcissistic," they say, and incapable of a transference or not capable of making use of a psychotherapeutic relationship.

Colleagues of the therapist may be uncooperative, discouraging, resentful, or even scornful of his or her efforts. The patient's condition is outside the bounds of what the therapist's training has led him to believe is treatable. Also, the patient may seem uncooperative and is not likely to let the therapist know when he is being helpful. The patient's family may seem overtly or covertly hostile to the therapist's efforts. This is because they are trying to cope with anxiety by showing hostility, anxiety that may not seem clear to them.

The patient may seem insensitive to everything except the therapist's weak spots. He may be fiendishly adept at arousing anxiety, guilt, anger, or feelings of incompetence. Yet if the therapist can tolerate discomfort and return to the patient, doing the best possible work given that setting and the limited time available, schizophrenic patients will recover. Luckily, the experience of having a patient who was considered hopeless but who recovered as a result of psychotherapy is a benign trauma from which the therapist rarely recovers. It is our hope that sharing our experiences will help to arrange that benign trauma a little more frequently.

2

Historical
Introduction

The current confusions as to cause and treatment of schizophrenia have been with us for a long time. From the days of the ancient Greeks onward, the causes of insanity were thought to be fearful experiences, possession by demons, curses inflicted by God or the gods, diseased brains, tainted families, and disordered metabolism (humors). Both scientific and magical theories may be used kindly or cruelly. Scientific treatments based on the empirical knowledge available to a period are not necessarily more effective than unscientific ones. Magical remedies are frequently selected on the basis of experience so that more helpful procedures may be continued, even if their original rationale would not be accepted by later generations. Thus, the use of tranquilizers by twentieth-century Western human beings came from nonliterate cultures that had used rauwolfia for centuries.

Early Treatment of Schizophrenic Patients

From ancient times onward, treatments for schizophrenia have ranged from kindness, and soothing medications, to restraints, cruelty, and even putting the unfortunate sufferer to death. The same belief as to causation, e.g., possesion by demons (which we now understand as "the split-off bad self" or "the introjected bad parent") could lead equally well either to a benign attempt to save the victim from the demon, or to a sadistic attempt to torture the victim in order to make his body inhospitable to the demon. The victim might even be murdered—either to save his soul in an after-life, or simply to punish him for having made a bargain with the demon. (We now understand these punitive procedures as the "treaters" punishing their own bad selves projected onto the patient, or destroying their own unconscious repressed tendencies.)

Punishing procedures, whether magical or "scientific," may be used with explicit recognition of their punitive aspect, or with a theory that suggests that the painful and/or frightening procedure is good for the patient. The ancient Greeks applied electric eels to the heads of some unfortunates. In the modern era, electric shock treatment has been used both as an "aversive stimulus" or because "epilepsy is inconsistent with schizophrenia." From the patient's standpoint, the rationale makes little difference.

For reasons that will become clear later in this book, pain, torture, or overwhelming fear will produce behavioral improvement in schizophrenic individuals. There is, thus, some empirical validity to the effectiveness of very painful or frightening treatments. Since schizophrenic patients are already frightened people, an immediate greater terror will often produce greater behavioral conformity. Unfortunately, this is the aim of many treatments, scientific and nonscientific alike, without the aim of cure, that is, without the aim of producing the capacity to live a relatively normal life in society.

Paradoxically, scientific theories may be used to justify cruelty, as in the use of aversive stimuli (pain) in behavior modification, even though the animal experiments on which the dominant learning theory of our time (that of Skinner) is based suggest that punishment is a poor basis for learning. Or in the use of dialysis machines to remove an unknown, hypothetical blood factor, as if it were not already well known that the dialysis machine is so unpleasant that many patients with defective kidneys who could live indefinitely with its help choose to die rather than to continue living by using it. Schizophrenic patients subjected to daily dialysis may well improve their behavior when placed on a once-per-month regime with the understanding that the daily dialysis will start again if the doctor decides they "need" it.

Equally paradoxically, magical beliefs may lead to benign and helpful treatments. Most striking was the founding of the shrine of St. Dympna at Gheel in Belgium around the seventh century. Because of the belief that there were magical restorative qualities inherent in the area where a miracle had occurred, seriously psychotic individuals have been brought to the town from the seventeenth century onward to this day. In order to stay in the vicinity of the "magic," the patients were left there by their own families to live with local families in a benign atmosphere, a practice which has continued. The benign human interaction led to a "magical" restoration in many cases.

The mass murders of so-called "witches" in the sixteenth and seventeenth centuries, the executions in Nazi Germany of mental patients, and the present-day sterilization of mental patients in some states in the United States—three "eugenic experiments" with differing rationales—all have proved the futility of such approaches. Not one decreased the incidence of mental disorders in the next generation.

Moral Treatment

The beginnings of modern psychiatry and modern treatment of mental illness were a result of the accession of Dr. Philippe Pinel (1745–1826) to the Bicêtre in Paris. It took the French Revolution to allow Pinel to introduce what he and similar workers referred to as "moral treatment." Textbooks report that he ended the humiliation and torture of patients. The patients were taken out of their chains, and many recovered. The early "moral treatment" practitioners were not by any means perfect, however. Pinel, who greatly improved the status of the patients under his care, nonetheless could not abide patients who were lazy and refused to work, patients who stole, and patients who were religious fanatics. He would regularly give up on such patients and maintain them in cells in the middle of the institution, which was hardly better than the treatment afforded all of the patients in the institution before he took charge (Magaro 1976).

Only recently has the effectiveness of Pinel's method and that of the other moral treatment therapists been rediscovered. In France, in Scotland, in England, and in the United States, where records have been kept of the discharge rates and recovery rates in the same hospitals during and after the moral treatment era, it is found that there were 60 to 80 percent discharge rates during the height of this period (i.e., the first part of the nineteenth century). Strangely enough, discharge rates dropped to 20 to 30 percent by the end of the nineteenth century, while psychiatry was congratulating itself on how scientific it was becoming and the great strides it was making. The truly scientific empiricism that would ask how many patients were getting better was absent during this period. The data on the effectiveness of moral treatment and the lack of effectiveness of its successors were not unearthed and discussed until the rate of discharge in the 1960s approached those achieved in the earlier era (Bockoven 1972).

We would normally assume that if a particular treatment is effective, it will be adopted, and certainly once adopted it will not be abandoned, unless a more effective treatment is developed. Unfortunately, this is not true. While there are other examples in the history of medicine, psychology, and psychiatry, moral treatment provides us with an instructive case history.

Its Nature

What *was* moral treatment? Moral treatment meant psychologic treatment; its principles were deceptively simple.

The first principle was to eliminate cruelty. Physical force was to be used only to prevent a patient from hurting himself or herself or someone else. It was not to be used as punishment, it was not to be used sadistically, nor was it to be used lightly. Self-evident as this humanitarian principle might seem, even today such a rule is difficult to enforce in most institutions. Frightened members of a hospital staff are often cruel. One of the benign side-effects of the introduction of tranquilizers in the twentieth century was the diminution of fear on the part of hospital personnel. With the assurance of a technique of control that does not require violent intervention, the reassured staff is more often able to be kind and humane.

The second principle was if you could not help the patient, don't do anything that would injure him. This is a sound principle of medicine dating back to Hippocrates, but one that is also hard to carry out consistently. Thus, the patients were not to be subjected to humiliation and contempt, or to physical cruelty.

The third principle of moral treatment was to keep accurate case histories. It was Pinel's view that his patients were sick people and that if he kept an accurate case history, or at least as accurate a history as could be obtained, he would learn something about his patient; he might eventually learn something about such patients in general.

The last principle, and the one that is responsible both for the power and the weakness of moral treatment, is that you must do what you can to understand the patient as an *individual human being*. Patients were to get individual attention and to be encouraged to live as normal a life as their condition and the institution permitted, with the aim of restoring them to a normal place in society. Productive work was seen as a good thing, just as it was viewed in the outside world. Depressing, destructive elements in the institution were to be minimized; productive, interesting elements were to be encouraged.

ITS IMPLEMENTATION

Doing your best to understand the patient as an individual human being required considerable specific attention to that individual person. The measures to be taken were, therefore, not clear. Moral treatment meant various things to various hospitals and to various practitioners. The common elements have been mentioned above.

Samuel Tuke (1784-1857), in England, had a version of moral treatment that emphasized tea parties. Tuke had noticed that psychoses were more common among the less affluent, and he believed that this could be explained by the fact that they had not had the privileges that the upper classes had had. His version of moral treatment included preparing the patient to act appropriately at a daily tea party. When the patient could dress, act, and talk appropriately in that setting, he was considered appropriately dischargeable. While this form of moral treatment may strike us as slightly absurd, nonetheless it is a fact that each patient got detailed individual attention, had a situation to look forward to, and a goal to be achieved. The criterion situation involved a somewhat elaborate interpersonal activity; this is certainly at least as good as many of the criteria currently used to assess mental and emotional functioning. Undoubtedly, Lewis Carroll was familiar with the mad tea parties of Tuke. In fact, "mad hatters" were not unusual; organic psychoses, resulting from the toxic materials used in their trade, were common among hatters.

ITS RESULTS

The effectiveness of moral treatment has been a matter of dispute. The most impressive figures come from those hospitals that practiced moral treatment and then discontinued it, but supposedly used the same criteria for discharge during both periods. Thus the Worcester (Massachusetts) State Hospital, for example, in the period 1833 to 1837 discharged as "recovered" 70 percent of those patients who had been ill less than 1 year, and 8 percent were discharged as "improved." In the years 1848 to 1857 the figures were nearly as good: 61 percent "recovered," and 5 percent "improved." By the end of the nineteenth century, the discharge rate as "recovered" was down to 20 to 30 percent.

Various critics have assailed the statistics, suggesting that some of the patients who were discharged as "recovered" came back to the hospital, and that there existed hospitals that claimed 100 percent recovery. The most influential criticism was that of Pliny Earle (1809–1892), who maintained that the discharge and recovery rates were inflated. But even Dr. Earle's own figures show a marked decrease in recovery rate in the subsequent period.

John G. Park, a contemporary of Earle, went over the Worcester (Mass.) State Hospital figures using his own stringent criteria of recovery rather than the hospital's. Using all admissions, not just first admissions, he reported a much lower recovery rate. In the period between 1833 and 1862, according to Park, the rate of recovery was only between 45 and 48 percent. Nonetheless, his figures show a steady decline, so that in the period 1882 to 1902 the recovery rate was approximately 20 percent. From 1920 to 1950, the recovery rate, using Park's criteria, was 10 to 15 percent. Thus, even the critics of moral treatment, while denying its high level of efficacy, report that the procedures employed after moral treatment were much less effective, even though these critics ignore the implications of those facts.

How then can it be that a treatment that was effective was succeeded by a treatment that was less effective, and no one noticed the difference? Actually, both psychiatry and society at large were congratulating themselves on how scientific and humanitarian psychiatric treatment was becoming.

THE FATE OF MORAL TREATMENT

The first cause of the abandonment of moral treatment was educational. The moral treatment practitioners did not bother to train a second generation in the principles of moral treatment. It is not clear whether this was because they felt that no special training was required, that common sense (whatever that means) would suffice, or because they thought moral treatment was an art that could not be taught. Whatever their reason, they were shortsighted, because when the first generation of moral treatment practitioners died, so did moral treatment. The lesson from this is that when we have evolved an effective treatment, teach it to others, so that they can build on what is known rather than beginning all over again on their own.

The second cause of the abandonment of moral treatment had to do with the sociology of scientific development. The keeping of accurate case histories on mental patients made possible the description of hypothesized disease entities which might be correlated with specific causes. An understanding of general paresis was, of course, the great triumph of this record-keeping. The discovery of a specific set of symptoms, with a specific outcome— progressive paralysis, dementia, paranoid delusions, with the motor symptoms progressing to death—eventually led to the discovery of the relationship of paresis to a previous history of syphilis. This led first to the malaria treatment for paresis, and eventually to the use of antibiotics, as in any other form of syphilitic infection. It should be noted that the remarkable discharge and recovery rates with moral treatment were achieved despite the fact that the patient population included those with organic psychoses, like general paresis, for which no such benign outcome is possible.

Unfortunately, paresis is unique among major causes of psychoses. The development by Emil Kraepelin (1856–1926) of disease entities and the frantic search for physical causes have not yielded consistent results that stand the test of time. The major breakthrough—the discovery of the physical cause for schizophrenia or for manic-depressive psychoses—is announced again and again and again, only to be given up with the passage of time and the accumulation of more information. Nonetheless, the tremendous strides that were occurring in physical medicine at that time, especially the discovery of physical disease entities, made anything that was not a search for the physical cause "unscientific." Psychiatry prided itself on how "scientific" it was, because it, too, had diagnostic categories, disease entities, and presumed physical or infectious causes. The fact that patients no longer got better was not relevant to the march of "science." As D. O. Hebb (1951) has suggested, one should always phrase a theory in psychology or psychiatry as if it represented known physiology. The same theory will be accepted if it is so phrased, and rejected if it is phrased in terms that do not represent physiologic entities, even if the physiology is entirely speculative.

The third cause of the abandonment of moral treatment was sociologic. Paradoxically, the abandonment of effective moral treatment came about through humanitarian reforms. In the United States, the reforms of Dorothea Dix (1802–1887) removed mental patients from the reformatories and jails and put them in mental hospitals. This vastly increased the number of known mental patients, and it became apparent that the bulk of severely disturbed mental patients were poor. It also became clear that immigrants had a higher rate of severe psychoses. The social status of the patient was dropping. Concomitant with this, the status of the physician was rising. This had several consequences.

The sheer number of patients in mental hospitals increased, and, hence, the number of patients per doctor increased in a way that made attention to individuals difficult, but this was easily rationalized. At this time (the latter half of the nineteenth century), social Darwinism was a dominant theory. The poor were poor because they deserved to be poor; the rich were rich because they deserved to be rich. It was presumed that these qualities were hereditary. Immigrant groups were poor and had less education. Their higher rates of insanity were presumed to be proof of defective stock. (Such arguments have been used in turn to describe Irish, Italian, Jewish, Chinese, and Japanese immigrants. Unfortunately, they are still used today to describe Black and Hispanic individuals. Each immigrant group in turn has been considered impossible to educate or to integrate. With the passage of time and availability of opportunities, the apparent basis for such judgments of each group has disappeared.)

Nonetheless in the nineteenth century the phrase "pauper immigrant insane" was used as if each of these was a crime. If these people were insane, it was not worth worrying about, because, even when not insane, the poor and the immigrants were not of much value anyway.

Previously in the United States, mental patients and their doctors were compatible with each other. They came from the same ethnic group as well as from the same social class. When the social class and ethnic group of the patients changed, they had much less in common with their doctors. With the enhanced status of the doctor and the decreased status of the patient, it was not worth the doctor's trouble to talk at length to any of them.

The final cause of the abandonment of moral treatment was economic. The large increase in the number of patients meant that a similarly large increase in the number of doctors and institutions would be required. Most of the advocates of moral treatment felt that no more than 200 patients could reasonably be treated in a single institution. The humanitarian reforms of Dorothea Dix had a paradoxical effect in that the numbers of patients to be taken care of required exceeding these bounds and undertaking a massive hospital construction program.

The new, indigent patients could not afford to pay for their own treatment, and so that burden fell upon state governments. State governments in the nineteenth century, as in the twentieth or any other century, were never overjoyed with new financial burdens; however, one state hospital superintendent, Pliny Earle, discovered a way to make the state hospital economically self-sufficient. His procedures were immediately popular with state legislatures, and he became the model of the state hospital superintendent.

Earle had begun as a moral treatment advocate. His version of moral treatment, however, was to give lectures to sizable numbers of patients assembled together in one place. That kind of moral treatment did not prove effective. He studied European hospitals and developed an admiration for the German institutions. They were well run and efficient, and the patients were well taken care of physically; the accounting department was particularly efficient. When Earle became superintendent of Northampton (Massachusetts) State Hospital, he instituted a hospital regime that was orderly and efficient. Patients were well cared for physically; the accounting department was equally efficient.

In keeping with the precepts of most moral treatment practitioners, Earle valued productive work; however, he relied on it in a way that was unique. He started a farm as a part of the hospital. The farm was so successful with patients doing the work that it paid the expenses of the institution. Soon all state mental hospitals had farms as part of their operation, and this continued well into the twentieth century.

At first, the farms could be justified as vocational rehabilitation, and they continued to be justified on this basis even though the United States became less and less a rural farming nation. With most patients coming from urban communities where farm skills were irrelevant to obtaining jobs, and with the increased efficiency of American farms, so that there was a surplus rather than a shortage of farm labor, it became harder and harder to maintain this rationale for the continuance of the state hospital farm. But the economics of the situation made the farm imperative.

If the farm was to support the institution, who was to be used as farm labor? One certainly does not hire laborers in the open market, for the state hospital farm then would be no more profitable than any other farm and would certainly not support the costs of the institution. If inmates are used to run the farm, the very sick cannot be used or the farm would not be productive. Indeed, the very sick would most likely come to physical harm since, as any farmer knows, farm work can be dangerous if one does not keep one's wits about one. Therefore, it was necessary to have a large number of inmates working on the farm who were not very sick. Under those circumstances it was not surprising that the low discharge and recovery rates were not a cause of great alarm; the patients were necessary if the system were to continue.

We now know that living in a total institution, like a state hospital, is destructive to the individual's capacity to function independently, unless something is being done in that institution which more than makes up for the noxious effects of living in it. Thus, it has been found that many of the incapacities of institutionalized mentally defective individuals were a result not of their low intelligence, but rather of the unfortunate fact of having lived in an institution for most of their lives.

Moral treatment was abandoned. People who could have been better were languishing in the institution. There were, however, significant advances in descriptive psychiatry.

Advances in Descriptive Psychiatry

The diagnostic entity of schizophrenia really began with the clear-cut diagnostic work of Kraepelin. Previously, Karl Ludwig Kahlbaum (1828–1899) had described catatonia and hebephrenia. Kraepelin placed these, together with the other syndromes we now would call schizophrenia, into a category which he termed *dementia raecox*. This was to distinguish it from the other group of frequent psychoses for which no clear-cut organic cause was then known, namely the manic-depressive psychoses. Dementia praecox was so named because the most frequent ages of onset were between 15 and 25 years of age. He described dementia praecox as having a progressive development to complete deterioration. He did differentiate the "disease" of paraphrenia, in which there was no decay of the personality, from dementia praecox proper.

Kraepelin's aim was to delineate the disease entities of psychiatry, each with a typical onset, course, and outcome, and thus lay the basis for the correlation with physical pathology. He originally believed schizophrenia to be caused by a straightforward organic pathologic condition in the brain; later, he decided that it was probably a metabolic problem; however, no firm evidence was ever assembled.

Kraepelin's concept of a clear-cut outcome to schizophrenia has had an unfortunately long tenure as a scientific "truth." As Ciompi (1980) has found in following schizophrenic patients for 40 years, the long-term course of the disorder is highly variable. There is not one, but eight to eleven "usual" courses, depending on how one classifies them. Ciompi found that the course of the "disease" of schizophrenia does not seem to follow that of a physiologic disease, but rather the order of the social crises in a human being's life experience. Nearly half of the patients were working 40 years after their first admission, and less than half were in the hospital. Because of the length of Ciompi's follow-up, these results can in no way be related to any "modern" treatment.

Eugen Bleuler, in his book *Dementia Praecox, or the Group of the Schizophrenias* (1911, English translation, 1950), provided the best descriptive psychiatric presentation of the schizophrenic disorders. It was clear to him that the schizophrenias were widely varied; his conclusion was that either schizophrenia was a series of diseases, or it was not a disease at all. This conclusion has escaped the notice of most readers. We have used Bleuler's concepts as the basis for our discussion of the nature of schizophrenia (Chap. 3), and hence will not discuss them here.

Bleuler and Jung were led by their studies of schizophrenic patients to take an interest in the work of Freud, but they both eventually disagreed to some extent with him. Bleuler tended to be ambivalent about the psychodynamic or psychologic treatment of these patients. At times one gets the impression of great pessimism, while at other times Bleuler's clinical work was rewarded with good therapeutic outcome.

This ambivalence runs through other psychodynamic workers. Thus, Carl Jung (1875–1961) showed an interest in schizophrenic individuals and was intrigued by the illumination that psychoanalysis, both of the Freudian variety and of his own conception, seemed to shed on the pathologic aspects of schizophrenia, but at the same time he grew pessimistic about his ability to intervene therapeutically. Yet even in the papers in which he suggests a metabolic process or organic basis, which make psychotherapy of limited value, Jung reports some striking therapeutic successes. Alfred Adler (1870–1937) and his followers, too, report some successes with psychotic patients.

In the mainstream of psychoanalysis, Freud took a pessimistic view of the psychodynamic treatment of schizophrenic patients, in part based on theoretical considerations. Freud felt that the libido was invested in the self and not available for a transference relationship. He considered that this was a technical obstacle around which someone might find a way. Nonetheless his co-workers, including Karl Abraham (1877–1925), early in the twentieth century began attempting the treatment of psychotic individuals and occasionally succeeded. Indeed, some of the hysterical patients that Freud described would probably be classified as borderline, or possibly ambulatory, schizophrenic individuals today. Paul Federn (1871–1950) worked extensively with schizophrenic patients; Editha Sterba treated psychotic and autistic children in the 1930s. Many other psychoanalytic workers began exploring these fields. In England, the Kleinians worked with psychotic individuals with some degree of success, using theories based on their work with very young children.

Sullivan's Psychologic Advances Regarding Schizophrenic Patients

Consistently successful psychotherapeutic work with schizophrenic patients seems to be most indebted to the work of Harry Stack Sullivan and Frieda Fromm-Reichmann in the United States. Starting in the 1930s, they worked with schizophrenic patients and developed a modified version of psychoanalytic technique that seemed to be very effective. Its drawbacks were that it took a great deal of time and patience. Reduced to an oversimplified schema, the treatment consisted of getting the schizophrenic patient to build a relationship with the psychoanalytic therapist, and then to use the therapist as a bridge to the external world. Sullivan and Fromm-Reichmann used an extended version of psychoanalytic theory, emphasizing interpersonal relations and early preverbal experience to understand the details of the experiences and symptoms of the schizophrenic individual.

Like all psychodynamic theorists, they based their treatment on an understanding of general human development. Sullivan discarded the libido theory, with its fixed quanta of energy as a conceptual model, and hence could understand the relationship between the therapist and schizophrenic patient as transference, irrespective of the nature of that relationship. Human beings cannot survive without relationships with other human beings. Sullivan understood the heart of psychoanalysis to be the description of the nature and history of those human relationships, internal and external.

With its emphasis on interpersonal relations, Sullivan's developmental stages were: infancy, childhood, juvenile, preadolescence, early adolescence, late adolescence, and maturity. He does not reject the zonal psychosexual stages (oral, anal, and genital); rather, he views the interpersonal reactions around these zones as most important psychologically.

He defined "infancy" as the preverbal period. Much of the conscious experience of the schizophrenic patient was hard to verbalize, because it never had been verbalized; that is, it was primarily a continuance of, or in some cases a regression to, the experiences of the preverbal period.

The "awe-full" affects of adulthood, especially frequent in psychosis, are the primitive affect experiences of the infant, reexperienced at a later age. Anxiety is felt to be uncontrollable, Sullivan hypothesized, because the infant feels anxious by empathy whenever the "mothering one" feels anxious. Thus, the infant's anxiety would, to a large extent, come and go without respect to the infant's efforts, except for their calming or disturbing effect on the mothering one.

Sullivan tried to reconstruct in detail from observations and retrograde material what the experiences of the preverbal period must have been. It was apparent to him that many of the "strange" experiences of the schizophrenic individual were reexperiences of the fragmented experiences of the preverbal infant. He described the development of a sense of self and of others out of the fragmented sensations of this period. Thus, for example, the experience of something feeling and being felt at the same time provided the primitive basis for body image and the development of what other analysts would term *ego boundaries*. One of his important conceptions is that the infant develops two separate concepts: the "good mother" and the "bad mother." These concepts are separately organized on the basis of the affective experience of the interaction with the mother and other caretakers.

Simultaneously, the infant evolves three concepts of self: the "good me," the "bad me," and the "not me." The separate development of the good me and the bad me refers to what later analysts refer to as "splitting," and the not me refers to what is repressed.

Childhood begins, for Sullivan, with the acquisition of language. This radically transforms not only communication with others, but also communication with self, including the provision of categories for thought. Experiences in childhood, therefore, become easier to think about and remember, as well as to communicate to others. Bad experiences in infancy may be partially remedied in childhood. Indeed, according to Sullivan, the transition to each of his stages provides an opportunity for the partial remedy of earlier developmental defects. One's understanding of one's experiences in childhood tends to coincide with those of the others in one's immediate environment, and one's concepts tend to coincide with specific objects or people. The conscious integration of the good and bad mother, and the clear differentiation of mother from father should be accomplished in this stage. In this stage, regression as a defense against anxiety is first noticeable.

The "juvenile" era, in Sullivan's schema, begins when playmates become important, not merely two children in the presence of each other, but *reacting* to each other. In this period, the child should learn to cooperate and also to compete, and to be comfortable with both of these types of behavior. From the juvenile era onward, Sullivan, unlike Freud, consistently emphasizes the importance of the development of relationships with peers, particularly peers outside the family. Freud worked only with neurotic patients, who had such relationships. Sullivan worked with schizophrenic patients, who lacked such relationships or had severe problems with them; he described the negative effect when age-appropriate peer relationships were lacking and the reparative effect when they were available to the patient.

"Preadolescence," in Sullivan's schema, is the stage at which one develops a close relationship with a "best friend" of the same sex. Here, one learns the interpersonal skills and satisfactions of a close mutual relationship with another human being. These skills make possible the later development of meaningful heterosexual relationships. Patients who have not passed through the preadolescent stage frequently go through it in therapy. The longing

for such a relationship often engenders supposedly homosexual
urges and their resultant anxieties; being accepted dispels loneliness.
Loneliness, according to Sullivan, is more unpleasant than anxiety,
and he sees this as a good thing, since it motivates reaching out,
even in the interpersonally inadequate individual; however, schizophrenic patients are usually so interpersonally inadequate that
loneliness is inescapable.

"Early adolescence," for Sullivan, is the beginning of the
sexual confusions that characterize adolescence. For most people,
this is accompanied by an increase of genital activities.

"Late adolescence," in Sullivan's schema, is the stage at
which the individual has achieved a more or less stable pattern of
sexual (genital) interaction that he knows to be his (or her)
preferred mode. Many people never reach late adolescence.
"Maturity," for Sullivan, is that period when the individual's
social, interpersonal, sexual, and vocational roles have been patterned into a more or less satisfying way of life.

Sullivan also describes the centrality of self-esteem, and
how the avoidance of anxiety and shame generated by possible
loss or damage to self-esteem generates neurotic and psychotic
symptoms.

Sullivan was alert to sociocultural influences. The Sullivan-
ians were among the first analysts to state that a homosexual
adaptation was not necessarily a sign of a pathologic condition, and
that the health or sickness of such a relationship needed to be
examined on its own merits, just as with heterosexual relations. As
Fromm-Reichmann, particularly, made clear, even a not altogether
healthy homosexual relationship was a step forward from a schizophrenic adaptation. In the 1930s, to take such a view of homosexuality required professional courage.

Sullivan used a language different from that of other psychoanalysts, but it would be a mistake to think of him as rejecting
Freud. He built on existing insights and clearly took into account
the earlier clinical description of psychosexual development, and
of oral, anal, and genital (including oedipal) problems.

The main rationale we would attribute to Sullivan for the
development of his own language was the need to escape the libido
theory. The "fixed quanta of energy" libido theory seemed to get
into trouble in two places. The first was the concept of narcissism:

If I love me, then I cannot love you. If I love you, I diminish my own self-love. This concept was based in part on the phenomenology of nineteenth-century romantic love. In fact, the general phenomenon is that one's self-love and other-love tend to vary directly, not inversely. One can respect others only to the extent that one respects oneself, and vice versa. To use Sullivan's words, "If all human beings are pigs, it does not feel very good to be the best of the pigs." Indeed, modern Freudian psychoanalytic thinking has come to the conclusion that the narcissist (the apparently self-loving individual who does not care for others) suffers from too little gratification of his self-esteem, which he is attempting unsuccessfully to remedy.

The second flaw Sullivan found with fixed quanta libido theory, as noted earlier, involved the transference of schizophrenic individuals. If the libido is withdrawn to the self in the "narcissistic neuroses" (schizophrenia, paranoia, and manic-depressive psychoses), no transference occurs. But if there is no fixed quanta of libido, transference may occur, and indeed it does. The only problem is the *nature* of that transference.

In terms of therapeutic technique, Sullivan and Fromm-Reichmann emphasized extraordinary patience and kindness in developing and maintaining an interpersonal relationship between therapist and patient. It was assumed that unresponsive patients knew the therapist was there and that negativistic and insulting patients were simply acting out defenses based on early hurts. The therapist may speculate aloud about processes which may be going on but which the patient does not verbalize. With schizophrenic individuals, Sullivan and Fromm-Reichmann recommended avoiding interpretations of unconscious material, on the assumption that the unconscious is already conscious; rather, they recommended paraphrasing the patient's conscious experience.

Throughout the therapy it is assumed that the therapist will be tactful, and will be directed by a dynamic understanding of the patient. Sullivan and Fromm-Reichmann found that problems with anger are even more important than sexual problems for schizophrenic patients. The importance of loneliness, the fear of loneliness, and the fear of closeness are to be dealt with. The psychotic phenomena should be made meaningful to the patients, as reactions to life problems, without accepting the psychotic distortions or promising reparations or an ideal world; simply promise a realistic world in which it is now possible to live nonpsychotically. The therapist should make every possible effort to deal with the patient as an adult and to encourage mature behavior. As the treatment progresses, it should become more like the psychoanalytic therapy of the neurotic patient. Treatment for schizophrenic patients, they found, was extremely time-consuming, but it was frequently successful. Most of what is called psychoanalytic therapy in other schools consists of independently discovering or translating the ideas and techniques of Sullivan and Fromm-Reichmann into the language of the alternative psychoanalytic school.

In recent times, the basis laid by Sullivan and Fromm-Reichmann and extended by other psychoanalytic workers in other languages has demonstrated that when knowledgeable and persistent work is attempted, patients recover. The remaining problems are twofold. (1) The treatment is slow and tedious, but this is a technical problem, and attempts have been made to speed up the process so as to make it economically feasible. Some of the attempts to accomplish this are described in this book. (2) The psychotherapy of psychotic individuals is not regularly a part of the training of treatment professionals, even those who have adequate training in psychotherapy with other types of patients. Unfortunately, even today only a minority of professionals in any of the mental health professions have adequate training in the treatment of psychotic individuals.

Concurrent "Advances" in the Somatic Treatment of Schizophrenic Patients

The rise of scientific psychiatry and the decline of moral treatment led to the myth that schizophrenic individuals are incurable. Concurrent with the psychologic advances being made by Sullivan and Fromm-Reichmann, organic psychiatrists were also trying to treat schizophrenic patients. Drastic somatic treatments were developed in the 1930s. Manfred Sakel (1938) proposed using insulin coma and reported extraordinarily successful results in 1933. Meduna (Meduna and Friedman 1939), in 1934, under the mistaken impression that epileptic individuals do not become schizophrenic and that schizophrenic individuals do not become epileptic, induced artificial epileptic seizures with metrazol and reported extraordinary results. Cerletti and Bini (Cerletti 1950), in order to provide a more controlled epileptic seizure, developed electric shock treatment shortly thereafter. It is an interesting footnote that Cerletti could never bring himself to use electric convulsion therapy (ECT) on any of his own private patients, that is, any patient whom he knew as a human being. Indeed, he spent the last part of his life in experiments on animals, hoping that shock treatment would stimulate the development of substances which would produce the same beneficial effects ECT seemed to have on patients. He hoped that a serum produced from shocked animals would dispense with the need to subject human beings to shock treatment.

These physical treatments were reported to have enormous benefit when first introduced. The importance of shock treatment for the psychiatrist without psychoanalytic or psychotherapeutic training is well described by Greenblatt (1977): "The treatment . . . was an unquestioned boon to psychiatry as a profession; psychiatry suddenly began to earn a little respect in medical circles and from the general public." As shock treatments have continued in use, their marvelous effects have diminished. Undoubtedly, this is because of the more careful scrutiny we have given the patients who have been subjected to them. For a full discussion of the limitations of shock treatment, the reader is referred to Friedberg (1975) and Breggin (1979).

Psychosurgery, particularly prefrontal lobotomy, was supposed to empty out the mental hospitals. Antonio de Egas Moniz, in 1949, was awarded the Nobel Prize for its development. This treatment has been largely abandoned, which seems to be a benefit to the patients.

These more drastic treatments were more in keeping with medical tradition and training. They did not require learning a whole new body of knowledge. They were simple. They required very little of the doctor's time. Consequently, they have been extremely popular.

Psychodynamics and psychotherapy represent a break in the continuity of the training of psychiatrists. The concepts and techniques are different from those used in other branches of medicine.

It is easier to build on previous learning. Moreover, psychodynamic concepts are often anxiety-provoking, insofar as they lead to an examination of one's own defenses. This is particularly true if one attempts to understand the extraordinary pain and discomfort of psychotic individuals. It therefore requires a willingness to tolerate such anxiety and a determination to learn what is necessary even if it does not build on previous training. Nor is there an economic reward for undergoing the difficulties of learning this kind of treatment.

As Hollingshead and Redlich described the situation in the 1950s, there were then, and to some extent still are, two professions of psychiatry in the United States: the *directive-organic* and the *analytic-psychotherapeutic.* Directive-organic psychiatrists have less training, earn more money, and consequently are far more numerous. Analytic-psychotherapeutic psychiatrists, because they must spend more time with each patient, earn less money even though they have more training. Consequently, they are far less numerous and tend to be found mainly in large cities or in the vicinity of universities. The situation has changed somewhat since the 1950s, but in the main, these conclusions remain valid.

Fortunately, there is a somatic treatment for schizophrenia that is consistent with general medical training, that is less drastic and less destructive than shock treatments and psychosurgery. During the 1950s the tranquilizer era began, and medication is now the major nonpsychotherapeutic treatment for schizophrenic patients.

Other Psychodynamic Contributions

Federn (1952) felt the tasks of therapy with schizophrenic patients to be reestablishing (or establishing) appropriate ego boundaries, strengthening a defective ego, and helping the defenses to work, that is, re-repressing id impulses so that the integrity of the personality could be maintained. He started by accepting and sharing the psychotic individual's perception of the world, and then helped the patient, whom he now understood, to face external reality and cope with his impulses. Schilder (1935) described the distortion of the body image, which forms the basis for the ego representation, and its implications for schizophrenic patients.

Parts of the self are repressed and/or projected in order to defend against feelings. He also attempted to describe schizophrenic logic, and felt hallucinations could be analyzed like dreams.

Rosenfeld (1965) and Segal (1950) have described the application of Kleinian concepts to schizophrenic patients. They stress projection and introjection of part-objects (e.g., good breast, bad breast, etc.) and particularly projective identification (a somewhat confusing concept describing a confused experience in which split-off parts of the self are fused with external part or whole objects) in their interpretations. They also stress the paranoid-schizoid position (of early infancy, where one fears being robbed of the inside of the body). Problems of rage and terror and the transference psychosis are given central attention. They believe frequent "deep" (i.e., infantile) interpretations are reassuring to the patient and maintain therapeutic contact. The patient progresses to a real analytic experience. The schizophrenic patient is well on the way to a neurotic integration when the patient's material primarily concerns the "depressive" position (the fantasy that the inside of the body is "bad") based on the integration of part-objects, including the good and bad mother and the good and bad self, and the consequent problems of anger and guilt.

Fairbairn (1954) and Guntrip (1969), in Scotland, formulated a somewhat different "object-relations" theory, in part out of their experience in treating schizophrenic patients. We have found their views helpful, and they are discussed in later chapters, as relevant to specific issues.

Perry (1961) has continued the effective development of Jungian psychoanalytic therapy with schizophrenic patients. Despite the difference in metaphor, the same issues are dealt with. It is notable that one of his recommendations about technique is that one should not "analyze the archetypes," but rather relate them to the patient's individual life. From our standpoint (and that of our most contemporary Freudian and Sullivanian analysts), that means interpreting the "archetype" (i.e., symbol), and that should be helpful.

The extension of the Sullivan, Fromm-Reichmann tradition is best exemplified in the work of Will and Searles. Will (1961) takes a somewhat existential position and relates the treatment of chronic schizophrenic patients to the therapist's acceptance, investigation of, and understanding of the human condition at its worst. Searles (1965) has documented in detail many aspects of schizophrenia, and, in particular, has described the countertransference with such patients in all its complexity and unpleasantness, as well as the transference, and he explains their relevance for understanding and treating these disorders.

Lidz (1973), perhaps the most insightful of contemporary writers on schizophrenic patients, is summarized in Chapter 5, in which the relationships between schizophrenic individuals and their families are discussed.

Kernberg (1975, 1976) has been particularly concerned with the treatment of patients with borderline conditions, who, he found, responded best to psychoanalytic therapy as opposed to psychoanalysis (which did not provide sufficient support) or supportive therapy (which did not uncover). He has attempted to integrate object-relations insights into American ego-analysis. In his theoretical understanding of borderline and schizophrenic patients Kernberg emphasizes the importance of "splitting" (of both self and object) as a defense mechanism, as opposed to repression, which requires an intact ego. Developmentally, oedipal conflicts occur only after major splitting has been resolved; character traits are seen as defenses against rage. Volkan (1976) describes essentially the same model applied to schizophrenic patients.

Sechehaye's (1951) unique contribution lies in the use of symbolic realization, with the therapist acting within the symbolic meaning of the psychotic material, rather than interpreting it, so as to undo early trauma. Rosen's (1953) contribution was the early use of "direct" (i.e., without associations) interpretations of psychotic material to foster a positive transference.

Eissler (1952) contributed some useful techniques, and first used the concept of "parameter" (intentional deviation from classic technique based on a psychodynamic understanding of the patient's needs). His most controversial (and perhaps most useful) contribution was his description of the "appropriate countertransference" for therapists of schizophrenic patients: an inability to accept failure in the treatment. He utilizes the traditional metapsychology of egopsychologic psychoanalysis to provide a sensitive clinical description of schizophrenic patients and their needs.

Affects lose their signal function and are traumatic. Anxiety is replaced by terror. "Neutralized" nonaffective energy is less available for thinking. "Deadness" is a defense against unbearable affect, and so-called "masochism" in schizophrenic patients is a defense against deadness (pain is better than death). The ego is lacking in structure and effective defense mechanisms. Consequently, not only is affect avoided or experienced as traumatic, but so are ordinary perceptions. New ego structure, including a clearer sense of identity, is developed in therapy by the healthy object-relationship with the analyst, which provides more mutual and appropriate "love" than any other for the patient, although it is not the symbolic all-gratifying "love" of the patient's fantasies. Eissler believed, "The schizophrenic patient must be sure beyond any doubt that he will have the opportunity of continuing his treatment independently of his ability to cooperate."

The initial "parameters" of not remaining silent, of providing unambivalent acceptance and greater activity, are removed as the patient builds ego-structure on the basis of the good object-relationship with the therapist, and the analysis can eventually proceed on classic terms to a successful outcome.

Arlow and Brenner (1964) helped to delineate the continuity in schizophrenic defenses with those of neurotic patients in ego-analytic terms. Giovacchini (1979), within the American ego-analytic tradition, attempts to synthesize the concepts of disparate schools of psychoanalytic thinking, particularly those of Fairbairn, to describe an appropriate office treatment of schizophrenic patients. Arieti (1955, 1974) and Bellak (1979) attempt to provide coordinated reviews of the range of perspectives on schizophrenia.

Gendlin (1967) sensitively describes appropriate procedures for the regressed schizophrenic patient. While Gendlin develops the client-centered or experiential theoretical framework, his discussion will seem comfortable to other psychodynamic therapists, and his suggestions, always couched in clear descriptions of the patient and of the therapist's experience, provide a good beginning for therapists of any school attempting to work with schizophrenic individuals. Because his clinical chapter appears in a research book, it has been overlooked by clinicians.

Gendlin makes clear that it is the therapist who is responsible for initiating the therapeutic process with schizophrenic patients and for continuing to provide the stimulus for the patient's moving the process forward. He views the therapist as doing this through the use of "reflection," by which he means the verbal reflection of unformed, preconscious, but felt emotional experience. Gendlin sees this as helping to expand the bounds of clear consciousness.

Gendlin acknowledges that schizophrenic patients may not give a very clear picture of what they are experiencing, or they may present the therapist with feelings that are difficult to understand or difficult to tolerate. Nonetheless, Gendlin believes that the patient can be met in a one-to-one encounter that has a positive thrust. In dealing with the schizophrenic patient, Gendlin finds it useful to utilize the "sensible person" assumption, by which he means that when speaking to the patient he always responds as if talking to a rational individual. He acknowledges that acting in this way with many schizophrenic patients often requires imagination, but, inevitably the patient confirms, at a later time, awareness of all that was said.

Contacts with the patient, according to Gendlin, do not need to be either 50 minutes in duration or nothing. Brief contacts can be helpful too, either because the situation is too painful to continue for long periods, because the patient wants a brief contact, or because the patient initiated a contact (as in the corridor or ward) at a time when it is not possible for the therapist to spend much time with him. He clarifies this issue in terms of the "continuing interaction" (the internalized relationship, which continues between actual encounters with the patient).

One response to a potentially violent patient, who angrily refuses to continue the hour-long session, can be to end the session early; however, the session should still be ended in an accepting manner, and interest in future interaction should be expressed by the therapist, as: "I will go away for now, if that is what you want, but I will be back to see if I can help." The therapist need not prolong any interview. The important thing is that the therapist will return, and, if the patient still rejects him, he may say something like: "I know you don't want to talk to me, but I think I can help." The therapist may even remain while the patient walks away.

Gendlin also emphasizes how the apparently irrelevant ramblings of the schizophrenic patient provide an important vehicle for initiating interpersonal interaction, if the therapist will deal with and respond to the fragments that make sense to him, fragments that are always part of the patient's talk. He writes: "The therapist's bit-by-bit solid grasp and response is (sic) like a pier in the patient's sea of autism and self-loss. As each bit is tied to another person who grasps it, the vast, lost, swampy weirdness goes out of things."

Gendlin frequently talks to the patient about feelings the patient has not experienced, or feelings he would have if in the patient's situation. He emphasizes the use of the inner processes of the therapist as essential to successful work, and places a high emphasis on truth as a guide, since the patient's reality has already been confused enough. He, like many therapists of schizophrenic patients, emphasizes the importance of making clear whose feelings are being discussed—the patient's or the therapist's—at any time.

Prouty (1976), a student of Gendlin's, has specified simple procedures that can be used by paraprofessionals or beginning therapists to develop a therapeutic relationship with totally uncommunicative schizophrenic individuals. These principles are: (1) situational reflection—telling the patient what he is doing and what the situation is; (2) body reflection—telling the patient what he is doing with his body or mirroring it with your own body, or both; (3) reflection of facial expression—since affects are centrally related to facial expression—telling the patient what feelings he seems to be experiencing on the basis of his facial expression; and (4) "word-for-word reflection"—repeating any words or sentences that make sense in chaotic verbalizations, even if this means repeating single words. These principles are usually sufficient to transform an unresponsive patient into a responsive one in a matter of hours.

We could endlessly describe one psychodynamic writer after another, compile infinite lists of how one set of concepts relates to another, or point out how sets of concepts differ or how they are related to someone's favored abstract model, e.g., Hartmann's (1964) or Rapaport's metapsychology (1967). We do not find this practical, however. Only when psychoanalytic concepts translate into aspects of the patient's developmental experience and the therapeutic interaction, including both the patient's and the therapist's experience of it, do we find them of general value.

Gunderson and Mosher (1975) report the views and discussions of five groups of contemporary psychoanalysts on the treatment of schizophrenia: the New England group, the Chicago group, the San Francisco group, the Washington-Baltimore group, and the Los Angeles group. The major clinical controversies are listed as past versus present versus future; reality versus fantasy; affects; exploration versus relationship; activity versus passivity; and regression. Yet these are the wrong issues. The task of therapy is to untangle the past from the present to make the future conceivable. Reality and fantasy are intertwined and must both be dealt with. Affects are central to all therapy, and emphasis on anger, despair, loneliness, terror, and shame are all necessary, as is the clarification of affect, and the acceptance of positive affect. Activity versus passivity is again the wrong question; the right one is what action is helpful, when is it helpful, and when is *not* doing anything helpful? Regression is inevitable; should one accept it fully or try to limit it? This has no general answer other than do what is necessary (i.e., unavoidable) or most helpful to a particular patient at a particular time.

The Continued Reluctance To Confront the Psychodynamic Treatment of Schizophrenia

Many therapists in psychology and psychiatry continue for a host of reasons to avoid treating schizophrenic individuals. The latest resistance is the "gifted therapist" theory. It is espoused by many who once simply denied psychotherapy as an effective treatment. This theory claims that there are some gifted individuals who can practice successful psychotherapy with schizophrenic patients and have done so, but it also claims that for the majority of mental health professionals, this is impossible.

While such a theory seems like a more favorable attitude toward psychotherapy than their former views, it is simply a new rationalization for continuing not to treat such patients. It implies that the gifted individuals are so rare that for all practical purposes, psychotherapy is ruled out. This view holds that the probability of finding individuals with such unique potential among professionals in training is so slight that training in the psychotherapy of schizophrenia need not be provided. This is *not* our finding, as we shall elucidate below.

The schizophrenic patient *is* treatable. He or she may not be easy to treat, but is not impossible to treat. It is our hope that by means of this book we can share what we have learned, so that the next generation of therapists can begin where we left off and need not repeat our mistakes.

It has also been said, as a rationalization justifying nontreatment, that only young therapists have the energy to work with schizophrenic patients, and that one needs a great deal of experience and training in order to help these patients and not to harm them. This sounds like the old stage magician's joke that anyone under 25 with 30 years' experience can do the trick. The truth is that young therapists have more energy, which is an asset in working with schizophrenic patients; therefore, they can afford to make more mistakes. As a person gets older, he has less energy, and therefore he must make fewer mistakes. It is imperative to learn more as one gets older. But, young or old, it *is* possible for therapists to do this kind of work if they wish to, and they *can* do it successfully.

3

Schizophrenia: Coping with a Terrible World

"He's never killed anyone, but he might. He gets behind another patient and chokes him, and we know about it because the guy's feet are waving in the air. He always lets the guy go when he's unconscious, but some day he might not let go in time."

The patient so described was a muscular man and was being treated in the chronic ward of the state hospital. He had a history of violent assaults, he moved quickly, and he was grossly incoherent. When he was not incoherent, he stuttered badly.

The psychiatric residents had selected this patient as the subject of a clinical demonstration of psychotherapeutic treatment of schizophrenic individuals. This seminar was disparate from the rest of their psychiatric training program. Each week the technical difficulties were discussed as if it were reasonable to expect them to be able to treat such patients psychotherapeutically. The residents had reason to be uncomfortable. They knew how to make a diagnosis. They knew how to write prescriptions and keep the patients tractable. They even knew how to use the shock machine. But psychotherapy with such severe patients was a demand for which their training had not really prepared them, and therefore it seemed unreasonable. The residents were expressing their covert hostility at the suggestion that they could talk to schizophrenic patients by choosing this particular patient for an interview. Most patients are not dangerous.

This patient had been treated for many years. There were no facts in his case history that would seem to account for his severe pathologic condition. The psychiatric and social work records were voluminous. He had grown up in a poor family. This *is* difficult; indeed, the rate of schizophrenia among the poorest sector of our population is 12 times as high as it is among the wealthier part of the population. But most poor people are not schizophrenic. This patient grew up in Detroit, which may be unfortunate, but it is not enough in itself to cause people to become schizophrenic. His father was an alcoholic. That is more difficult, but it is still not enough to account for schizophrenia.

His childhood, as reported, was unexceptional, except for a speech disorder which appeared while he was in junior high school and which did not disappear with speech therapy. The first indication of a serious emotional difficulty, according to the case history, was noted in the army. He appeared at sick call with a venereal disease, and the site of infection was his mouth. A few days later he assaulted a stranger and nearly killed him. He was given a general discharge from the army very quickly.

His history subsequently was that of assaulting a stranger, going into the hospital, being very disorganized, slowly pulling together over a period of years, being discharged, within a short time again assaulting someone, and going back into the hospital. His pathologic condition was extreme, and yet there was nothing in his life history that would seem to account for it.

A short series of interviews, however, brought to light a few details of his life that somehow had escaped the attention of previous professionals. In the first session, the issue of his choking people was dealt with. One always deals with the issue of preventing homicide first, if there is any evidence that this is a danger. The next highest priority is preventing suicide, if there is evidence that this is a danger; all other issues are tertiary. (Of course, the most effective way to prevent a suicide or homicide is to understand the psychodynamics and deal appropriately in therapy with these issues.)

As the therapist (Karon) continued to reintroduce the issue of choking, bit by bit the incoherent verbalizations of the patient began to make sense. What was reconstructed with him was that as a young child his mother would place a cloth around his neck and choke him briefly for minor offenses, like not eating. When you cannot breathe, you panic. This is a useful, innate mechanism that keeps infants from suffocating; they kick off the blankets when they can't breathe. But choking as minor punishment, of course, left the patient terrified. After this material had been reconstructed and discussed with the patient, there was presumptive evidence that our reconstruction was correct: this grossly ill man ceased choking other patients. Such a dramatic change in pathologic behavior usually means that the therapist is probably correct in what he is working on.

The symptom represented his attempt to master the early traumatic experiences by reenacting them; he would play the mother and the victim unwittingly played himself. He was proving that his mother never would really have killed him. He always dropped the other man as soon as he was unconscious. A symbolic act, however, as in this kind of symptom, no matter how often repeated, never does undo the original trauma, because it is not connected consciously with the original problem. Only when the relationship between the symbolic act (or symptom) and the original trauma is reconnected in consciousness can the person really overcome it. What is unconscious does not change.

Already, we had a very different view of this man's life from what was contained in the record. A second insight occurred in a session which began with his yelling:

"Why did you do it to me, Dad?"

"Do what?"

"You know what you did to me!"

"How old were you?"

"You know I was 8 years old."

Further questions elicited the fact that he had been 8 years old when "I", (i.e., the father) came home drunk and anally raped him. This is more than just an alcoholic father. Most fathers, alcoholic or not, would not rape their children. Most rapists would not rape their sons.

Incidentally, it took a genius like Freud to discover the concept of transference, because neurotic persons, like you and us, are very subtle in what we do, and our transferences look realistic. But

it has always been a matter of great puzzlement to us that people
who work with psychotic patients have ignored psychoanalytic
insights when such patients often present the material in such
dramatic and unmistakeable fashion. It takes no genius to know
that when the patient calls you "Dad" or "Mom" (often without
regard to your sex) he is transferring feelings from the past. Of
course, if we were organically oriented, we might only conclude
the patient was "not oriented," or was "confused."

A third bit of information came to light. The patient stuttered
badly when he was not grossly incoherent; from the standpoint of
psychotherapy, this is, of course, a resistance, and it was necessary
to attempt to deal with it. We do not ordinarily do speech therapy
or work with stutterers. Luckily, the dynamics of this man's
stuttering are not typical of stutterers in general. (We are told by
people who have had extensive experience with such cases that
this patient became a stutterer in a very unusual way. Certainly
we would not want anyone to apply our insight into this patient's
problem to his friends who stutter.)

This man's stuttering had a traumatic origin. In a therapy
session, he began to stutter, and then came out with a few phrases
of real Latin. When the therapist was in high school, he was told
that if he wanted to go to college he should study Latin. He
studied Latin for 4 years, and this session was the *one* time in his
professional career that it has been of value. I thought: "How does
this uneducated man from Detroit know Latin?" It took me a while
to figure out the obvious, that he must have been an altar boy. In
typically subtle fashion, the therapist asked, "Were you an altar
boy?"

The stuttering became overwhelming. The patient said, "You
swallow a snake, and then you stutter; you mustn't let anyone
know about it."

If we were behavior modifiers, we might think this concerned
his experiences with snakes. But we are not. To a psychoanalytic
therapist familiar with the language of dreams, the problem this
man might be struggling with seemed clear. Moreover, that it came
to light in connection with being an altar boy and elicited enormous amounts of guilt suggested more of the context.

The interpretation offered was: "I know you sucked the
priest's cock, and it's all right. Anybody as hungry as you were

would have done the same thing." The man immediately stopped stuttering, and while the stutter occasionally recurred, it was always possible to stop it by saying, "I know what you did with the priest, and it's all right. Anyone as hungry as you were would have done the same thing."

In case the reader did not notice, this is an oral interpretation of an apparently genital phenomenon, something that is characteristic of schizophrenic patients. They are more concerned with the early mother-child relationship and survival than they are about later sexual development and the conflicts realistically related thereto. Thus, just as we have learned to consider other things psychoanalytically as symbolic of sexual activity, sexual activity itself may represent earlier, more basic problems, and in these patients usually does. The penis may represent the breast; the vagina and the anus may represent a mouth. The basic battles of survival and of nurturance from early childhood may be seen reenacted in what looks like sexual activity, or sexual ideas and concerns. The clue that the homosexual activity connected with being an altar boy likely involved a priest rather than another altar boy was the intensity of the patient's guilt, plus the evidence of previous homosexual experience with the original father figure.

These strange words will make more sense as you proceed further into the book. The language in which the interpretation was phrased is emotionally meaningful to the patient (Ferenczi 1911, in Ferenczi 1950), even if it is not that of polite company, scientific discussions, or the usual psychoanalytic session. One should, as far as one can, match one's language to that in which the patient feels and thinks, because the therapy goes faster. Of course, all of us are sometimes more pedantic or more vulgar than our patients, but they will forgive us such human imperfection, while appreciating our attempt to do justice to their feelings.

What is important to note is that the voluminous records on this severely ill man revealed nothing that would account for his illness, but even a short reasonable attempt to understand what was going on revealed three critical facts, which no longer make his pathologic condition excessive: his mother choked him for minor offenses, his father anally raped him, and, when he turned to God, even God, in the form of a priest, took advantage of him.

Wouldn't anyone be psychotic living such a life? It should be noted, of course, that it is not merely that his mother choked him once, or his father raped him once, but what kind of mother would choke her child under any circumstances? What kind of a father would rape his son under any circumstances? What does living with these people for a lifetime do to you?

In every case, when we talk with the patient and think about his symptoms in the light of the material he produces in therapy, the pathologic condition is always equal to the life history, as experienced by the patient, both in severity and in specific details. When collateral information is obtainable, it invariably confirms the accuracy of the reconstructions from therapy, not necessarily as first mentioned by the patient, but as clarified in the therapeutic process. The one consistent distortion that often remains is that what is recalled or reconstructed as a single event or trauma is almost always a summary of recurring events with similar emotional meaning to the patient.

In every case we have treated, the individual had lived a life that we could not conceive of living without developing his symptoms. In not one case was a genetic factor or a physiologic factor needed to account for the symptoms. That does not mean that if you have a superficial interview with the individual or with his family you will necessarily find how that life really was experienced by the individual. There are studies in the literature which report that the families and life histories of schizophrenic patients are not different from those of other people, but in such studies the patients were not carefully examined. More recently, there are studies like those of Lidz, which indicate that the families are clearly quite different (e.g., Yi-Chuang 1962; Lidz 1973).

This is why we are skeptical of physiologic and genetic speculations, unless they are bolstered by strong evidence of a specific mechanism which can be demonstrated. Despite an enormous amount of literature, such evidence is still lacking. Genetic and physiologic theories are usually generated by investigators who have never talked or listened to any schizophrenic individual for any length of time. In a few cases, they have attempted therapy under difficult circumstances hampered by critically inaccurate theories. They have concluded that because they were unsuccessful, the patient must be untreatable. Physiologic and/or genetic deficits are the traditional all-purpose explanations for therapeutic failure in psychiatry and psychology. Such views, even with inadequate evidence, are more comforting, and hence more dangerous to the growth of scientific knowledge than an honest statement of ignorance.

The Nature of Schizophrenia

Bleuler (1911; English translation, 1950) initiated the term *schizophrenia* to describe the "splitting" of the mental functions and the split from reality. He concluded, in that classic monograph summarizing his observations on such patients, that either this was a group of diseases, or no disease at all. That conclusion has been largely forgotten, although its truth is obvious when one works with patients who are called schizophrenic. They are a widely varying group of human beings. Symptoms vary, degree of impairment varies, and even their variability varies.

What do they have in common? First of all, they are very sick. Those whom we call clearly schizophrenic are usually easily noticeable by their grossly impaired reactions to normal life. It is also the case, however, that the word "schizophrenic" has been used to cover other patients, such as those who are able to function marginally, but have some symptoms severely discrepant from normal life, or those who may usually appear normal, but at some times function more like the typical schizophrenic individual than like a neurotic or normal individual, that is, who use regression as a defense more readily than most people.

Insofar as there are common defining characteristics, Bleuler's original three criteria make good sense: (1) thought disorder—inability to think logically when one wants to, (2) affect disorder—apparently inappropriate affect or apparent absence of affect, (3) autism—withdrawal from relationships with other people. From a descriptive standpoint, these symptoms are central in establishing the diagnosis. They are usually accompanied by more dramatic symptoms, which Bleuler called secondary—like hallucinations, delusions, catatonic postures, inability to take care of oneself, strange verbalizations—which because of the severity with which they impair one's life easily form the basis for the diagnosis, but which are not present in all cases. In any event, descriptive psychiatry is not sufficient to understand what is going on.

The classic distinctions between paranoid, catatonic, hebephrenic, and simple schizophrenic refer to symptom complexes which may differ at different times in the patient's life. The dichotomy between process and reactive schizophrenic patients turns out upon empirical investigation to be a continuum. Moreover, every apparently "process" or "bad premorbid adjustment" schizophrenic person undergoes critical life crises, and every "reactive" or "good premorbid adjustment" schizophrenic person has undergone a life history that has made him vulnerable. It is nonetheless true that it is generally easier to restore a function than to help produce it where it has never existed, and therefore, the distinction between developmental arrest and regressive symptom is clinically useful. It is also a fact that acuteness of onset of a symptom is usually related to better prognosis.

All of the symptoms of schizophrenia may be understood, however, as attempts to deal with terror (anxiety seems too mild a term) of a chronic kind. Human beings do not tolerate chronic terror well.

Unfortunately, so-called schizophrenic symptoms, or defenses against terror, have a tendency to make the problem worse. Thus, for example, withdrawal from people reduces one's immediate fear of people, but it makes it harder to overcome the fear of people, or the thought disorder, or the apparent inappropriateness of one's affect by decreasing corrective experience. Similarly, the thought disorder and/or inappropriate affect and/or delusions and hallucinations make it difficult to relate to people. Those people who have tended to use any of these in attenuated form as characteristic adjustive mechanisms are more likely to use them dramatically in the so-called schizophrenic "break." In psychoanalytic terms, they are more likely to use regression as a defense.

Terror and the Schizophrenic Patient

There is nothing in the schizophrenic reactions which you will not find in the potentiality of all human beings. Any of us can and will develop so-called schizophrenic symptoms under enough stress of the right kind. As Bettelheim has noted, he has never seen anything in a schizophrenic person that he had not seen in normal people in a concentration camp. What varies from person to person is how much stress it takes, and what kind of stress. It seems as if the major determinants of these quantitative and qualitative differences are one's childhood experiences (as understood by the child, not necessarily as understood by an outside observer).

In World War II, every soldier who underwent a particular battlefield experience developed schizophrenic symptoms. The precipitating situation was very simple. The soldier was under fire and in danger of being killed. He dug a foxhole under fire as quickly as he could, one just barely big enough to get into. He crawled into it and stayed there. He didn't eat or drink. He urinated and defecated on himself, because there was no other place to urinate or defecate without being killed. If the situation lasted for several days, every single soldier appeared classically schizophrenic when the shooting stopped, and his buddies came up to him. That is, when these patients were finally rescued, they exhibited Bleuler's primary symptoms, plus hallucinations, delusions and/or catatonic symptoms.

While these patients looked like very severe schizophrenic individuals, if they were reasonably healthy before this trauma they recovered spontaneously with rest. The term *schizophreniform psychosis* was used at first to describe these patients, people who look in every way as if they are classic schizophrenic types, but who have a very good prognosis for spontaneous recovery (Bellak 1948; Grinker and Spiegel 1965). It was then believed that no schizophrenic patient ever recovered—a recurring view in the mythology of psychiatry—hence they must be suffering from something else. Now we see in these patients simply one example of schizophrenic symptoms that occur in people who are reasonably healthy but subjected to unusual terror.

Most of us will never be in that kind of stress, and most of us will never be schizophrenic. It is nonetheless true that the more severe one's environment, the more probable schizophrenic reactions will be. This is evidenced by the marked differences in the incidence of schizophrenia according to socioeconomic class of family of origin (Srole et al. 1962). Within the lowest socioeconomic class, those individuals who develop schizophrenic symptoms are, in general, living under more stress than those who do not; they attempt to cope by strategies that make their situations realistically worse (Rogler and Hollingshead 1965).

But most of the patients who break down under the stresses of normal life have been prepared for such a breakdown by a childhood that has made them vulnérable. The patient has suffered from a series of subtle and unsubtle rejections all his life. These lead to the formation of a set of fantasies, conscious and unconscious, which then influence how later experience is perceived; further fantasies develop, which eventually, of course, lead to a way of understanding the world which is intolerable (Karon and Rosberg 1958a, 1958b; Rosberg and Karon 1958, 1959).

Ordinary stresess in life may lead to a breakdown, if one's life history gives that stress terrifying meaning. Thus, for example, people feel bad when their parents die, but they do not ordinarily become psychotic. One patient, whose father died when the patient was 16, began to hallucinate the voices of drowned people in lakes as he drove past. He did not tell anyone about these hallucinations and continued to live a superficially normal life for a year or so, until he refused to go to school. He was eventually brought to a psychiatrist, who could not understand the patient and put him in a hospital for observation, where it became apparent that he was continuously hallucinating. The patient spent the next 16 years in and out of mental hospitals. He was never discharged, but he was a genius at escaping. His mother would send him money to live on until the next voluntary or involuntary hospitalization.

It is well known that people sometimes have conscious or unconscious death wishes toward a relative who dies. The actual death of the relative is then taken as evidence that one's wishes were in some way involved, and the patients develop symptoms as a result of guilt or the fear of punishment. This has even found its way into the mass media, as in the motion picture *The Snake Pit*.

The therapist's suspicions were aroused, however, when he learned that the mother repeated approximately once a week to her adult paranoid son: "You don't think you killed your father, do you? No one thinks you killed your father." Or she would say, "No one holds you responsible for your father dying." Somehow these reassurances did not reassure.

What was reconstructed in therapy was this: throughout most of his childhood the patient had struggled with his mixed and conflicting loyalties to his mother and his father. His father was, emotionally speaking, much weaker than his mother, but also less destructive. The patient referred to this conflict as "The Civil War." (Usually "Civil War" delusions refer to the feeling that one must love one's mother and hate one's father or love one's father and hate one's mother, but not both.) He finally chose his father, and his father died shortly thereafter. The father died under unusual circumstances, probably a suicide. The mother, who was psychologically sophisticated in a superficial way, did not tell the boy how his father died "to save him from worrying."

What was reconstructed in therapy was not that the patient wanted his father to die, but that he had chosen his father over his mother, and then the father had died under apparently mysterious circumstances. He felt that his mother had killed his father, and that he was next on the firing line. Such fantasies are sufficiently frequent that they should be considered in light of the patient's material whenever there is a psychotic reaction to the death of a parent.

His terror was assuaged by the wish-fulfilling hallucination ("hearing the voices of drowned people"), which reassured him that death was not real, that people were still alive even if they were dead. A wish-fulfilling hallucination, of course, is simply a way of staving off the chronic terror that the patient feels, and it is at most partially successful. Even the choice of defense was not random: his father had had a strong interest in spiritualism, it was learned.

It would be a mistake in understanding this man to assume that these dynamics were only the result of the trauma of the father's death. In fact, they were set by a series of problems that began in infancy and lasted throughout his life. They began with his earliest fear as an infant that he would be killed by being abandoned, allowed to starve, poisoned, etc.

Of course, no infant has a conscious, clearly verbalized view of these fears and experiences. Rather, such experiences are diffuse and only gradually conceptualized; they begin in tensions communicated by the parent through the physical handling of the infant. The fears may in part be self-generated, that is, responses to intrabodily reactions and discomforts, to which the ministration of the parents should promote relief. But the anxious or angry parent communicates these parental feelings, even if unconscious, through the way in which they handle the child. Spitz (1965), for example, has demonstrated how the unconscious anger and anxiousness of the parent is reflected in jerky, angular, tense movements, not noticeable to the ordinary eye, but easily discernible under slow-motion photography, and easily felt by the infant, whose sensitivity to motion and position is acute. It is not accidental that Sullivan, who pioneered in the treatment of schizophrenia, wrote elaborately about the preverbal period of infancy as the source of the "awe-full" experiences of the psychotic. He suggested, correctly, that the "indescribable" character of some of the symptoms had an early derivation. Even the Kleinian description of early internal object-relations we would understand as a clear conscious conceptualization, for therapeutic purposes, of experiences which are in fact not clearly and consciously conceptualized by the infant. Of course, the reconstruction of the psychology of early infancy, while it must be attempted, is sufficiently uncertain that there is room for legitimate clinical difference of opinion.

All children experience terror and helplessness, and see the world as dangerous. These fears are naturally associated with the parents, the most important elements of the infant's world. For children who grow up relatively normal, the parents are a source of support in overcoming these infantile fears. Each achievement of independence further helps to increase the growing child's sense of being able to ensure its own safety and satisfaction. But for schizophrenic individuals the reassurance never comes. The parent, most typically unconsciously, continues to relate in an ambivalent manner which does not lead to reduced anxiety or to confidence about a stable, secure world. Each advance that the child makes toward independence may be reacted to by the parent in such a way as to make independence seem more dangerous than prolonged helplessness. The short-term adjustive strategies that work under such pressures are frequently poor long-term adaptations to living.

Catatonic Stupor from an Evolutionary Perspective

The role of terror in the formation of schizophrenic symptoms is well illustrated by catatonic reactions. The catatonic stupor is perhaps the most dramatic of the schizophrenic reactions. It was originally conceptualized as a separate disease by Karl Ludwig

Kahlbaum (1828–1899), and later integrated as one of the major forms of schizophrenia by Eugen Bleuler. Biologic speculations about catatonia as a "disease" have been rampant, and generally they have not been sustained by continued investigation. For example, 30 years ago, the drug bulbocapnine was noted to cause muscular rigidity; research was undertaken to investigate "bulbocapnine catatonia" in animals, but, the bulbocapnine-induced rigidity was in many ways unlike the schizophrenic reaction, and no trace of bulbocapnine has ever been found in the bodies of schizophrenic human beings. It is now clear that catatonia is not a disease, but an adaptive response to terror, of which all humans, indeed nearly all animals, are capable.

As is well known, catatonic human beings seem impervious to their surroundings. They can be subjected to great pain without responding. They appear to be in a state of stupor. They are immobile, unresponsive, and either rigid or waxily flexible. They sometimes come out of the stupor unpredictably and go into a frenzy of violent activity.

Strangely enough, while in the catatonic stupor, these patients are also characterized by a very rapid pulse, which seems discrepant with their appearance and functioning. Moreover, despite their apparent inattentiveness and unresponsiveness, there is clinical evidence that they are aware of their surroundings. Many clinicians (e.g., Fromm-Reichmann) have noted that recovered catatonic patients tell them about the conversations and events that occurred around them when they were in the catatonic state. Further evidence of the patient's awareness lies in the fact that persistent psychotherapeutic work based on the assumption that the catatonic individual hears and understands the therapist leads to clinical improvement and termination of the stupor (e.g., Rosberg and Karon 1958, Karon and VandenBos 1972).

The "comparative method" (Denny and Ratner 1970) for investigating and understanding behaviors across a large number of species with respect to both form and function from an evolutionary perspective has led to a body of data on animal behavior that sheds new and important light on the meaning and nature of the catatonic stupor.

A wide variety of species demonstrate a similar "immobility" response. For example, an alligator placed on its back becomes immobile and waxily flexible. Rabbits, which are an unusually squirmy and uncooperative experimental animal, become pliant and immobile when restrained upside-down on a V-board. Investigation of a wide variety of mammal, reptile, and even insect species has revealed how widespread this phenomenon is: lions, pigs, monkeys, cattle, horses, mice, rats, fox, coyotes, goats, guinea pigs; swans, chickens, owls, and over twenty other species of birds; snakes, frogs, chameleons, and alligators; octopus, angelfish, and toadfish; cockroaches, spiders, mantids, and other insects (Ratner 1967). The only exceptions were domestic dogs and cats and regularly handled laboratory white rats. Rats from laboratories where they are not regularly and gently handled do demonstrate the immobility response. Although such a phenomenon is well known to animal researchers and veterinarians who make use of it as a practical expedient in handling animals, why this should occur and what function it serves for the animal has been by no means clear.

The most frequent explanation was that the animal was "hypnotized." Aside from the immobility and apparent imperviousness to pain, however, the animal does not seem like a hypnotized subject. There certainly is nothing like the usual induction procedures used with human beings, and heightened suggestibility can hardly be invoked, even among animals who have worked with trainers and hence can understand commands.

While painful and even fatal wounds can be inflicted without reaction during immobility, pupillary reflexes to light remain (Ratner 1967). Conditioning experiments, moreover, reveal the effects of conditioning carried out while the animal was in this immobility state; this would seem to indicate that there is indeed awareness of stimuli, even though there is no external response or sign of awareness. Moreover, despite the animal's trancelike or stuporous appearance, the animals are characterized by a rapid heartbeat, until just before termination of the immobility (Ratner 1967). The animals come out of this state with full functioning, in a split second. Attempts by experimenters to predict from external signs when an animal will come out of this state and regain mobility have been fruitless. For example, a group of birds in an immobile state were placed on a table, and an attempt was made by standing over the table to catch them when they came out of it. Not one of the birds was caught.

An animal's prior experiences with the test situation, with the experimenters, and with prior testing for immobility reactions influence the intensity of the catatoniclike response. Daily handling and/or taming of the animal before testing decreases the intensity of the response (Ratner and Thompson 1960). Repeated testing under exactly similar conditions at an interval of once a day will decrease the intensity of the response, but changing any aspect of the situation will reintensify the reaction.

The stimulus element producing the most dramatic increase was to change the experimenter (Gilman et al. 1950). Test trials in which the animal is immediately reimmobilized increases the duration of the reaction; repeating such procedures with guinea pigs for 2 hours increases the duration of immobility from 30 seconds to 2 hours (Liberson 1948).

The adaptive significance of this response in animals is that it is the last stage of defense of a prey under attack by a predator. Almost all species are prey for some other predator species. Most predators will kill prey, but not eat it if they are not hungry. They will store their prey for later.

In observing the behavior of animals under attack by predators, each prey species has a characteristic sequence of adaptive responses as the predator gets closer and closer to killing and eating the prey (Ratner 1975). Some of these responses tend to save the life of the individual, and other responses tend to preserve the lives of other members of the species. Both types of responses would obviously be selected for by evolution.

After all other predeath adaptive responses, such as squawking, distress cries, distraction (in order to lead the predator away from other members of the species), aggression (either individual or mob), and feigned injury, have been exhausted, the last response of each species examined has been to "die," that is, to go into the "immobility reaction." Unlike the usual mock death, which occurs earlier in the adaptive sequence, the individual does not seem under voluntary control. In this immobility state, the individual can be subjected to great pain and appears, from the standpoint of the predator, to be a dead animal.

Thus, in one laboratory experiment, frogs were released in the presence of a ferret. The ferret chewed the leg of one frog, or ate the eye of another, with not one flicker of movement from either frog, while they were in this peculiar state. Every frog under attack went into the immobility state before its real death. The ferret ate what it wanted and stored the frog, partially mutilated, for later. In the laboratory experiments, 70 percent of the frogs survived and, with no warning, hopped off to escape death, but in a mutilated condition.

Obviously, if in the natural environment even 30 percent of the animals survived to one more breeding, the effect on evolution would be massive. The immobility or catatonic response, therefore, is adaptive and life-saving, both for the individual and for the species. Since almost all species are, or have been, prey for other species, almost all species have this response evolutionarily built in. This includes human beings.

It is clear that the reason this catatonic stupor in animals does not occur with domestic dogs and cats and white rats used to gentle handling is because these animals are not in the clutches of an unfriendly predator. Presumably, the reason most species (for example, alligators) go into immobility reaction on being turned upside down, is because no such animal who had any control of the situation would be in this posture. In the natural environment, it would mean that a predator has the animal helpless and restrained.

Many years ago, Frieda Fromm-Reichmann reported the conscious experience of catatonic patients to be that they would die if they moved. Unfortunately, human beings are highly symbolic animals, and we can feel we are at death's door under circumstances that are remote from actual physical danger.

Thus, a very disturbed adolescent who had previously been treated unsuccessfully at a series of institutions for disturbed children was living at home while continuing treatment with a not altogether competent therapist. The patient revealed homosexual episodes to that therapist, who relayed this information to the parents. The parents said to the patient, "Let's go for a ride." (This was in the 1940s, when gangster movies were common.) They put him in the back seat of their black Cadillac, while they sat in the front, and discussed him, saying, "What shall we do with him?" They agreed aloud, "We must get rid of him." (By which, they consciously meant, put him in another institution. Their unconscious may well have been more in keeping with the patient's interpretation.) When the ride was over, they were surprised to discover him in the back seat catatonic. Ten years later, the meaning of this chain of events was discovered during the process of his successful psychotherapy.

As a second example, a schizophrenic woman in her 30s, functioning on a borderline level, was raped. She went to the emergency room of the hospital at which she had been treated for emotional problems. After being physically examined, she was given tranquilizers and was told she could stay overnight. There was no discussion of the rape or her feelings about it. In the morning she was discharged with still no opportunity for any kind of therapeutic discussion. As she left the hospital, she became catatonic just outside the door, only to be brought back in and readmitted.

She was angry both at being raped and at not being offered any help in dealing with it. "I couldn't move. I was surprised I couldn't move. It was like something big was going to come down out of the sky and kill me." (While it would be tempting to speculate phylogenetically, it is probably more accurate that she was terrified that her anger might lead to retaliation, which of course in childhood would have come from above—from one's towering parents.) She felt as though she was going to be killed. The patient felt she could not go back to her parents' house even though she still lived with them, because the rape made her sexually culpable in their eyes. Furthermore, she had wanted help from the hospital, but they had refused either to shelter her or provide psychotherapy. The result was that she was a helpless child abandoned to a dangerous world where rapists and other vicious people can prey on people who receive no help and no support, and where people cannot even get angry because they do not receive any help. This was a repetition of her childhood feelings—of not being able to depend on her parents, of being in danger, of being abandoned (for a child, abandonment means death), of not being able to be angry about what she was not getting for fear that she would certainly be killed for being angry, and that any kind of sexual activity, even being raped, was morally culpable. The provision of even minimal counseling could have avoided a psychotic break, at least at that time.

The catatonic stupor is an emergency reaction. It is the last stage in one's biologic defenses against what seems like an inescapable threat of violent death, a defense which throughout human evolution has been effective, or partially successful, in saving the individual's life when all else has failed.

Affect Disorder in Schizophrenia

There have been numerous attempts to explain why schizophrenic patients have no affect or, less usually, inappropriate affect. These explanations, like so many explanations of aspects of schizophrenic disorders, founder upon inconsistent experimental findings. The reason for this is very simple. The patient is *not* without affect.

The schizophrenic patient lives in a chronic terror state, which is so strong that other affects do not appear. If your life is organized around staying alive, you may not have much time for excitement, sadness, disappointment, intrigue, joy, or any of the other more subtle feelings of human existence.

Like most true theoretical statements, this leads directly to appropriate psychotherapeutic technique. A way of achieving therapeutic access to schizophrenic patients, no matter how sick, is to let the patient know some time in the first session that you are not going to let anyone kill them. This is always a good idea. Even patients who seem intractable can be seen to react to that statement, if to nothing else that the therapist says in the first hour. This is because it is directly addressed to that with which they are most centrally struggling. It is not accidental that all the medications that tend, at least temporarily, to help schizophrenic patients, the so-called antipsychotic medications (or, as they used to be called, major tranquilizers) are medications that reduce terror.

Just as absent affect has to be understood as apparently absent affect, so "inappropriate affect" has to be understood as apparently inappropriate affect. Not to do so leads one's theories far astray. Thus, Sarnoff A. Mednick has attempted to explain the inappropriate affect in schizophrenia in learning theory terms as the result of reduced anxiety. He used the example of Norman Cameron's patient who was told that his brother had died in an automobile accident while driving to the hospital to visit him. The patient looked out the window and said: "What a beautiful day it is today." It was assumed this was an inappropriate affect, as well as a confused cognition. With no further information about the patient, it was argued that when the patient replaced an appropriate affect and cognition with inappropriate ones, the reduction in anxiety reinforced the "irrelevancies," and that this could explain schizophrenic symptoms.

But anyone with a modicum of knowledge either of psychoanalysis or of child development in general knows that the feelings of brothers for each other are ambivalent, and that sibling rivalry is something with which every child, even in the best of homes, has to learn to cope. It is a glib assumption that if the patient feels it was a beautiful day when his brother died, it is necessarily an inappropriate affect, just because society officially prefers to believe all relatives love each other. It may be inappropriate from a socially desirable standpoint, but certainly not necessarily from an empirical one.

As any psychoanalytic therapist knows, the patients do use denial, repression, and reaction-formation, but the end products of symptom-formation, the symptoms themselves, are not irrelevant; they provide the beginning for the investigation both of the defenses and of the impulses, feelings, and conflicts defended against by the symptoms.

Thought Disorder in Schizophrenia

There exists a large body of literature that attempts to establish the nature of the schizophrenic thought disorder, some of which deals with it as the central symptom. Certainly, it is one of the central symptoms of schizophrenia, but not the only one. Highly sophisticated principles such as Von Domarus's principle (equivalence of predicates), double-bind theory, etc., have been elaborated at great lengths (cf. Arieti). But experimental validations do not indicate that the thought disorder is as simple or as consistent as these explanations by a simple principle would lead one to believe.

It is clear that schizophrenic people are not always illogical. Nor does their thought disorder consistently follow any simple rules of "illogic" or "paleologic." They become illogical when the content of their speech or thought is in some way connected with something frightening. Again and again, it has been our experience that things which have specific meaning for a patient have been

overlooked because they seemed like a "characteristic" of the
disease. Such "throwing away of data" is one of the justifications
for the recent critiques of the "medical model." For example, early
in my (Karon's) experience, a patient was described, with no
further comments, at a case conference as "confused," because he
drank from his own urinal. A later paranoid patient explained such
a symptom when he said, "If you only drink your own urine and
only eat your own feces, you will never die." This view of self-
sufficiency as a defense against death is not uncommon, and ought
to be investigated with any patient who manifests that symptom.

The most illuminating description of the schizophrenic
thought disorder is given by Theodore Lidz (1973), who started
his researches in schizophrenia by investigating thought disorders,
and came to the conclusion that the thought disorder in schizophrenia is not the same as that in organic disorders, a conclusion
also reached earlier by Kurt Goldstein (1954). Lidz suggests, in
agreement with Wynne and Singer (1963a, 1963b), that the schizophrenic thought disorders can best be subsumed under the rubric
"egocentric overinclusiveness," that is, the feeling that things
which logically are not related to the self *are* related to the self, or
that things which realistically one cannot influence *are* being
influenced by one's actions.

An even more careful scrutiny, he points out, of the patient's
material and the relationships with his or her family revealed that
what looks like "egocentric" thought really is "parent-centric"
thought, and that it has to do with attempting to resolve the
relationship, real and fantasied, between the patient and his
parents.

In understanding the schizophrenic patient's thought disorder there are two additional considerations. The first of these is
that the parents themselves frequently teach concepts that do not
have the same meaning to other people as they do to themselves
(cf. Lidz 1973). For example, all parents teach their children that
parents love their children. A schizophrenic patient, therefore,
may report being loved even by a parent who actually has made
attempts to murder him. This makes the world seem a very confusing and dangerous place to the patient because he thinks that
any kind of love relationship has to be broken off to preserve his

life. It is also very confusing for the therapist to try to understand what is going on in the patient's mind, but the therapist for schizophrenic patients must tolerate the confusion that occurs and will occur for a long time. It occurs simply because he assumes that words have the same meaning to him and to the patient, and of course they do not.

A second characteristic of schizophrenic thought is that under stress the patient regresses and uses modes of thought that were more typical of an earlier period in life, or were dreamlike, and that this varies over time between and within sessions, depending on the degree of anxiety with which the patient is attempting to cope.

Rudolf Ekstein (1971) has pointed out that while there is no general schizophrenic language, each patient has a meaningful personal language which the therapist must learn. That language may seem incomprehensible, but that is only because we do not know it yet. It is a common, but fairly naive, assumption that what we do not understand is necessarily meaningless. The strange verbalizations, the "word salad," the words which themselves seem meaningless or incomprehensible, as in the patients we designate "hebephrenic," all turn out to be meaningful; they just require patience to learn what that meaning may be. Needless to say, the same is true of the idiosyncratic use of words in the autistic child and, indeed, in all schizophrenic people.

CONCRETE VERSUS ABSTRACT

How misleading systematic research can be is illustrated by the concept of "concrete" versus "abstract" responses. Kurt Goldstein (1954) while he was clear that schizophrenic thought disorders were different from organic thought disorders, nonetheless termed both kinds of problems *concrete*. A typical item used to measure concrete thinking is the ball and field test. A circle is drawn on a piece of paper and the patient is asked, "You have lost a ball in here. How would you go about finding it?"

"I have not lost a ball," is a response that is uniformly classified as "concrete." It is easy to confirm that this response occurs more often with schizophrenic people or brain-damaged patients than with normal individuals. Thus, one of our paranoid-schizophrenic patients would give such a response. Not only would he say, "I have not lost a ball," he would scream it and put his hands over his genitals.

This man was not lacking in the ability to form an abstraction, rather the examiner had raised a terrifying issue of life and death significance for the patient. He had to be concerned with that issue rather than with the task that the examiner thought he was setting for him. In other contexts, this particular patient handled abstractions very well, was very fond of philosophy, and was generally better able to manipulate abstract ideas than most of the people who had attempted to treat him. In fact, he confided in therapy, "I like abstract ideas, but I am not too much concerned about their empirical referents." In short, he used abstractions for defensive purposes.

It is generally true that schizophrenic patients will be concrete or abstract, depending upon what best serves the purpose of defending them against anxiety. Most hospitalized patients are less educated than the doctors who treat them, and "concrete" communications best serve the purpose of defending against anxiety. Occasional bright paranoid individuals are encountered, however, who use abstraction as their best defense and do not wish to be troubled with the concrete realities because reality arouses too much anxiety.

THE "DOUBLE" AND "SINGLE" BIND

It has been observed that many parents of schizophrenic patients make mutually contradictory demands of the patient, the so-called "double-bind." Experimental research reveals, however, that all people, normal and schizophrenic, have difficulty with "double-bind" situations and that clearly diagnosed schizophrenic people tend to have more trouble coping with almost any problem than "normal" individuals, but that schizophrenic people do not have an exaggerated vulnerability to "double-binds" (Potash 1964). It is simply one way of being a psychologically unhelpful parent. While we see double-bind theory as a specific example of a wider spectrum of psychonoxious interactions, it must be admitted that the "double-bind" view derives from and leads to paying careful attention to the interaction patterns within the patient's family, and understanding interactions is central to understanding the so-called schizophrenic process.

Clinically, many of our schizophrenic patients suffer from "single-binds"; for example, their parents have led them to believe their existence is a crime. There is no comfortable sane way of accommodating oneself to such a belief.

PARANOID THOUGHT DISORDERS

It is well known that Freud derived the origin of many paranoid delusions from defenses against homosexual impulses. Almost never reported in secondary sources, however, is Freud's explanation of the source of these urgent homosexual impulses; neither is his explanation of the apparent contradictions to his views. Moreover, Freud himself did not explain the systematic character of paranoid delusions which forms such an integral part of their nature.

Freud described, in the language of the libido theory, the fact that the schizophrenic patient felt withdrawn from relations with other people. In trying to relate again, it is easier to relate to someone of the same sex. This is because members of the same sex are more like oneself and also because developmentally one learned to relate to peers of the same sex before one learned to relate to the opposite sex. Unfortunately, the appearance of this self-curative impulse, this strong urge to relate to someone of the same sex, is experienced by the patient as something taboo: "My God, I'm a homosexual." Thus, the frequent paranoid delusions may be understood as different ways of denying or rather contradicting the sentence (in the case of the male patient) "I love him."

The most common dynamic is "I do not love him, I hate him" (a reaction formation into paranoid hate). One cannot, however, irrationally hate people, so this is typically projected into "He hates me." If he hates me, then, of course, I can hate him, and if I hate him, no one need think that I love him. This is the most usual dynamic for paranoid hate and feelings of persecution. Of course other delusions may be formed. The homosexual impulse itself may be projected: "I do not love him. He loves me." This is the kind of patient who is perpetually concerned with homosexual threats from others. "I do not love him, I love her" leads to delusions of erotomania. "I do not love him—she loves him," leads to delusions of jealousy. "I do not love him, I love me" leads to delusions of grandeur. Of course, these sentences are simplified verbal representations of a process of symptom-formation which is unconscious.

What is missing from secondary sources, but not from Freud, is the understanding that the strong "homosexual" urge is itself the paradoxical result of an attempted self-curative process. Thus, for a therapist to treat the paranoid delusion as only reflecting a homosexual impulse is not only bad treatment because it is tactless, and experienced by the patient as insulting, but also because it is inaccurate.

It is frequently pointed out as a criticism of Freud's view that female paranoid patients usually have male persecutors rather than female persecutors in their delusional systems. Clinically this tends to be true, and, not surprisingly enough, Freud described this himself and explained its dynamics on the basis of clinical material from a female paranoid patient. His view was that there was always an earlier version of the symptom in which the persecutor was female, and this was transformed as the symptoms become elaborated into a male persecutor as a further stage of disguise. In our clinical experience, Freud's reconstruction is correct.

This is a special case of a more general phenomenon. Paranoid delusions get more complex and disguised the longer they exist. Frequently, with patients who have been schizophrenic for a long time, the paranoid delusions do not simply disappear in therapy, but transform into earlier versions. When one reaches the simpler version that the patient suffered during his first "break," one often has the feeling, "It was *so* clear. Why didn't anyone understand?"

There is much about paranoid symptoms, however, which Freud did not explain. Even in the case of Schreber, there are many symptoms that Freud does not explain. Careful examination of the clinical material, of Schreber's childhood, and of the facts about his father reveals that much of the paranoid system is simply transference, that is, descriptions of real events, and childhood feelings about real events that occurred with his father, transposed to the outside world and to God. Thus, Schreber's delusion of a metal band being applied to his forehead by God "lovingly" is simply a repetition of the metal band which formed part of devices that Schreber's father, a famous pediatrician, had invented to ensure that children would have to sit or lie straight to improve their posture. Schreber's father even advised that these devices (which by modern standards we would consider torture devices) should be applied "lovingly," as he himself did. For a careful and insightful consideration of this case, the reader is referred to Niederland (1959a, 1959b, 1972).

The point that many paranoid symptoms can be best understood as transference is generally valid. Thus, the feeling of being persecuted and the specific nature of that persecution may be a straightforward transference reaction. "My mother hates me" may be true, as well as the thinly disguised "The queen of England hates me," or the most general "Everyone hates me" (i.e., everyone of importance in childhood). Of course, while the well-informed therapist may know the meaning of such statements, transference is a defense, and the patient will remain unaware of its meaning without an interpretation.

At no point does Freud explain the systematization which we take as the hallmark of paranoid disorders. Certain characteristics of the paranoid system have become clear to us over the years in clinical work. First of all, patients we call paranoid or paranoid schizophrenic are not the only patients who have paranoid systems. All schizophrenic patients have a paranoid system. Those whom we call catatonic will not communicate it (or anything else) to us. Those whom we call hebephrenic do not communicate to us in a way that we can understand. In both cases, when we do understand them, we find a paranoid system. As a matter of fact, all of us have a paranoid system, that is, a systematic understanding of our world and our experiences. The reason that you and I do not understand each other as paranoid is that our systematic understanding of the world is very much the same. If you believe the world is flat, your views are not paranoid if the year happens to be 1400. If the year happens to be 1975, you are at least suspect. The belief is the same—it is the level of shared knowledge and assumptions which is different.

The people we call schizophrenic have had lives which are different and experiences which are different, and, therefore, their systematic understanding of the world in which they live has to be different. The patients we call paranoid or paranoid schizophrenic generally are the brighter patients, who therefore have developed a better systematic explanation of their experiences and consequently do not need to develop the more regressed symptoms of the patients we call hebephrenic or catatonic. While this seems to be true clinically, it was possible to check on this in a systematic way. When all state hospital admissions in a New England state for 2 years were used (Albert Rabin, Personal Communication, 1962), it was found that IQ test scores of patients diagnosed as true paranoid tend to be higher than those of patients diagnosed as paranoid schizophrenic, which tend to be higher than those of all other schizophrenic patients.

One of the fictions about paranoid systems is that they are extremely stable and cannot be changed. A careful systematic attempt to understand a paranoid system in detail will reveal that it changes from week to week and even from day to day, especially when it undergoes mutual scrutiny by a patient and an interested psychotherapist. The paranoid system does not quite fit reality, and therefore enormous repair work is continuously being done by the patient to make it fit. The work gets frenetic when there is a therapist who continually brings the inconsistencies with reality to the patient's attention in a sympathetic way. The reason for the myth that paranoid systems are unchanged is that they are so different from the set of beliefs the rest of us have that it seems as if they do not change, and they are rarely investigated in careful detail.

SCHIZOPHRENIC LANGUAGE

While the literature frequently suggests a so-called schizophrenic language, many students find that it does not appear when they listen to patients carefully. One linguist, listening to tapes of psychotherapy sessions from the Michigan State Psychotherapy Project, and trying to investigate schizophrenic language, said, "But these people don't talk like schizophrenics." Indeed they did not, because the therapy helped them to make sense out of their lives and symptoms. They did talk like schizophrenic individuals when their anxieties overwhelmed them.

The search for formal, syntactic, or grammatic principles peculiar to schizophrenic patients is frequently motivated by a wish to find an impaired physiologic mechanism, and distracts from paying careful attention to the content of the schizophrenic patient's communication.

Hallucinations

Hallucinations may be readily understood by a body of literature which already exists. Freud's description of dreams characterizes hallucinations completely, except that the motivation has to be stronger to produce a dream when you are wide awake. It is true that schizophrenic hallucinations tend to be predominantly auditory rather than visual, although all sense modalities may be involved at times in the symptoms. As with dreams, associations should always be obtained, if possible.

The utility of a knowledge of elementary dream theory in understanding hallucinations can be exemplified by a hallucination which puzzled the patient's resident. The patient reported being terrified by the face of the woman outside the barred window of his room. He said that she was a total stranger, and he had no associations to her. But a knowledge of the theory of dreams might lead one to recall Freud's statement that a total stranger in a dream is always someone very close to the dreamer, so close that the dreamer would not fail to recognize the person. The meaning of the hallucination becomes clear: he wishes that he were afraid of a total stranger outside the barred windows of his room rather than being afraid of his own mother who had free access to his room, even in the hospital.

While an all too brief summary of applicable dream theory is to be found in the technique chapter, the novice therapist would be well advised to know as much about dreams as is to be found in Part II of Freud's *General Introductory Lectures* and in the first chapter of the *New Introductory Lectures*. For the novice, it will be useful in reading Freud to know that the libido theory is at most a useful metaphor which breaks down in certain places which will be described later in this book. The collective unconscious does not seem to have any validity and, therefore, symbols that are based on the collective unconscious are to be treated with caution. Nor are symbols based on the origins of words to be taken at face value. Freud's patients frequently were educated at the Gymnasia and had studied many years of Latin and Greek. They required no racial or collective unconscious to be able to form symbols out of word origins. Symbolic interpretations are not universal; nonetheless they remain good clinical guesses based on prior clinical experience, which can be utilized when associations are not forthcoming.

Those symbols which are most valid are based on the biologic nature of human beings and hence universal in each one's own experience. In all cultures, the male genitals have three parts, are intrusive, are roughly snakelike; in all cultures the female genitals are an enclosure; in all cultures children are smaller than adults and adults control them.

Autism: Withdrawal from People

Autism, or withdrawal from people, has a number of sources. The family has typically encouraged the preschizophrenic child not to form relations and identifications outside the family. This prevents the ordinary corrective identifications that all of us use to correct the "warps" in our family. Hence, any problems in the preschizophrenic child's family get magnified in their impact.

In addition, the patient is frightened of interpersonal interactions on the basis of his or her relations inside the family, usually beginning in infancy and usually continuing throughout life, and they generalize (transfers) to people outside the family, believing them to be as difficult and dangerous to deal with, and in the very same ways.

The patient is often struggling to become a separate psychologic entity from one or both parents, typically the mother. The struggle not to be devoured, absorbed, engulfed, and the wish to split off, conflict with the fear of being abandoned to die and the fear of being isolated forever. This becomes a central conflict around which much of the pathology, and even some of the healthy development, can be understood (cf. Mahler, et al. 1975; Fairbairn 1954; Guntrip 1969). Each new "object-relationship," that is, relationship with a person, raises again the specter of being involved in the same overwhelming panic-inducing conflict. To perceive a new "good object" correctly as "good" means having to face the awareness that the parents were by comparison "bad," and having to face the anxiety that provokes. (Of course, "bad," as used here, refers to the patient's feelings and/or the consequences of the original parental relation, not to moral qualities of the parent.) Therefore, interpersonal interaction is entered into with the greatest of trepidation.

It is easy to see that taking the view that schizophrenia arises out of the adaptations to one's life places these symptoms in a very different perspective, one which, however, fits with all the currently available data. The most important thing for a therapist to remember is that every one of the symptoms of schizophrenia is meaningful and is embedded in the life history of the patient. There is a difference between something being meaningless and its meaning being obscure. The working assumption that every symptom is meaningful soon leads the therapist to tolerate a chronic state of confusion and bit by bit to understand what is going on.

Physiologic Distractions

An enormous body of research literature exists, much of it superficially rigorous, which attempts to explain the symptoms or characteristics of schizophrenia. What is remarkable is how unconvincing and contradictory most of that literature is.

The most common hypotheses are genetic or physiologic. While accurate information about genetic mechanisms or physiology is always of value, these hypotheses tend to be accepted prematurely and with insufficient data. The danger in such genetic and physiologic studies is that they may be used, as they have been in the past (Kallman 1938), as an excuse for psychotherapeutic pessimism, although that is not a rigorously necessary conclusion, even if genetic and/or physiologic factors were clearly demonstrated.

Every organ system in the human body has been claimed to be the cause of schizophrenia. These findings rarely replicate and never last more than 5 years (Bellak 1948, 1958; Bellak and Loeb 1969b; Kety 1959a, 1959b; Wyatt, Termini, and Davis 1971). At this point, it is difficult to take them seriously unless they do. There is even one investigator who always gets national publicity whenever he discovers "the physiological basis for schizophrenia": he makes this discovery approximately every 3 years. In each instance, the data never replicate at other institutions.

The typical fate of physiologic theories may be exemplified by a theory which seemed compelling in the 1950s. Reputable researchers seemed to have established a slower rate of synaptic transmission and a related difference in 11-oxysteroid and 17-keto-steroid metabolism in schizophrenic individuals. Both were attributed to a malfunctioning adrenal cortex. The critical experiment was performed, excising the adrenal cortex of each patient, and placing the patients on cortisone. The result, unfortunately, was a group of schizophrenic patients who now needed to be maintained on cortisone.

The biochemical inquiries are often at a level of subtlety readily influenced by diet. Many of the supposed findings in the literature are based on the fact that the patients' diets in a particular institution were different from those of their control subjects.

One endocrinologic finding that seems to hold up is that approximately 10 percent of schizophrenic patients have underactive thyroids; this is a considerably more frequent incidence than in the general population. These patients, like anyone with an underactive thyroid, show improved functioning when the deficit is remedied. Anything that makes coping more difficult will increase the rate of schizophrenia.

What other findings remain seem to be components of the normal terror syndrome. Careful physiologic work thus tends to be consistent with psychodynamic observations.

Investigators, physiologic and psychologic, frequently report using elaborate experimental techniques requiring considerable cooperation from the subject. They never report a single patient who could not take or would not take their procedures. Anyone with a clinical knowledge of schizophrenic patients will be suspicious of such research. It would be more convincing if they reported the percentage of people who could not or would not take their procedures and stated the characteristics of the patients who did not complete the procedure. On the Michigan State Psychotherapy Project, we found that, before therapy, 30 percent of our schizophrenic subjects could not give a Rorschach that could be scored. Yet, almost any kind of response to the Rorschach cards can be scored. It is not a crime to use an experimental procedure that not all patients can take. It is a scientific crime to pretend that such phenomena do not exist if you are really trying to explicate the puzzles of the real world. In addition, apparently rigorous research may be misleading, because it does not ask the right questions or consider the context in which the patient is living.

For example, in the mid-1950s, an article in a prestigious journal reported altered time perceptions in schizophrenic individuals, supposedly related to physiologic mechanisms underlying the disorder. The empirical evidence was merely that the patients answered questions about time inaccurately ("What day of the week is it? What month is it?" etc.). Curious about this, Karon asked a chronic paranoid-schizophrenic patient, who was watching TV, if he ever got confused about what day of the week it was, what month it was, etc.

"Sure."

"When?"

"When I was in the State Hospital."

"Why was that?"

"What difference did it make?"

"Do you know what day it is now?"

"Sure."

"What day is it?"

"Today is the day Sid Caesar comes on."

That is, there was a difference between days that were functionally relevant to him now. Patients are often in living situations other than State Hospitals where the same events occur in the same order every day, so distinctions that are relevant to most of us have little importance for them. The same phenomenon is observed in campers in the wilderness, where a day is a day, and which day of an arbitrary calendar is irrelevant.

If you are so terrorized by a thought that your life is organized around dealing with what seems to be *the only* life and death issue, which day of the week it is, and many other matters, may seem irrelevant and unimportant, even if it is functionally relevant to others in that setting. If you ask someone an irrelevant question when they are concerned with more important issues, you may get anything back. Sullivan pointed out that much of the confusion in

the experimental literature on schizophrenia could be understood
if one realized that the schizophrenic patient frequently says whatever he thinks will get you to leave him alone.

The general finding in experimental investigations is that, on
the average, schizophrenic persons do worse in everything, usually
with greater variability than normal controls, both between subjects and within the subject's performance.

Early in his career, Karon considered, with some physiologic
researchers, the possibility of treating severely regressed patients
on whom careful assessments had been made of those physiologic
functions where there were established differences between
schizophrenic and normal individuals. As the patient improved,
it would then be possible to determine whether the physiology
changed with clinical improvement, or whether the organism
learned to function normally despite physiologic impairment. In
either case, we would learn something important about the human
organism and the relation between some physiologic and psychologic functions. Unfortunately, neither then nor now does sufficient consensus about physiologic disturbance exist to make that
research possible.

Genetic Distractions

It has been well known for a long time that children of
schizophrenic persons have a higher probability of becoming schizophrenic, and that, in general, close relatives of schizophrenic
persons are more likely to become schizophrenic. For a long time,
not only was this information considered sufficient to establish
schizophrenia as a genetic disorder, but it unfortunately became
part of the diagnostic process in doubtful cases, so that it became a
self-fulfilling prophecy.

This problem is still with us. In the American Psychiatric
Association *Diagnostic Statistical Manual III*, it is proposed to
include "familial" factors in the diagnostic manual. While the
psychiatrist is instructed "not to use" this information officially,
it is included for convenience.

Just how pernicious this can be is exemplified by the so-called
"Wolf-man" (a patient of Freud's whose pseudonym derives from
a dream about wolves). Before being treated by Freud, this patient

was treated as an inpatient by Emil Kraepelin, who diagnosed him as manic-depressive because he was intermittently elated and depressed without being able to give an adequate explanation, and his father had been a manic-depressive, which confirmed the diagnosis.

In fact, he was in love with a nurse. When she acted interested, like all lovers, he became elated. When, fearing for her job, she rejected him, he was, like all lovers, depressed. And he could not tell Kraepelin, who was in charge, because she would be fired. Hence, his "meaningless" mood swings.

Obviously, increased incidence of a disorder in close relatives is compatible with both genetic and psychodynamic causal hypotheses. One useful consequence of the awareness of familial incidence is to identify children who are at higher risk. As Manfred Bleuler (1971) has pointed out, effective preventive intervention is possible: by providing brief counseling to the children of schizophrenic parents one can effectively reduce their vulnerability.

In the quest for more scientific certainty about genetic factors, identical twins have been compared with fraternal twins, and, in general, found to be more often concordant with respect to schizophrenia; however, while it is clear that discordance between identical twins must be a result of environmental factors, it is not clear that similarity between identical twins must be directly a result of genetic factors, since identical twins are more often treated like a single individual even by their parents, and there are special psychologic reactions to being an identical twin (Burlingham 1952; Nolan 1960).

The statistical indexes (h^2, intraclass correlation, etc.) ordinarily used in twin studies to apportion variance give an appearance of precision which is somewhat of an illusion; they include the effects of social reactions to a hereditary disfigurement as genetic variance (ignoring the environmental link in the chain of causality, since the causal mechanism is not investigated). Moreover, these indexes usually include only environmental variations, which differ for twins raised together, and they exclude such environmental variation as that between siblings of different ages, let alone between different families and different cultures. Moreover, the statistical indexes will vary with the range of variation of the population studied (Karon and Saunders 1958).

As the difficulty in disentangling genetic and environmental influences became increasingly apparent to researchers, adopted individuals seemed a promising avenue of research. Scandinavian countries provided records that could be used for such purposes. Thus, Kety (Rosenthal and Kety 1968) found that adopted parents and siblings of schizophrenic people have a lower incidence of schizophrenia than biologic parents and siblings. This was reported as evidence for a genetic point of view, which it is if one assumes adoptions are random. But very few agencies in any country would permit a schizophrenic parent to adopt a child, and very few families with one or more schizophrenic children would want to adopt another child. Thus, the findings would occur even if there were no genetic factors.

The accepted "definitive" studies have been those that investigated the rate of schizophrenia in children adopted at an early age whose biologic parents were schizophrenic as compared to those whose biologic parents were not (e.g., Heston 1966, 1970). The rate of schizophrenia is dramatically higher (approximately 10 percent) in the adopted offspring of schizophrenic biologic parents. While the rate of psychopathology is reported to be higher in the parents who adopted children from schizophrenic natural parents, it is not sufficiently higher to account for the difference in the incidence of schizophrenia.

Such a finding, however, confuses pathology (the degree of one's own symptoms) with "pathogenesis" (the degree to which one produces pathology in others). Such an assumption is natural for a geneticist unfamiliar with psychodynamics. The psychologic, psychiatric, and psychoanalytic literature readily reveals that the characteristics of a parent that make children vulnerable to schizophrenia are not the same as schizophrenic symptoms, and in some cases actually protect the parent against such a breakdown. Clinically, there are some people who seem reasonably healthy when examined psychiatrically, but whose unconscious involuntary interaction with their children may be psychologically extremely difficult to grow up with, and others who may even be overtly psychotic, but who largely shield the child from the harmful effects of their pathologic condition. This will be discussed further in Chapter 5.

Lyman Wynne and Margaret Singer in a series of studies (e.g., Singer and Wynne 1965a, 1965b) have found that parents whose children become schizophrenic tend to show a characteristic thought disorder, which is not identical with that of grossly psychotic people, but which is measurable, and Singer and Wynne (1966) have devised scoring keys for the Rorschach and TAT. Wender, Rosenthal, Zahn, and Kety (1971) gave Rorschachs to adoptive parents who had adopted children either of biologic parents who were normal or of biologic parents who were schizophrenic. They reported, like Heston, an increase in the frequency of schizophrenia (approximately 10 percent) in adopted children whose biologic parents were schizophrenic (Wender 1969), as opposed to those whose biologic parents were normal. They also reported no difference in thought disorder on the Rorschach between the parents who adopted children from schizophrenic natural parents, and the parents who adopted children from "normal" natural parents. Hence, they argue the increased incidence of schizophrenia could only be accounted for by genetics.

When the Rorschachs were scored blindly by Singer using the appropriate key, however, only those parents whose adoptive offspring became schizophrenic showed the specific kind of thought disorder found in natural parents whose offspring became schizophrenic (Lidz 1973, p. 66). Hence, no genetic factor would be required to account for the findings. Rather, one would begin to ask what are the nonrandom factors in adoption in Scandinavia that lead parents who are "pathogenic" to be more likely to adopt children born to parents who are "schizophrenic."

Wender, Rosenthal, and Kety (1975, 1976) have argued that this is not the case, and only genetics can explain the differences, since word-association tests, MMPIs, and TATs did not differentiate the two sets of adoptive parents. But no serious investigator has ever suggested that word-association tests or MMPIs would differentiate parents of schizophrenic children. As for the TAT, these investigators took no chance of Margaret Singer being able blindly to identify the adoptive parents whose children became schizophrenic—they never sent her that data. (The Wynne and Singer scoring is sufficiently complex that other researchers have reported it took a year to develop reliable scoring by raters other than Wynne and Singer themselves.) Nor did they use the "Pathogenesis" TAT scale, which, according to Mitchell (1969, 1970), even more strongly differentiates parents of schizophrenic children from parents of normal children than the Wynne and Singer TAT scale, even though its use was suggested to Rosenthal and Kety by Karon in 1969.

Why children whose biologic parents were schizophrenic should be more likely to be adopted by psychologically destructive individuals is an interesting question. First of all, only about 10 percent of the "adopted-away" children of biologic parents who were schizophrenic became schizophrenic themselves. More than that percentage of adoptions are not handled through agencies. A review of our own schizophrenic patients who were adopted reveals that they were adopted by relatives, or friends of the family, or even bought on the "black market." Further, adoption workers tell us that it is absurd to think of adoptions handled through agencies as ever being random. Anywhere in Europe, where the "genetic taint" of madness has been accepted for centuries, most families would not accept a child from schizophrenic parents, and an adoption worker would try to find a family that might not object, possibly because of some preexisting emotional problems in relatives.

There have also been some attempts to locate separated identical twins adopted in the first year of life. But such cases are rare, and the facts are hard to establish. Thus, cases have been reported as separated when they were not separated, or when they were separated later in childhood, or raised by close relatives. Some of the other anomalies that are revealed by close inspection of the genetic data are discussed by Lidz (1977).

In short, the genetic literature reveals a frantic search for a simple explanation that can be used as an excuse for avoiding the painful task of understanding the patient and the difficult work of treating them, as well as an excuse for therapeutic failure. A more admirable motive is the compassionate wish to relieve parental guilt feelings.

But what if we accept at face value the studies that suggest there is a genetic component to schizophrenia (e.g., Rosenthal and Kety 1968)? These studies do not show that schizophrenia is inherited or that there is a known mechanism or known gene for schizophrenia, but only suggest some unknown inherited factor or factors that tend to increase the frequency of schizophrenia. If we assume that schizophrenia consists of extreme methods of adaptation, part of the potentialities of all human beings, anything that makes life adjustment more difficult is going to increase the rate of schizophrenia. Thus, it is known that the rate of schizophrenia among the poorest socioeconomic class is 12 times as high as it is among the highest socioeconomic class, using the Yale five-class system of classification, simply because life is tougher for the poor in our society (Hollingshead and Redlich 1958). It is also known that the psychosis rate is higher if you are discriminated against (Karon 1975).

There are many inherited factors that make adjustment more difficult: a crooked nose, a humpback, an underactive thyroid, and any number of things that we do not know. The sum total of such effects would well account for the kind of genetic findings that have been reported, namely, that, if the assumptions of the genetic researchers are accepted, about 10 percent of the variance of the disorder can be accounted for by genetic factors. That is all that has been demonstrated.

It is hoped that further research will take the form of postulating specific causal mechanisms—genetic, environmental, or interactional—which can be directly confirmed or invalidated.

Research on genetics and physiology should not be discontinued, particularly as the biochemistry of the genes is increasingly open to direct investigation, but, tentative indirect findings and speculative explanations should not be used as though they were facts, to justify ineffective clinical treatment, clinical inaction, or "genetic" counseling (as opposed to psychotherapeutic preventive efforts with patient and offspring).

4

Developmental
Aspects of
Schizophrenia

Psychotic breaks do not occur overnight. But in many instances the patient and the family talk about the psychotic break, or even experience it, as if it were an unique experience with no pre-history, discontinuous with their earlier life. The vulnerabilities for such an acute emotional reaction are set up from the earliest days of life, however.

Insofar as schizophrenic people are widely varying people, and the families of schizophrenic people are equally widely varied, the specific developmental problems, that is, problems in child-hood which have lasting effects, also vary. All of the psycho-dynamic and developmental problems that are found in other patients may be found here. Nonetheless, there are certain prob-lems that are so frequent in these patients that the clinician is well advised to be aware of them.

Overview

At this point it is probably worthwhile to present a brief simplified outline of the most usual developmental dynamics of schizophrenia, as we understand them. Because of the need to be brief, the description here of the parent sounds unduly harsh.

73

But the parental dynamics described are largely unconscious; that is, they represent a symptom of which the parent as well as the child is the victim. While they are modal, they may not apply in every case. All of these issues will be clarified later. Some psychoanalytic readers may find the language unacceptable, but the differences among psychoanalytic theorists frequently lie in the conceptual language used, and the processes described here clearly emerge in the clinical writings of Sullivan, Klein, Rosenfeld, Searles, Fairbairn, Guntrip, Kernberg, Volkan, Wolman, Jacobson, Mahler, Lidz, and others.

Schizophrenic pathology is usually the result of a pattern of unconsciously malevolent parenting from the earliest days of infancy onward. It is not merely the result of isolated traumatic experiences, but of a pattern of pressures that continues throughout childhood in somewhat changing form. The basic problems that begin in infancy are strengthened rather than reduced by the continuing interactions between the preschizophrenic child and his or her parents, particularly the mother. The child is the victim of a series of subtle and unsubtle rejections, the end effect of which is to make him or her feel worthless, unlovable. But to be literally unlovable means that mother will not love you, that she will abandon you and, to the infant, this means pain and death. This is the infantile terror that lurks behind the schizophrenic symptoms. The schizophrenic individual's whole life is organized around the need to defend psychologically against this danger.

The schizophrenogenic mother (Karon 1960; Karon and Rosberg 1958a) feels inadequate and compensates for her inadequacies by making demands on the child in terms of her own pathologic needs, without regard for the welfare of the child whenever their needs conflict. In many respects, the underlying problems of the schizophrenogenic mother are similar to those of the schizophrenic individual, but she defends against her anxiety by *unintentionally* destroying the child. Her relationship to the child is typically one of dominating dependence, whereby she dominates the child in order to force the child to satisfy her dependency needs. This pathologic relationship may be general, that is, with all her children, or it may be specific, i.e., only with sons, only with daughters, only the oldest child, etc. Frequently, the mother feels that this child is her favorite, which is understandable, since this child helped her maintain her own psychic equilibrium.

The pathologic pressures are not subtle, but a casual observer may miss them. These pressures are mainly to be found in the mother's unconscious, but involuntary manifestations can be noted in the verbal and behavioral reactions to the child. Consciously, the mother, in many cases, manifests (not only to others, but to herself) an attitude of apparent benevolence. Where the mother does not even derive pathologic satisfaction from the child, it is likely that the result is not schizophrenia in the child, but the sub-syndrome of infantile autism, where the acute symptoms begin in infancy, provided that, for external reasons, the child is kept alive (Bettelheim 1956).

One of the preschizophrenic child's attempts to deal with this problem is to deny the "bad" mother. Unfortunately, this defense is self-defeating. Despite such a denial, the mother still rejects her child and the more "ideal" the rejecting mother, the worse the child must be. The child tries to find something wrong with himself or herself to explain the feeling of rejection, but, when he or she changes whatever is thought to be wrong, the rejection remains. The child's only solution is never to change, or to attempt to change in some way that is unchangeable. Either of these maneuvers allows the reassuring belief that, if he or she did change, everything would be all right (and therefore that the mother really does love the child, except for this unfortunate circumstance). The child also looks around for a second "mother" who can provide what the original mother did not—he or she will turn to the father, to siblings, to others—but the schizophrenic symptoms are evidence that the child never succeeds in finding a benign mother image in these other persons. Rather he or she usually finds new versions of old problems. Typically, schizophrenic and the preschizophrenic individuals try all of the defenses described above frantically and unsuccessfully.

The problems of the schizophrenic person are basically oral in the sense that they were first manifested in the relationship between mother and child in the early oral period. But these problems are not primarily zone-related. Rather, it is the pattern of relationships which is primary, and the same psychologic battles are fought successively on the oral, anal, and genital battlegrounds.

The psychologic life of any individual may be described in terms of the fantasy structures, which are formed on the basis of experience and of previous fantasy structures. We interpret our experiences of the present on the basis of the fantasy structures—conscious and unconscious—which are formed in the past. It is in the nature of the fantasy structures and of their relationship to each other that we see the effects of childhood experiences upon the schizophrenic individual. When his life situation, as given meaning by his conscious and unconscious fantasy structures, gives rise to a terror against which he cannot defend except by gross distortions of reality, hallucinations, paranoid delusions, becoming mute, and so forth, we call him blatantly psychotic.

Before the Beginning

It is nice to be a wanted child and to be wanted just for yourself. Unfortunately, this is an uncommon experience even among people who do not become schizophrenic. Anything that makes life more difficult will affect the rate of schizophrenia. If the parent's reasons for having a child leave the parent with a residue of resentment and frustration, it will make life more difficult for the child.

Unfortunately, parents sometimes have children or adopt children for reasons that have nothing to do directly with wanting a child or wanting to raise a child. Sometimes having a child is a way of getting or formalizing a relationship, "He (or she) won't leave me, if I have a child (she has my child)." Sometimes the fantasy takes the form, "No one could love me, but if I have his child (she has my child), he (she) could love me for the child." The pregnancy fantasy may have as its motive a feeling that at least I will have a part of the person who left me (or whom I left). Even when there is no prospect of a permanent relationship, psychoanalysts have observed that separation regularly arouses pregnancy fantasies, frequently even in male patients.

Sometimes a pregnancy is a way of arranging a marriage. It is well known that one out of six American marriages start with a pregnancy. This is not a new phenomenon. In the 1600s, the records of the Puritan Church in New England indicate that one out of six couples publicly confessed to fornication before getting married, which was necessary if the "premature" child was to be baptized. This time-honored American custom of pregnant marriage continues unabated. It is not necessarily destructive if the people would have gotten married in any event or if, as sometimes occurs, they use the pregnancy to convince their parents that a marriage is not such a bad thing.

Many unwed fathers-to-be can be manipulated by guilt into marrying a woman he has "wronged," but people who are manipulated by guilt are angry, and they generally get even. The unwed mother, too, may feel guilty. If the couple marry, no one need feel guilty. The marriage may be used as an alibi (or even a legitimate reason) for giving up important aspirations and goals by one marriage partner or the other. Realistically or not, one partner may then be blamed by the other for the loss of the aspirations that have been surrendered. It is typical for the "injured" partner to get even with the spouse for whom he or she "has given up so much." Unfortunately, while the suffering of the spouse may be great, there is an even more vulnerable person in the family. The hostility of each parent toward the spouse is frequently directed toward that helpless person, the child, who is seen as "the cause of it all." Moreover the child is often reacted to as if he or she were the other parent.

Sometimes a child is used to maintain a marriage, or to justify the potential mother's role in the family. Unfortunately, once the child exists, the parents are faced with the realistic difficulties of raising a child, even though they may have little or ambivalent motivation for dealing with these difficulties effectively. Thus, for example, one early childhood schizophrenic person was an adopted child. During the psychotherapy of the parents, it became clear that the mother had felt that the father was uninterested in her. In order to maintain the marriage, the mother insisted upon adopting a child. The father went along with her request in order to keep her happy. Since both parents were emotionally ungiving individuals, they had trouble obtaining a child through ordinary channels; however, the father had no difficulty buying a child on the black market. This he felt should keep his wife "quiet." The wife accepted the child, and then found that it did nothing for her marriage. She was then in the position of having a child to raise with no real reason for wanting to raise the child.

There are other fantasies and dynamics related to having a child which can be articulated. They occur in the parents of normal children, as well as in the parents of schizophrenic children. The difference lies in how the fantasies are manifested in relation to the child, that is, whether they lead to constructive interaction or to interactions that neglect the child's needs.

For example, a person may want to have a child to prove that she really is a woman, or conversely, he is a man. Or one may be trying to give birth to oneself, to become one's own mother (or father). This may lead to either benign or pathogenic handling of the child, depending on whether the unconscious dynamic is undoing the bad parts of one's childhood, or simply repeating them as the active rather than passive participant. Or, the fantasy may be to give birth to oneself as perfect—the child one felt one ought to have been to be loved. But no child, like no adult, is perfect. The resulting inevitable disillusionment may lead the parent to unreasonable resentment or even rejection of the child.

Along with the need to give birth to one's self, is the need, frequently seen in women, to change sex or become a boy by giving birth to a boy. In such a case, the boy is not merely her child, but, in the mother's unconscious, herself reborn as a boy. If, in such a situation, the woman has a daughter, this dynamic can lead to an irrational rejection of the girl, as if to be a woman is to be defective. The impact on the daughter is nothing short of catastrophic.

One can also attempt to prove the acceptability of one's sexual identity by training the opposite-sexed child to prove how wretched it is to be the child's sex, or by treating the child as if his or her sexual identity is unacceptable. Thus, Robert Stoller (1968) reports male transsexuals to result from a concatenation of three factors: a very attractive male baby, a physically or emotionally absent father, and a mother who relatively unambivalently raises the child as a girl in the beginning years. The unconscious meaning of the child to her is a feminized penis.

A same-sexed child's sexual identity may be undermined to bolster the sexual identity of a parent. Most often it is a father whose unconscious fantasy seems to be "At least compared to my son, I am a man." These correlative dynamics in his mother and father, respectively, were clear in the case of an effeminate schizophrenic man whose parents and older sisters rewarded him consistently whenever he proved incompetent, and rejected him whenever he acted successful or independent. The sisters, on the other hand, were consistently encouraged to independence and competence, both by the parents and each other. None of the daughters became schizophrenic, but their sons did.

The traumas of one's own childhood may be recreated so as to be mastered. As mentioned above, this can be destructive when the mastery consists only of playing the active rather than the passive role in traumatic events of one's childhood (cf. Fraiberg et al. 1975). Thus, it is well known that the parent who was a physically abused child tends to physically abuse his or her own child. This phenomenon is more general than just physical abuse. It has even been our experience that patients will explain being mistreated by their own parents because of their mishandling of their own children, reversing the direction of time and causality. This puzzling psychodynamic makes good sense when we take into account the endurance of the infantile need to preserve the fantasy of the "good" mother at all costs.

A child may be conceived for the benefit of someone else, most typically someone from a parent's family of origin. Having a child of one's own may be required in order to be recognized as emancipated from some families. In other situations, where the parent's own existence had served to justify the mother's role in the family, there may be a need to have a child to provide her with a replacement. This is most frequently observed with either the oldest or the youngest child in the family. Similarly, a child may be conceived as a representative or a replacement of someone else. This might be the parent's dead grandmother or grandfather, his own parents, or to replace a dead sibling. Such a situation is devastating to children because they are treated as if they were someone else and not individuals with identities of their own. Moreover, a child conceived for such a purpose is frequently a great disappointment. No matter what one does, one is *not* the dead child (or dead relative). The parents may express this resentment by letting the child know he or she is a replacement, setting off the fantasy that "they do not really like me, I am just a spare tire." Or even the delusional belief that one is the dead person.

The motive for having a child may be merely the wish to be pregnant. For such mothers, giving birth to a child and having a child is not the desired state. On the contrary, it is a disappointment, and the child will be rejected. In its most devastating form, the wish to be pregnant, arising from severely unfulfilled oral needs, results in a postpartum psychosis in the mother (Rosberg and Karon 1959). The psychotic state which ensues is felt by the child as a rejection. A severe physical illness of the mother may have the same unfortunate effect. The infant, whose legitimate dependency needs are enormous, is deprived of attention from the mother for as long as the psychotic state (or illness) lasts. In many instances the effect on the child can be long-lasting, even lifelong.

A mother may suffer a postpartum psychosis and yet the child may emerge relatively unscathed, if the psychotic symptoms do not impair the concurrent and later mothering. Moreover, the later attitude of the mother (and father) mitigates or intensifies the effect on the child. If the mother lets the child know that his or her birth was a catastrophe, or the family projects the responsibility for the mother's illness on the child, the resultant feeling is, "I am unlovable and so destructive that I bring terrible things on anyone who is close to me. My crime was being born." Some such feelings may occur without prompting, but "You drove me crazy" or "I have never been physically well since you were born," repeated throughout childhood, does not foster normal development.

These are a variety of situations that lead parents to have a child with little or no desire to relate to that child as an unique individual. Such dynamics can be seen in many parents. In milder forms, these do not necessarily lead to schizophrenia, but they are likely to lead to severe symptoms in the offspring when such dynamics are essential to the parents' adjustment, and are not attenuated by healthier motives. Of course, it would be absurd to attribute a lifetime of pathology as severe as schizophrenia to one pathogenic factor or destructive event. It is the cumulative effect of a lifetime of such pressures that determines the ultimate degree of pathology.

Oral Trauma

When the mother's ambivalence, anxiety, or rage at having to "parent" is present from the very beginning of the patient's life, the child's earliest experience of the mother may be bodily sensations of discomfort and pain while being handled and fed, as well as physical discomfort while not being handled and not being fed. As Spitz (1965) has described, when the mother is angry at the child, even when she tries not to show it or reacts with saccharine sweetness, the infant reacts as if it was devastated. The child feels the hostility and anxiety in the mother. While it has been tempting for psychologic theorists to talk about empathy as if it were magical, no such transcendental principle is required. Spitz (1965) has shown that slow-motion motion pictures of mothers handling infants reveal that mothers who are even unconsciously angry move in a jerky, "angular" way as opposed to the smooth motions of the normal mother. Young infants are very sensitive to motion and position. They readily pick up the difference in the mother's way of moving, react to it, and are traumatized by it. The fact that an adult observer cannot see with the naked eye the difference in the way the mother moves does not prevent that difference from having demonstrated impact on the child.

Whether one takes the view that the early infant has elaborate structured fantasies, conscious and unconscious, as do the Kleinian analysts, or one takes the view that the mental life is unstructured at first and only gradually becomes more structured into conscious and unconscious fantasies that are clearly delineated, as do most ego-analytic analysts, is not, in our opinion, the important issue. What is important is that the early experiences of life do have an impact that make the child vulnerable, and that these experiences successively become delineated sharply into conscious and unconscious fantasies, whether or not they were originally so delineated.

The destructive pressures of the early mother-child or parent-child relationship do not begin and cease in infancy, but begin in infancy and continue in modified forms throughout childhood. It is difficult if not impossible to be sure at what point the destructive impact was felt, or when the complex fantasies of childhood first originated. What is important is that the pressures had an effect, and that fantasies were formed which determined much of the individual's life and psychopathology. These fantasies can be unearthed and understood and placed within a realistic causal nexus of the child's reaction to its life history.

Erikson (1963) describes, in his ego-psychologic terms, the attitude learned in this early oral period as "basic trust." The schizophrenic individual has not had the chance to learn this attitude toward other people from a satisfying, secure early mother-child relationship. ("Mother" is used in the sense of functional role, not necessarily biologic status.) Nor does the schizophrenic individual ever learn to develop this on the basis of later experiences. It is our view that later experiences can make up for what is missing in an earlier developmental phase; it just becomes progressively more difficult the older and more structurally organized a human being is. A solid base for later development is usually missing in the patients who become schizophrenic.

Apparent Contradictions in the Literature

From the psychoanalytic exploration of human beings, it has been obvious that the oral period (roughly the first year of life) and events connected with it (sucking, eating, biting, and hence activities concerning the mouth, and concerning dependent relationships) are very important in human development. Touching and handling are as important in this period as the actual mouth activities. Nonetheless, the first year is still referred to by psychoanalysts as the oral period, and activities connected with the mouth are an important part of it. The best summary of what we know of the first year of life is given by Spitz (1965).

The importance and complexity of the psychologic processes that have been called "oral" are attested to by their recent elaboration and refinement in the writings on "narcissism" and on the development of the self and objects by Kernberg and Kohut, on "psychologic birth" by Mahler, as well as the Kleinian developmental theories. Symbiosis, separation, individuation, conceptualization of the self and others ("object-representation"), internalized "objects," and mental "structures" all begin and develop in this period; these are characteristics that endure throughout life (in fact, because they become at some point unconscious and hence unchanging).

Schizophrenia, because of its severity, seems clearly to evolve from problems that originate early in life, including those of the oral period. Yet the experimental literature that has tried to relate problems in later life, which are oral in the psychoanalytic sense, in a simple manner to events concerning feeding or events of the first year of life does not show a remarkably strong relationship.

Insofar as there is an apparent contradiction between the experimental literature and the clinical literature, one or the other must be wrong. After all, there is only one real world. This is true not only with respect to schizophrenia, but in any field; however, these discrepancies are often most apparent and puzzling in the literature on schizophrenia.

There is confusion about what constitutes the "oral trauma" by both clinicians and researchers. Usually the oral trauma is interpreted as the age of weaning; sometimes it is more sophisticatedly interpreted as the abruptness of weaning, with the awareness that an abrupt weaning that is late is more traumatic than an abrupt weaning that is early. The relationship between oral trauma defined as just weaning-related experience and so-called oral pathology is not striking in the research literature, but clinically, it seems clear that psychologic reactions to events during the entire early period of life concerning the mouth and eating are important in mental development, especially as one listens to schizophrenic patients. Hence, psychoanalytic therapists tend to stress oral problems in working with schizophrenic patients.

The same patient who heard voices of drowned people after his father's death clearly had oral pathology. First, he was schizophrenic, which suggests oral problems. Second, he went on hunger strikes. Third, he was afraid of being poisoned. He would not drink milk at the beginning of treatment. He reported, "The Athenian girls are laughing at me. They say their breasts are poisoned." One day a woman with a rather well-endowed bosom walked by him. He made frantic wiping gestures from his side. Afterward he said, "She approached me with her breast, and I got a pain in my side."

He would at times sit cross-legged and make a clicking noise with his tongue, which sounded like a child sucking at the breast. He said he was saying the word "best," but he could not say it fast enough, so the clicking noise substituted for it. The word "best," according to him was short for "make the world best." Further associations seem to indicate "best" represented the breast in his fantasies.

Despite these symptoms, his mother reported that she had breast-fed him for a full year and she had weaned him gradually. Where then could there be an oral trauma?

The mother, who was familiar with psychoanalytic concepts, asked her adult son, "Didn't I give you enough milk?" and he said something that an organic psychiatrist would interpret as irrelevant.

He looked up at the sky and repeated a statement he occasionally made about one of his delusions: "The cow gave her calf milk and then kicked it. She shouldn't do that. It's something that happened hundreds of times in the history of the world."

If one pays attention to what the patient says, the mystery is unraveled. The language is easy to understand, if one assumes it is meaningfully related to the patient. The history of the world is obviously his history. The cow is his mother, and he is saying that every time she fed him, she got angry. This then was his oral trauma.

As mentioned above, if the mother is angry when she feeds an infant, the infant reacts as if it is being traumatized. "Poison" is simply something that you eat, and you get hurt afterward. Every time his mother fed him, he got hurt. This happened in infancy, but it never changed. Such a traumatic interaction repeated for years is far more potent than any single traumatic event. This sequence was still observable when the patient was in his midthirties. The mother took care of the treatment house to save expenses, and every time she cooked a meal, and he ate, there was a quarrel afterward. If she didn't cook (sometimes the attendants cooked), there was no quarrel. If he did not eat (sometimes he was on a hunger strike) even when she did cook, there was no quarrel. But if she cooked and he ate, there was a quarrel. The quarrel was not about eating. It was about something different each time. Nonetheless, over a 6-month period when they were under observation, the sequence was invariable.

It must not be thought that this mother understood what she was doing. When she had to feed, the demand "feed-me, mother-me" produced anxiety. When she was anxious, she became angry. When she was angry, anything became the pretext for a quarrel. Consciously, the mother was making every effort to be helpful to her sick son. Unconsciously, she was repeating the trauma.

The son also was not consciously aware of this sequence. He was only conscious of the delusion that the cow gave her calf milk and then kicked it, but he would deny that this had anything to do with his life.

One of the myths about the treatment of schizophrenia is that schizophrenic patients are conscious of their problems and that only the relationship with reality needs to be worked with. In fact, what they have is not the unconscious fully in consciousness, but rather a consciousness dominated by the unconscious in the same way that the manifest content of a dream is dominated by the unconscious. The content may be apparent to the observer, but not necessarily to the patient.

If you discuss this material with the patient, he says "I try to talk about history, and all you want to do is tell dirty stories about me and my mother." Nonetheless, if you can get the patient to relate his delusional material to the reality situation from which it derives and help him to see and cope with his feelings, he need not cope with them by means of his symbolic schizophrenic symptoms.

This does not mean that by asking the schizophrenic to make the connection, he will spontaneously do so. That task belongs to the therapist, and as the therapist persistently relates such material to the patient's life, the patient will begin to see the utility of understanding the realistic basis of his ideas and feelings and begins to make similar connections himself.

Oral Problems in Genital Disguise

Schizophrenic patients frequently talk about genital problems, that is, sexual problems in the ordinary sense. It is tempting to deal with these problems as if they were sexual problems in the ordinary adult sense. Indeed, some psychoanalysts treat genital conflicts as if these were the "deepest," most central issues in treatment. This in part accounts for the common misunderstanding that the unconscious is conscious and that interpretation is of no value in dealing with schizophrenic patients (Fenichel 1945). It is felt that these central genital conflicts are already in consciousness, but to discuss them is of no value to the patient. The problem is that the apparently genital material is symbolic of the more central earlier oral problems of survival, originating in the earliest periods of life. To deal with the genital disguises of oral problems as genital material is of no more value than to deal with symbolic material representing genital conflicts as if it only concerned the things used as symbols. Whatever it is that patients are concerned with, we must help them to understand. Of course, schizophrenic patients do have real sexual conflicts, so do all of us, but most of the pain and concern have to do with more fundamental issues of survival and relatedness, intactness of the inside and outside of the body, and intactness of the identity.

The Draining Fantasy

The oral, anal, and genital phases of psychoanalytic theory may best be understood as battlegrounds on which essentially the same battles for survival get successively played out in different versions for schizophrenic patients. Consider one infantile fear that frequently needs to be understood in dealing with schizophrenic patients, the fear that the inside of the body will be drained and emptied.

The earliest version has to do with the oral experience of the stomach becoming more and more empty as time goes on. Just as other sensations are more acute, so hunger is more intense and fearful in infancy, and the infant cannot sufficiently span time well enough to feel sure of the predictable replenishment. Ordinary infants, however, feel good when mother feeds them and develop a sense of predictability and trust toward the mothering one, and hence toward people in general in a later stage in life. The preschizophrenic infant is apt to find mothering less dependable, and not even to feel good when being fed, because of the anger and fear in the mother, communicated by the way she handles the child.

The anal version of the draining fantasy is that the mother now demands that you give up what is inside your body. The mother that was less helpful in the oral period is also apt to be less considerate or even cruel in toilet training. She may hit the child, leave the child on the toilet for long periods of time, threaten the child, or use enemas (often experienced as "rape" by the child) and laxatives, which rob the child of feelings of self-control. The child feels again that the inside of the body does not belong to him or her.

The genital version of the same draining fantasy is that the inside of the body will be drained through the genitals. This is particularly striking in male patients, who may even describe a wish to be castrated in order not to be drained. Indeed, male schizophrenic patients who cut off their own penises almost always are struggling with the draining fantasy and defending themselves in what by normal standards is a grotesque means.

Female patients occasionally describe the genital version of the draining fantasy in the form of the "vacuum cleaner" penis hollowing them out. More usually women describe it in terms of being drained of their feelings and having nothing left inside them.

The male or female patient may also talk about being swallowed up by the mother's vagina, either in direct terms, or as symbolized in dreams, hallucinations, or fantasies. The important issue is to know that a draining fantasy exists and to be ready to discuss it with the patient if it seems relevant. To talk to a patient who is struggling with a genitally disguised draining fantasy about Oedipal conflicts in the ordinary sense is of no value whatsoever.

Knowledge of the draining fantasy may make explicable symptoms which are otherwise strange. Thus, a patient in his twenties had several psychotic breaks, each precipitated by his wife's demand for sex. According to the ward notes, the treatment staff were unable to get him to talk coherently.

During the initial interview, after providing background information in response to structured questions, he was asked, "What seems to be the trouble, what can I help you with?"

"I'm tired."

"Are you on medication?"

"Yes."

"Well, medication can cause tiredness. When you go off the medication, you will know."

"Yeah."

"Is there anything else?"

"I don't know."

"Why are you in the hospital?"

"I was wandering the street. Didn't know where I was."

"What happened just before that?"

"I don't know. I guess my wife asked for sex and I ran out of the house."

"Why?"

"I don't know." He seemed ashamed, as if he were afraid, as he later said he was, that this made him not masculine.

A woman's demand for sex does not ordinarily precipitate a psychotic break. A potent underlying dynamic must be involved, and the draining fantasy seemed an obvious possibility.

For some patients, it might be possible to talk of "draining" immediately if one believed the patient might understand it. In this case it seemed more likely to be understood if phrased more generally.

"I have the feeling your wife was always making demands on you that were too much, that you couldn't meet." He responded to this coherently, although he defended his wife.

Further discussion revealed that his wife demanded that he hold two jobs, while she remain unemployed, and he felt inadequate because he found complying with her "legitimate" demand too exhausting. The therapist reiterated that the wife's demands were excessive. He then revealed that she refused to use contraception. Even in the first session, the therapist pointed out that it made good responsible sense not to have sex without contraception unless one is in a position to take care of the resulting child. "The fact is that you felt so guilty about it that you had to go crazy in order to do what was sensible."

The Split Between the "Good" Mother and the "Bad" Mother

Various theorists (Sullivan, Klein, Kernberg, etc.) have called attention to the fact that the patient has at least two different images of the mothering person, namely "the good mother" and "the bad mother." Frequently attention is called to the defense mechanism of *splitting*, but the term is misleading. It does not refer to separating unitary phenomena, but to never having integrated them in the first place. The initial situation of infancy is that the mother (or mothering person) feels so good to the infant when she is being "good" and feels so bad to the infant when she is being "bad" that the experiences seem so different that it is as if there were two different people—one being good and the other being bad. Therefore, it is easier for the infant to coalesce these emotional experiences of bad mothering into one image, and of good mothering into a separate image than to form ambivalent images which correspond one-to-one with the real people in one's environment. The development of internalized images that correspond to the actual people rather than to emotional experiences is a later achievement in the mental life of the normal infant. The schizophrenic patient may never have achieved this, or may regress to a split image under stress, or may preserve both split and integrated parent images in the unconscious.

There is a similar "splitting" or nonintegration of the good and bad self-image, and of the affects that are related to both internalized parent and self-images. The recent concern with splitting in treating borderline and schizophrenic patients arose to explain the patient's rapid shifting between incompatible attitudes toward the therapist in the therapy hour, and toward other people in their current life.

The patient tries to maintain the view that the real mother, or mothering person, or current authority figure, is the "perfectly good mother" of the original infant representation, and that the malevolent or "bad mother" does not exist. But an unrealistically perfect mother cannot be maintained. An unrealistically "good" self-image may temporarily solve the problem, but it does not change the reaction of the original mother or of current reality figures.

An image of an unrealistic hostile mother may be maintained, but this is too dangerous. As Fairbairn (1954) has pointed out, the most terrifying idea for any human being is that they are really helplessly at the mercy of a malevolent object (person), and that this started in infancy. To believe one's mother is really bad, or, later, one's parents, is to be in a situation of hopeless terror. One technique of denying the bad parent is to change the "unconditionally bad" parent to a "conditionally bad" one. "They only treat me this way because . . ." If one can find one's crime, one finds psychologic, if not realistic, security. It is better to feel guilty than helpless. The problem is that one cannot correct this crime which supposedly accounts for the rejection, without becoming aware that the "perfect" mother is not perfect, and that she still rejects you. On the other hand, if one does not remedy the crime, one is in danger of being abandoned, kicked out, rejected, or killed for the crime. One may also use a supposed personal defect or flaw in the same way.

This may lead to acting out whatever the crime might be, committing new crimes, acting "crazy," needing to be "perfect" (one will, of course, fail), having to be God, or changing sex. All of these maneuvers are guaranteed to fall short, while the attempt at achieving them reduces anxiety.

There are three infantile terrors that persist in adult schizophrenic individuals which were most clearly delineated by the Fairbairn (1954) and Guntrip (1969) object-relations perspective. The first is what Fairbairn characterizes as the "depressive anxiety," the fear that one's anger will "destroy the object," by which he means destroy the "good mother," either by actually destroying her, by causing her to abandon the child, or by changing her from the "good mother" to the "bad mother." This starts early in infancy. The infantile reality basis for this fear is the mother's reaction to an angry child. Of course, fantasies concerning the "good" and the "bad" mother are activated by any important relationship, male or female, in later childhood and adult life. Even more serious is what he terms the "schizoid anxiety," the fear that one's love will "destroy the object." The reality basis for this fear is that an infant's love is demanding, and the mother may not react to those demands well. If one fears one's love will destroy, close relations with people are not possible. The "depressive anxiety" is less crippling because it allows for close relations with people if one avoids anger. Guntrip (1969) has added "defensive withdrawal" from the object (person) and the fear that one's withdrawal will be so great that one will never find one's way back to relations with other people. Similar processes, of course, are described in other psychoanalytic languages, for example, Mahler's description (Mahler et al., 1975) of the process of psychologic separation in early childhood in ego-analytic language.

Of course, these "depressive" or "schizoid" anxieties are not limited to the patients carrying those diagnostic labels, but are part of the human dilemma, to be found most intensely and destructively in schizophrenic patients.

The earliest experience of the infant probably does not clearly differentiate the external world from the self-image. This differentiation is gradually learned on the basis of independence of action and consequence. Parents of schizophrenic and preschizophrenic children blur the distinctions between parent and child, and the gradual psychologic separation of identities is thwarted. The adult patient may then merge with the parent or parent-substitute as a defense against abandonment, and flee or attack as a defense against annihilation by absorption into the parent (or later reality figures, including the therapist).

Growing up consists of a series of vacillations between the need for independence and the need for security. The child needs to depend and to have that dependency accepted. If the child is secure, independence becomes a need. This needs to be accepted also. The good parent facilitates and accepts both of these. If the child is anxious, or faced with problems, he needs to depend. Parents of neurotic and psychotic offspring tend to interfere with this healthy vacillation by not providing security and permitting dependency when it is needed, or not permitting independence when the child moves in such directions. The preschizophrenic child develops the fantasy that to depend is to be a "monster-child"—deserving of punishment or death, or to be independent is to be an "uncaring or even hostile bastard"—deserving of rejection or exile to a dangerous world.

Unfortunately, the only stable adaptation that one can live with comfortably is to bring one's fantasies into closer and closer harmony with reality. This requires conscious experience. A clear view of the defects as well as strengths of one's parents allows one to enjoy better adult relationships of one's own choosing, and possibly even a better relationship with the parents.

The Anal Battleground

Of all the psychosexual stages, the anal period is most clearly a battleground. Here the child both relinquishes autonomy and gains it. The parents struggle for control, or if you prefer, the civilization of the child. Western civilization requires more stringent toilet training than almost all other known societies (Whiting and Child 1953). One of the ways in which our society has been influenced by psychoanalytic understanding is that, in general, we have become kinder about toilet training. This influence has come about through the writing of Spock and similar psychoanalytically influenced child-rearing experts.

Nonetheless, it is understandable that toilet training should become a battleground. Feces are almost by definition unpleasant substances, and all parents are relieved when their children no longer require them to deal with dirty diapers. Insofar as the parents' positive gratification and commitment to the process of child rearing are less, the frustration and unpleasantness of the urinally and anally incompetent infant will be more frustrating and irritating to them. There will be greater urgency on the part of the parents to make the child more convenient. Moreover, a parent's anxiety and guilt about her or his own toilet training will exacerbate the severity with which she or he handles such development with the child.

These conflicts are well known, have been described psychoanalytically in understanding neurotic symptoms, and have been particularly related to the development of compulsive symptomatology. Compulsive symptoms occurring in schizophrenic patients frequently have an anal basis. In other words, the dynamics of a specific symptom, such as an obsessive-compulsive symptom, occurring in a schizophrenic patient is apt to be the same as those underlying that symptom when it occurs by itself. Of course, the dynamics of compulsive symptoms have more to do with the defense mechanisms of reaction-formation, undoing, and isolation, and with the warded-off impulse, usually anger, than to the anal period.

Because of the severity of the schizophrenic individual's life, the pathology resulting from toilet training may be fundamental. The child may learn not that you produce feces which have to be eliminated in a particularly socially acceptable way, but rather that the inside of your body is filled with evil, or even that all of your body is evil, and that this terrible stuff is at least the core of your identity, if not all of it, and that being tolerated by other people consists of never letting them know how awful you are. The frustrations of toilet training lead to anger, and the anger gets identified with this awful stuff inside your body which must be hidden from the outside world for anyone to tolerate you. The young child does not know that everybody defecates. The preschizophrenic child in particular is apt to believe that he or she is uniquely evil, rotten, and "shitty." Such lessons do not make later development easy.

Giving up control of one's feces always involves a certain loss of autonomy, but in some families this loss of autonomy is maximized. As we said before, the use of enemas, laxatives, and stringent battles where the child is left on the potty for hours until he or she defecates when mother decides he or she should, can leave lasting emotional scars in terms of not being in control of one's own body. It is one thing to learn that bowel control is essential to being a healthy adult human being; it is another to learn that feces are extremely dangerous. This can lead to hypochondriacal fears in adulthood. Severe toilet training may lead to the belief that one ought not to defecate at all. The experience of enemas may lead to fantasies about rape and homosexuality that seem strange when they appear in the patient's later fantasies, dreams, or hallucinations.

The reader will recognize that the draining fantasy discussed earlier is reminiscent of the dynamics of the paranoid position described by Klein (1948) and Rosenfeld (1965), and the anal dynamics described here are reminiscent of the depressive position. While these descriptions of the origin are different (and unfortunately difficult to establish beyond doubt), clinically it is important to deal with these dynamics, whatever one's conceptual framework. The patient, with the therapist's aid, will, of course, modify the specific interpretation and conceptual framework of the therapist to fit his or her unique psychic situation.

Genital Battles

Genital development, that is, ordinary sexual development in common-sense terms, is a focal area of conflict in our culture. It is not surprising that schizophrenic people, who have more difficulty with every problem in general, should also have more difficulty in that area of life which is most fraught with difficulty for all Americans. The fantasies that are involved in genital sexual development for schizophrenic patients include primarily oral (penis being a symbolic breast, and vagina a symbolic mouth), and even anal fantasies (i.e., semen, menstrual fluid, and vaginal lubrication are feces, or "dirty stuff").

A sexual relation with a woman is commonly experienced by male schizophrenic individuals as having to "feed" her, but they feel unable to "feed" anyone. This is closely related to the draining fantasy. The problem with the mother is often fantasied in terms of "What do I have to give her in order to get something?" or to use Silverberg's (1952) term, the "quid pro quo" fantasy. "If I have to feed her, I must, but I can't," is the feeling, and therefore, women are dangerous. The fear is that the female genital will either devour, castrate, or drain the patient through his penis.

The young child sees the genitals of the adult members of the family or fantasizes about them. For the little boy, the hugeness of the female genitals, that is, his mother's genitals, leads to the fear they will engulf and devour him. The boy compares himself with the enormous genital of his father and feels forever inadequate. For the female child, the mother's genitals may also be feared as devouring. She may experience her lack of a penis in oral terms as not being able to "feed" (meet the needs of) her mother. The enormous size of the father's penis leads the little girl to fear that she will be ripped open, since the child does not know of the elasticity of the genitals and in her fantasies male genitals grow in proportion to her own size (Bonaparte 1953). The unconscious never seems to realize that as we change, the relative size of our own genitals compared to others changes as well.

The classic Oedipal fantasies, of course, do occur in schizophrenic patients, but they are less frightening than other fantasies for the patients. One can almost say that the patient is getting better when the traditional Oedipal fantasies are of central importance. Indeed, schizophrenic patients report that they were never sure that their parent of the opposite sex would have objected to an incestuous sexual relationship.

The parents of schizophrenic individuals tend to be unusually puritanical in their child rearing, or to be unusually provocative. In either case, they set no livable standards. There are two ways for a parent to be unhelpful with respect to sex: to seduce the child, or to be so afraid of one's own sexual impulses toward the child that one denies the child normal affection. Among the parents of schizophrenic children we find both patterns, or strange admixtures within the parent's behaviors. Normally, children depend on their parents to provide affection without undue sexualization, and to object to sexual activity within the family. When the parents do not play these appropriate roles, the only person attempting to control the child's impulses is the child, and this is a heavy and frightening burden.

Masturbation Conflicts

The parents of schizophrenic individuals are extremely unlikely to have helped the child to understand that masturbation is a normal part of growing up. Spitz (1965) found that infants who touch their genitals were those who were better developed and who had a better relationship with their parents, a finding which has been largely ignored. Most people in our society have been exposed to antimasturbation propaganda. These pressures are not exclusive for preschizophrenic individuals, but this inappropriate information leading to inappropriate guilt is one more pressure that the therapist must alleviate.

Both male and female patients may feel they have injured themselves physically by masturbating, or driven themselves crazy, depending on the kind of antimasturbation training they have experienced. Surprisingly often, boys have had direct castration threats made "jokingly," usually by the mother and usually in connection with masturbation. Sexually uninstructed girls frequently believe (consciously or unconsciously) that menstruation is the result of injuries they have done to themselves by masturbating.

Anal factors are also involved in masturbation guilt—sex, sexual activity, and sexual lubrications are dirty. Similarly, menstruation may be experienced (consciously or unconsciously) as a failure of toilet training.

Patients may feel that sexual excitement has driven them crazy, or that they masturbate only because they are crazy. In either case, it is important to correct their misinformation.

While the psychoanalytic literature discusses masturbation conflicts in terms of Oedipal fantasies and guilt about Oedipal conflict, it is our experience with schizophrenic patients that the conflict and guilt are much simpler and more central. The patients' feeling is that their bodies and their genitals do not belong to them. They do not have the right to use their genitals or their bodies for their own pleasure. The fantasy is that they ought to use their genitals or their bodies for the pleasure of their parent, particularly their mother, or not at all. When the preschizophrenic child is caught masturbating, and is made to feel guilty about the pleasure he or she derives, the child can understand this as similar to the older experience of wanting the pleasure of being orally filled up, and being made to feel guilty about it. Feeling good about themselves is made to feel like a crime, or at best something that can be tolerated only if the mother condones it.

The parent who has been afraid of being a separate individual cannot allow the child to be a separate individual, yet genital development, starting with masturbation, requires privacy. Privacy implies that the child is a separate individual who has separate experiences, for whom separateness is legitimate. Helpful parents accept such a notion, and know that private experiences are a necessary part of growing up. Unhelpful parents act as if "togetherness forever" were a reasonable way of life. Such a view is always motivated by the parents' own unindividuated childhood. The development of interest in someone of the opposite sex outside the family is also seen as a threat by the parent who cannot afford to have an individuated child.

The family uses the normal societal taboos and anxieties about sex and dating as an excuse for exerting unusual control or arousing unusual guilt. Their own conscience is assuaged because they are doing it in the interest of morality and of making the child a good person. Very few Americans entirely overcome their anxieties and guilt about their own adolescence and sexual development. It is common for these same anxieties to reappear when their children are going through the same developmental stage. The parents of schizophrenic offspring, however, become unusually intrusive in the private life of the child. They may monitor telephone calls, or decide which friends the child shall or shall not associate with (even into the "child's" thirties). They may decide what kind of clothes the child should wear long after this custom is age-appropriate. In general, the parent who cannot afford to separate will use any apparently reasonable excuse to lay down limits and controls. The child dare not refuse these intrusions, made "in the child's best interest."

Sexually Traumatic Incidents

Real traumatic events may not come to light for a long time, even with intensive therapy. This does not mean that they did not occur. There is a growing awareness that overt incest does occur and is often not reported.

A discovery of Freud's, e.g., that the seduction memories of his conversion hysteria patients were more often (but not always) fantasies rather than real events, led many therapists to discount such reports not only in hysteria, but in all patients. With schizophrenic patients, however, the majority of reports of traumatic experiences, including seductions and rapes, refer to real events. When not consummated, such material is related to parental interactions based on the fantasies of the parents.

The most common overt incest is brother-sister; it is also the most frequent form of incest discussed in therapy. The next most common is father-daughter. The least common are mother-son, brother-brother, sister-sister, mother-daughter, and father-son. These apparent frequencies also reflect the degree of taboo or guilt in our society.

There are, of course, blurrings in our evaluation and in that of the patient as to what constitutes sexuality or incest, as opposed to childhood play or curiosity, in the interaction between children. Sometimes sibling incest if nonexploitative, mutual, and undiscovered may have been a relatively supportive element in an otherwise rejecting environment, but the patient may struggle both with fear of detection and with the guilt that there was pleasure either in the activity or in the relationship. It is useful to educate the patient about the normality of sexual curiosity and exploration in childhood in our sexually conflicted society, and that it is not a crime and that one need not feel guilty about being a child in this respect, or any other, irrespective of the parents' views on the matter.

When brother-sister incest occurs in a family, schizophrenic or not, it has been our experience that the parents psychologically are involved, while maintaining to themselves that they are not. The psychologic function served is to ward off the parents' guilt about each of their sexual feelings toward their own children. "It is those dirty kids who are doing those awful things, not me," is the defensive feeling.

For example, one set of puritanical parents placed a 13-year-old boy and an 11-year-old girl in the same double bed all winter "to save heating costs." When the inevitable sexual play occurred, it was, of course, not mentioned to the parents. Eventually the little girl mentioned it to her mother, who said, "How could you do a thing like that to your brother?" implying the little girl's guilt. The patient felt overwhelmingly guilty. At times she considered the possibility that the brother might be responsible rather than she.

But only in therapy, when it was pointed out by the therapist, did she examine the possibility that the parents unconsciously had arranged it. She reluctantly agreed that the parents knew, as well as she and the therapist knew, that two children of that age, sleeping in the same bed all winter, would be certain to play sexually sooner or later.

When parent-child (usually father-daughter) incest occurs, exploitation of a child by an adult obviously is involved. What is particularly destructive is that this adult should have been one of the two especially trustworthy people in the world. Such occurrences of incest vary in terms of use of force or cruelty or apparent benevolence; they vary even in degree of awareness by the parent of its deviance or benevolence. But in every case there is exploitation, and a blurring of the appropriate boundaries between the role of child and adult, lover and parent. This is not helpful to either sexual adjustment or healthy psychologic maturation. When parent-child incest has occurred, it is useful to help the patient deal with his or her rage that the parent did not act like a parent.

There are ample studies showing that, where father-daughter incest occurs, the mother is in some psychologic sense also involved. Again, she usually responds to the daughter with something like, "Don't let the neighbors know," rather than responding to her daughter's needs for reassurance or protection.

Thus, for example, a 14-year-old girl complained to her mother that the stepfather was having sex with her and had been for 3 years. The mother's initial reaction was shock, then anger, and then to "do the right thing"—call the police. Within 48 hours, however, the mother was no longer interested in pressing charges

against her husband, was fearful he would leave her, was presenting her daughter to neighbors as a probable liar, despite the fact that
the other (natural) daughter, age 11, had since informed the mother
that the father was doing the same thing with her. Moreover, the
mother was again leaving her husband alone with the 14-year-old
while she and the younger daughter went grocery shopping.

The incest with the older child had started when the father's
business was failing; he felt insecure and inadequate. The wife felt
threatened by the loss of financial security owing to his business
reverses, and blamed her husband for "upsetting" her. She could
not be supportive of him, and absented herself from the home at
PTA meetings and art classes. She was frightened. Her father had
deserted the family when she was 8, and her first husband had
deserted her (and the oldest child). She feared losing this husband
too. The husband turned to the daughter. With her, he felt adequate
and supported. The daughter adapted to the situation, in some ways
enjoyed it, and learned to use it to her advantage. She would have
sex with her stepfather to get permission for special events. This
"permission-obtaining" practice had gone on for several years. All
of the children knew about it and talked about it together. It kept
the father in the family and protected the mother from losing him,
as long as she did not know about it.

Everything was "in balance" until two things happened: the
father became sexually involved with his own (younger) child as
well, and after having intercourse with the older daughter, refused
her permission to go to a party (because he feared losing her to a
teenage boy). The 14-year-old was furious at losing her special
status and advantages, and wanted to get even with the father (and
the mother, and the sister), so she told the mother. The mother
felt guilty and called the police. But quickly her defenses re-
established and she began to deny the events and present her
daughter as a liar.

This quick reversal is typical of mothers whose daughters are
sexually involved with the father. It preserves the equilibrium and
allays the mother's anxiety—not only the superficial one about
someone breaking our ordinary sexual taboos, but their deeper fear
of being abandoned. Surprisingly, the mother's failure to provide
protection and acceptance is frequently experienced as more
destructive than the incestuous experience itself.

Such denial by the family is why superficial clinical investigation may not reveal an activity that is known at some level to everyone. All are more comfortable if they believe, or think everyone else believes, the child is simply "crazy" or a "liar" who tries to "embarrass us after all we have done for her."

Mother-son, father-son, and mother-daughter incest are rarely commented about, but that does not necessarily mean they never occur.

One adult male schizophrenic patient had a history of acting out in bizarre ways with women, and of being violent with women as well as men. After unsuccessful treatment with medications for many years, he was finally taken off all medication and started on psychotherapy. The patient was seen 3 times a week. Very quickly his thoughts, as well as his behavior, began to be much more orderly.

A year after therapy had begun, he reported an incident in which a woman suggested she perform fellatio on him. He described feeling very angry at her. The therapist asked why. The patient finally said, "She shouldn't do that—there's something wrong with a woman like that. It would be all right if I told her I wanted her to do it, but it wouldn't be all right for her to want to do it."

This still seemed puzzling to the therapist, who questioned it. The patient finally said, "My mother warned me about such women. She told me there are bad women in the world, and you must be careful. She said you know what they will do—they will do this to you." She had then performed fellatio on her 12-year-old son.

Up to this point, the things he had said about his mother would have led one to believe she was puritanical. He was always offended by any slightly negative reference about her. He would say, "Your mother is right—she knows what is good and bad, just as the Bible does." From his fragmented recollections, it eventually became clear that his mother had been, at least at times, a prostitute. Nonetheless, he reported how difficult it was to keep from getting violent with the therapist, because the therapist did not share his idealized view of his mother.

The only case of externally corroborated mother-daughter incest in our experience was not disclosed to the therapist by either mother or daughter until several years into therapy, even though the incestuous experiences were frequent, and other very disturbing material had been disclosed earlier. The point is that just because material is disturbing, against the social mores, or unusual, does not mean it is impossible or untrue. Nor, because it is not disclosed early in treatment, does it even mean that the patient does not know about it. The fragmented, delusional, or distorted communications and experiences can only be sifted through by a therapist who can tolerate the possibility that such things might have happened.

In each case, the willingness of the therapist to hear anything, explore and clarify the meaning of anything, is helpful; together, patient and therapist can not only reconstruct the events and the feelings associated, but the intermeshed psychologic determinants within all of the family members, so that the patient no longer is simply "crazy" for no reason, nor so awful that they are beyond another human being's understanding. Rather, they see their symptoms as the inevitable result of the lives they have led, the "best of a bad bargain," to use Freud's phrase, and no longer necessary. As their life and symptoms become meaningful, the patient is able to accept the therapist's view that one can learn from them, and grow psychologically.

Superego Formation

It is clear that schizophrenic individuals have unusual consciences, usually excessively strict, but also unrealistic and often "strange" in its areas and manner of application. This is readily understandable by considering the formation of the conscience, or in psychoanalytic terms, the superego.

The conscience is not an innate characteristic of human beings, or the "still small voice of God." It is the result of what real people have really done, as interpreted by a child. What is innate is the capacity for superego formation. The child learns to adapt to reality by internalizing the parents. "Good" and "bad" are whatever mother, and later, the parents, say is "good" or "bad." To prevent having difficulties with the most important part of the child's reality—its parents—the child now "tells" itself what the parents would, and avoids troubles with the parents. This is an enormous advantage, a giant stride toward relative independence.

There is a danger, however. Insofar as parental demands were unreasonable, one's conscience is unreasonable. Moreover, the

Freudian concept of the superego may be misleading in that it sounds integrated. But one may well function as if there were more than one superego with conflicting demands, since it is based on the internalization of different people. Thus, one borderline patient was a successful truck driver, but was depressed, and became a successful college teacher, but became anxious. His mother had felt that any man who, like his father, worked at a job where he got his hands dirty, was worthless. His father felt that any man who did not get his hands dirty, like a teacher, was a "fairy." Between them there was no room for a human being.

It is now beginning to be well recognized that borderline and psychotic patients usually have unintegrated superegos, which can be conceptualized in various ways, such as "split" superegos, or different internalized "objects."

Corrective Identifications

In normal development, children relate to people outside the family, and identify with them as part of the normal process of growing up. Every family has warps. No one has ever had a perfect set of parents or a perfect family. The identifications outside the family allow us to correct these warps to a large extent. Parents who permit relations outside the family are faced by occasional rebellions and values and behaviors of which they do not altogether approve, but these are needed by the child to correct the weaknesses of their experiences in the family.

Freud does not speak of such processes extensively, because he treated primarily neurotic patients who had had such corrective experiences. Sullivan (1953), on the other hand, who worked extensively with schizophrenic patients, was the first to draw attention clearly to the fact that later identifications could correct earlier problems. Other theorists who have worked with schizophrenic patients (Searles 1965; Lidz 1973) have also called attention to the importance of the existence or nonexistence of these relations outside the family and their corrective value.

Children who are prone to become schizophrenic are generally the product of a family who systematically discourage relationships and identifications outside the family. From our standpoint, this is simply an important example of a more general destructive parental dynamic—the repeated predominance of parental needs over child needs. The unconscious motive for this restriction is to maintain the child as a source of reassurance against the parent's anxiety. This anxiety may be about separation, or it may be about losing control of the child, or it may be about the child challenging an emotionally necessary belief of the parent. The parent may be afraid the child will do something the parent has done or may fear doing, and about which the parent feels guilty or anxious. Preventing corrective identifications is particularly destructive, because it magnifies the effect of any problem that already exists. In our experience, those people with severely destructive parents who do not become schizophrenic have always been saved by such corrective identification with people outside the immediate family.

A treatment program with considerable promise, Soteria House, makes use to a large extent of corrective identifications. The evidence to date suggests that schizophrenic patients derive considerably more benefit from an interactive residential setting with healthy peers, who will accept temporary regression without requiring it (Mosher 1975, 1975a), than from traditional hospitals and medication.

With schizophrenic individuals, one of the critical developments that must occur is new corrective identifications. Most central is the identification with the therapist in what has been previously termed *reverse transference*, that is, the internalization into the ego (as a model for the self) and into the superego (as a replacement for the parents' values) of the therapist as a model, and the relationship with the therapist as a model for human relationships. Moreover, the therapist opens the way for new corrective identifications with other people, outside of therapy. Among the new superego values is the one of rejecting even the therapist's values when they are personally inappropriate.

Hostility and Other Affects

The most problematic affect for schizophrenics is anger. The character structure of borderline and psychotic individuals and many of the symptoms can be understood as a defense against rage.

Biologically, anger is an innate response in all human beings to being hurt; it is also an effective motivation for corrective action. In the families of preschizophrenic children, however, even minor irritation or an ordinary self-assertion may have been reacted to as if it were murderous rage. The child internalizes that value.

Of course, in early childhood (and in the unconscious throughout life), anger actually tends to be experienced as uncontrollable rage. If minor anger and self-assertion are reacted to by the parents in childhood, by the external environment late in life, or by the superego (the internalized parents) as intolerably dangerous, the frustrations of life increase, and the bottled-up anger becomes more intense and feels increasingly dangerous.

Moreover, every child starts out equating thoughts with action. The benign parent helps the child differentiate thoughts and feelings from actions, and differentiate degrees of action in terms of seriousness of consequence. The "pathogenic" parent reacts to angry feelings as if they were murderous physical assaults that both parent and child must be afraid of. Actions may be responded to without regard for the seriousness of realistic consequences. One family may treat a minor disagreement by the child as horrifying, and another family an actual murderous assault by either parent or child as unimportant. And sometimes both occur in the same family.

Parents do not like to have their children angry with them. Most children learn that you do not express direct hatred or anger at your parents. In most families, the children, with or without awareness, channel their anger into indirect avenues (e.g., griping, throwing stones at a tree, or fantasy). In the preschizophrenic family, however, even the most indirect expression of anger may be responded to as if it were a direct assault. For example, one set of parents, after any angry encounter, followed the child around and accused him of wanting to murder the parents whenever the child began vigorous physical activity. The child was not permitted to sublimate.

Interestingly enough, such parents may never recognize their own anger or may describe their anger at the child as something else (discipline, education, a joke). The injunction never to be angry usually, however, applies only to the patient, the child in the family. In the parent's view, if the parent was angry at the child, it was justified. This is the world view that the parent transmits. If the child is angry at the parent, it is unjustified, either a crime or a symptom. When the parent reacts to something, no matter how innocuous, as a grievous fault or major symptom, the patient accepts this evaluation rather than his own; this often plays a role in later symptom formation.

The patient may ultimately need to project the anger by means of an hallucination and see it not as one's own anger, but that of hallucinated people, hiding behind trees or walls, talking about how angry they were, and how they wanted to kill the patient or the patient's parents. The defensive use of projection has obviously been taught. The patient punished for anger at a parent may hallucinate voices from another room, projected from Martians, from the television set, from people one does not know, saying that one is angry. One may make an accusation to someone (e.g., the police, the landlord, the neighbors) about the supposed persecutors and then feel enormous guilt, that the accusation has done something terrible and evil.

This may be understood as an attempt to resolve the problem. The conflict is displaced onto the less frightening strangers or television set, but also there is a part of such a guilty patient that knows that the television set, the strangers, really are not doing these things, that the accusations really are unjustified, and therefore that one is sick to feel the way one feels. The feeling that he has caused damage reflects the parents' earlier attitudes, and justifies them, and if one has done wrong, one has no reason to resent one's parents' disapproval.

Patients may hear voices which are annoyed at them, in ways that their parents have been annoyed at them. The patients thus maintain the familiar relationship. It may be unsatisfying, but it is not total abandonment. The voices may be accusatory, or simply grumbling in an unclear way, as parents sometimes do.

For example, one mother, while cleaning the house, regularly grumbled aloud. It was not clear to the child whether or not this was an angry comment about him. Yet the child felt that in some way he was responsible and ought to be able to do something to satisfy her, in part because that would mean she was concerned with him, rather than preoccupied, and in part because she probably was annoyed with him.

After all, children do dirty houses, and parents do clean up after them in all families. Children get hungry, and parents feed them. Children get sick, and parents have to take care of them. These are normal parts of being a child and of being a parent, but, schizophrenic patients have never been allowed to feel that the normal processes of being a child was something to which they are entitled. Their demands on their parents to be parents were treated as excessive and unreasonable, something of which they should be ashamed.

Nearly every child from time to time confronts a parent with a rebellious accusation, which is not tolerated by the preschizophrenic child's parents. In adolescence, it is normal for children to become even more rebellious. Parents find this frustrating, but most parents tolerate it. Most knowledgeable professionals do not get concerned by an increase in rebelliousness in a teenager, but would get concerned if there was no increase in the teenage years, because it provides a vehicle for the process of individualization and separation.

The parent of a schizophrenic, however, reacts differently. The rebellion is treated as a major crime. The patient then feels that any expression of hostility is something so horrible and irrational that nothing can forgive it or eradicate it. Thus, a teenager who, after a prolonged and morbidly symbiotic relationship with his mother, got overtly angry for the first time and swore at her in his mid-teens, was immediately proclaimed to be crazy by his mother, who then sought treatment for herself. She never acted as though the (morbid) symbiotic dependency was something about which to be concerned. The minor rebellion would probably annoy most parents (and parents of teenagers are frequently observed to be annoyed), but they would certainly not react to it as evidence of severe or damaging illness.

The psychotic defenses against anger, including repression, splitting, isolation, projection, etc., are motivated by the fear of retaliatory annihilation, or by the fear of destroying the good "object" (mothering person) and hence being abandoned to die. Even mild feelings of annoyance (conscious or unconscious) under such circumstances may produce dramatic symptoms. Human beings do not have the capacity to repress only one affect. The struggle against hostility can deaden one's whole affective experience.

Crying has a special place in human affective development. From the standpoint of evolution, the probability of survival of the human infant was greatly enhanced by his or her capacity to cry—that is, to communicate distress by a signal that makes any adult in the vicinity uncomfortable. The adults can make themselves comfortable by attending to the child's needs.

Unfortunately, this mechanism can backfire. Many infant murders have occurred because the parents "couldn't stand the kid's crying any more." Less destructively, the parent may express his rage by punishing the child severely but not lethally.

As in most aspects of child rearing, the more crying was punished in the parents' own childhood, the more harshly they tend to deal with it in their children.

In early infancy, however, crying is a prototype of all affect, and what the infant learns about crying generalizes to all affects. Often, when patients cry in therapy it is a signal of the reawakening of their awareness of their affective experience. The later the punishment, physical or social, of crying, the less generalized its effects.

There is more than a taboo on hostility and crying in pre-schizophrenic families. There is often a taboo on all or most affects. This, like so much of "pathogenesis," is just an exaggeration of a general problem in our culture (Tomkins 1962, 1963). Even fear may not be recognized because it is bad, "childish," unmanly, or stupid.

Unfortunately, if a person does not know what his or her feelings are, it is impossible to know what is really going on, and hence act rationally or constructively to change one's life. As Tomkins has shown, the affects, rather than being irrational, are essential components of normal effective motivation and realistic thinking. Insofar as one does not know one's feelings, one is losing essential information about what is going on both in the outside world and intra-psychically.

Tomkins' (1962, 1963) theory of affects suggests the following taxonomy: interest-excitement, enjoyment-joy, surprise-startle, fear-terror, distress-anguish, anger-rage, shyness-shame-humiliation, and contempt-disgust. Obviously, the experiences of the schizophrenic patients have led to overwhelming terror as a symptom, but it has also been characteristic of their experiences in life compared to nonschizophrenic individuals. Humiliation and self-contempt, too, play a major role in the affective life of the preschizophrenic individual, given the kinds of life experiences described above.

The two positive affects, interest-excitement and enjoyment-joy, are under-represented in their experiences, in part because an excited child makes noise, which may be resented by parents ("If one is happy, the gods will be angry"), but more because interest-excitement is a response to new experiences and the preschizophrenic child usually has been taught that new experiences are likely to be dangerous or bad. Enjoyment-joy, too, has been under-experienced, since it is related to warm interpersonal relations, and in the preschizophrenic experience close social bonds have been less often unambivalently pleasant.

The Self and Self-esteem

We all need to know who we are and that we are worthwhile. Included in this is competence—knowing that we can do things effectively, and that it is a good thing to be effective.

Needless to say, such healthy feelings are all undeveloped in borderline and psychotic patients. Although Sullivan (1953), and even Freud, made insightful observations with respect to these aspects of development, it is only recently in the work of Kohut (1971, 1977) and Kernberg (1975, 1976) that they have received focused attention by most psychotherapists.

It is hard to know who you are if the distinction between you and your parents as separate entities, between being a child and being a parent, between being yourself and being some other real or fantasized person, and whether you are a boy or a girl, is blurred by your parents. Such blurring in one or more of these respects is frequent in the lives of our patients.

The concept of "narcissism" used to be used by psychoanalysts as a pejorative term denoting psychopathology, usually with the implication that it resulted from too much gratification in early childhood, leading to insufficient motivation for developing a realistic perception of the world and a capacity to delay gratification. This was extended to severe pathology like schizophrenia by psychoanalysts who never treated such patients.

Even if we accept the view that the development of the "reality principle" (balancing one satisfaction against another in terms of reality to maximize overall satisfaction) requires frustration, there is more than enough frustration in the best of infancies for this purpose. The biologic nature of human beings is such that one need conflicts with another: one cannot urinate and still be dry, one cannot cry frequently and always have a kind mother attending to one's needs, etc.

"Narcissism" in the sense of the "spoiled" child does result from overindulgence. But as reported in Levy's (1943) widely cited (albeit inaccurately) study of maternal overprotection, overprotective mothers who are not unusually hostile, result in symptomatically annoying "spoiled" children. These children tend not to respond to psychotherapy because neither mother nor child wants the situation to change, but they tend to improve and mature ("grow out of it") without therapy, and they have a lower rate of serious psychosis than the general population.

Most understandings of Freud's views on narcissism neglect the concept of legitimate narcissistic gratification. When one has had insufficient legitimate gratification, the resultant narcissistic injury leads to pathologic reparation attempts.

Kohut's (1971, 1977) contributions may be understood as a development of this neglected view, as it applies to "narcissistic" and borderline individuals.

The worthwhileness of the preschizophrenic child, of who he or she is, including gender identity, and of what he or she does, has not been adequately appreciated by the parents, for one reason or another, and consequently has not been internalized as a clear sense of self and of self-esteem.

Even obvious competence may not have been reacted to as worthwhile because it raised the possibility of either separation from or competition with the parent.

5

Parents and Schizophrenia

In our society, there is a general belief that parents have an enormous impact on children, which to a large extent is obviously true. No one in our society really knows what the ideal way is to raise a child, however. Even the so-called experts disagree, as can readily be ascertained by going to the child-care section of any bookstore or library. Radically different advice for handling almost any situation is given by professionals with apparently solid credentials.

There are some areas of child rearing about which we know a great deal, but they are only islands of knowledge. We generally know more about how to produce pathologic conditions than health. Good mental health professionals could probably tell you one or more ways to raise your child to ensure that they would develop any particular symptom. It is the other question—what is the reasonable way to raise normal children—about which there is disagreement. If this is true for the mental health professionals, it is true for parents as well.

All parents make mistakes. Luckily, human beings are very rugged. What seems to destroy a child is not a single mistake, but parents who seem dedicated to that mistake, who make the same

111

mistake over and over again and act as if they were determined never to discover or permit the child to discover that the parents might have made a mistake. Obviously, such unfortunate consistency should be thought of as a symptom, with unconscious dynamics, motivated by anxiety, as are most symptoms.

Parents of Schizophrenics Are Not Criminals

It cannot be said too many times that parents of schizophrenics are not evil people. In some psychologic discussions, the parent of a schizophrenic is described in a way that would make you think the author was referring to a criminal. Fortunately, most professionals are not that simple-minded.

But the parent who talks to a professional saying, "You are accusing me of destroying my child," is as much dealing with self-accusation as with any perceived accusation from the professional, and the wise professional will deal with this guilt feeling. Moreover, the parent has usually raised the child to the best of his or her knowledge or capacity.

Most parents dealing with the awful problem of living with a severely disturbed child, even a grown-up severely disturbed child, who seek help and try to understand how this could happen, do feel like criminals. Because of their own self-rebukes, they hear any implication that they are in some way involved in their child's pathologic condition as meaning that they are really criminals. The disturbance of the child is so massive that the parents feel there is no way they could be involved, unless what they had done was itself massive, and they are not consciously aware of anything they have done that could be that destructive.

Of course, the confusion arises from the fact that the destructive pressures from the parents in the majority of schizophrenic cases lies in the parents' unconscious. The destructive pressures on the child are a symptom of the parents—a symptom for which the parents are no more to blame than the hysterical patient is for having a paralyzed arm, or the obsessive patient for needing to carry out a ritual, or the schizophrenic patient for hallucinating. This symptom, however, arouses more guilt if it is recognized, because it directly affects another person, indeed, a loved one, and affects him or her in a severely destructive way.

The parents are engaged in a struggle, to live with and provide for a very sick, puzzling, and difficult child. The treatment of the child often means intense personal and psychologic discomfort for the parents, because it means changing techniques of adaptation that have worked for them; yet parents will go to extraordinary lengths to see that their child gets help, and to do what has to be done for the child's best interest. This is realistically admirable.

It is nonetheless understandable that some therapists feel hostile toward the parents of schizophrenic offspring. The therapist sees the parents through the eyes of the patient, sees the terribly devastated life and the pain and sees how the reactions of the parents over a lifetime have helped to produce this devastation. The therapist empathizes with the rage and pain of the patient. That is why it is often easier to have a different staff member work with the parents, if continuing therapy of the parents is undertaken, since the other staff member does not have the same immediate emotional identification with the pain of the child and can more readily see the parents as themselves victims, coping as best they can with the problems of their own childhood and with their responsibilities as adults.

It is important to remember that in most cases whatever part of the parents is involved in and needs the symptoms of the child is unconscious, and no one is responsible for his or her unconscious, since no one can control anything until after it becomes conscious. The conscious rational part of the parents does not want and does not understand the patient's symptoms. The parents may be less anxious at the thought that it is the child and not the parent who is sick. Accepting the child's healthy development, like normal masturbation, independence, need for privacy, etc., may have required accepting things in the child which would have created enormous anxieties in the parents, but all of these conflicts are unconscious. Part of the help a professional can give is to bring these matters tactfully into conscious awareness, and hence conscious control, but this requires adept handling. It is easy to traumatize the parents. It is even easier to irritate them so that they become the therapist's enemies rather than the therapist's allies. Changing the destructive part of the parents' interaction with the child means changing a symptom; consequently, unconsciously motivated resistance is to be expected.

For example, one mother of a schizophrenic child, knowing that I (Karon) felt there was parental involvement in the vulnerability to schizophrenic symptoms, said, "Parents of schizophrenics should be shot." The woman seemed to be almost shaking with anger.

"No, parents of schizophrenics should be given counseling." She relaxed and smiled. She had expressed the intense hostility she thought I felt toward her and was relieved when she was offered help. While it is difficult enough to get the schizophrenic patient to accept you as being on his or her side, it is even more difficult for the family to get the feeling that you are on their side, particularly after the therapy begins.

Parents of schizophrenic children vary in how amenable they are to help. Ordinarily, when, as a professional, one suggests, "It is very difficult to be a good mother, and I'd like to be of help," most mothers are relieved.

But one mother of eight, four of whom had been hospitalized as schizophrenic, smiled when she was offered help, "Oh no, Doctor. You don't understand. It's very easy to be a good mother."

She was very resistant to any kind of therapeutic assistance. We had just begun to talk when she immediately perceived what the problem might be. She said, even though I (Karon) had never raised the issue of her relationship to her parents, "You are trying to make me hate my mother, and I won't do it." She correctly perceived that her difficulties in being an adequate mother were related to the inadequate mothering she had herself received, but that was a relationship that she was not ready or willing to explore. It was easier for her simply to act out the trauma by repeating it again and again with her own children, this time with herself as the active rather than passive member of the pair. The result was tragic.

Difficulties in Assessing Specific Dynamics

In trying to understand the familial pressures that predispose a child to serious psychopathology, the clinician and researcher alike are struck by the fact that some families seem obviously pathologic, and it is not surprising that the children develop severe symptoms. If a schizophrenic child is raised by parents who feel there is nothing strange about burning a young child with matches to teach him the danger of fire, because the parent was treated that way himself as a child, the child's susceptibility to terror is not surprising. The majority of parents in our society would consider this grossly unreasonable and cruel. Similarly, some schizophrenic individuals come from families in which thought patterns and the ways in which the family deals with each other are clearly bizarre. Such families literally teach the pathology.

But there are families in which some of the members seem normal and others pathologic. Occasionally, a seemingly "good parent" has a schizophrenic child, and only one child in the family is schizophrenic. The symptoms of the child seem surprising because of the apparent health of the family. Moreover, there are even families that seem pathologic, but the children survive and are psychologically healthy. One is tempted to dismiss the problem with "innate biologic susceptibility." Such a glib explanation would make careful examination unnecessary, but it does not seem plausible when the family interactions are given careful scrutiny. Close screening reveals subtle isolated "family-syncratic" thought disorder shared by the "normal" members of the family of a schizophrenic child, with the symptomatic child playing a special role in the familial interactions.

In such seemingly "good" families, the parents will often report that their house is a stable middle-class home and that they have provided materially for the child and been concerned about him or her. The patient, too, will tell you that he or she has had a good home and good parents. A routine social history frequently may not reveal anything that will explain the disorder. In some cases, the pathologic pressures become obvious only when the patient is treated or observed over a period of time. The key may occasionally be obtained in detailed interviews which review all of the events in the family, not just events the family presents as pertinent.

One set of parents brought their adult schizophrenic son for evaluation. They were proud of their "good middle-class way of life" and the material benefits they had given him. They could not understand why he was catatonic. When the three of them were interviewed together, the son sat rigidly and said nothing. The parents talked about him in the third person as if he were not there. Each member of the family was then interviewed alone. As soon as the parents were absent, the apparently catatonic man talked freely and responsively. As soon as the parents entered the room again, he relapsed into his stonelike appearance and unresponsive posture. This dramatic difference in symptoms clearly indicated the relationship that existed between his family and him. None of us, even if we had a sick child, would refer to him in the third person if he were there. We would try to bring him into the conversation; we would acknowledge that he ought to speak for himself and be included in any discussion of him. These parents habitually dealt with him on this level, because at some level there was a part of them that wished he were as inactive as a stone and as little trouble.

Lidz (1973), whose studies of the families of schizophrenic individuals reveal pathology-producing patterns of interaction in every such family, reports that many of the families were referred to his project because the referring psychiatrist felt the referred family was so healthy that they could not have played any significant role in producing the designated patient's pathologic condition.

The schizophrenic person may hold a special meaning or position within the family, e.g., the oldest child or the youngest child, the only boy, or the only girl, or the first boy, or the first girl. The special significance of the individual to the family may come from events that were happening at the time of birth. The patient may be the child the mother had at the time the father was having an affair. A not uncommon pattern is that the child was born in close proximity to the death of a grandparent, about whom there were ambivalent feelings. The parent may act out these feelings in relationship to the child.

The family members may confuse therapists (or researchers) because they know more than they acknowledge. Sometimes they suppress what they know because they believe it to be irrelevant, or too shameful. Adelaide Johnson and her co-workers (Beckett et al. 1956) conducted an interesting investigation. Each member of families of schizophrenic patients was taken into therapy with a different therapist. The therapists for a given family compared notes. If traumatic events were mentioned by one member of the family, each of the therapists then probed their patients and were able either to confirm or not confirm its actuality. In each family, there were disturbing events that every member of the family knew about, but these were not disclosed initially to either the patient's therapist or anyone on the treatment team.

Interestingly enough, if the designated patient mentioned the traumas, they were most likely to mention them as delusions, misinterpretations, or false memories. "This didn't really happen, but I keep thinking it happened." These workers found that after verification, it was extremely useful to bring the patient back into touch with reality: "Improbable as it may seem, this really did happen to you."

Sometimes the family may have rational reasons for withholding information. Patients who are lower on the socioeconomic ladder have good reason to be distrustful of authorities with respect to information that could get them into legal difficulties. Patients from any socioeconomic class may be fearful of their reputation in the community. One family with a 19-year-old schizophrenic daughter did not reveal that the stepfather had seduced her, that the mother was training her to be a prostitute, and that the patient and her sister had had an ongoing homosexual relationship for many years. All of these were legally defined crimes, and understandably no member of the family wanted to go to jail. But it was difficult to understand the daughter's symptoms until this information came to light in therapy.

Positive statements by a schizophrenic patient about how good a parent he or she has had cannot be taken at face value. The child has had no one outside the family to compare. The parent has always said, "I am a good parent, and think how awful it would be if you had a bad one." The patient, for security, has maintained this fantasy and tries to maintain it with desperation.

Probably no parent treats all of his children in the same way. The child who becomes schizophrenic, with nonschizophrenic siblings, has not been treated exactly the same as the other children. Paradoxically, the mother will often report in private that the schizophrenic child is or was her favorite. She may even say she had to be careful not to show her favoritism too much. An objective account of the handling of the patient as compared to other children readily reveals differences in what actually occurred that would hardly be called favors. The reason the "favorite" is the sick individual is that the mother has unconsciously used this particular child psychologically to maintain her own adjustment; that is, without the mother's being aware of it, this child has reduced some of the mother's important anxieties. Therefore the child is her favorite, but what that means is an intimate psychologic intertwining in which the child's needs do not determine how they interact.

In one case, the mother had toilet-trained her "favorite" harshly, and, without being aware of his feelings, terrorized him into compliance by 6 months of age. The "less favored" child was treated more gently; as late as 5 years of age, he was not beaten for "accidents." This information was at no point volunteered by the mother. She nonetheless confirmed it in answer to specific questions, after it had been reconstructed in her "favorite's" therapy. While she had gone to great lengths to cooperate with treatment, the initial and continuing social history data only included information in which the "favorite" had been treated at least as well or better than his nonschizophrenic brother. It is not unusual that parents of schizophrenic children will "gloss over" major differences in the handling of two children in general terms as being "similar" or both having been handled "well."

Sometimes a mother may relate psychologically to the child in such a manner that she becomes worthwhile on the basis of the child's achievement, but the child does not become worthwhile on the basis of his own achievement. This process is illustrated by a family in which there were two sons, one of whom became a businessman and made a lot of money, and the other became a college professor and also did very well. When talking separately to the parents, the businessman heard only about his brother's brilliance, and the college professor heard only about how much money his brother made and was asked why he earned so little. Both of them felt worthless; both of them eventually had psychotic breaks. Meanwhile, the mother, who was neither able to be an intellectual nor to earn a lot of money, was able to maintain her self-esteem at the cost of her children's self-esteem. She did not know she was being destructive. She probably was not even aware that she was defending her own self-esteem, fending off her own feelings of her inadequacy compared to the achievements of her sons.

Another example of this is a patient with artistic ability whose mother took his paintings, from childhood on, even though he begged her permission to keep them. She showed them to her friends, rationalized to herself and to her son that she was only trying to show how proud she was of him. She derived the satisfaction of the attention and praise the paintings received. Her son's achievement tended to make her feel good about herself. At another level, however, it still touched off her envious rivalry. The son, however, got no direct gratification and believed that people admired his work solely because of his mother. Before intensive therapy, he had developed no realistic view of his talent. As he said to his therapist, "If it wasn't for my mother, nobody would think I was worthwhile." The mother in her need to feel worthwhile, also bragged about nonexistent achievements of her son, so that the therapist was surprised to find out that his art was really extraordinarily good.

An adult catatonic patient was the second of a family of eleven children of whom he was the only reportedly sick individual. He made bizarre gestures, involving among other things his neck and face: he habitually turned to one side and bent his neck. When the family was interviewed, they said that he had never made unusual gestures before he came into the hospital. After several weeks of psychotherapy, the patient seemed in pretty good shape, and the relatives visited him in the hospital. The therapist observed them from across the room and noted that as the patient talked with his family, he began to relapse into his dramatic gestures and posturings. As the parents were leaving, the therapist stopped them and asked, "How did your son seem today."

"Very good," they said.

"Did he seem sick?"

"Not at all," they said.

"Did he make any peculiar signs or gestures?"

"Oh no, he's like he always is—very healthy."

The therapist then asked about his neck postures and imitated the patient.

The mother said, "Oh well, he's done that a lot. We thought he did that because he sleeps on a couch that is too short for him."

The patient, who was in his mid-20s had been removed from school at the age of 16, that is, as soon as it was legal to do so. His parents had taken him directly to the employment office of an automobile factory. He had worked on the assembly line ever since. His entire salary was turned over to the mother, and neither the mother nor the father held a full-time job. The largest salary in the household was that of the patient. His oldest brother had been allowed to keep the money he made, however, and eventually to leave the household. The younger children derived some security from the patient. As long as he went to work, brought the money home, gave it to his mother to help support the household (keeping only a small allowance), and, despite working very hard at an arduous job, was content to sleep on a couch which was too short for him, he was considered healthy; that is, he met the needs of the family as a system. Indeed, he met the needs of everybody except himself.

It was only when he refused to go to work that he was brought to the hospital. As in many poor families, clothes were highly valued. The patient had bought some new clothes out of his small allowance and he cherished them. His older brother, who was not required to turn his income over to the family and was bigger than he, borrowed them and, of course, split them. The patient was told by his mother that he must not complain and that it was all right. This was the point at which he stopped going to work. The posturing of his neck was his physical way of complaining about the fact that he had no adequate place to sleep, but such complaints were just as ignored as more realistic verbal complaints would have been; at least he was not punished.

Traumatic events are frequently seemingly little things that are continued over a lifetime. The woman who got angry every time she fed her son is a good example. This destructive pressure was not something of which she was aware. All she knew was she had had a quarrel that day with her son, and she had felt annoyed with him that day. No one of these quarrels would in itself have had any permanent effect. It is the fact that from infancy to adulthood, whenever she fed him, anger was communicated either by the way she had handled him as an infant or by her quarreling with him as a child and later as an adult. This persisting inevitable pattern of hostility under specific circumstances produced in the son the persisting symptomatic feeling that all food was poisoned.

In schizophrenia, it is important to remember that this pervasive quality of the interpersonal pressure is central to the development of severe symptoms. A specific single traumatic incident is usually an intense and dramatic presentation of a chronic problem. Part of the confusion about the nature of traumatic events and pressures arises from the fact that the one major difference between what is reconstructed in a careful psychoanalytic therapy and what really happened is that what is remembered as a single event is always a summary of many events with similar meaning. There is increasing acknowledgment of this with neurotic patients, as well as with schizophrenic patients.

As noted earlier, Freud's discovery that the repressed seduction fantasies of conversion-hysteric female patients in the Victorian era were most often fantasies, led us astray. Later analysts have interpreted this as if he said in all cases, hysteric or not, you are dealing with a fantasy. In schizophrenic persons, the fantasies of seduction, of rape, and of torture most often turn out to be based upon an interpretation of real events. The way the patient first tells about it may not be realistic, but after he has discussed it with the therapist a number of times, what will be reconstructed will turn out to be real events, or misunderstanding of real events. Schizophrenia is a much more serious disorder than conversion-hysteria, and big effects do not result from little causes.

Some of our psychoanalytic colleagues, when we have discussed the families of schizophrenic patients, have objected and said that they have seen neurotic patients whose families were every bit as destructive in their impact as those described; however, there is a critical difference. For these neurotic patients, there is always one or more people outside the family who provide much of what the parents have not provided, but, as mentioned previously, the families of individuals who ultimately become schizophrenic systematically discourage contacts with people outside the family—that is, they discourage the identification with and the learning from peers and adults outside the family.

Parental Determinants of Disordered Behavior

The specific symptoms of schizophrenia are exceedingly varied and the people called schizophrenic are an exceedingly varied group of people. Since this is so, the particular parental pressures that have led to such disordered behavior would also be expected to be exceedingly varied. This is, in fact, the case. One parent may beat a patient unmercifully to teach him an important lesson. Another parent may teach a grossly distorted view of the outside world, because the parent believes it. Another parent may starve a patient to teach the child not to be greedy, and still another intrusively stuff a patient with food to reassure themselves that they care about the child. Indeed, the various specific behaviors of parents that are destructive are almost endless.

The parental pressures that tend to produce schizophrenia are not themselves necessarily schizophrenic symptoms. This distinction has not been understood by genetic researchers. They tend to look for schizophrenia in the parent as being the cause of schizophrenia in the offspring, even when they are supposedly investigating psychologic pressures, not genes. It is true that schizophrenic individuals are very difficult to live with and consequently may produce a higher rate of psychologic disorder in their children. It is also true that their children identify with them, as all children identify to some extent with their parents. But the specific pressures that lead to schizophrenia are different from schizophrenic pathology itself. There exist people whose functioning in other contexts is healthy, who are nonetheless "pathogenic" parents. There also exist severely schizophrenic individuals whose parenting is surprisingly unaffected by their pathologic condition. Admittedly, as with any complex task, the sicker one is, the harder it is not to be destructive in the complex interaction of parenting.

We have tried to conceptualize, at a very general level, what it is that produces schizophrenia. While some parents of schizophrenic offspring are obviously unpleasant people, most parents of schizophrenics are not consciously destructive and would not harm their child if they had conscious control of the process. The parent whose offspring tends to become schizophrenic has used that child to solve his own psychologic problems. Therefore, we conceptualize it as follows: to what degree does the parent act in terms of the child's needs or his own when the two sets of needs conflict?

To measure this tendency, the unconscious functioning of the individual should be investigated. Therefore to examine this process, we defined a score for the TAT. The stories could be scored when there was a potential conflict between the needs of the dominant person and the needs of the dependent person. The degree to which the dominant person takes the dependent person's needs into account is scored: "pathogenic" (the dominant person does *not* take the dependent person's needs into account), "benign" (the dominant person *does* take the dependent person's needs into account), or "unscorable." A pathogenesis score is derived by the formula: number of pathogenic stories divided by the total number of scorable stories, that is, stories scored either pathogenic or benign.

In a series of studies, blindly scored TATs differentiated parents of schizophrenic children from parents of normal children. In the original study, Meyer and Karon (1967) had found almost no overlap between the mothers of schizophrenic children and the mothers of normal children in this psychologic trait. This was replicated by Mitchell (1968). In a further study, Mitchell (1969) scored TATs gathered by Singer and Wynne (1965a, 1965b) and found that both fathers and mothers of schizophrenic children were more "pathogenic" than parents of normal children.

In another study, on adult schizophrenic individuals, the degree of maternal pathogenesis correlated with the severity of patient pathology (Nichols 1970). This was a very stringent test. Since all the patients were schizophrenic, the range of variation was small. Statistically, a reduced range of variation tends to make all correlation coefficients smaller.

Interestingly enough, Mitchell (1969) found that on the average the mothers were more pathogenic than the fathers. Here we see a congruence between clinical work and research when appropriately carried out. From the early days of psychotherapy with schizophrenic persons onward, those psychotherapists who have done intensive work have talked about the role the mother has played in producing the pathologic condition. This has been doubted by people who felt that it was unfair to mothers, and by people who felt that childhood could not be that important, and by people who preferred to believe that schizophrenia was a mystery. The research evidence is that, for schizophrenic individuals from intact families, not only are the mothers more important because mothers are more important for both healthy and unhealthy development than fathers for most children in our way of organizing the family, but also because, on the average, the mothers of schizophrenic children do tend to be somewhat more destructive in their impact than the fathers of schizophrenic children, even though these fathers may be more destructive than normal fathers.

An interesting sidelight on this is that Mitchell found the reverse to be true for delinquents, namely that the fathers tended to be more "pathogenic" in this specific sense than the mothers, who were more nearly like the mothers of "normals." A male delinquent from an intact family tends to have a sense of identity (which one would expect with a better relationship with the mother), but to have trouble with social controls (which one would expect with an impaired relationship with the father). This latter finding has been replicated.

Pathogenesis has also been found to differentiate child-abusive mothers from normal mothers, and child-abusive fathers from normal fathers, in both black and white populations (Melnick and Hurley 1969; Evans 1976).

In our studies of psychotherapy, as described in Chapter 10, pathogenesis has been used to examine the TATs of therapists, where it was found that "pathogenesis" differentiated ineffective from effective therapists. This should not be surprising. Therapy, like being a parent, is a situation in which one person has a dominant role in determining what happens, but what occurs is supposedly for the benefit of the dependent person. If the therapist is meeting his or her own needs unconsciously and not the needs of the patient, not much therapy is likely to be accomplished.

Do Children Teach Parents To Be Destructive?

In every case in our experience the schizophrenic individual's life has been such as to make his or her pathologic condition inevitable, and in most cases that means that the parents have been unconsciously "pathogenic." If even one parent is both strong and "benign," a schizophrenic outcome is improbable. As the evidence for unusual dynamics in the families of schizophrenic persons has accumulated, two alternative explanations of these data have emerged. One is genetic: schizophrenia, sometimes in mild form, leads to schizophrenia. But "pathogenesis" as we have defined it, and "parental communication deviance," as Wynne and Singer

(1963b) have described it, have been found to be more closely and consistently related to schizophrenia in the offspring than specifically schizophrenic traits, whether observed behaviorally or measured in psychologic tests.

The second alternative explanation is that the deviant child elicits deviant behavior from the parent. There is, of course, a certain amount of truth to this. Living with a very sick person is frustrating and may well exhaust a parent's tolerance and capacity to cope rationally.

Nonetheless, if one examines the specifics of the parent-child interaction, the specifically destructive interactions are usually such that no child could have taught them to the parent. The research problem is that the specifically destructive behavior varies from family to family.

Thus, no child teaches a mother to hold his hand in a flame for a minor offense, or to toilet-train the child by 6 months of age with severe measures, or from infancy on to get angry whenever she feeds him.

The one prospective study of the impact of family deviance to date (Doane, West, Goldstein, Rodnick, and Jones 1980) reports on the families of maladjusted but not psychotic adolescents. They measured Singer and Wynne's (1965a, 1965b) schizophrenia-producing communication deviance from the parent's TATs and so-called "expressed emotionality" (i.e., intrusive hostility) of the parents, a variable reported (Vaughn and Leff 1976) to be characteristic of parents whose schizophrenic offspring tend to be rehospitalized early. If both of these parental measures were in the schizophrenia-producing direction, all the offspring were, 5 years later, diagnosed as schizophrenic or borderline. If neither variable was in the schizophrenia-producing direction, none of the offspring was schizophrenic or borderline. If the parental measures were not both in the same direction, there was an intermediate frequency of severe pathologic conditions.

Some Aspects of Family Dynamics

The views of Lidz (1973) are so cogent that they are worth briefly summarizing. We human beings depend upon our families to provide positive support and pressure to make it possible to grow up as independent human beings. When the family fails to provide the proper nurturance, support, identifications, and acculturation, we do not develop the strengths and abilities to make an adult individuated adaptation. The family that produces schizophrenic patients, according to Lidz, consists of disturbing and, sometimes, disturbed people. That is not to say that they are consciously malevolent people; on the contrary, they are typically very upset by the patient's illness.

All of us depend on our families to teach us cognitive categories similar to those used by other people in our culture. Lidz finds that families of schizophrenic offspring tend to teach cognitive categories which differ in meaning from those of people outside the family. Lidz describes two types of schizophrenia-producing families, which he terms the "skewed" and "schismatic." The skewed family is oriented around the needs of one of the parents, usually the mother. A distorted view of the world, of family life, and of how children should be raised is accepted by the other spouse and by the children. These distortions are needed by the dominant parent to maintain the parent's own psychologic survival. The parent does not differentiate the child from the self in any clear way. Usually the schizophrenic child is a boy in such families.

The schismatic family involves two parents, each of whom attempts to impose his own distorted view of the world, family life, and of the proper way to raise children upon the family. No consensus is arrived at by the parents, and the child internalizes two conflicting parental introjects. Usually the schizophrenic child in such a family is female.

In both types of families, the differences between parents and children, between male and female roles, and between the self and the other are blurred and confused. In the skewed family, the overidentification of the mother with her son, who is among other things the man she could not be, is very common. In the schismatic family, the identification of the daughter with the mother is made difficult by the mother's own derogation of her sex role, plus the father's derogation of the mother. These may account for the apparent sex-specific destructive effects.

The schizophrenic thought disorder, Lidz points out, is central to the pathology, and is clearly not like any organic thought disorder. He characterizes it as "egocentric overinclusiveness." By this he means the belief that everything that happens is related to one's self, and the belief that one can influence all sorts of outside events over which one has no realistic control.

In the so-called schizophrenic state, the patient's thoughts are thoroughly dominated by this egocentric overinclusiveness. But this is an adaptation to which the patient has been sensitized by a family that itself shares the same kind of thought disorder, but to an attenuated degree and usually restricted to intrafamilial transactions. The patient for most of his life is not so much egocentric as "parent-centric" in his or her functioning; that is, the patient's deficits are those required to make up the deficits in parental functioning. Such functioning on the part of the patient, however, appears to be egocentric from the standpoint of the rest of the world, particularly when it becomes so severe that it is no longer a viable way of life.

Lidz differentiates schizophrenic people into developmental versus regressive disorders in that some patients never have developed capacities, while others attain more mature functioning and then, under stress, regress to a prior level of more primitive intellectual functioning. What for a potentially schizophrenic individual might comprise an intolerable stress, however, may be no more than the normal stresses of human life for people with a different life history: the problems of independence and separation from one's family at adolescence, the need to be able to relate to people outside the family, the need to develop closeness and sexuality with other human beings, and/or the need to find a career and an adult way of life in the outside world.

Some Common Patterns of Bad Parenting

Frequently, there is a reversal of roles in families of schizophrenic individuals, so that the child feels as if he or she ought to be able to parent the parents, and that the parent should be able to enjoy the psychologic status of a child, and, if not, the parent is being unjustly used.

With male schizophrenic patients, the unconscious need of the "pathogenic" mother is usually to maintain control of her boy so that he never becomes independent of her. He may be allowed to become competent in some ways, but not to the point where it would lead him to separate and depart. Even his competence is used as a necessary addition to her fulfilling her own narcissistic needs.

This frequent pattern of destructive mothering is paralleled by a different pattern of "pathogenic" fathering. The father is generally not troubled about separation; in fact, in many cases, the father would just as soon the son did not bother him. The father's need is to set up competitions in the areas in which he feels inadequate. The role of the son is to lose that competition. If the father is unsure of his masculinity, the son is to be feminine or a homosexual. If the father is unsure of his intellectual competence, the son is to be "dumb." If the father is not sure of his ability to hold a job, the son is to be occupationally inadequate. The son's inadequacy reassures the father and makes the child necessary for the father's adjustment.

The fathers of schizophrenic children of either sex often express their "pathogenesis" by emotional absence, thus not providing an alternative relationship or model for the child. They do not interfere with even obviously hurtful practices of the mother, either because of "weakness," or because "one shouldn't argue in front of the children." Projective examinations generally reveal that, dynamically, such a father is just as "pathogenic" as the mother, allowing her to act out the destructiveness he might otherwise act out himself.

In our experience with female schizophrenic patients, this sex-role typing of the pernicious interaction does not seem as clear-cut. As in so many other issues of developmental psychology, the pressures involved in the development of schizophrenia in females are not as clearly patterned and tend to be more confusing. Mothers do seem to have more conflict about psychologic separation (that is, of identity), but both the fathers and mothers may equally generate problems with independence. The fathers may, however, be physically or emotionally absent. Competition in areas of anxiety may occur with either parent. A mother may reject the daughter as a child, but exploit her as a caretaker for younger siblings, or even for her. Sexuality is even more of a conflict than it is for males. The fathers either become seductive, or more frequently, emotionally withdrawn from the girl, for fear of their own sexual fantasies. The little girl almost never understands why she has been rejected.

Advising the Parents

Parents of schizophrenic children, whether being seen in treatment for themselves or in consultation regarding their child, may ask if they have caused their child's problems. They feel guilty. Like all patients, parents project onto the therapist the condemning superego based on the punitive part of their own parents. It is well known that in therapy every interpretation is twisted into an accusation; likewise, every bit of advice we give to parents is frequently twisted into an accusation.

But "In what way have I been culpable?" is not a fruitful question. Rather, we want to focus the parents on "What should I do now, given what has happened, and what I now want to happen." It is important to help them talk about how frustrated they are dealing with a child whom they see as headstrong, out of touch with reality, and demanding totally unrealistic things. There is generally considerable truth in their complaints.

There are clinicians who intentionally intensify the guilt in order to get cooperation (or a high fee), but cooperation elicited through guilt is not recommended here, any more than in other relationships. Inevitably, it leads to anger, denial, and sabotage of the therapy. There are other clinicians who bolster the parents' self-esteem by telling them they have nothing to do with the child's problem, even if the clinician believes otherwise. This makes it difficult to investigate and change current parental practices later.

In most cases in which the parents initially cooperated, but later disrupted therapy, either the parents and the therapist colluded to avoid the issue, or the therapist blatantly lied to the parents about their involvement.

In our opinion, the proper approach, when parents ask about their role in the child's problems and it is too early to know, is to say: "I don't know. It may take us a long time to know exactly what caused your child's symptoms; however, it is our job to find out. Even if your child had no symptoms, being a parent is very difficult. When your child has problems, it is even more difficult, and I would like to be of use to you." It is helpful simply to add: "I don't know yet, but what do you think?"

The therapist thus is honest about how much he specifically knows, and yet he is not denying the possibility of some involvement by the parents. After all, the degree and nature of parental involvement will not be clearly understood until a good deal of work has been accomplished. Moreover, there are some cases of unusually severe life circumstances in which parental involvement is minimal. This honesty and uncertainty leave the door open for the parents to raise specific concerns later, and makes it easier for the therapist to raise such issues at a later point in therapy, if it would be useful. Obviously, there is more need for the therapist to have contact with the parents if the patient lives with them, and with a severely disturbed younger child living at home the concomitant treatment of the parents is an absolute necessity.

Over time, the schizophrenic offspring and their parents have developed a complex relationship. By the time a therapist typically sees them, the child's behavior confirms the parents' conscious experience of the child as crazy and unrealistic. The child's symptoms and other interactions with the parents express a mixture of hostility and compliance which is very frustrating. Indeed, a superficial evaluation of the parent-child interaction would lead to the conclusion that the parents were simply being victimized. The therapist must help the parents to handle their frustration with their difficult child. As he talks with them about what they are doing, he clarifies what is appropriate or inappropriate and helps them move to doing things with the child in different, more positive ways. Alleviating their realistic discomfort provides the leverage for the therapist to have an impact.

But when the child begins to change, the parents frequently panic. They now confront the anxiety and guilt they have been avoiding through their previous handling of the child. The therapist must take the lead in discussing what the child's changing behavior and the parents' reactions do and do not mean, consciously and unconsciously. The therapist needs to have prepared for this by having begun the relationship in a way that allows such discussions. The therapist also needs to function as a benign parent figure for the parents, providing emotional support during this difficult transition.

The therapist's view of human nature and of normal development needs to be communicated to the parents, including the role of the unconscious. Particularly important for the parent as well as for the child is the differentiation between thoughts and actions, the harmlessness of all thoughts and feelings, and the evaluation of actions by the seriousness of consequences. The importance of privacy, the normality of anger, crying, sexual feelings and curiosity including masturbation, must be discussed, as relevant.

The therapeutic view of child rearing that long-run goals should outweigh short-term inconveniences should be communicated to the parents. Thus, for example, the mother who is afraid of being kind to her child ("too kind," according to her), because her relatives will disapprove and think she "spoils" him, should be enlightened about probable long-term effects, so her guilt over kindness can be alleviated. She needs to be told that the evidence (e.g., Levy 1943) is that "spoiling" a child by overindulging or being too "kind" tends to produce a nuisance in the short run, but the problems are readily overcome in the long run, while excessive deprivation or severity tends to produce chronic problems. Therefore, when in doubt, err in the direction of kindness.

Of course, it is not kind to undercut independence. Parents need to be told that independence is best achieved from a position of security, that human beings want security and will accept control when they are afraid, and feel burdened by control when they feel safe and want independence. It is important that they understand children vacillate between wanting security and wanting independence. Ideally, the parent needs to provide security when the child wants dependence and freedom when the child wants independence. Both preventing independence and not providing security are hurtful, and, of course, teaching the skills that make independence possible is essential, as well as having independence as an important value.

Most parents want their children to be well behaved. The role of discipline in the socialization process is troublesome to most parents. They often feel some guilt about physical discipline and yet feel they have no alternatives. Like all problems, these are more serious for the parents of schizophrenic children and they need concrete help. Consider the father who beats his child for swearing. Both the issue of swearing and the issue of beating need to be discussed. The father's concern about swearing can be refocused: "Do you know any grown-ups who don't swear?"

Father, surprised (as if it's a new idea): "No."

"Then the problem isn't to teach him not to swear. That's not possible. The problem is to teach him when to swear, and when not to swear." This is a paradigm for discussing many issues (e.g., sex, cleanliness, card-playing, dancing, alcohol, etc.) namely, what is a reasonably socialized adult like, rather than an overconforming "perfect" child.

Beating is an issue in its own right. Serious physical injury is never to be tolerated. The parents must be told that it is possible to raise children without ever hitting them, usually a new idea to them, and that the therapist would like them to consider, with his help, other ways of handling specific problems. It is also important, however, to let them know that very few parents are capable of never hitting their children, despite their best intentions. Otherwise the parents hear the therapist condemning them, or as being unrealistic. The therapist's emphasis on long-term consequences permits the therapist to point out that physical punishment is the fastest way to stop an immediate problem but tends to make the general discipline problem worse. In dealing with parents, it is essential for the therapist to try not to be seen as the condemning superego, or as someone whose standards are impossible to live up to. He should, of course, deal with the most serious destructive situations first, and expect only gradual and imperfect compliance on the part of the parents with any suggestions.

Parents need to be told that all children want their parents to like them, no matter how much the children's behavior seems to belie that. This powerful lever is there, if the parents will make use of it constructively. Punishment frequently serves primarily as a communication about what the parent does and does not want. Therefore, the parent can learn to communicate his or her wishes in other ways, often more direct and differentiated, as in verbal communication. Of course, inconsistent reactions or consistent unconsciously motivated reinforcements in the "undesired" direction will produce unwanted counter-reactions by the child.

We frequently tell parents that they can have any kind of specific improved behavior from the child they want if they will be absolutely consistent in their reaction for a minimum of 6 months. It is not unusual for them to say, "But it's not worth it," which immediately places the so-called major problem in perspective.

There is no single bit of advice more useful to most parents who are having difficulties with their children (or who are concerned about their children's difficulties) than to suggest that every week each parent separately make some time available to the child that the child can depend on. The time is best spent with each child alone, although with large families that may not be practical. The child should have the right to cancel, but not the parent. When this is done, the disappearance of apparently "serious and unsolvable" problems is often dramatic. In some schizophrenic cases, there is a nonexistent father-son relationship which both would like, but feel they ought not to have, and that the "other" would not want, and only the authority of the therapist can permit the relationship to develop (generally over the mother's objections). In other schizophrenic cases there is a mother or father who withdraws from the child because the parent feels he is emotionally hurtful and he is trying to save his child (cf. Searles 1965), who can be helped in re-establishing a relationship. Such advice, however, is unnecessary for most of the parents of schizophrenic children because of the elaborate psychodynamic intertwining that already exists. Rather, the problem is encouraging the parents to allow meaningful contacts outside the family.

In advising parents, and in working with families of schizophrenic adults, one's primary goal must be to prepare the child (or adult patient) for the role of a healthy independent adult. The secondary, short-term goal is to produce a temporary living situation that is tolerable for all concerned. (Normal child rearing is, of course, a temporary situation, although it is not always conceptualized that way.)

6

Psychotherapeutic Technique with the Schizophrenic Patient

There are many ways to treat schizophrenic patients successfully with psychotherapy. Differing theoretical and technical approaches can be successful, but there are also many ways to fail. The fact that different practitioners frequently talk in different languages and say different things with certainty is confusing, especially to the novice therapist. Moreover, words or actions that have different meanings to the therapist may have the same meaning to the patient.

To sort out the technical literature on schizophrenia, one must transcend the language. What are the therapists saying, if anything? What must the patients have said to give rise to these abstractions? What does the therapist say to the patient? Given what the therapist said, what might the patient have heard? Finally, avoid those experts on schizophrenia who describe the optimal technique on the basis of an abstract theory not derived from their own clinical experience. Unfortunately, the field abounds with such advice. Many of the so-called experts on the treatment of schizophrenia do not actually treat schizophrenic patients.

It is not our intention to describe the entire process of psychotherapy, rather, to supplement the insights that the serious psychotherapist already has. Schizophrenic patients do not remain distinctively schizophrenic as the therapeutic process unfolds. After all, the processes are not unique to schizophrenia, only their severity. As psychotherapy progresses, the symptoms become less and less serious, and hence less unique. The psychotherapy becomes more and more what one is accustomed to practicing with other patients. For the borderline patient who regresses easily, and hence varies dramatically in level of functioning, the technique should be appropriate to the patient's functioning at that moment.

Noncommunication and the Schizophrenic Patient

Schizophrenic patients are geniuses at not communicating clearly. They do not even tell the therapist that he is helping them, because they are afraid it will be used against them. Therapists who have only worked with neurotic patients are not prepared for working a long time without direct feedback from the patient.

For example, a 10-year-old paranoid schizophrenic boy, after being in treatment between 8 to 12 months, described a dream. I (Karon) commented about it, but the patient said nothing. I added, "Well, maybe I'm wrong."

A slight smile appeared on the patient's lips, "How often do you think you've been wrong, Doc?"

"I don't know. Perhaps half the things I say to you don't fit."

Broader smile, "You haven't been wrong yet, Doc."

What a beautiful statement of positive transference! This, however, was the first time this patient had ever indicated that anything had been correct.

Why should this be? Another child patient made this very clear. The child had been adopted by two parents, each independently sterile. (These parents would make one believe in psychogenic sterility, because the odds of biologically sterile people meeting by chance and marrying are very slight.) Each of them, on a psychodynamic level, was a person who literally could not give to anyone, although neither was aware of this. The adoptive father had solved the severe economic deprivation of his childhood by eventually becoming a slum landlord. The mother had adopted the child to save her marriage and was disillusioned that having the child had not done so. By the age of 7, the boy was adapting on a psychotic level.

An indication of the adoptive father's pathologic condition may be given by the following conversation. After 6 months of treatment, I told the parents that the problem for which they originally brought the boy to treatment was now gone. Originally, the school could not tolerate him even in kindergarten. He now was adapting to the first grade, and was doing adequate work, only slightly below his ability. "However," I said to the father, "he now has a symptom, which is at least as serious—namely, that he can only relate to other children by hurting them or being hurt by them."

"What," asked the father, "is sick about that?"

In dealing with the father, I asked him if he ever hit the child. "No," he said. "Well, almost never."

"How often is that?"

"Almost never."

"Well, how often is that?"

"Well," he said eventually, upon further questioning, "two or three times a week." Compared to his own childhood, where he had been beaten two or three times a day, that, indeed, seemed like almost never.

Many years ago, Harry Stack Sullivan (1953) said that if you wished to produce a malevolent adult, hurt him every time he wants love. Like so many things that Harry Stack Sullivan said, this statement is true.

In discussing the issue of punishment with the mother, I asked whether there could not be some other method of punishment besides hitting the child.

"But," she said, "You don't understand. He never lets us know what he likes. If we knew what he liked, we'd take it away from him, but he never lets us know what he likes." This mother clearly let us know why it is that so many of our schizophrenic patients do not tell us things very clearly.

As therapists, we are not used to continuing to work for months, or perhaps even years, without clear statements from the patient, such as: "You are helping me." "You are not helping me in this way." "You are doing this." "This is going on." It is very frustrating.

Psychoanalytic Theory and Therapeutic Practice

THE ROLE OF THEORY

Theory is essential to the therapist. Its value lies in generating hypotheses about what is occurring in the patient, from even small cues. This allows the therapist to begin meaningful and relevant work with a schizophrenic patient. As in all cases, the therapist listens to the patient and modifies his or her initial hypotheses on the basis of clinical data, until his understanding is accurate. Of course, this requires tolerating not knowing with certainty what is occurring, and tolerating the discovery that his initial formulation was wrong. Never should a therapist be so smugly satisfied with his theoretical reconstructions that he is unconcerned about the patient's progress.

Theory belongs in the mind of the practitioner, and is communicated to the patient only if it can be made meaningful and useful to him (c.f., the discussion of "educative comments" in the treatment of the economically poor patients, Chapter 8). In general, psychoanalytic theory does not directly dictate method. Theory tells you what you want to accomplish, not necessarily how. There is a variety of ways to accomplish almost anything in an interpersonal situation. The critical issues are to get some idea of what is occurring in the patient, to know what it is that you are trying to do, and what you are doing in order to accomplish this. If the therapist keeps these in mind, he will be effective. While we will make very specific statements about what to do, only a fool would think that there is only one way to communicate a message, which is what psychotherapists do.

THE NATURE OF PSYCHOANALYTIC THEORY

As orthodox an analyst as Otto Fenichel (1939), when considering the issue of whether alternative practical procedures were "psychoanalytic," said that anything you do is psychoanalysis, if you know why you are doing it. We assume he meant that if you have some idea why you are doing it, what it is you expect to accomplish, you can then evaluate whether it worked or not. If it is not effective, you can change it. If you do something simply because it feels good, you have no idea why it was or was not effective.

That does not mean that you will not react spontaneously, just that you will think about what you do. Indeed, it is a mistake with borderline and psychotic patients to be overly deliberate. It is better to act and be "off the mark" or even inappropriate than to wait a long time to be "right." You will seem so stilted and inhuman to the patient that he will not be able to relate to you. If you feel you have acted inappropriately, you can discuss that with the patient. After all, if you can make mistakes, so can the patient. It does the patient no good to think that the therapist believes so strongly in his own Godlike omnipotence that he, like the patient's parents, cannot be challenged. The patient must not think that no good person ever really makes mistakes. No matter what the therapist says, the patient learns from an apparently infallible therapist that the fallible patient is defective.

Your tool in effective psychotherapeutic work will always be your own personality. For example, the therapist who naturally never swears should not swear for the benefit of the patient. The therapist who swears easily ought not to inhibit it too much because he thinks therapists do not use that kind of language, unless he is dealing with a patient who, he has reason to believe, would be shocked by such language. With the average patient, such a restriction of language would make the therapist appear stilted. The schizophrenic patient would respond to that stiltedness, but not know what it means; he probably would not ask, and fill in the ambiguity with transference feelings (generally negative).

The most important parts of psychoanalytic theory are also the most fundamental. In some psychoanalytic discussions, that which is most abstract, that which sounds most like physics, seems to be the most valued. Unfortunately, those are the parts of the theory that are least useful. The most useful parts of psychoanalytic theory are the ideas about the unconscious and consciousness, the relationship of childhood to adulthood, symbolism, displacement, and defense mechanisms. These fundamental statements about the human organism are central to everything you do as a therapist. As we get more and more abstract, we get less and less that is directly clinically useful.

It is a mistake to assume that psychoanalytic theory is *a* theory, that is, a single, cohesive body of theory that is unambiguous, covering all situations. Psychoanalytic theory is a set of theories evolved by a large number of workers, the fundamental contributions, of course, being those of Freud. It is clear that Freud's own contributions were never entirely integrated. The general psychoanalytic way of looking at human beings is in terms of development and of the relationship between the conscious and the unconscious.

This is clearly different from purely biochemical (psychology is unimportant), or behavioristic (thoughts and feelings are not important), or phenomenologic (the unconscious is not important), or cognitive-behavioral (feelings and the unconscious are not important), or Gestalt (the unconscious of the therapist is not important), or transactional analytic (anything that is complicated is not important) approaches to understanding human beings. Nonetheless, all of these derive more from psychoanalysis than their practitioners are willing to admit. If one follows their evolution, particularly in the hands of practitioners, you find many disguised psychoanalytic ideas and techniques.

Some parts of psychoanalytic theory are very specific, while others are general. Both are clinically useful. For example, a very practical clue to unraveling the meaning of a dream is, "To whom did you tell your dreams?" If a patient reports telling a dream to someone the next morning, the dream concerns that person (Ferenczi 1953). On the other hand, psychoanalytic theory includes principles as general as: "Any problem which we cannot solve directly, undoubtedly has unconscious components." Or, Freud's dictum, "One always interprets from the surface," that is, starts with reality and explores the realistic reasons for a symptom or a phenomenon, and gets into the unconscious after exhausting more superficial reasons, an approach that makes sense to the patient.

Fundamental is the view that every symptom and every verbalization of the patient, indeed every action as well, is meaningful. Although neither you nor the patient may know the meaning, examination will eventually reveal the meaning to both of you. A useful assumption is that every piece of data (verbal and non-verbal) in a clinical hour might be related to everything else in that clinical hour. The relationship may not be clear, or even important. But this may help to make sense of a puzzling hour. It is also axiomatic that associations are meaningful, whether you or the patient understand that meaning immediately; that transference reactions are inevitable, and are at the core of what is occurring; that human beings have a childhood, and that childhood is terribly important in understanding their later life, far more important than the patients can imagine.

Psychoanalytic theory says that human beings carry their childhood with them in their unconscious. When a patient talks about any kind of problem or interpersonal encounter, which seems excessively anxiety-provoking or is routinely handled poorly, the therapist should always wonder of what this might be a reenactment. Indeed, even if the patient insists that the current problem is unique, the therapist should consider that it is a recurring problem.

For example, a schizophrenic patient, after years of "supportive" treatment and medication, said in the first interview of her intensive treatment that she was afraid that "the government will deport me. Can they do that?"

"They only deport people who aren't citizens."

"Oh. But they say they will tear up my birth certificate."

It takes no great stretch of imagination to tell her that "the government you are concerned with is the government of your family, your mother and father. You must have felt they would throw you out of the family."

"No."

"What's on the birth certificate?"

"Who my parents are."

"Well?"

"They did threaten to tear up my birth certificate this week when they were mad at me."

"I think that's the government that you were afraid would deport you, don't you?"

"How come my other doctors never talked like that?"

THE UNCONSCIOUS AND SCHIZOPHRENIA

The most fundamental concept in psychoanalysis is the unconscious. One of the current misconceptions, even among sophisticated therapists, about the nature of schizophrenia is that the repressions are undone, and that the schizophrenic patient is aware of his unconscious. Neither of these statements is true, in our experience.

The schizophrenic patient has a consciousness which is dominated by the unconscious, but he is not aware of the unconscious itself. Thus, for example, the patient may be aware that, "The Athenian girls are laughing at me. They say their breasts are poisoned," or, more transparently, "The cow gave her calf milk and then kicked it. She shouldn't do that. It's something that happened hundreds of times in the history of the world," but he is not aware of his own unconscious feeling that his mother got angry and thus hurt him after every time she fed him, which is at the basis of his poisoned milk fantasy. He does not consciously relate the first hallucination to his mother, and the second one he does not see as having any relationship to himself at all. "It's just a fact. It has nothing to do with me," is his response when any attempt is made to relate it to his life.

No one is more afraid of the contents of their unconscious than a schizophrenic patient. The repressions are strong, but brittle. Under stress, the unconscious may break through, and then be repressed again. Part of the reason for the impression that the repressions are undone in schizophrenia lies in the fact that certain impulses and ideas which are repressed in normal individuals become conscious in the schizophrenic. This material, which is often treated as "deep" in the analysis of neurotic patients, represents for these patients nothing but another set of defenses against being aware of their real problems. Thus, Oedipal fantasies may be conscious, but the classic Oedipus complex does not have, for these patients, the significance originally ascribed to it by Freud. Instead, it serves as a defense against deeper and more frightening problems (Rosberg and Karon 1958), as we discussed in Chapter 4.

Typically, the distortions of schizophrenic individuals are attempts to deal with their problems symbolically. The essence of the symbol is that the contents of the unconscious are expressed, and yet the individual is preserved from the awareness of what he is expressing. The schizophrenic person is constantly trying to solve his problems, but he is too frightened of them to deal with them directly; he represses the real problems and deals with the symbols. This affords him a measure of relief, but he cannot solve his problems on a symbolic level.

In several schizophrenic patients whom we have treated, both acute and chronic, it was clear that an overwhelming conscious fear of death immediately preceded the psychotic break. In other patients, this was not clearly established, but Bettelheim (1956) seems to support the generality of this finding. It is certainly clear that every schizophrenic patient believes that he could not live without his symptoms. Anything that endangers his psychotic adjustment is felt as a threat to life. Consequently, there is a qualitative difference between the resistance of the psychotic and the resistance of the neurotic patient.

RESISTANCE

The resistance of the neurotic person is mainly unconscious. He or she will consciously cooperate with the therapist to a large extent. Nonetheless, you can feel the anxiety "around the corner" whenever significant material begins to come to the surface. The neurotic symptoms represent "solutions" to the patient's problems. When the therapist interferes with these neurotic solutions, the patient feels anxious. This anxiety is based on the fear of being in the situation or faced with the dilemmas that have been avoided by means of the symptoms. The therapist may know that a better solution to the underlying problems is available, but the patient does not. He is not even aware of the problems he has solved by means of the symptoms. It is only after the specific problems that were unconscious have been made conscious that the patient is capable of seeing a healthier resolution for them is possible. Nonetheless, he consciously hopes it is possible to alleviate his symptoms by psychotherapy and, on the whole, he consciously cooperates in the process of psychotherapy in order to alleviate the conscious distress he suffers from his symptoms.

In contrast, the resistance of the psychotic patient is not only unconscious, but also conscious. Anxiety seems too mild a term to describe the fear of the psychotic. Terror is more appropriate. The patient literally believes he cannot live without his symptoms and, when the therapist attempts to interfere with them, the therapist is raising the threat of death. If the patient cooperates, it is either an attempt to get the therapist to leave him alone, or, at best, it is a desperate plea for help by someone whose own resources have come to an end and who does not know what else to do. The help he wants has to do with the supposed source of his terror and not with his psychosis. Consciously, he does not want to get better in the sense of losing his psychotic symptoms. After all, why should he or she die for you?

This difference in the resistance gives rise to the basic difference between the psychotherapy of neurosis and psychosis. In the psychotherapy, or psychoanalysis, of a neurotic patient, the work is mutual—the two of you, patient and therapist, are engaged in the work together. Despite the resistance, the patient is engaged in forwarding the work. Although through transference, the therapist is magnified larger than life, this distortion is analyzed. The therapist at no time acts out the distorted role. For the most part, the work is mutual. Eventually, the patient is doing the bulk of the work on his own problems and you are helping him. When he reaches the point at which he no longer needs your assistance, the therapy is terminated.

In the psychotherapy of a psychotic patient, the work is not mutual. The therapist imposes the therapy on a somewhat unwilling patient. It is true that if the therapist is nonthreatening, if the therapist tries not to interfere with the symptoms and does not interpret, and if the therapist is willing to wait long enough, eventually the transference needs are such that a therapeutic relationship can be built in which the therapy is not being imposed on an unwilling patient. Such an approach is advocated by Fromm-Reichmann (1947, 1950). Any hope of a brief course of therapy must be discarded, it seems to us, with such an approach. It is only after considerable progress has been made in the therapy that the psychotherapeutic work can really become mutual.

TRANSFERENCE AND THE SCHIZOPHRENIC PATIENT

The patient is threatened by the possibility that the therapist will take away the psychosis. This would stir up an intolerable terror except for the protection that the therapist also provides. This protection is worth, from the patient's standpoint, some cooperation.

Thus, *the first function of the transference relationship* in the psychotherapy of schizophrenia is to provide sufficient protection and gratification to overcome the conscious resistance of the patient. The patient's search for a new "mother" continues in his illness; he is, therefore, susceptible to building a relationship with the therapist. When Freud said that schizophrenic patients did not form a transference, he meant they did not spontaneously develop a therapeutically usable transference, that is, a transference of positive, trusting dependence on the therapist which can be used as a motive for therapy. Since the childhoods of schizophrenic patients have been so undependable, they have trouble forming a strong, so-called positive transference to the therapist. The therapist for a schizophrenic patient, however, can help this process by being a strong, protective, more gratifying figure than he would be in the therapy of a neurotic patient. He must actually provide more gratification and protection. It is not necessary or useful to be too subtle with schizophrenic patients, since they fill in ambiguities with the destructive aspects of their parents. This is, after all, a transference relationship, and the patient will eventually see in it the malevolent characteristics of his past relationships. Further, despite his initial response to a benign relationship, he will eventually try to disrupt it, under the unconscious pressure to prove that all people are bad, and therefore preserve the fantasy that, as compared with all others at least, mother was good. The mother or father may have aided such a defensive maneuver by directly teaching that people outside the family are worse, dangerous, or untrustworthy. Both the need to disrupt relationships and the direct manifestations of the disruptive transference should be interpreted to the patient as soon as they are evident.

The transference relationship has two further functions in the psychotherapy of schizophrenia. *The second function* of the transference relationship is to permit insight. This is identical with its function in the analysis of neurotic patients. The patient relives feelings and experiences from the past, particularly those concerning his parents, thus providing an enormous source of information as to what his life history and problems were really like. Transference means the repetition of events and feelings from the past as if the past were the present. People do this not only in analysis, but in their everyday life. Transference always seems as if it were current reality. Neurotic patients are very subtle. It took a genius like Freud to discover transference. Psychotic patients are not subtle, as, for example, the patients who call the therapist "Dad," or "Mom." The transference permits an accurate reconstruction of the problems in their past and provides material for bringing to light some of the most important unconscious problems.

Understanding the transference with psychotic patients is very important. Freud's discussions are misleading in that he sometimes talks of transference as if it were something that occurred only in analysis. This, of course, is not true, and even in the early psychoanalytic discussions (e.g., Ferenczi 1950a), one clearly finds that transference, like other defenses, is discussed as occurring not only in therapy, but outside of it. The difference is that the therapist pays attention to it, studies it, and uses it therapeutically. Indeed, much of the pathology of schizophrenic patients is nothing but transference to the world at large. As mentioned earlier, Niederland (1959a, 1959b, 1972) has pointed out that in the Schreber case (Freud 1911b), much of the delusional material which Freud does not explain, consists of nothing but repetitions of what we would consider torture devices that Schreber's father actually used upon him as a child. (Schreber's father was a famous pediatrician who believed posture was very important, and invented certain devices to make children sit or lie straight.)

The third function of the transference relationship is to provide a model for identification, both identification into the superego, and identification into the ego. In any psychotherapy, the patient replaces, to some extent, the original mothering pattern with the more benign patterns of "mothering" he has received at the hands of the therapist. Thus, the strong transference relationship allows the therapist to provide a new model of how the patient is to treat himself, and with this model the patient can free himself from his old patterns. The image of the therapist thus gets taken into, and modifies, the superego, but it is also taken as a model to some extent for the ego itself. This process is something that occurs in all therapy (c.f., L. Horwitz [1974]), although we do not always like to admit it. But in the treatment of schizophrenic patients, it is of particular importance, because of the defective models of identification available in the patient's early life, and the lack of corrective identifications outside the family earlier in the patient's life.

In the beginning of the therapy, the first function of the transference—providing protection and dependency gratification—is the most important. As the patient sees that he can face today what terrified him yesterday, he fights less against the process of therapy, and this function of the transference becomes less important. Nonetheless, the patient will return to the sessions, implicitly (and sometimes explicitly) saying "Yes, you have helped me. Can't we stop analyzing now?" As the therapy progresses, he takes a larger share in forwarding the work until both therapist and patient are working together on the patient's problems. When the patient no longer needs to see the therapist as omnipotent, and can regard him as a near equal, the psychotherapy is no longer distinguishable from that of the neurotic patient. As with a neurotic patient, it is hoped that the therapy continues forever: only the external therapist's aid is relinquished.

The most frequent errors in the treatment of schizophrenia lie in refusing to be strong and active when the patient's anxieties demand it, or, having played such a role, to refuse to relinquish it when the patient no longer needs it. It is the job of the therapist to allow the patient to grow; he cannot grow if the therapist refuses ever to accept him as an equal human being. If the therapist, upon whom he now depends, is unwilling to let him grow up, the therapist is repeating the traumas of his childhood and he cannot grow up. He may lose some of his psychotic symptoms, but he will always remain a dependent child tied to the infantilizing therapist.

AMBIGUOUS COMMUNICATION

While for the neurotic individual it is of some advantage to be ambiguous, it is clear that for the psychotic individual the ambiguous therapist is a hostile, malevolent, destructive therapist because patients can only fill in the gaps with their transferences. The useful part of ambiguity in psychotherapy is that it allows the transference freer play. In the case of people whose lives have been so awful that they have to function on a psychotic level, those transferences are going to be malevolent, destructive, and awful. Therefore ambiguity in the therapist's communication is a threat.

For example, a patient asked early in the hour for an extra session on a weekend. I (Karon) said, "I will do it if I can work it out; I'll have to think about it and call you back after this hour." As the session progressed, the patient got angrier and angrier and finally burst out in a physical assault.

At the time I was puzzled. My children knew that "Possibly, I'll see if I can work it out," means "yes, it's only a question of feasibility." The patient's childhood was such that "possibly" had meant "no." His parents never clearly said "no" so that he could get angry at them. To the patient, I was saying "no, but I'm not even going to tell you that," and that is what made the patient furious. If you are going to say "no" to a psychotic or borderline patient, say "no." If you cannot decide at that moment, give the patient a clear idea of exactly when you will make the decision. Preferably, the decision should be made before the patient leaves the session.

Never promise a patient more than you can deliver. If you are in doubt, say "no." Nobody ever feels bad about being told "no" and later being told, "I have reconsidered this and I can do for you what I earlier did not think I could do." On the other hand, everyone feels furious about being given something, counting on it, and then having it taken away unpredictably. This is particularly true for our psychotic patients because that is the story of their lives.

THERAPEUTIC OPTIMISM

One of the most potent forces the therapist has to offer is his informed optimism about a condition which the patient, and, unfortunately, all too many other professionals before the therapist have treated as hopeless, incurable, or, at best, a horrible burden which must be borne without cease for the rest of the patient's life.

The therapist must be that strong, optimistic individual who is not going to be deterred by the magnitude of the problems or overwhelmed by them. It is not necessary to pretend to have instant solutions to all problems; indeed, it is not helpful since that is a lie.

It is not untrue, however, that if the therapist and the patient continue working as well as possible, the odds are very strong that the patient will improve and the major problems will be resolved. This is a stance that is very difficult for the inexperienced therapist, or for the experienced therapist who has only had failures with such patients. The reasons for his failures may have been because he was working in settings and with supervision that ensured such failure. There is clear experimental evidence (Arnold Goldstein 1962) that therapists who expect no improvement tend to have patients who do not improve, and that therapists who expect their patients to improve tend to have patients who do. In part, that is owing to the fact that people's expectations are based on their previous results, but it is more directly related to whether the therapist communicates to the patient an attitude of hope or hopelessness; this is critically important to the patient.

This does not mean that the therapist should hold out a simplistic hope to the patient that if he will just hang on, everything will be better. Rather, the therapist should present the view that with continued contact, work, exploring and understanding the experiences of the patient's childhood, and understanding how the patient struggles internally with his thoughts and feelings, the patient will increasingly be able to understand his life, thoughts, and feelings, be able to function better, and be happier.

Being optimistic does not mean that the therapist denies to the patient the seriousness of the problem or the amount of time and effort that it will require of the two of them. Being optimistic means being honest both with himself and with the patient about the seriousness of the problem and continuing to work despite the fact that there is no rapid or immediate change and despite the fact that it is very frustrating. If the therapist lets the patient know that they both have hard work ahead, but it will be worthwhile, it is easier for both the therapist and the patient to continue working in the face of difficulty. When you allow the patient to think that the work is going to be easy and quick, or that it will be fruitless, you are only setting the patient up for another failure.

There is a world of difference between a hard job and an impossible one. The patient will undertake a hard job when he senses that the therapist is ready for the work. The patient will shrink from an impossible one and stay as sick as is necessary for his or her apparent well-being.

After having successfully treated one or more severely disturbed individuals, it is possible for the therapist to be realistically optimistic in the face of the most intimidating sets of symptoms. It may be necessary, however, for a supervisor who has successfully treated seriously ill people to provide the motivational support to sustain the novice therapist. Luckily, most novice therapists have a certain degree of optimism which their supervisor can either bolster or destroy. Unfortunately, there are many therapists whose initial experiences in doing therapy or whose personal therapy has been so unsuccessful that their optimism about the effectiveness of psychotherapy is destroyed, perhaps forever.

Aspects of the Treatment Process

Therapy may begin in a number of ways. Therapists argue for and against the need for an initial accurate case history, the advantages of an unstructured or structured initial interview, and the importance of having or not having psychologic testing. Yet none of these is the critical issue in the psychotherapy of schizophrenic patients.

The critical issue is how to come into meaningful contact with the patient. The therapist knows his purpose is to help the patient, but the schizophrenic patient may not be sure of that. This is more than just a transference problem.

This is also a service delivery problem. The current mental health system is structured in such a way that it rewards quantity, not quality, of care. Even private practitioners are rewarded economically for high-volume, low-quality treatment or diagnostic procedures: shock treatments, medication practices, 15-minute psychiatric "evaluations," etc. Thus, most schizophrenic patients are likely to have encountered previous mental health professionals whose aims, consciously or unconsciously, were not primarily to help the patient, but to get the "job" done—to put in so many hours, to process so many patients, to get the case load reduced, to "treat" the patient with as little involvement as possible, or to find out particular pieces of information that someone else needs.

These unhelpful contacts of the patient may have begun early in life with a school social worker or a mental health professional involved in some preschool screening. Further, the yearly turnover of psychiatric residents, psychology interns, and other staff members in most public institutions may mean that, even if the patient has had a meaningful and helpful previous relationship, it was taken away. Unfortunately, the separation from each specific psychotherapy relationship is not typically used as material for psychotherapeutic work. Realistically, therefore, such a patient has reason to be suspicious of entering a new relationship, in addition to transference problems.

Successful psychotherapy with schizophrenic patients requires a therapist who is dedicated to such efforts. Effective psychotherapy, in general, is a difficult, demanding, and tiring task. In treating schizophrenic individuals, the difficulties and the demands on the therapist are also tiring and many times greater. It is essential that the therapist be someone who wants to do this kind of work, is willing to make the commitment, and is working in a setting which, at least, permits it; it is hoped that the setting encourages such treatment. Therapists who do not want to work in therapy do not help patients (Malan 1963; May 1968; Karon and VandenBos 1972), and they soon become processors of patients, not therapists.

Of course, the patient's transferences are apt to be of hostile or inadequately helpful people, namely the parental figures transplanted onto the therapist, even when the patient is, in fact, being helped. Help itself may be experienced by the patient as overcontrol. The therapist may be seen as psychologically merging with the patient and undercutting the patient's judgment in order to prevent his independence, as the parental figures may have done.

Moreover, if one of the parents has been helpful and the other not, it is not uncommon for the less helpful parent to have labeled the helpful parent's behavior as destructive. For example, if a mother who cannot relate well to her son notices that the father enjoys spending time with the boy, and the boy enjoys it, she may suggest to either or both of them that her husband must have homosexual problems. Similarly, parents who themselves are overly restrictive and who permit no play that might make the house untidy, may notice that their little girl goes next door, where the mother is kinder to her own children and their friends. The restrictive mother may spend a good deal of time telling her child how terrible the people next door are, and what a bad mother her friend has, since the friend's house is often a mess. These psychologically poisoned explanations of the good things in the world help to keep the patient trapped in the parent's world, enhancing the power and hence the psychologic security of the parent. But these internalized beliefs are clung to by the patients as part of the only meaningful relationship the patient has had, and they continue to poison their explanation of what is going on, even in therapy. The therapist must, nonetheless, try to build a relationship not knowing what malevolent interpretation the patient will construct of the therapeutic intervention.

It would be good to have a simple theory and a simple technique that could be mechanically applied without emotional involvement, anxiety, self-doubt, or impatience. Unfortunately, no such technique exists, at least not one that is successful. The schizophrenic patient, as we have shown, is a frightened human being who does not entirely understand what is happening, who is afraid to communicate clearly because that may be used against him, who typically is angry because he has been hurt so badly although he is afraid to express the anger directly or toward the instigator (in many cases a patient is not even consciously aware of who the instigator of the anger really is). He either expresses the anger violently or in a covert way, and "inexplicably" shifts attitudes and behavior dramatically during a single interview as well as between sessions.

The therapist will be puzzled and confused, and he must tolerate his own confusion. He will resonate to the patient's anger, depression, and fear. In all the problem areas of life in which the therapist has experienced difficulty, the patient is likely to have had even more, so that the therapist will find himself having to confront those areas of life in which he is still uncomfortable; however, the therapist will find that the patient's difficulty is many times greater than that of the therapist.

In the first meeting with a severely disturbed patient, emotional contact must be established. This is sometimes done in very active ways, or it may be done quietly by being very attentive to the patient's experience and conveying understanding. For many schizophrenic patients, it is extremely useful somewhere in the first hour to say that you will not let anyone kill him (or her).

In the early years, I (Karon) used a very dramatic technique. In recent years, I have used a more relaxed technique; however, both techniques were successful. The issue of activity-passivity in the sense of physical activity or drama is really not the critical issue in the psychotherapy of schizophrenic patients. The critical issue is what is communicated to the patient by whatever the therapist does or does not do. Schizophrenic individuals are good at not getting in contact with people, so in the initial sessions it is important for the therapist to establish his existence and real desire to communicate and help. In the initial phases of treatment, he may have to see the patient three or more times per week to establish himself genuinely as both a reality figure and a trans-ference figure in the patient's life.

DIAGNOSIS VERSUS UNDERSTANDING

With most patients, one can begin work by no more elaborate or technical procedure than simply asking, "What seems to be the trouble?" or "How can I be helpful to you?" Most schizophrenic patients will begin to tell you the problem, even many patients who are supposedly uncommunicative, incoherent, or "lacking insight." The aim is to find something which, from the patient's standpoint, is a problem or which does not make sense to him, something with which the therapist can provide help. If you allow yourself to be distracted by the need for an accurate medical diagnosis, you may prevent the patient from telling you the problem.

Sometimes diagnostic questions make a difference, but in many settings, the first 2, 3, or 4 hours with the patient may be spent trying to decide where along the borders of the standard diagnostic categories the patient is to be located, even though the differential diagnosis may have no implications for what the thera-pist should do. The patient picks up the notion that the therapist is concerned with something, but it does not seem to be with help-ing. The patient reacts. After all, he knows how to deal with people like that, people who become intensely involved with you in order to do something else, which they never clearly communicate to you, all the while telling you it is for your own benefit. In many cases, that has been the story of his or her whole childhood.

Thus, a patient who had been ineffectively treated for many years, was said not to know he was ill, and it was said also that he would not cooperate with treatment; he was supposed to have no insight into his illness. In the first session, when asked what seemed to be the problem, he said, "I have trouble with my anger. I hurt people." When the therapist (Karon) agreed that the violence he described sounded like a problem and asked if he wanted help with it, he said, "Of course I want help with it. I don't want to hurt people."

Yet the hospital and previous psychiatrists had called him "uncooperative" and described him as having no insight into his problems. It is true that if you asked him whether he was paranoid or schizophrenic, he would get very angry at you and not accept such words. Why should he? What benefits derive from accepting a "diagnosis?" From his standpoint, the primary consequence of accepting the "diagnosis" would be to legitimize the right of others to make decisions about his life. On the other hand, when a therapist says to him, "What's your problem?" and he says, "I hurt people even though I don't want to," and the therapist offers to deal with that problem, the patient suddenly becomes part of a working alliance. He has told the therapist what he should be working with, if he wants to be helpful to the patient, and his values are not wrong. It is a goal with which all of us would agree, and it should be the central focus of the initial stage of therapy.

Of course, all professional training requires that one learn how to classify patients using standard diagnostic nomenclature, such as DSM-III. That is all right, but it should not get in the way of treatment. Understanding a patient primarily in terms of the standardized diagnostic categories, and expecting the patient to value such labeling, is like a man who for convenience takes black and white photographs and is annoyed that other people will not describe butterflies in terms of shades of gray.

For example, one man kept saying, "There's something wrong with my head." His resident simply concluded he had somatic delusions, and not that he was asking for help with his disordered thoughts. Ward reviews centered on whether his was really a schizophrenic or a schizo-affective disorder. It was more important to know that this man was married, and Black (which observations were in the chart) and that he was a youngest child, had a sister, and that his brother was lighter-skinned than he (which observations were not in the chart) in order to be able to help him. The human experience, and hence the schizophrenic experience, which after all is the human experience in great trouble, is highly varied. When we compress our understanding of human beings into a nomenclature, we are throwing away most of what is happening.

This is not to say that it is not useful to have some basic information about the patient. If this information is not readily available, we ask the patient about his age, religion, occupation, education, marital status, the occupation and the education of his spouse, the age and sex of his children, the age and sex of his siblings, and who besides his parents and siblings lived with the family during his childhood. Obviously one does not use these stilted words in phrasing the questions, but rather something like, "How old are you?" "What do you do for a living?" "How far did you get in school?" "Are you married?" "Do you have any brothers or sisters?" Such phrasings do not sound to the patient as though he or she is considered less than human.

Such structured questions at the beginning of a first interview usually make it easy for the frightened patient to respond. There is no threat in the question. The answer is generally simple, factual, and usually nonthreatening. Borderline and psychotic patients generally function better (because of less threat) in structured situations. Of course, if the patient is unable or unwilling to answer these questions, we do not pursue them.

This information will help us (and consequently help the patient) to make realistic sense out of the apparently unrealistic material. Often, however, the patient in the course of answering such simple informational questions reveals essential problematic areas of his life.

Thus, a supposedly uncommunicative teenage schizophrenic patient reported, one at a time, the names and ages of her eight younger siblings.

"That's a lot of kids."

"It's enough."

"Being the oldest girl in a large family is a lot of responsibility."

And at this point the patient smiled and seemed to react as if the therapist were on her side.

The therapist's goals in the early sessions are to learn something about the patient and to get across the idea that he can help. Interestingly enough, current research (Luborsky 1977) seems to indicate that psychotherapy with neurotic individuals will not be helpful unless the patient, early in therapy, understands that the therapist will either "help with my difficulties" or "help me to work with him in solving my difficulties." Unless the patient gets the idea that this person called therapist actually has something to offer and will offer it, nothing therapeutic happens (e.g., Grinspoon et al. 1972). Luborsky tentatively conceptualized this as a patient variable, although we see it as a therapist variable.

Our view is that most psychotic patients clearly do not come in with the expectation that the therapist will be of any help. It is the therapist's job to create the therapeutic alliance by every possible means. Strangely enough, it often is not that much work.

The advice, given above, that most schizophrenic patients will talk freely if asked what seems to be the trouble, and if they are actually listened to when they do talk, may seem oversimplified. Yet we have seen patients listed on the ward charts as "totally uncommunicative," only to have the patient speak meaningfully when asked, "What seems to be the trouble?" Indeed, when we were invited as consultants to interview the "most difficult and uncommunicative" patient, to teach residents and graduate students how to deal with recalcitrance, we have been embarrassed by having the patients talk openly.

There are, of course, patients with whom we have to spend hundreds of hours before getting real communication. But such patients are really very rare. Most of the patients who are called uncommunicative turn out not to be, if allowed to talk about the issues that are of concern to them.

Very rare, even today, is an even minimal attempt to communicate with the patient, exemplified by Merriam's account of his experiences as a patient (Merriam 1976). Of course, when the patient communicates, he may communicate in ways that the therapist does not understand. The natural tendency of the therapist who has been taught that he must understand everything is to get rid of the patient, because he is making him feel inadequate, or for the therapist to remain quiet, meaning to the patient, "I have nothing to give you."

In the process of establishing a therapeutic relationship with the patient, it is important not to defend previous mental health professionals or the practices of the institution with which the therapist is affiliated. It is impossible to know what other professionals have done with your patient. It is also impossible to know what other staff members at your institution have done. The most that can be done is to say to the patient, "That is very surprising, because that would be a very bad thing for a therapist to do," or "That must have been awful, and I am surprised that he or she did that."

All involuntary commitments are just that, involuntary commitments, and the patient usually sees himself as being misused. Very often "voluntary" commitments are equally involuntary from the standpoint of the patient. Some family member or other authority figure has said he must go into the hospital. The patient did not want to go into the hospital, would not willingly go in the hospital, but was such a fearful, intimidated person that he did what he was told to do—and hated it. Most inpatient settings are experienced by patients as not very pleasant places to be, as prisons. It is all right to help the patient put that into words. Usually only very sick patients find mental hospitals congenial environments.

The hospitalized patient who "doesn't belong here," has at least one problem that the therapist can offer help with—how to deal with people so as not to be hospitalized.

SOME PRINCIPLES OF INTERPRETATION

What to interpret, and when, are central issues in any psychotherapy. Straightforward but conflicting simple sets of explicit rules can easily be found in the literature. Unfortunately, no one of these is uniformly clinically effective.

Thus, Kleinian analysts feel that if the patient is overly disturbed, the therapist has not interpreted deeply enough fast enough. Ego-analysts feel that an overly disturbed patient means that the therapist has interpreted too deeply too quickly. Premature interpretations are felt also to forestall the possibility of the patient's realizing on the basis of his own material that these interpretations are true.

While simple explicit rules do not seem to be clinically useful, there are some valid general principles.

The first principle is to interpret from the surface in the sense of exhausting reality factors and realistic explanations first. Few patients are willing to consider psychodynamic factors until common sense explanations are found wanting.

As to whether to interpret early or late, deep or shallow, defense or impulse, the most generally valid rule, albeit imprecise, is that one interprets what one believes the patient can make use of at that time. What the patient can make use of, and when, is always a clinical judgment that may be in error.

There are some times when a "deep" interpretation, even in the first sessions, will make sense out of experiences which otherwise overwhelm the patient; there are other times when the same interpretation would be incomprehensible to the patient.

The second valid clinical principle is that the therapist never does for a patient what the patient can do for himself. An insight he discovers is far more potent than a similar interpretation from the therapist, but how much the patient is able to discover is again a clinical judgment. Valid insights by the patient should be always valued and encouraged. But early in the therapy of a schizophrenic patient (that is, when the patient is more psychotic), more will need to be formulated by the therapist than later, when the patient's functioning (and hence therapy) is on a neurotic level. Even when the formulation is entirely that of the therapist, it is only therapeutic when the patient's experience confirms it.

A good interpretation directs the patient's attention to those experiences which confirm the accuracy of the interpretation. As Richard Sterba has so vividly described in clinical seminars, a bad interpretation is like saying "Look at that plane in the sky," when the patient sees nothing. A good interpretation is like saying "Look at that airplane over the top branch of the tree by the barn," and the patient looks and says "Yes" when he sees the moving speck.

A Case of Childhood "Schizophrenia" Cured in One Session

A 7-year-old boy was brought in for an evaluation because he was compulsively splashing water on his face and soaking his hands every half hour, as many as 20 to 30 times a day. He would wake up in the middle of the night to do the same thing. If he was told to stop, he would just ignore admonition. If the parents attempted to restrain him, he would go into a rage and violently fight their attempts to stop him. If they succeeded in restraining him, he would talk about "the worms." The parents could not determine what he was concerned about, other than the fact that there were "worms" beneath his skin. This had been going on for several weeks, and was intensifying. The family physician felt that the child was clearly psychotic and would require psychiatric hospitalization. He suggested that the "schizophrenic" child be seen, as a formality, by a local psychologist for a preadmission evaluation.

In talking with the mother, I found little that was unusual about either the father or the mother's handling of this child, or the two siblings. All of the children's early development and school performance appeared normal. The only disturbing event was that the parents were in a stormy process of divorce. It had been pending for about 6 months. The father and mother were having a difficult time separating from each other. They argued over whose fault the divorce was, and over the property settlement. These arguments included acting out by both parents: they would taunt each other, follow each other around, go to each other's residence at night, look in to see what was happening, and smash a window if they did not like what they saw.

The patient and the other children found this nerve-wracking. On numerous occasions the children witnessed intense verbal arguments and even physical fights between their parents. They had the frightening experience of playing quietly in their own living room and looking up to see a face staring in the window. Any child would feel anxious.

Each child had been taken to the family physician at one point or another, because the school officials saw them as quite "nervous." The physician, too, told the children that they were "nervous," and they had been placed on minor tranquilizers.

When seen for intake, the boy was attentive and obviously bright. He was friendly and cooperative, and sat in the chair like a very proud and grown-up 7-year-old. He talked freely about the fact that he was worried about "the worms." He was also obviously scared. He was no more articulate about the "worms under the skin" with the psychologist than he had been with his mother or the physician.

As is often the case when I (VandenBos) am stumped, I changed the subject. I asked him about what was going on in his life. He immediately told me that his mother and father were getting a divorce. He talked about some of the things that had gone on between them, and how frightened he was about them. This then led me to ask him whether he was nervous and had he talked to anybody about it. He said, "I talked to the doctor, and he told me I have bad nerves."

"What does that mean?"

"The doctor told me it was something like worms under my skin."

Being a kid who had been fishing, he knew what worms were, and he also knew what they looked like when they were left on the seat of a boat and they dried up and burst open. He was afraid that his nerves were like worms and that they were "bad," that is, they were going to dry up and crack open. He was terrified of this, and so he splashed water on his hands and on his face to keep his bad nerves wet, so that they would not burst open and his hands and face become a mass of pus.

"Big people," I told him, "sometimes talk in funny ways. What big people mean when they say 'you have bad nerves' is that you're nervous or upset about something, and that you have mixed feelings, and that you're scared, and that one of the ways that people deal with this is by feeling jumpy or shaky." I further explained to him how this was not abnormal, and certainly did not mean that his nerves were going to dry up and burst open.

The physician had tried to explain physiology to a 7-year-old boy by the unfortunate analogy that nerves were like worms crawling under the skin. The child had a vivid graphic image of real worms crawling around underneath the surface of his skin, which would terrify anyone. After this brief discussion, he stopped looking nervous and anxious. He and the therapist spent the rest of the session talking about five or six of the recent scary incidents. A second appointment was set up for him.

The mother called the day before the second appointment and said the symptoms had totally ceased. She said her son had been talking about his fears, and had engaged the other children in talking about how scary it was to have mom and dad doing the things that they were doing. All of the kids were feeling better and less anxious now that they were talking about these things. The mother was even able to recognize this as evidence of how frightening their situation had been for the children, and approached the father about this matter. As a result, they did cut down the level of fighting with each other, and were controlling some of their acting-out behavior (following each other, etc.). The mother did not bring the child in for the second appointment because she could find no reason to do so. Follow-up inquiries to the school and the mother about 4 months later showed that the improved condition of the child continued.

If the child's world had not been sufficiently entered, he would have been hospitalized. The usual procedure of tranquilization plus the trauma of hospitalization, for a 7-year-old, would in themselves have produced symptomatology that would have confirmed the diagnosis, as we have seen in other cases. The long-term effect on the child's life might well have been unfortunate.

Assessing Therapeutic Improvement

If the therapist works in a hospital in which the mythology is that schizophrenic patients cannot benefit from psychotherapy he can work effectively and never know it; he can go away assuming that the work was of no value. As mentioned above, the patient frequently does not tell the therapist. Very often, it is the ward staff, if the patient is in the hospital, or the family, if not, who may report changes in the patient's behavior. From them come the indications that the therapist has helped the patient. Otherwise, the therapist has to rely on his past experience or his supervisor to sustain his therapeutic effort, with little or no feedback from the patient. He needs to know that if he continues to do reasonable things long enough, the patient will improve, even though the patient does not say so, and even though much of what the therapist does will be "wrong," since the patient is not communicating clearly.

In some cases, a therapist knows he is helping a patient from the nature of the patient's complaints. For example, a patient who sounds quite sick during her therapy hours even now, finally says, "You know, I don't talk this way anywhere else. You know what would happen to me if I talked this way anywhere else?" She is quite right. But she was not that careful when treatment originally began.

More importantly, she complains, "You haven't helped me because I really don't like the guy that I am now sleeping with, and I really don't enjoy sex very much." These complaints, which should be taken seriously, nonetheless, tell us that she has made enormous progress. When she started treatment, she felt that no man would come within 50 feet of her. She later felt that when she dated a man, if she said no, he would kill her. She also felt that if she did go to bed with a man, he would kill her. For her to have her present problems means that she has made enormous progress.

Further, she says, "You haven't helped me, because I want more time off from work to take college courses, and they say they can't spare me. And I'm having trouble with my courses and I'll lose my B average." At the beginning of therapy, she was about to be fired. Now, they find her so valuable, they do not want to give her more time off. Moreover, she is taking college courses, and has a B average to lose. Yet, if one were to judge from her communications in therapy, one would believe that she was incapable of such a performance. In a very real sense, she is at her sickest during the psychotherapy hour, which is fine because there we use the psychopathology to gain more and more insight into her life and problems and to enhance the process of growth.

It should be clear from this discussion why it is useful to have a great deal of experience, or to have a supervisor who has had a great deal of experience with schizophrenic patients. If such is the case, one can sustain the motivation to do meaningful psychotherapeutic work, even without clear feedback, until the benefit is clearly manifested. Of course, enduring efforts will not be necessary for all patients before they show improvement. Acute psychotic reactions show dramatic improvement in the first five sessions, and the vast majority of hospitalized schizophrenic patients will be able to function as outpatients with 2 months of five-time-per-week treatment.

Our repeated advice about the importance of relevant supervision and experience concerns us, however, because it can be misconstrued as meaning that only someone with a great deal of experience, training, and supervision should attempt to treat schizophrenic patients. It is common to define the therapy for schizophrenic patients in such a way that it seems as though almost no one should attempt to treat such patients. In most settings, inexperienced therapists are all that are available, and we would not discourage them. Luckily, the energy, enthusiasm, and optimism of the younger therapist is helpful, and will compensate for many of their errors. The less energetic older therapist can afford fewer mistakes. In any setting, any therapist should attempt to provide the best treatment of which he or she is capable, and seek out relevant training insofar as it is available. If one does what one can, surprisingly often it will be enough.

IMPROVEMENT AS A PROBLEM

When a schizophrenic patient improves, this often, in fact, creates new problems, since the details of his life may change drastically. The patient may then paradoxically develop new symptoms in response to the anxiety generated by the changes attendant on improvement, or the possibility of these changes. He may feel ashamed that he cannot cope with what he believes "anyone" should be able to cope with. The therapist should be aware of this, and try to help the patient anticipate and deal consciously with these new problems.

A bizarre frightening person does not have to worry about sexual advances, or the frustration of sexual rejection. A chronic patient on welfare or disability does not have to worry about the pressures of holding a job. Someone who has been hospitalized or in a board-and-care home for a long period of time does not need to know how to socialize, react spontaneously, develop recreational interests, or make the myriad choices involved in independent living. Even the normal effort and frustration of regular employment may be a new experience for the patient.

Disability pensions (e.g., from the VA or Social Security) may be canceled if a patient holds a job. Patients may develop new symptoms for no apparent reason when they reach the point where they must decide whether to risk holding a job or not. Their fear is that they will get a job, lose their pension, and then lose the job. Unfortunately, they solve this problem in their characteristic psychotic fashion, by developing a symptom instead of making a conscious choice, and they may not mention the dilemma in therapy unless the therapist is alert to it.

Unfortunately, the agency may in fact act in an arbitrary fashion. It is useful, however, for the therapist to help the patient find out what the actual policies of the specific agency are. Then the realistic anxiety and realistic alternatives can be discussed and separated from unrealistic fears, tentative conscious decisions can be made, and the treatment process can be continued.

Similar conflicts occur in other spheres of life. A woman in her twenties seemed to recover after prolonged hospitalization, was discharged, attempted suicide, and was rehospitalized as blatantly psychotic. In the hospital, she began to make a rapid recovery. The treatment staff was concerned about the safety of discharging her, particularly because she had given them no coherent explanation of the suicide attempt and psychotic break.

Examination revealed a fear of abandonment combined with a fear of sexual intercourse. Her husband visited regularly when she was in the hospital, but, of course, made no sexual overtures. When she was discharged, however, she would either have to engage in sex or risk a divorce. Either was intolerable.

Symptoms were avoided on discharge by providing outpatient psychotherapy for her, plus counseling for the husband. He was given direct advice not to abandon her, or press her insistently about sex for the first few months until psychotherapy had had a chance to take effect, and he readily cooperated.

SOME WAYS OF BEING HELPFUL

In talking with the schizophrenic patient, we often refer to "giving," and the word "giving" is not chosen at random. It really is a question of giving and taking, of dynamics going back to the early mother-child relationship. The typical schizophrenic patient has felt deprived all his life. It is important that the therapist do whatever possible to be perceived as a giver and not a taker, and to be perceived as a nonpunisher and nonpoisoner. The contrary view has been seriously put forth (Wexler 1951) that the therapist should initially be the punitive superego, because the patient can relate more easily and comfortably to such a superego figure. Then the therapist should change, thus transforming the superego. But we find such an approach artificial, uncongenial to our temperament, and not necessary.

We find it useful to give the patient a cup of coffee. We like coffee, drink it during difficult sessions, and it would be unkind not to share with the patient. The patient thus gets direct oral gratification without interpretation. Patients frequently reject it and distrust it, but feel good about having something to reject. The important thing is that the rejection comes from the patient, not from the therapist, a theme which could be repeated endlessly in different phases of therapy and in differing contexts. Such an apparently superficial detail is really a therapeutic working-through of the separation-individuation process, which should have been accomplished in childhood (Mahler, Pino, and Bergaman 1975).

The therapist must talk freely, and try to be helpful on the verbal level. Even words may be experienced by the patient as a medium of exchange which can be given and taken. The therapist must be seen as someone who does not demand, but gives. When he asks for information, he should try to make it clear that it is only in order to be helpful. Frequently, the patient has practical problems, with which the therapist can be helpful. The patient's knowledge of the world is usually more limited than that of the therapist for symptomatic, cultural, or even accidental reasons. If the therapist can offer usable information, that helps to establish him or her as a helpful person.

But a therapist must not assume that since he has given the patient a solution to a problem, the problem is solved. On the contrary, the patient will frequently be unable to make use of what the therapist has imparted. The noncritical discussion of this inability leads directly into productive psychotherapy.

Frequently, the patient will raise a practical problem that he is not really interested in solving. There is an easy way to assess this. For example, if the patient says he cannot sleep at night, the therapist might well say, "That's something I should be able to help you with, if you like."

It is a good idea to stop at that point. The therapist indicates in a tentative way that there is something he could provide, and he leaves the option to the patient. If the patient never returns to that issue, he does not really want advice about it. If he is interested in it, he will come back to it, and the therapist can give him appropriate advice. In that way, a relationship is being established by helping the patient. If he does not want help with that problem, that means there is something more important that he really does want help with. Ordinarily, it is not for the therapist to decide what the patient needs help with the most. Of course, some patients may interpret not returning to the issue as meaning they are not supposed to. If it is not clear what the patient wants, the therapist may appropriately ask, before the session is over, "Is this something you want me to help you with today?" This may lead to a discussion of the problem, or a discussion of the difficulty in asking for help, or a decision to defer this specific problem to a later session. Obviously, if the therapist is concerned that the patient may murder someone or commit suicide, it is up to him to focus on those issues immediately, but beyond this, he should focus on what the patient feels he wants help with.

Similarly, when the patient expresses pessimism, "I cannot get better," or says, "Nobody knows why one hears voices," it is useful for the therapist to say, "That's not true." In the latter example, he could go on to say, "We know a great deal. We know why people hear voices." But, he does not explain why people hear voices unless the patient shows an interest in following up that lead. The main purpose may have been to say, "you don't know anything," not real curiosity about what causes voices. Indeed, the patient may already suspect what causes the voices, but he may not be ready to explore this, because it now serves as a defense which he cannot afford to give up yet. Nonetheless, it is useful for the therapist to pinpoint to the patient things that he can help with, such as "Your sex life isn't too good, that's something we should be able to help you with."

It is not necessary to explore the issue immediately, unless the therapist feels that is the patient's central concern. But he plants the idea that the symptom is not a fact, that it is not hopeless, that these are things that can be helped. Statements of the sort, "Well, any decent therapist should be able to help you with that," are very helpful. Such comments implant the idea that not only is help being offered, but the help is not magical, it is just the result of adequate training.

Sometimes patients do not see anything for which they need help. In such instances, at least they can tell the therapist how they got to his office and why people think they need help, but strangely enough, it is not uncommon for patients to be ignorant of why they have been sent. Nobody has ever told them. The family or other referral source was afraid that the patient would get upset. In such situations, it is best to tell patients what is known. Even if they get upset by accurate information, where better could they get upset than with a therapist?

There are many schizophrenic patients, however, to whom the therapist need only say, "All I have to offer you is understanding, but that's really a great deal," and they react to it as if he had offered them the Holy Grail. They are impressed when, indeed, he does understand something of their life. Strangely enough, the therapist may have understood something common to all human beings, but which they, because of their life experience, do not understand as common to all human beings. Their reaction is similar to his own reaction when, for example, he first read one of the great classics of literature, such as Dostoevski, and said "My god, this man knows something of my life, my experience, or my thoughts that I thought nobody but me knew."

The patient has that same kind of "aha" reaction when the therapist understands something about him, which is basically human. All patients, but particularly schizophrenic patients, do not think of themselves as basically human. They think they are something different from all other people, and that other people could never comprehend their defects, difficulties, and anxieties. Of course, this does not mean that simply saying, "You're just like everybody else" will help. But it is useful for patients to get a sense that they experience part of the human condition.

Some patients do not talk or answer your questions, or they act bizarre. In such cases, the therapist can point out what they are doing, and that most people would consider it crazy. After all, people who do not talk when spoken to are considered either crazy or insulting by most people. The therapist can point out that people often are unkind to people who are acting crazy, because such behavior scares them. When people are scared, they are often mean. Patients generally do not have much trouble noticing that people are mean to them, unless those people happen to be in their own family. They usually believe that people are unkind to them because of their thoughts and are unaware that others are reacting to their obviously "weird" behavior.

Most patients do talk. If the therapist asks, they will tell him enough about what seems to be the trouble to begin a working relationship. Often they tell him a specific symptom or personal problem, about which he can give them direct advice. By doing so, he not only helps them with an immediate real problem, but demonstrates that he knows something and that there is something for them to gain by talking with him.

It is important, from the very first session, for the therapist to make clear to the patient that anything can be talked about with him: any thoughts, any feelings, any actions. Nothing is taboo. Even if the thought, feeling, or action is different from what the therapist likes to hear, or the patient thinks he would like to hear, or is inconsistent with his advice, it can and should be discussed. The therapist should make it clear that he will not punish or reject the patient. Only if patients have permission to talk about anything, can they learn what is realistic and what is not, or what is good advice and what is not.

Commonly, the schizophrenic patient fears talking not merely because the therapist will disapprove of what he says, but also because he fears that talking about a feeling, or even thinking it means acting on it, or that the thought or feeling itself is an action with immediate consequences in the external world. His family have commonly treated thoughts as being equivalent to actions.

Again and again the therapist must make the distinction between thoughts and actions, as, "It is all right to feel anything. The only thing you have to control are your actions, because they are the only things that have consequences in the outside world." This must be mentioned early in therapy, and repeated as it seems relevant, as is inevitable.

In the first session with a schizophrenic patient, and frequently thereafter, the therapist is almost certain to feel confused. Being confused would hardly seem a virtue. Yet the ability to tolerate confusion is an absolute essential in working with schizophrenic patients. They have spent a lifetime trying not to communicate clearly, because they dare not. The therapist must be able to tolerate uncertainty and make clear that it is all right for the patient not to trust him enough to communicate clearly. He will eventually.

That does not mean that the therapist must not understand the patient; he obviously prefers understanding to not understanding. He will understand a great deal, because he understands a great deal about human beings and he understands a great deal about sick people. The sicker human beings are, the more alike they are. The therapist knows the patient is very terrified and is trying to cope with that terror. The therapist does not know the details of the patient's life, or how he has experienced those events, but he does know that the life history must account for the symptoms. If the patient tells him anything, he can begin to make sense out of it. If he can make any of it meaningful, it is more than other professionals have ever done, and more than the patient has ever been able to do. The patient will forgive the therapist's errors.

When a therapist gives advice, he makes it clear that it is not a crime to ignore it, just as when he gives an explanation, or interpretation, the patient does not have to accept it. The therapist lets the patient know the therapist believes his advice will be useful; otherwise he would not give it. He must also let the patient know that the patient does not have to follow it. The therapist suggests that the patient do what makes sense to him at the time. The therapist also suggests that the patient discuss later in therapy whatever he has actually chosen to do.

It is important early in therapy to introduce the idea that "mistakes" are extremely useful. The therapist presents the attitude that there is no such thing as a mistake, once one is in therapy, because one learns from everything. He tells the patient, "You know, our society is crazy because it doesn't teach that bright people make more mistakes than stupid people. Stupid people make a mistake and say, 'Oh my God, I'm stupid' and stop doing it. Bright people make more mistakes, because they do something new; then they learn, which means they make fewer mistakes. Once they learn to do something, they start doing something else and start making mistakes all over again. There is no way not to make mistakes other than to stop doing things."

The patient, of course, will not believe him. He thinks the therapist will criticize him, punish him, and abandon him, if he does not do exactly what the therapist tells him to do. Only gradually will the patient make the startling and pleasant discovery that this relationship is not predicated on his pretending to obey the therapist's evey word. When the patient starts to confess that he feels guilty about lying to authority figures because he has not done something he was told to do, supposedly "in his own best interest," he is talking about transference issues. The therapist should discuss these feelings, and their childhood origin, to teach the patient to trust his own experience, to judge "prescribed choices" by their consequences, and to see the value of relating his current dilemmas to childhood.

When a patient chooses to do something different from what the therapist has suggested and it proves to be a better choice, it is an extremely therapeutic experience, if the therapist is genuinely delighted with it. Frequently, the patient has information the therapist does not have, which clearly changes what is appropriate. Even very sick patients may develop creative adaptations far better than any of the therapist's suggestions. When this occurs, it should be reinforced. Such an attitude contrasts sharply with the attitude of the overprotective, symbiotic, or authoritarian parent.

The general rule of thumb is that one does not do for a patient that which the patient can do for himself. If a patient does not know how to do something or is momentarily overwhelmed, however, the therapist can always help out. He gives the patient the help needed at that moment, but uses that instance as a learning experience. This is perhaps an oversimplified sequence, but during the course of treatment the therapist may help the patient and talk about it afterward. The second stage is when the patient does what the therapist did earlier and can talk about it. The third stage is when the patient knows how to learn what to do, and, as always, discusses it.

CONFIDENTIALITY

Very critical in the development of the therapeutic relationship is establishing limits of confidentiality. This is particularly important with the schizophrenic patient who usually has not had his privacy respected in any sphere of life. Since we tell patients that it is all right to think or say anything in therapy, we also tell them what they say belongs to them. It is part of their thoughts, and no one has a right to know their thoughts, not even therapists, except that we think we can help them. We will not transmit any information without their knowledge and consent, even the fact that they are in therapy.

We usually tell patients who worry about confidentiality that even the FBI cannot get that information, and that in several past contacts the FBI has respected our unwillingness to disclose even whether someone was in therapy. These days patients have heard of Ellsberg's psychiatrist. We generally use this as an example of someone professionally ethical; even the Federal Government conducting a burglary could not find out whether Ellsberg was in therapy, let alone any other information.

If there is a third-party payer, whether insurance company, government agency, or family member, it is important to make clear to the schizophrenic patient how confidentiality will be handled. For insurance and government agencies, we discuss with the patient any necessary forms. In general, we feel that third-party requests for a diagnosis, prognosis, recommended course of treatment, and information as to whether the patient is coming for therapy or not are reasonable requests. Routine minor forms that are repeated, like billing, need not be individually approved, as long as the patient knows what information is being transmitted and has approved. The first time we actually complete such a routine form we show it and discuss it with the patient as a way of demonstrating our attitude about confidentiality. While the need of insurance companies and government agencies for diagnoses is understandable, it is well known that very few responsible psychiatrists or psychologists give diagnoses with potential for damaging their patients, unless the "damaging" diagnosis has already been given. A label of "schizophrenia" can come back to haunt a child or adult for the rest of his life, even after he has been cured. Employers and university admission officers respond to what they believe the labels mean, rather than to the actual behavior of this person. Most insurance plans are handled through employers, and it is not good treatment to get your patient fired or passed over for promotion.

We make clear that detailed, nonroutine, personal information is transmitted only with the patient's approval, after he has
reviewed and approved a draft of any written communication. The
issue of confidentiality is a responsibility to the patient, not the
therapist. Checking any communication with the patient allows the
therapist to get his view. The patient has the right to release his
own information, with, of course, the therapist's advice as to the
likely consequences of sharing that information. Sometimes it is to
the patient's advantage for the therapist to share information with
a draft board, judge, probation officer, school administrator, or
employer. Patients are often less concerned than we think they
will be. But most important is the fact that they know they are in
charge of what happens to them.

When another agency calls for information, the therapist
does not just answer or refuse. He obtains information. What do
they need to know? What do they need to decide? How does his
information relate to what they need to decide? How will it help or
hurt the patient? Then the therapist arranges to call them back
after he has talked with the patient. Even if the patient has already
given the other agency a release, the therapist should talk with the
patient (if he is still in treatment) before releasing the information.

There may be times when sharing information without prior
discussion is obviously in the patient's best interests. In such
cases, the therapist always discusses what he has said with the
patient afterward. For example, a prosecutor may call and ask, "Is
this man a patient of yours?"

"Why are you asking?"

"He was arrested, but we think he needs treatment. He said
he's a patient of yours, and we'd like to cooperate."

"Yes, he's being seen."

"We feel it doesn't make sense to jail him. He needs treatment. We will either dismiss the charges, or recommend a suspended sentence. What do you think?"

"I think you're right. That makes good sense."

Some of the bases for such departures from confidentiality
are: (1) the patient has already indicated a willingness to share the
information, (2) sharing the information is likely to be clearly in
the patient's interest, (3) the information is such that this particular patient would have no qualms about sharing it, (4) delaying

answering might be harmful to the patient's interests, and (5) the information requested is general. Such discussions, without prior detailed permission, should be kept brief, and should be unusual. When in doubt, absolute confidentiality is the best policy.

In the case of an inquiry that the therapist cannot answer, it is even more important to find out the inquirer's concern than it is to tell him what cannot be done. What they ask is frequently not what they want. In one case, a police agency called about a potentially violent crisis involving a patient but asked, "Is Bob Smith a patient of yours? One of the officers thought he recognized him. He's threatening to kill us." The therapist (Vanden-Bos) responded: "I really can't tell you that, but, it sounds like you have an explosive situation on your hands. Tell me more about it. Maybe I can help."

A therapist working in a hospital, community mental health center, or other institutional setting must complete particular kinds of documentation. Nonetheless the therapist can tell the patient how much confidentiality he does have. Therapists often feel uncomfortable at telling their patients that their records are not fully confidential. Patients are not generally concerned about whether or not the Auditor General comes in to make sure that the file fee sheet balances with their ledger card. Patients are concerned about whether or not the therapist is going to tell people their private thoughts. Even therapists in public institutions can answer these concerns by telling them what will and will not be documented.

It is important to discuss confidentiality. Once the issue has been raised, the patient will at least partially believe the therapist. Moreover, it demonstrates that the issue can be discussed. Frequently, a patient will assume without discussing it that the therapist does not keep secrets, because others have conspired against him. Potentially disturbing information about the limits of confidentiality is less disturbing when discussed openly, than when discovered. Moreover, if the therapist has admitted limits to confidentiality, it makes his or her statements about what is confidential more credible.

For example, if a therapist tape-records therapy for research or supervision purposes, it is important to tell the patient, explain the purpose, who will hear it, and when it will be erased. The tape recorder should be in clear view, and it is recommended that the therapist tell the patient it is a tape recorder, point out the microphone, and start it with the patient there. From that point on, the therapist should ignore the tape recorder for the rest of the session. To fuss over the tape recorder once the session is started communicates the feeling that the tape recording is more important than the therapy. Any check of the tape recorder should be done before the patient gets there. If the therapist has begun the hour and is not sure, he should forget about it. If the tape recorder is out in the open, if the patient's questions about it are answered, and if once the hour begins the tape recorder is forgotten by the therapist, it will be forgotten by the patient. After all, the patient wants to trust the therapist at some level.

Supervision can easily be explained by, "I wish to get the opinion of a more experienced colleague about the work we're doing so as to make sure that if I make any mistakes I will know about them and correct them. After all, I want to be the best therapist I can." Such a statement may sound naive, but it is on the mark, it is honest, and patients understand it.

Patients are rarely upset by consultations as long as the purpose of the consultation is made clear. For example, if a patient has had a heart attack and the therapist is a nonmedical therapist, setting up a consultation with an appropriate physician to help evaluate the possible role of emotional factors is more successful if the patient is told that it is going to be done. Patients are relieved that the therapist can recognize there are limits to his knowledge, and that he gets appropriate information when he has reached those limits. Such behavior by the therapist is particularly helpful to psychotic people. They are not used to having someone deal openly with the fact that no one person knows everything, and that the appropriate use of resources is a realistic part of functioning. To them, the use of resources has always been a confession of inadequacy. The transference basis of this is that their parents covered their inadequacies by pretending to be omniscient, and by pouncing on the weakness of the child, as if it represented defectiveness rather than the normal state of someone who has not yet learned something.

It is our procedure, once therapy has started, to tell patients of any conversation we have with family members or others concerned with them. We tell the patient, "I do not owe a bond of confidentiality to the other people, because they are not my patients. Only you are my patient. What you say to me is absolutely confidential, but what other people say to me about you and what I say to them I will tell you. This is the only way I can work." We do allow parents, or spouses, one confidential interview before therapy begins. We also encourage parents, or spouses, to contact us when they are worried or frightened, but we tell the parent or spouse that the later contacts are not confidential, and advise them to let the patient know whenever we talk.

If someone else in the family is going to be in treatment with another therapist, both patients should be told whether or not the therapists will consult with each other, and what information will be exchanged. When a family session is planned, the patient should be asked if there is anything he prefers not to be brought up. That request should either be respected, or the patient informed about why it is important to talk about it. Talking about why the therapist thinks it is important to talk with a family member about some problem is as important as doing it, because you will find out and explore the patient's fears about what the family would do if they knew.

One interesting case where confidentiality was central to therapeutic progress involved a social agency which sent a patient and, as part of their routine procedures, requested information on the case. The patient had been seen at a community mental health center and refused to return. She seemed not to trust them or anyone else. Supposedly, she was very difficult (this is often the criteria for requesting us to see patients). I (Karon) called the agency while the patient was present, and said, "I don't really think you want me; because I will not give you reports on what the patient says." The agency worker was upset, because it violated usual agency procedures. After consulting with his supervisor, he asked for a meeting with me. I agreed, provided the patient sat in on it. The three of us met and agreed to an initial written evaluation, as required by the agency. (This was already written, and the patient had already gone over it in private with me, and we had deleted several sentences to which she objected.) In addition, the agency wanted a statement that the patient had attended her sessions, and that the therapy was going satisfactorily. I told the patient that I thought that was reasonable, because the agency was paying for the therapy. The patient agreed that that amount of information was legitimate.

Once this was settled, it turned out that the critical current life problem that had precipitated the symptoms was an affair the patient had had with a married man; the affair had broken up. The patient was afraid the welfare agency would take a puritanical view and discontinue aid to her if they knew about it. It became clear that my apparently intransigent attitude about confidentiality was critical in transforming the uncooperative patient into someone who wanted help and could make use of it.

Understanding and Handling Dramatic Symptoms

It can be a bewildering experience to deal with a hallucination, delusional belief, or paranoid system. How does one talk to a patient whose experiences are bizarre? How does one deal with the patient who will not talk to you? How does one deal with a patient who seems potentially violent? Such questions trouble all of us. Yet, it is clear that a reasonable psychodynamic orientation provides sufficient knowledge of the human condition to deal with a great deal of this.

HALLUCINATIONS

One simple explanation for many hallucinations is that the patient is lonely. The voices represent somebody who cares about him. Even malevolent voices are better than being alone. Any child would rather be punished than ignored, and any adult, sick or well, still carries the seeds of his childhood within himself.

It is well known that schizophrenic patients have predominantly auditory hallucinations. Eugen Bleuler pointed this out as a characteristic of the disorders. Almost all schizophrenic patients hear voices. Visual phenomena, while they may be present, are less prominent.

One of the differential diagnostic criteria for suspecting organic involvement is when a patient describes predominantly visual phenomena, particularly moving animals in color. When such material arises it is reasonable to consider the possibility that he may be suffering from a toxic psychosis; and thus, he should be asked about his use of alcohol and/or other drugs. This elementary fact, which has been known clinically for a very long time, was ignored by researchers who tried to tie schizophrenia to LSD and other chemical substances. The chemically induced psychoses had all the characteristics of other toxic psychoses, namely a predominance of visual phenomena. The schizophrenias, which occur without such substances, are still as they always have been, predominantly auditory in their hallucinatory symptoms.

The meaning of this is that schizophrenia is basically an interpersonal disorder. We know that children or adults who are deaf tend to have more psychologic problems than people who are blind. Blind people are more physically incapacitated, but deaf people are cut off from human beings. The reason the hallucinations in schizophrenia tend to be auditory is because the problems that lead to schizophrenia are not primarily physical, but are the result of disturbed relations with other people, and it is these disturbed relations with which the patient is trying to cope and to resolve.

The hallucination has exactly the same structure as a dream. Therefore, hallucinatory material—whether auditory, visual, odoriferous, or any other—should be treated like a dream; that is, it should be associated to, made sense of, and brought meaningfully into the context of the patient's problem. As a therapist, one cannot deal with what one does not know or see or hear. The first thing to do is ask the patient to tell you what he sees or hears. Until then you cannot do anything. We encourage patients to tell us about hallucinations, indicating that they are even more useful than dreams. Second, attempt to get associations to the elements of the hallucination, as to a dream. Some very disturbed patients may be unable or unwilling to associate, but many patients will, even when very disturbed. Further, if you know something about the patient, it is usually much easier to interpret an hallucination than it is to interpret a dream, because the motivation has to be much stronger to hallucinate, that is, to have a dream, when you are wide awake.

There is a view among many psychologists that the hallucinatory material and the delusional material should be ignored. The patient should be directed toward reality and not encouraged to explore the hallucinations. Such a view is a mistake. It is like the view that it is not necessary to talk about dreams in doing psychotherapy. It is true you need not, but you are throwing away an extraordinarily valuable tool. Of course, the patient may not see any connection between the hallucinations and his current problems in life, any more than patients ordinarily see the connection between their dreams and their current difficulties, but the therapist should point out that hallucinatory material is useful and meaningful and he should help the patient make use of it.

It may be useful to outline, albeit all too briefly, Freud's theory of dreams, which is equally applicable to hallucinations. The dream has the purpose of keeping the dreamer asleep in the face of disturbances, of which for therapy the most important are conscious, preconscious, and unconscious wishes. The hallucinations, too, consist of wish fulfillments. The dream is constructed from memories of the previous day and earlier memories going back to childhood. In psychotherapy, the dream takes on a new function as a medium of communication to the therapist of what needs to be worked on. This can be seen as a special case of Ferenczi's (1953) insight that when a patient has an urge to tell a dream to someone, that person is involved in some way in the dream.

Obviously, the hallucination does not preserve sleep, but it does deal with disturbing impulses. Freud's distinction between the manifest and latent content is critical. The manifest content of a dream (or hallucination) is the dream (or hallucination) as it is experienced or as it is remembered; the latent content is what it is all about. Wishes that are acceptable to the patient will be expressed openly in the dream. In general, the more unacceptable to the dreamer (or the dreamer's superego) the impulse, the more disguised its expression.

To gather information about the latent content of a dream (or hallucination), the therapist asks the dreamer, "What comes to mind?" for each detail of the dream. "It doesn't have to make sense, and there aren't any bad thoughts; what comes to mind?" Alternatively, he may ask what comes to mind about the dream (or hallucination) as a whole without asking about each detail. Or he may ask about a particularly striking detail.

For the dream (but *not* for the hallucination), the therapist may ask for associations by saying, "Every dream involves something from the previous day. What from the previous day seems involved in this dream?" Often this is the fastest way to get associative material concerning early childhood, as Freud pointed out.

The distortions in transforming the latent content into the manifest content of a dream (or hallucination) can be summarized as: (1) condensation—many elements of the latent content are represented by a single element of the manifest content, or its converse, and many elements of the manifest content represent a single element of the latent content, e.g., a patient feels her body to be "hard, like it is made of wood," relating to (a) if you are hard you can't be hurt, (b) men's bodies are hard like wood, (c) penises are hard like wood, (d) she wishes she were a man, (e) her mother and father would prefer a son, (f) sex is all right if you are a man and dangerous if you are a woman, (g) anger makes you hard, and hence strong, safe, and good, (h) men are angry, (i) sex and anger are the same thing; (2) displacement—something which belongs in one place is expressed in the dream or hallucination but in the wrong place or in connection with the wrong thing (e.g., a man who is angry at his wife dreams of her being killed by a hit-and-run driver despite the patient's best efforts to save her); and (3) plastic or visual representation—abstract ideas represented by things which can be seen (e.g., a dream of digging a trench a second time relating to "retrenching" one's finances).

Freud points out that further changes are made in remembering or in telling the dream (or hallucination) so that the manifest dream (or hallucination) will seem to make better sense. We called this secondary elaboration, since it did not have to do with the dream as originally experienced.

The subject of symbolism is usually misunderstood, as we have noted earlier. There are no universal symbols. Of course, one always uses the patient's associations, if they are obtainable. Obtained associations to classically understood symbols frequently are the usual symbolic meaning. When the patient cannot, or will not, give associations, then, as Freud pointed out, we can surmise that the associations would be disturbing. The number of things which are very disturbing to human beings is sufficiently limited that we can fall back on our clinical experience (i.e., symbolic interpretations) for a good clinical guess as to the probable meaning of the dream (or hallucination).

Certain experiences are universal because of the biologic nature of human beings. Specific contents, which are particularly apt for the expression of common conflicts, will be frequently used as symbols. There are other symbols which are commonly used, but only by people sharing a particular culture in which they make sense.

Because of the nature of the human genitals, the male genitals will frequently be symbolized by the number three (because of the three parts), elongated objects, piercing objects, weapons, guns, or snakes (which are roughly penis-shaped, capable of elongation, and frequently dangerous); the female genitalia will frequently be symbolized by caves, containers, boxes, jars, vases, etc. Children will be represented by small things, small animals, insects, or even worms. Parents may be symbolized by giants or politically powerful figures like generals, presidents, kings, and queens.

Because of the frequency of the number three as a symbol, the number four will often represent escape to a world without penises and without sexuality (in the words of a patient: "Perfection is turning three's into four's").

Running water may represent urine, and coming out of the water, birth. This is, in part, because of the frequency with which children, unfamiliar with the concept of semen, conceive of intercourse as the man urinating inside the woman.

Language styles and slang expressions may shape the symbols patients use. In a culture where "bird" is a slang expression for penis, it is a frequently used dream symbol; in a culture where "bird" is a slang expression for woman, it is rarely used as a penis symbol. (Although some patients who are impressed with the elongated neck of some birds may still use such symbolism.)

Even the snake symbol, which has been widely noted as a phallic symbol in many cultures, may have other meanings. It may symbolize a biting creature—whether one's own wish to bite, or the mother, or women in general. It may represent a combination of the devouring mother and the sexually threatening father, and, for at least one patient, it symbolized his wife, whom he thought of as "a snake in the grass."

How a terrifying hallucination might be a wish-fulfillment is well explained by the same principles that Freud used to explain the nightmare. (1) The wish-fulfillment refers to the latent content and not to the manifest content. (2) The dream (or the hallucination) is an attempted wish-fulfillment, but the attempt may fail. In the case of the nightmare, the anxiety may wake up the patient, and the wish-fulfillment may be the awareness "It's only a dream," a reassurance which unfortunately is only partially true. In those patients who are aware that they hallucinate, the awareness "It's only a hallucination," may similarly be reassuring. (3) The wish may be a wish for punishment. (4) A lesser fear may be substituted for a greater one. Finally, the general rule that the more unacceptable a wish is to the dreamer the more disguised will be its expression in the dream has this major exception: an unacceptable impulse may be expressed directly if it is accompanied by sufficient anxiety. The intense negative affect serves the purpose of disguise. If it is so unpleasant to the dreamer, it surely cannot be the dreamer's wish! These same mechanisms can readily be recognized in hallucinations.

A terrifying hallucination or a recurrent nightmare becomes a symptom in its own right, and proper interpretive work will relieve that symptom as the issues are dealt with consciously.

It is, of course, extremely important to help the patient see that the hallucinations are not real, that they do not represent real persons, but rather material from his unconscious. The patient at first will not accept such a view. When the patient accepts such a view, the therapist has already undercut some of the function of the hallucinations, and the patient is already moving with him toward health.

Patients may not tell the therapist about their hallucinations for some time. This is because they do not trust him. Indeed, the hallucinations may even say, "Do not tell him about this." In some cases, we have only become aware of the fact that the patient hallucinated because the patient referred to strange things we ourselves had supposedly said. For example, when I (Karon) asked one outpatient, "When did I say this to you?" He answered, "When I was in my bedroom."

In still other instances, we have had patients who actually hallucinated the therapist giving interpretation during the therapeutic hour. This may make therapy a somewhat chaotic process. It may take a long time before this comes to light. Unfortunately, hallucinatory interpretations are almost always 180 degrees opposed to anything the therapist would ever say; however, when patients do have such hallucinations, you can interpret the transference material and infer childhood experiences with a significant parental figure, most typically the mother, very easily.

In general, in dealing with hallucinations, we get across to the patient our general view of the power of psychotherapy, namely that the very difficulties and symptoms that the patient experiences are the lever we are going to teach the patient to use to help his or her growth. The problems become the means of solutions. Difficulties, rather than being dead ends or catastrophes, become the building blocks from which the patient can learn and grow. It is the difference between learning from your mistakes that everything is hopeless and that you are bad or worthless, and learning from your mistakes something about what causes you to make mistakes and what difficulties might arise again and why, and consequently what might be done to change them. Eventually, the patient realizes that this is not merely a view of therapy, but rather a general view of life, and one which, unfortunately, our culture rarely teaches.

What do you communicate to the patient about a hallucination? You communicate whatever part of your understanding of their hallucination you feel the patient can make use of. It would be nice to give you pedagogically simple principles, but unfortunately such principles do not have clinical validity. Some examples may help, however.

A psychotic woman, age 20, whose father's death had occurred 6 months previously, hallucinated seeing a priest and having a conversation with him, even though he was 500 miles away. It was easy to interpret that, "You must have wanted him to be here." She then revealed having hallucinations about her father for which the same interpretation was offered.

While this did not rid the patient of hallucinations, it opened up the issue of her longing for her father, her longing to be accepted by a father-figure, her loneliness, her fear of death, and the fact that she handled this by hallucinatory wish fulfillments, which could then be talked about.

Another patient, a paranoid schizophrenic in his mid-30s, said to me (Karon), "Bridey Murphy says she is going to kill you today."

I said to him, "Why do you want to kill me?"

He responded defensively, "I don't want to kill you, Bridey Murphy does. You can't hold me responsible for what she says."

Since he had been in therapy with me a while, I said to him, "Do I hold you responsible for what she says?"

"No."

"What do I hold you responsible for?"

"For believing her."

"That's right, you cannot help hearing voices. That is not under your control. But you can control whether you accept it as real, or whether you treat it as something to be understood, something caused by your unconscious which has a lot of very useful information. Hallucinations are even better than dreams, because they often lead to the conflicts much more directly."

He said, "But suppose it is real?"

"All right, I'll tell you what. If it's real—when did she say that she was going to kill me? Here's my schedule for today. Make sure you tell her, and if I'm dead, we can stop therapy. But if I'm not dead, we'll double the length of the therapy sessions."

"None of your goddamn bets."

"It doesn't sound as if you really believe her."

"Well, none of your goddamn bets anyway."

"What comes to mind when you think of Bridey Murphy?"

Bridey Murphy turned out to be a condensation of two people, himself and his mother, both of whom were very, very angry at me. After all, his paranoid delusions had preserved his life, or so he believed, and I was asking him to give them up. His mother was hostile to me because his paranoid delusions and sickness played a role in maintaining her own functioning, and she was being called upon to change her adjustment as he got better. Moreover, his awareness of his mother's hostility to me was related to his feelings of her hostility to his father and to his belief that she had caused his father's death (although it was not interpreted on this level at that time). What was interpreted to the patient by the therapist at that time was only his anger and his mother's anger.

The voice of God is an hallucination to be dealt with tactfully. Direct challenges that the voice really is not that of God can provoke violent attacks on the therapist. After all, God represents everything good. The therapist seems to be trying to take God away from the patient, and crusades have been fought for lesser injuries.

Listen to the material carefully. Sometimes one can say, without directly referring to the "Godly" experience, "I wonder if your mother used to say . . . [whatever it is that "God" said]."

Often a patient who would resent a direct challenge will immediately accept the statement as true, sometimes adding, "But how did you know?" even though the patient had just finished describing "God's" statement. After these parallels have been explored, it is sometimes possible to point out and get acceptance to the notion that people occasionally impute to God things their mother or father said to them when they were very young.

If the voice is challenged, it should only be because it has said something clearly destructive and you (the therapist) cannot believe that God is destructive.

DELUSIONS

What about delusions? Again one can only deal with what one hears. The first thing to do is to get the patient to describe the delusion to you, and you must try to look at the delusion through the eyes of the patient. What does it mean? What sense does it make? Why would anyone believe this to be true?

It is important that the therapist not conclude too quickly that a delusion is a delusion, just because it sounds weird or distant from his own experience. Take the attitude with the patient that you would take with yourself if you had a weird belief: "Why do I think this is so, what is the evidence?"

One female patient talked about the heroin dealers who were hiding in her basement and who would kill her if she revealed their presence. She had, in fact, rented out her basement to four men, who, it later turned out, were heroin dealers. If she had attempted to turn them in, they would undoubtedly have attempted to kill her. When a patient reports something that sounds frightening and unrealistic, this does not necessarily mean it is a delusion. The therapist always addresses what the evidence is, and what the data are.

After all, one is teaching the patient how to think, and it is permissible to gather evidence on anything. All thoughts are, after all, capable of being thought in the world that all real therapists live in, just as all feelings are capable of being felt. If it seems likely that some thought is delusional, review the evidence and consider with the patient other possible ways to understand the situation. Sometimes the patient will accept the idea that there might be other explanations and is willing to continue gathering information.

Sometimes the patient will even say, "I know this is not true, but I believe it." Then they are in good shape, because you can explore the patient's associations as if the delusional belief were a dream and discover together why they might have come to this belief, even when not true.

But in some cases, the patient is adamant. Then you have to accept the delusion tentatively or at least go along with it, continue to gather information, and encourage the patient to continue gathering relevant information. The more the patient deals with the delusion as if it were a realistic belief and reviews relevant information, the more likely the discrepancies are to come to the surface. Instead of being able to ignore discrepancies by focusing only on the conflict with the disbeliever, the patient who reviews his beliefs with an interested listener becomes more and more concerned with the inevitable discrepancies between his beliefs and the evidence. As these discrepancies become enough of a problem, the patient eventually will be interested in analyzing what is going on, that is, discovering the origin and purpose of his delusions in a way that makes consistent sense.

If the patient asks whether his delusion is true, you may say directly "No, it's not true," if you think he can hear you. More often you may say, "There is no way that I could possibly know whether this is true or not" (which in most cases is a fact), "but tell me moﬁe about it."

If the patient makes a claim which can be put to an immediate test, try to do so. For example, if he says that he is about to be killed in 10 minutes, you can flatly say, "This is not true, and let us test it out right now."

If he says, "I am God," you can say that you really do not believe that because, if he were God, he could do—[something, which you name]. You choose a test that the patient could readily carry out, and which he will accept as in God's power. For example, you can say, "If you were God, you could walk on air."

One patient said, taken aback, "Where did you get that idea."

"Well, God is infinity, and anyone who's infinity can walk on air."

"Who says so?"

"Well you've read the mystics, all the mystic theorists say so." (The patient prided himself on his knowledge as compared to psychologists and psychiatrists.)

"Which one?

"Nicholas Flamel and Guillaume de Paris. You've read them, haven't you?"

"Of course."

Strangely enough, some patients, like this one, will seriously attempt to walk on air, and, of course, fail. You continue with the patient in the notion that you will always be in favor of gathering evidence.

Sometimes the patient has a delusional belief which is not really delusional at all; rather, it is a problem of language or lack of shared knowledge. For example, the psychiatric residents at a medical school presented a patient for consultation who supposedly had no insight; he had been hospitalized a number of times and treated with medication. The resident "treating" him was wondering whether or not he was treatable. The patient heard voices and supposedly had a somatic delusion. The somatic delusion was, "There is something wrong with my head and I need an operation." He readily revealed this when asked what seemed to be the trouble. When I said, "Of course, there's something wrong with your head, if you hear voices. The only operation you need is to talk to someone about your problems and what makes the voices appear. Are you interested?"

The patient who supposedly was uncooperative, relaxed, smiled, and said, "Yes, that sounds like a good idea." An uneducated man has no way of knowing that hallucinations can be caused by emotional problems, and he is accurate in perceiving that his head, i.e., brain, is not functioning the way other people's do, because they do not hear voices.

DELUSIONAL AFFECT

In deciphering hallucinations and delusions, it is helpful to remember that feelings are always justified. The hallucination, delusion, or in some cases, irrational behavior, expresses an appropriate feeling in an inappropriate way. Sometimes, the feelings are clearly and correctly expressed, but about inappropriate objects (e.g., the telephone company computer). Sometimes the situation is straight from the patient's current life, but "who is feeling what" is reversed, or the feeling is exaggerated so as to seem irrational. By presenting the feeling in an inappropriate manner, the patient is attempting to get external confirmation that the feeling itself is inappropriate, or even get punishment for having the feeling. The patient will not only seduce himself, he will seduce many therapists into telling him how irrational his feelings are. The important thing is to get around that, not to be made the primitive, punishing superego that the patient works so hard at getting you to be.

Affect is central to any real psychotherapy, particularly psychoanalytic psychotherapy. Freud thought this was so axiomatic that he did not always make it explicit. When asked about it, he said, "What else could psychoanalysis be about, except feelings?"

In some psychoanalytic circles, however, abstractions have intervened, and the feelings of the patient are not always given the appropriate attention. This is, of course, characteristic of our culture, which to a large extent tries to deal with emotions as being irrational. Indeed, some psychology textbooks have taken the position that emotions are irrational, or even defined them as "disordered behavior."

This set the stage for Carl Rogers (1942, 1961) to rediscover that emotions are important for psychotherapists to consider, because they are important for human beings to consider. The most adequate psychologic theory of emotions has been developed by Tomkins (1962, 1963). It is quite clear that, far from being irrational, emotions are a central part of the adaptive mechanisms of human beings. Thought without emotion is not adaptive.

Emotions tell us something important about what is going on. If we are angry, it is because we have been hurt. If we are frightened, it is because there is something to be afraid of. If we are happy, it is because something good is taking place. If we are sad, it is because something bad is taking place, and so on. In therapy, we encourage patients to pay attention to their feelings. When they do, they suddenly realize that all sorts of things that are important are happening, but they have been taught to ignore them.

The handling of affect is, of course, specific to the patient's life and family. People internalize what they have been taught to internalize, as described earlier. If they were taught not to feel, they try not to feel. If they were taught to ignore their feelings, they do not pay attention to feelings, or they may isolate. Punishment for crying early in life may lead to guilt or anxiety about crying as well as guilt for having or showing any strong affect. Whatever way they handle their feelings was originally an adaptive response to being a child in a particular family, because our feelings are never always what our parents would like our feelings to be. Frequently, patients have been taught either to ignore their feelings, or to believe the feelings are irrational, or different from what they actually are.

The therapist knows better. We teach the patient that there is no such thing as an irrational affect. If they are angry, they have been hurt. If they are frightened, there is something to be frightened of. If what they are angry or frightened about is not in consciousness, it is unconscious, but it is nonetheless real. If it is not in the present, it is in the past, and something in the present is symbolic of it.

Much of the instigation for affect will turn out to be realistic in the present, however. Even "normal" people have apparently irrational affect which, upon investigation, turns out to be realistic. You may feel anxious "for no reason" while driving, only to discover that half the cars that pass you are off the road in the next 2 miles; that is, the feeling of anxiety may be in response to a preconscious awareness that the car is not handling the way it should and road conditions are not quite as good as they seem to be. Such discoveries are not infrequent in normal people, but the more you have been taught not to pay appropriate attention to your feelings, the more you are cut off from what is happening around you.

Probably the most problematic affect of all for schizophrenic individuals, and hence for therapists of schizophrenic patients is anger, or to put it as it is felt (and defended against) murderous rage. Our patients, because their lives have been worse than the lives of most people, have more rage than most people and are more terrified of dealing with it; however, if you are aware of your anger, you can control it. If you repress it, it will control you. This is only a slight paraphrase of Freud's general statement about the unconscious. Consciousness is an enourmously important asset of a human being. Yet it is frequently overlooked by psychotherapists when dealing with rage because rage frightens them as well as other people. The therapist is afraid of the patient's losing control.

If the therapist makes clear the distinction between feeling (or thought) and action, he or she can teach the patient that feeling the rage, no matter how murderous, and talking about it, makes it easier not to act dangerously. "You can control your own actions, if you don't try to control your thoughts." This allows the patient to gain control of his own actions. With patients of a lower socioeconomic class, it is important to say, "It is all right to *feel* angry," rather than saying "It is all right to *get* angry," since "getting angry" means behaving angrily (e.g., hitting someone).

To return to the first principle, feelings are always justified. When a patient doubts the appropriateness of a feeling, the therapist can say: The feelings are justified. The situation, of course, may not be the one that you are concerned with, but the feelings are accurate. The question is, what was the situation in which you really initially felt this way, when those feelings were appropriate?

If you know something of the patient's life, or if you have a cooperative patient, or both, you may readily find the answer as soon as you begin to ask that kind of question. Of course, you will both look for the historical antecedent, as well as the current event which resonates with the earlier experiences and the feelings they produced.

OTHER DRAMATIC SYMPTOMS

The patient in a catatonic stupor, as we have mentioned earlier, hears and sees everything that goes on around him. Therefore, to begin therapy with such a patient, it is only necessary to talk persistently in as meaningful a way as possible. Since we know that the patient is terrified, we should reassure him that we will not let anyone kill him. We then talk about his problems to the best of our knowledge. When we feel tired, we stop the session for that day, and tell him we will continue tommorrow (or whenever the next session is scheduled). Sessions should last at least 30 minutes. It is a rare catatonic patient who can stand being talked to for many such sessions without beginning to talk in return.

The patient who is mute, though not catatonic, should also be treated by being talked to. If necessary, the therapist talks continuously for the whole session and does so for as many therapeutic sessions as are necessary. This may sould like an arduous task, but if the therapist uses theory (that is, what we know of human beings in general and schizophrenic patients in particular), only a scrap of data about this specific person is needed for the therapist to be able to talk at length about possible problems.

One mute patient was being talked to session after session. I (Karon) said, "We will talk as long as it is necessary. I once had a patient who did not talk for 6 months, and I had to do all the talking." The patient blurted out, "My God, why would you do that!" The thought of listening to his therapist for 6 continuous months of therapy was more than he could bear.

The patient who talks in a weird, strange manner should be listened to carefully. Sometimes we can figure out what he is talking about, sometimes we cannot. When such patients seem to be trying to communicate, the therapist should try to listen. Patients frequently talk gobbledygook, in the midst of which they sneak in a realistic statement about themselves or their lives. The therapist is supposed to miss this. Picking up such statements and treating them seriously moves the therapy appreciably. For example, a patient continuously talked in neologisms. Even when he used ordinary words he used them with different meanings. In the middle of talking strangely about mystic experiences, he said, "My mother never loved me. She did not like taking care of a child."

Then he went on with his mystic neologisms. He was surprised that the therapist picked up his straightforward statement of his problem, because this had not been his experience in earlier attempts at therapy. He had always succeeded in throwing therapists off the trail by being irritatingly confusing and boring. Like all symptoms, this permitted him to express both sides of the conflict: he could express his resentment at his mother openly, and at the same time demonstrate that she wasn't bad, because it was all "crazy talk."

When patients make strange gestures, the therapist should pay attention to them. Gestures are meaningful as well as words, and the therapist should try to understand the meaning. General psychoanalytic understanding or previous experience with schizophrenic patients may suggest possible meanings; for example, since male patients who make a long, narrow opening between their thumb and forefinger or who burn themselves with cigarettes have taught us that these are attempts to create symbolic vaginas on their own bodies and magically to become women, who get fed through the vagina (symbolic mouth), it is easy to guess what the meaning of such behavior might be with the next patient. In other cases, the gesture may not be meaningful to the therapist, but he can ask the patient and the associative material may make it clear. Thus, the patient who bowed from the waist revealed when asked that it represented his balancing between fear and loneliness. Such meanings may be unconscious, or may be conscious to the patient, but not communicated to the therapist. In either case, it is useful to bring the meaning into conscious consideration in the therapy. The symbols that neurotic patients use in their dreams and to some extent in their symptoms, psychotic patients use not only in their hallucinations, but in their verbalizations and in their motoric gestures.

The Threatening Patient

Some schizophrenic patients have a past history of irrational violence. With such patients it is very useful to structure their handling of aggression early in the therapy. "Sooner or later you will feel angry at me and feel like hitting me. It is very important that you tell me about it. You will learn a lot from it, but do not hit me. Here we talk, not fight." Such comments frequently relieve patients who are potentially violent. They are often frightened of what they do to other people and see their choice as simply containment or explosion. Knowing there is a third option, talking, is a relief to them. Of course, this comment should be repeated whenever appropriate (e.g., when the therapist is scared).

The patient who directly threatens the therapist is frightening. The aim of the therapist should be to find out what it is that is sending the patient into a panic, to prevent the patient from hurting the therapist, and, it is hoped, to prevent the patient from being hurt or hurting himself. The therapist should try to make the patient feel that this is not a crisis in which the patient has to prove that he is a man by assaulting the therapist or someone else. The therapist should be careful not to injure the narcissism of the patient by making sarcastic, insulting, or denigrating remarks which the patient will feel the need to avenge.

When confronted with a threatening patient, even one with a gun or knife, many therapists find that the knowledge that the patient is almost always more frightened than they are and is making threats as a way of putting distance between himself and others is often useful. Saying to the patient, "I know you're frightened. I won't hurt you, and I won't let anyone else hurt you," may allow the patient to retreat from his stance of threat. Such patients will often then respond to a straightforward request, "Please put the gun down."

This information is particularly useful to police officers. They frequently confront a person who is frightened and is afraid that the police are going to punish him because they have had angry thoughts, have thought about doing something violent, or have made verbal threats as a way of attempting to keep people away. Police officers should protect other people. It is often useful for them to know that the threatening person feels threatened. Offering that person protection and telling him that the police are not going to beat him up will aid the police in disarming him and avoiding a violent encounter.

The patient who brings a dangerous weapon to the therapy hour should be discouraged. For example, a female patient brought a knife to an outpatient hour and said, holding out a check for her past bill, "Why don't you get your pay?"

The therapist said, "I don't need money that much."

"What's the matter—are you scared?"

"I do not enjoy fighting with people. You must put that knife down if you want to work with me. If you want a therapist who will fight with you, I will be glad to recommend you to someone else."

The patient stabbed the treatment chair, then sat down in the chair and apologized profusely for ruining the furniture. The therapist said, as any reasonable person would, "Better the chair than me." This was a value system that the patient could not understand, since it was exactly the opposite of her parents' values, namely, the furniture was very valuable, but her life and the life of one of the parents were not considered valuable. Intrafamilial violence was frequent in her childhood. She accused the therapist of cruelty because he would send her away rather than permit violence.

In the next session, she held the knife in her lap while she talked. The therapist said, "You know, you will have to stop bringing that knife to the therapy hour, because all I do is think about the knife, and I don't hear a word that you're saying." The patient got angry, and said that was unreasonable.

"If you wish to bring a knife to your therapy hour, you'll have to get another therapist, and I will be glad to make some referrals." The patient found this very unreasonable, and the discussion of this continued for the rest of that hour. At the end of his work day, when the therapist left his office, he discovered the knife on the front seat of his car. The patient obviously had made a choice. Two weeks later, however, the patient requested the return of her knife and became irate that the therapist refused. She said, "It's my property. Give it back to me." The therapist appropriately interpreted to her what returning that knife would mean, namely, condoning the use of violence, which he certainly did not.

The threat of violence never recurred; however, the incident allowed the therapist to discuss her parental topsy-turvy set of values and how different they were, not only from the therapist's values, but those of most people in our society. The patient found this hard to believe, but it related to many of her central feelings that the whole world was very dangerous and that strangers would or might kill her over trivia, such as being told that they had over-charged her a nickel.

When the therapist realizes that direct or implied threats are im-mobilizing him clinically, he must raise the issue. An illustration of this involved a patient who was a plainclothes police officer. For the first several sessions, he came to his appointments with a sports coat on. The therapist was unaware of the fact that he was wearing a shoulder holster and pistol. As the patient began to feel anxious because of the material that was being dealt with, he began to display the pistol on some occasions by not wearing a sports coat and wearing a belt holster. The implication was clear. The therapist, however, still felt comfortable as he frequently worked with police officers and was used to being unarmed in the presence of armed officers. After a few more weeks, however, the patient began to come in with the flap over the revolver open, so that the pistol was easily accessible. At this point, the implied threat was clear and the therapist uncomfortable, so he indicated that the patient would need to come to the appointment without his revolver because it was distracting to him. The patient protested that he was required by law to carry his revolver at all times. The therapist suggested that he leave the revolver with the receptionist, as there was no other way out of the therapist's office. Even if he was called on in an emergency, he could easily retrieve his revolver. He did not like this option but accepted it; after three sessions of discussion he acknowledged the anger and anxiety that he was feeling in therapy and agreed to lock the revolver in the trunk of his car before coming to his appointments.

It is sometimes the case that a particularly violent person has been overpowered by the police and brought to the emergency room still thrashing and screaming. The temptation is to give him a sedative and talk to him when he has been "calmed down." If the therapist can tolerate the ranting and screaming and is willing to address the fears and rage involved in what the patient is saying, he can frequently hear very clearly at that time what the central concerns of the patient are. A real therapeutic relationship can begin. It is to be recommended that one try to engage the patient in such a dialogue without medication, even if the patient is so overwhelmed and overwhelming that no one dares to let him out of restraints. It is, of course, permissible to do therapy with the patient in restraints. That is better than constantly worrying about one's own physical well-being.

Better than restraints is a therapist and assistant or several therapists holding a potentially violent patient, one on each arm. Such a procedure is risky unless the other person is someone in whom you have a great deal of confidence, however. If two adult males who have confidence in each other each hold an arm of the patient while one tries to talk to him, this is sufficient to control almost any patient, no matter how strong. The fact that the control is exerted directly and not through artificial means helps the patient make meaningful emotional contact with the therapist. It clarifies the notion that the very disturbed patient's murderous rage, which he is as much afraid of as you are, is not really going to be allowed to be dangerous to anyone, or to prevent the continuance of the therapy. Engaging the patient in a therapeutic dialogue which makes physical encounters unnecessary is preferred to all forms of physical restraint.

There are therapists who are comfortable countering the physically intimidating patient by the technique of being even more physically intimidating themselves. This often has useful consequences, because the patient now feels that there is someone he can depend on who is stronger than he is and that he cannot use a defense which ordinarily immobilizes the treatment. Most therapists, however, will not be comfortable with such approaches.

If it looks as though a physical confrontation might be necessary, it is useful to have two or more people available so that the patient does not see it as a test of mettle. Second, physical violence in general should be used as the method of last resort rather than the first.

ACUTE SCHIZOPHRENIC REACTIONS

The term *acute schizophrenic reaction* refers to those cases in which blatant psychotic symptoms—lack of contact with reality, hallucinations, and so forth—have appeared only a short time before the patient was seen by the therapist. This type of patient is differentiated from the chronic schizophrenic patient whose symptoms have endured a long time in blatant form. We shall attempt to describe therapeutic devices aimed specifically at rapidly resolving the acute symptoms, that is, ending hallucinations, and restoring sufficient contact with reality so that the person can live and carry on his day-to-day activities effectively without losing control, and continue to make progress with further psychotherapy while living as a human being in the outside world.

The therapist's first step in rapidly resolving the psychotic symptoms of an acute schizophrenic reaction is to establish emotional contact with the patient. In some cases in which the patient is desperate and seeks help, this can be accomplished, as we have said, by nothing more than asking the patient what his problems are. On the other hand, establishing contact may be extremely difficult as, for example, with a mute patient, or an evasive patient who talks but not about his problems or pathologic condition. In such cases, the therapist is thrown back upon his ingenuity and knowledge somehow to establish emotional contact, and quickly. Just being with a patient for a period of time during which it is obvious that you are trying to reach him, will eventually lead to such an emotional contact; thus, no effort to make a meaningful contact with a patient is entirely wasted. But if rapid therapeutic improvement is needed, for example, to prevent hospitalization, it is important to make this contact as rapidly as possible.

One way to establish such contact is for the therapist to tell the patient about something that consciously bothers the patient, but which he has never told the therapist. For example, with one evasive patient, who was willing to talk but not about any of his problems, it was possible to establish emotional contact by asking him how he felt after he had had intercourse with a girl.

"Good."

"Really?"

"Yeah."

"That's funny. Didn't you feel empty, kind of hollowed out and drained?" The patient looked startled. So the therapist added: "Don't you know why that is?" At this point the patient was ready to talk about something that bothered him, and to listen and respond meaningfully.

Another technique is to give the patient a so-called "direct" interpretation of the unconscious meaning of some aspect of his pathologic condition. If the interpretation is correct, this will temporarily undo the disguise function of the symbolic expressions which have been interpreted; this particular symbolic resolution of his problems becomes ineffectual and in his desperation he may be ready to turn to the therapist for help.

We must be willing to be mistaken, but we can use what we know to attempt to disrupt a stalemate. Inasmuch as the psychotic patient will settle for a standstill, it is up to the therapist to find a way to keep the therapy progressing. Sometimes direct questions about possible problems are the best approach. One technique useful with patients who are capable of and willing to talk to the therapist in a more or less continuing fashion is to ask for the patient's earliest childhood memory and allow the patient to continue his recollections from there. Frequently, this leads directly to the patient's central problems.

Free association, if the patient is capable of it, not only helps to uncover repressed material, but it also serves to give the patient practice in letting his thoughts wander freely, while the presence and interventions of the therapist reassure him that the situation will not get out of control. The usual objection that borderline or psychotic patients must not free associate because they will uncover material they cannot handle does not hold if the patient has a strong relationship with the therapist.

If the therapist (and other staff members) can tolerate the acute patient who screams wildly without immediate medication, the patient will be heard to scream his major concerns very clearly. By responding appropriately, the therapist can give the patient the feeling that he is being understood, that he is in a safe and helpful place, and that a therapeutic relationship is beginning. Frequently, this suffices to restore self-controlled behavior.

Aside from the importance of rapidly establishing and maintaining the emotional contact, the principles of treatment for acute reactions are the same as those we have discussed in general. Particularly important are making the distinction between thoughts and actions, and the acceptability of all feelings, but particularly anger.

Two illustrative acute cases may be helpful. The psychotic reformatory inmate will be recalled. This patient had nightmares and hallucinations of his stepmother beating him. He wanted to know whether he should escape and kill her. "I get these nightmares. I keep getting the same dream over and over every night, my stepmother beating me with a stick. I wake up and it keeps on going. I still get the nightmare. She keeps on beating me after I wake up. What I want to know is, if I run away from here and kill her, will the dream stop?"

Rapid improvement came about when he was asked, "Who told you it was wrong to kill her?" He was nonplussed. Unconsciously, he wanted to be punished. He wanted to be told he must not kill his stepmother, that he was evil, and that she was, consequently, good.

"No one," he finally stammered.

"Somebody must have told you it was wrong. Who says it's wrong to want to kill a bitch like that. The old bitch deserves to die, for what she did to you." At this point, the patient began to tell me about his childhood and that his stepmother had, in fact, been cruel to him. After I had insisted that it was right to want to kill her, I could then go on to differentiate thoughts from actions.

"The only reason for not killing her is that you'll get caught. If you're willing to die in order to kill her, she must be more important than you are. That sounds stupid to me. (But note—I did not say 'bad'.) It would be stupid to do it, but you certainly should *want* to kill a bitch like that."

I explained to him then and later that it was natural and healthy to hate. "Any time anyone hurts you, you hate them, you want to kill them. And that's healthy." It is our experience that genuinely homicidal patients do not consciously hate. The crucial step was to decrease the patient's feelings of guilt about his own hostility.

On the fourth day of psychotherapy, he reported that the nightmares had ceased, both while he was awake and while he was asleep. The patient continued to make progress in once-a-week psychotherapy until he was released with the strong recommendation that he continue psychotherapy on the outside.

A 19-year-old was arrested, and, while in the local jail awaiting transfer, attempted suicide. He had been arrested 5 times previously. It later came to light that he was hallucinating, was overtly homosexual, was an alcoholic, and was "experimenting" with codeine.

In the first session, he told me (Karon) that he had thought the psychologist might be able to help him, but that he had changed his mind.

"There's nothing you can do for me. I'm praying to God about 15 times a day and I don't think I need your help. So there's no point in talking to you."

"As long as you're here, you might just as well talk to me anyway. It can't do any harm."

"What am I in for?"

"Don't you know?"

"No."

I checked his record and found that he had broken parole by failing to report and by changing his address without notifying his parole office. When I informed him of this, he denied it.

"That's a lie. I didn't move. I was just walking. For 5 days I just kept walking. I didn't sleep. I didn't stop or stay anywhere. I was just walking."

When I accepted his statement, he went on to tell me a little about his life. He had been in jail on a number of previous occasions. He told me about his previous crimes, mainly thievery. He said he was an alcoholic and had tried Alcoholics Anonymous on his last reformatory sentence, but it had not helped. He did not know why he had tried to commit suicide, but "it had," he said, "just seemed right." We talked a little longer. I mentioned that it was all right for him to have any kind of thoughts, to think anything. After we had discussed this awhile, I suggested he come back to my office the next day.

On the second day, he told me a little more about himself. He said that he had never felt safe without a gun in his pocket since he was 10 years old, and that he had a gun in his pocket when he was walking the streets before he was arrested this time. He was waiting for the "voices" to tell him when to start shooting. He did not know when it would be, but he thought it would likely occur in a bus station. Anyway, the "voices" would know and tell him.

He told me about his girl. He met her while he was on parole. She had first been "going out" with another parolee, a friend of his. The friend had "slapped her around," and the patient had intervened. Then he began to "go out" with her. She induced him to "get a bunch of my friends together, all of us parolees, and beat up the other guy. Now he's got his friends and the word is out to get me."

The patient was afraid to set foot in the city in which his erstwhile friend lived. "They'll kill me. I know those guys and they don't play games."

Meanwhile, he was having sexual relations with the girl regularly, but he heard that she was seeing the first boy again. When he heard this, he decided that, "All my troubles were her fault. I could have gone back to jail, and all my friends too, if they [the police] found out about the fight. All on account of her. So I decided to kill her."

"I went to a drugstore to get some poison, but they wouldn't sell it to me. So I got an icepick and I put it in my pocket and I was going to go to her house and ring the doorbell. And when she answered it, put it right here." He pointed to his Adam's apple.

"When I got to her house, I rang the doorbell. She opened the door and instead of killing her, I was disgusting."

"What do you mean?"

"I was disgusting. I just did that same dirty old thing."

"What do you mean?"

"You know. I went to bed with her. If I was a man, I would have killed her. I was disgusting."

He was told that he was not disgusting, that it was a good thing he had not killed her since, if he had, there would have been no chance for anyone to help him. "But I don't think it was her you really wanted to kill. Wasn't there somebody else you wanted to kill?"

"Who do you mean?"

"Well, it was probably somebody female," I suggested.

"Maybe it was the other girl."

"What other girl?"

"The last time. The first girl I ever got into bed with. I took her out all the time, and we were going to be married and then I got arrested. And when I got out of jail, she was married to someone else. I asked one of her friends if she loved him and she said she'd learn to love him. That seems funny to me."

"And maybe you were angry at her for leaving you for another man, and when your new girl did the same thing, it was like living it over."

He agreed and said that it might have been the first girl whom he wanted to kill. He was then asked to go back even further.

"But I think that's still not the whole story. I think there's somebody earlier. Somebody who also left you for another man. And it was easier to kill your girl than to face the idea that you want to kill her."

"That's all there was. There ain't any girl before the first one. Just two of them, that's all."

"But the girl you really want to kill is your mother. Didn't you ever feel that she left you?"

"When the old man came back."

"Came back?"

"He used to take off and just leave her and the kids. He'd take up with some woman or just go off and leave her. And when he was gone, she'd tell me I was the man in the house."

"And you'd feel like you were married to her."

"Yeah. And then he'd come back. And she'd always take him back."

"And you were a kid again."

"Yeah. I was nothing when he was around."

"Then you must have wanted to kill her for that. That's reasonable enough. When first one girl and then the other left you, it was like your mother all over again. And it was your mother you wanted to kill."

We went on to discuss the idea that it was all right for him to want to kill somebody, how you always want to kill someone, when they hurt you.

It was in the third session that he told me about the dream. "What do you do to get rid of a nightmare?" he asked.

"You tell it to me so that we can analyze it."

"Well, I get this dream about once a week, since I was eight. I trip and fall, and then it's like nothing human. I fall and I don't feel nothing and it's dark and I get smaller and smaller until there's nothing."

His associations to "trip" and to "fall" were the same: falling in the gutter like a drunk, taking codeine, falling down, doing something bad sexually, getting into trouble with the law, being a homosexual. To "It's like nothing human" and "I don't feel nothing," he associated insanity and death. To getting "smaller," he had no associations.

The dream was interpreted as follows (guessing at the symbolism of getting "smaller"). It was pointed out that his associations to tripping and falling were, in fact, all the ways he got into trouble—by getting drunk, taking codeine, getting into trouble with the law, doing something bad sexually, being a homosexual— all of these were his problems. Each of them was a way of "falling down." Similarly, he had tried to commit suicide and he was going insane, but the dream is a wish and therefore he wanted to "fall down." Each of these ways of falling down, I continued, had a purpose—getting smaller represented a wish to become a child again so he could get the love he wanted but never got from his mother. All of these ways of falling down were ways of proving to himself that he was bad, that this mother was right in not loving him, and, therefore, if he were good, she would have loved him and still might.

"But you can't ever stop falling down, or you'll find out she doesn't love you at all, no matter what you do. When you were an infant, you might die if she didn't love you, and therefore you will do anything rather than face that fact."

Not only did the nightmare never recur, but a marked change in pathology occurred at that point. The next day's session began as follows:

"Doc, this is crazy. Here I am in jail. I don't know how long I'm in for, at least a year. I am in with a crew of gorillas. [He had been assigned to the cottage reserved for the toughest inmates.] Yet I feel freer than I ever felt in my whole life. I'm happier and freer than I've ever been. It's crazy."

He was continued in psychotherapy on a once-a-week basis after the first week. After the first interval of a week, he told me:

"You know, it's funny, it's like all my life I've been in terror, there was a door closed and it was bulging at the seams and I was afraid it would break open. Now the door is wide open. Occasionally something comes out that scares the hell out of me but I can deal with it. And I'm free. It was worth going to jail for this."

Eventually, he was released, found a job, and was looking for a therapist with whom to continue further psychotherapy when last heard from.

SEXUAL CONFLICTS IN SCHIZOPHRENIC INDIVIDUALS

The therapist must continually aim at decreasing the patient's feelings of anxiety, guilt, sin, and worthlessness. He should emphasize to the patient that only when someone has actually been hurt is there any reason for feeling guilty. Closely related to this is the handling of sexual problems.

The therapist should tell the patient directly, when the subject of masturbation is discussed, that it is not harmful. The therapist should unequivocally indicate that it is neither harmful nor morally wrong. Masturbation is simply something people do if they do not have anything better to do. No one has ever been hurt psychologically or physically by masturbation. Even today, female patients often believe they have injured themselves by masturbating or that menstrual bleeding is caused by such masturbation injuries. The patient should be told that nearly everyone has masturbated, including those who say it is evil, and that the therapist heartily approves of the patient masturbating. The patient has a right to enjoy himself. Reassurance and the verbal lifting of moral bans, to be effective, must not be lukewarm or ambiguous (Ellis 1959).

It is amazing how much subjective relief is often experienced by patients as a result of surface reassurance. For many patients, it may not be necessary to go deeper into the unconscious significance of masturbation. Where the surface reassurance brings no relief, one should go deeper. We have found that, in such cases, the unconscious significance of masturbation is not incest but treason —that is, there is the fantasy that their body, genitals, and/or (in the case of the male) their sexual products rightfully belong to the overwhelming demanding mother, and the wicked patient is using them for his or her own pleasure. The therapist can bring this fantasy to light, and then tell the patient that his penis, her vagina, or their body really belongs to them, and to nobody else, and only they have a right to them.

The patient's fear and guilt about heterosexual relations should be similarly handled by means of surface reassurance, information, and the uncovering of unconscious fantasies. While some patients seem to find surface reassurance sufficient to allay their fears and guilt over masturbation, however, heterosexual problems seem always to require an examination of the related unconscious fantasies. The therapist should point out in no uncertain terms that sexual intercourse is fun and that it is part of the pleasure of being alive. This is the only reason for having intercourse. The patient should be told emphatically that if he or she enjoys it he or she should engage in intercourse; if they will not enjoy it, they need not engage in it. It is a matter of concern only to the two people involved.

Of course, it is unjustified to hurt an innocent person. Therefore, the patient should take precautions against having children unless the couple want them, and, of course, rape is no more justified than beating someone for any other purpose.

It is useful to have such patients describe their ideas of the nature of intercourse and of reproduction. Their misconceptions can be pointed out and these distorted notions taken as a springboard for exploring their unconscious sexual fantasies. The unconscious fantasies that are most pertinent are the incestuous desire for the mother or father, the *quid pro quo* fantasy (Silverberg 1952), oral feeding fantasies (either directly or with the penis representing a breast, and the vagina or anus representing a mouth), and the draining fantasy.

The fear of being castrated or killed by the opposite-sexed parent (the Oedipus complex) is frequently present as a problem, but also as a solution to the more central earlier problems. For male patients as well as female patients, the fear of the more important parent, the mother, tends to be defended against by displacement to the less important (for survival of the infant) parent, the father. Female patients also may be concerned with the fear of being ripped open by the fantasied huge penis.

While the therapist should deal with whatever the patient presents, he should remember that problems of survival are the critical ones for schizophrenic individuals, and those are the issues to focus on when the material is capable of alternative interpretations.

Homosexual urges and the defenses against homosexual urges appear to be universal in schizophrenic patients. The therapist should make the patient aware of his or her homosexual urges, that is, urges to be of the opposite sex, not to be of their own sex, to have intercourse with members of their own sex, or not to have intercourse with members of the opposite sex. The failure to analyze these urges is one of the surest ways to disrupt the therapy. The three most usual mistakes in handling these problems are: (1) failing to make the patient aware of his homosexual urges; (2) making the patient aware of these urges but stopping there as if these urges were rock bottom; or (3) to derive them from the classic Oedipus situation, that is, the fear of incest with the mother and castration by the father, or the fear of incest with the father and retaliation by the mother.

If the homosexual urges are not brought into consciousness, those symptoms that serve as a defense against this awareness cannot be resolved. Further, any interference with these symptoms may lead to a homosexual panic. If the homosexual urges are brought into awareness but not investigated further, the patient will go into a homosexual panic at that point and regress clinically. As for the classic Oedipal interpretations, these do not seem to be the source of the homosexual urges in schizophrenia, and consequently such interpretations do not seem to help the patient with these problems, although they may be relevant later in therapy when the patient is psychosexually more mature.

It is useful to tell the patient that he or she is not really a homosexual but that they are afraid they might be. The therapist should explore the unconscious fantasies which underlie these urges: the need for love, the search for a relationship with an emotionally estranged same-sexed parent, the search for a new mother, the penis-breast equation, the wish to meet the parents' needs, the need to change something unchangeable, the wish to be one's own mother, and the draining fantasy.

One puzzling question is what determines the development of a homosexual acting-out pattern, as in the homosexual neurotic patient, as opposed to the development of paranoid defenses against homosexual urges. The answer seems to lie in the degree of terrorization. The homosexual neurotic patient expresses, among other things, aggression toward the mother figure in the homosexual activity. The paranoid schizophrenic individual is so terrified of the overwhelming, destructive mother figure that he or she cannot regularly commit such a gross act of treason as to give his or her body or sexual products to a homosexual partner instead of to her. (Similar "treason" fantasies may also be aroused by hetero-sexual activity.)

Of course, homosexual activity, as Fromm-Reichmann (1950) pointed out long ago, is a move toward health, as compared to schizophrenic withdrawal. Homosexual relations should be judged by the same criteria of health or sickness as other human relation-ships, namely by consequences for the patient and others. Whether a patient remains homosexual or not is too important a decision for the therapist to make. The attitude must be of helping the patient understand as much as possible, but not requiring any particular sexual orientation. Otherwise, one cannot help the patient who wants to remain homosexual, or the patient who wants to be heterosexual, but is afraid he or she cannot be.

Patients who have not yet had homosexual relations but who consider the idea should be discouraged on the basis that they will feel guilty about doing so, but factual reassurances about the frequent occurrence in childhood or adolescence of homosexual activities in heterosexual individuals is important so as to permit the guilt-laden patient to discuss such activity. Also, it is useful to let the patient know that if he or she were a "real" homosexual, it would be no tragedy: a homosexual way of life is common and livable in our present society, although there are still some disad-vantages. Unfortunately, paranoidal patients are rarely willing even to consider this reassurance.

Treatment Decisions

There are several practical decisions that confront therapists: whether or not to hospitalize, when to discharge, whether or not to use adjunctive medication, the number of sessions to schedule per week, and the use of the telephone.

The decision to hospitalize is based on whether the patient needs it, wants it, and whether there is an alternative feasible living arrangement. In considering hospitalization, one must be concerned with the question of under what circumstances this patient can be discharged. Hospitalization frequently means permission to regress. If patients are already regressing to the point at which their ordinary environment cannot tolerate them or adequately protect them, providing a safe environment in which to regress is helpful. If the hospital is realistically a better environment than the one with which the patients will have to cope on discharge, however, hospitalization may be a serious mistake, and more active efforts than usual to keep them in their usual environment should be considered.

The general principle is that patients' problems are best worked out when they are living as nearly normally as they are capable of doing, and are attempting to cope, no matter how ineffectively, with the problems they need to solve. Whether on a neurotic or psychotic level, giving up the attempt to function in a "normal" setting is generally countertherapeutic. For example, it is generally bad advice to tell students to drop out of school or leave school until their problems are solved, if they can function, however marginally, in the school setting. Similarly, a patient ought not to be encouraged to quit his or her job, or stop caring for the children or household, or ask for a "less demanding" (lower ranked) job, if it seems possible to maintain functioning.

The therapist must permit and help the patient with regression, but must not require or idealize it. Often hospitalization is experienced as a demand from the therapist or parents to regress, and be a "crippled" person (i.e., a person who is not expected to be fully socially responsible and to whom concessions must be continuously and perpetually made).

In most states involuntary commitment now requires that patients be dangerous to someone else or themselves, as indicated by overt acts (including not being able to take care of themselves). These regulations were a needed corrective to earlier abuses of the civil rights of patients. Some professionals have argued that it is impossible to treat psychotic patients under such laws. The fact of the matter is that most psychotic patients will cooperate with treatment if it is offered. A hospital that only processes and medicates, or even abuses (e.g., shocks or lobotomizes) patients may well have difficulty obtaining voluntary cooperation, and deserves to have difficulty.

Hospitalization should be seen as an extraordinary inter-vention. Hospitalization does provide a secure place for people who are actively suicidal, actively homicidal, or in danger of being killed. It can provide a temporary escape from acute stresses and it can temporarily allow severely disturbed behavior with no long-lasting consequences for the patient. The patient can be watched if necessary, and is available for intensive therapy.

It is a disservice to hospitalize a patient and then see that patient only once a week. Hospitalized patients should be seen daily in at least 30-minute sessions. Since what psychiatric hospitals have to offer to patients is limited, most psychotic patients do not need hospitalization. Frequently, relatives or friends will be willing to tolerate an annoying or inconvenient patient if they know the patient is in treatment and their tolerance is therapeutic and temporary. In our experience, the vast majority of schizophrenic patients who were not in the hospital when they began psycho-therapy never required hospitalization.

If a person hospitalizes a patient, or places the patient in some other artificial living environment, he must be sure that the staff will cooperate with the treatment. The private-for-profit "board and care" homes as an alternative to hospitalization, while ap-parently successful in pilot projects with motivated operators, have turned out to be disappointing when instituted on a large scale. Unreasonably rigid schedules and rules (e.g., in bed by 9 p.m.), insistence on high-dosage medication, discouragement of normal independence and adult activities (e.g., employment and sexuality), interference with psychotherapy, and resistance to turnover, that is, patient reentry into the real world, are all too frequent.

Discharge from the hospital should be made as rapidly as the patient can tolerate it. We feel strongly that the same therapist should see the patient in and out of the hospital if this is at all possible. Otherwise, close cooperation should be maintained.

Acutely psychotic patients who require hospitalization will have progressed sufficiently without medication in 5-day-per-week therapy to be discharged within 2 weeks. Even the bulk of more chronic patients will take no longer than 8 weeks.

We prefer not to use adjunctive medication. When medication is not used, any improvement that occurs is obviously the result of underlying changes. These changes result in enduring improvement.

There is an alternative way to work. The therapist can begin with the patient on medication, since that makes the patient more tolerable to the therapist, to the staff, and to the family. Then, the therapist can gradually decrease and discontinue the medication as rapidly as the patient can tolerate it, while focusing on psychotherapeutic work. The therapist should not be seduced by the behavioral control produced by the medication, or permit the patient to be seduced by it. Long-term use of medication, particularly in high doses, is not adequate treatment and is neurologically dangerous (e.g., tardive dyskinesia).

Medication produces behavioral control, and an apparent change in the thought disorder by damping the disruptive affects of fear and anger. But medication slows down underlying personality changes resulting from psychotherapy, since part of the process of change in psychotherapy depends on emotional reactions and having to deal with them. Data regarding this, and the long-term consequences of using or not using adjunctive medication, are discussed later in the report of the Michigan State Psychotherapy Project. The improvement in the thought disorder with psychotherapy was slower (less) when the patients were also on medication. In the long run, this had consequences for rehospitalization.

Patients who are already on medication are told that we will not take it away from them, but that they will soon see that they do not need it. They are told that psychotherapy sessions will have more effect if they are not on medication, but that we will not ask them to trust psychotherapy over medication until they are ready.

A surprising number of patients will tell you that they have already stopped taking their medication anyway, but they dared not tell their doctor for fear he would hospitalize them again, or at least be angry. They often express relief at not having to lie anymore. It is frequently estimated that only one out of three patients supposedly on psychotropic medication is actually using the medication as prescribed. Even when patients are actually on medication, most of them are relieved to have permission to stop. Such side-effects as impotence, impaired thinking, drowsiness, tremors, and dry mouth are frequently experienced as unpleasant.

Of course, patients do derive security from the medication, and we allow them the choice of keeping their medication and using it when they feel a need. They often report dramatic immediate relief from a single pill when under stress, undoubtedly largely a placebo effect.

If a patient is on medication, the best way to help him stop is to suggest skipping the dose just before a psychotherapy hour. One can then discuss any apparent changes. This gives the patient the feeling that he is not alone when solving the problem of coping without medication. The next step is to ask him to skip his medication for a day before his next therapy session. Progressively, this increases until the patient is off medication. Of course, a reasonable alternative is to reduce the dosage gradually, but we have found the above procedure more meaningful to the patient.

For any kind of psychotherapy in any kind of setting, the more time one can make available the more effective it is. How frequent the sessions are is more important than their length. The minimum necessary to let a psychotic patient know that the therapist is making a real effort to communicate is 30-minute sessions, however, and sometimes 30 minutes is about as much time as the therapist can tolerate with a particular patient.

If you hospitalize patients, as we said earlier, you should see them daily. In any event, five sessions in the first week is a good way of starting psychotherapy with a psychotic patient. Even in a community mental health center, where once-a-week treatment is usual, beginning intensively with schizophrenic patients will establish the relationship and increase the rate of progress not only initially but overall, even though the continuing treatment is once a week. In our experience, nothing fruitful can be done on less than a weekly basis. That is not to say, however, that intermittent psychologically oriented crisis intervention (e.g., a small number of closely spaced sessions) may not be very useful.

Most therapists find it strange that the offer of help, or of more help, in the form of continued psychotherapy, or more sessions per week, may frighten many patients, who frequently interpret such offers as indications that the therapist thinks of them as very sick, and they fear that the therapist may take such drastic action as to hospitalize them against their will. Such frequency of session may also be frightening to the schizophrenic patient because of the closeness it involves. Whatever the patient's interpretation of offers of help, the therapist should explore and discuss it.

When a schizophrenic patient is experiencing acute stress, the mere knowledge that he can reach his therapist if he has to is therapeutic, reassuring, and calming. We give our severely disturbed patients our home telephone numbers as well as the office telephone number. Neither of us uses mechanical answering devices or an answering service. We specifically tell our patients that in a crisis they can call us at any time of the day or night. We tell them that if they cannot reach us, to call again in an hour, and to keep doing that until they reach us. If they finally reach us in the very early hours of the morning, it is not disturbing as we will have been home less than an hour. We even explain that we have a bedside telephone so that being disturbed by a distraught patient is no more inconvenient than absolutely necessary.

The telephone has symbolic value as well as functional utility. It is a means and a symbol of maintaining communication and contact, even at a distance. The important thing is that it gives the patient the feeling that help is available if it is necessary. With this reassurance, the patient can handle many problems that he could not otherwise bear. Patients are usually able to handle the situation without calling.

There are some patients who abuse this privilege, and use it as a form of hostility, but they are extremely rare; however, they are easily managed in a relatively short period of time. It is only necessary to ask (if it is not already clear), "But why are you calling me?" The patient who is genuinely in need of you will tell you. The patient who evades the issue is being hostile and this needs to be pointed out and dealt with in the next therapy session. It is our experience that most patients view these telephone calls as a privilege and do not take advantage of it. It is usually more difficult to get patients to make the telephone call when they are distraught than it is to get them to desist when it is not necessary.

7

Countertransference:
What Am I Doing Here?

Why do so many mental health professionals believe that schizophrenic individuals are "untreatable"? In part, this is because they
were taught to believe it. In part, this is because many of them
have attempted psychotherapy with schizophrenic patients and
failed. But does this alone account for their belief? We think not.

Counter-Resistance and the
Psychotic Individual

We do not wish to see ourselves as being like the patient.
It is too painful. The psychotic patient frequently is so sick
that he or she barely seems human. This presents a peculiar
problem. Much "better" to assume that what they are saying
or doing has some root that need not be understood, that it is
"characteristic of the disease," or that, at most, it should be
given a label.

The material that the schizophrenic patient brings to the
surface relates to the therapist's own unconscious conflicts as
well as to the patient's, and that which is in the therapist's unconscious, just as that which is in anyone else's unconscious,

is there because he does not wish to deal with it. In the neurotic patient, the therapist can control the dosage level. The neurotic person brings up conflicts in ways sufficiently socialized to be bearable. At worst, there is time to discourage the patient from exploring specific problems with such subtlety that neither therapist nor patient need be aware of it. Obviously, insofar as the patient and therapist collude in such maneuvers, the therapy is limited in effectiveness.

But the psychotic patient may explode with material—material so vivid that it cannot be mistaken, and yet we dare not recognize it. We may feel overwhelmed. Our own defenses are under stress. Even the therapist's unconscious attempts subtly to sidetrack the patient frequently do not work any more than therapeutic attempts to cope with it.

That psychotic patients present material in its rawest and least socially acceptable form is not an accident. This serves the purpose of resistance by frightening and "grossing out" the therapist. If the patient can get the therapist to treat the material (and the patient) as offensive and reprehensible, the therapist will become the patient's ally in maintaining the psychotic adjustment.

Such unacceptable material may involve early infantile wishes to destroy the parents, to devour the parents, to murder one's siblings, to involve one's self in sexual or pseudosexual activities of a socially unacceptable sort, to experience and defend one's self against such terrors as being mutilated, castrated, drained, exploded, poisoned, starved, deserted, and left to die.

Frequently the patient presents the frightening material in an intermediate degree of clarity, with an ambivalent hope that the therapist will get into it and help him, as well as that the therapist will be frightened into leaving it alone. The therapist is confronted with his own dilemma: Should he deal with it deeply, knowing that he is opening a Pandora's box, or should he try to keep it under wraps, knowing that to do so may be to tell the patient that the therapist is as scared of this material as the patient is. The therapist's choice will vary from hour to hour and from patient to patient. It is always decided in the light of what the therapist is able to tolerate, and what he feels the patient is able to tolerate at that moment.

Typical First Attempts

Consider the situation under which most therapists attempt to treat their first schizophrenic patient. The therapist is typically in a setting in which he or she is called upon to work miracles in an incredibly limited time. He may be in the short-term intake ward of a large city hospital, where he may be expected to see as many as 10 new patients in a week's time, where gathering information rather than providing treatment is the job priority. Or, he may be in a community mental health center where between 20 or 25 patients per therapist are seen each week in treatment that ends after 12 sessions. Or, he may be in a long-term psychiatric hospital where both staff and patients are in agreement that nobody gets better here. In any of these settings, psychotherapy may not be valued. Also, it may be considered window dressing. A therapist may be required to combine the therapeutic work with the patient with such procedures as medication or electroconvulsive shock treatments, even though these procedures may interfere with the psychotherapy, and the novice therapist may not yet know that such procedures interfere with psychotherapy.

Therefore, the therapist who attempts to treat a schizophrenic patient may do so without emotional, clinical, or administrative support. The likelihood of "failure" under such conditions is high. This can have devastating consequences on the willingness of the therapist to undertake such treatment again.

Colleagues share tales of the schizophrenic patient's "untreatability" and the disasters that result when people attempt to undertake such "wasted" work, rationalizing the sense of uselessness, frustration, and inadequacy that they experienced before they gave up working with such difficult and disturbed patients. The therapist frequently has no one to turn to for emotional support when he is in need of it, or for technical suggestions.

One's colleagues can be helpful, if they value psychotherapy, believe psychotherapy to be useful for schizophrenic patients, use their own errors as a basis for learning, are not threatened by the success of colleagues even in areas in which they themselves may not be competent and, at best, know how to work successfully with schizophrenic patients themselves. What the therapist needs is support in his frustration and confusion at working with such a difficult and puzzling patient and help in tolerating the uncertainty of not knowing, while being encouraged to conceptualize the patient's material without premature and rigid certainty.

The Pervasive Sense of Fruitlessness

Only a fool is certain that he knows what is happening with a schizophrenic patient the first time they meet. All the therapist can be certain of is that the patient is afraid. The patient does not tell him clearly what is happening. The therapist must feel puzzled and confused and the novice is tempted to believe that this reflects some inadequacy of his own. The confusion of the therapist is the direct result of the confusion of the patient and of the patient's inability to communicate even about those things which are clear to him. The term *inability*, as used here, refers not only to that which the patient cannot do but also to that which the patient could do if he were not afraid that it would cause him great pain, trouble, or suffering.

Both novices and experienced therapists working with schizophrenic patients will experience such unpleasant feelings that to avoid these feelings the psychotherapists avoid the patients. Therapists, like most people, do not like to feel that they are unkind or that they irrationally hate particular patients. They do not like to think they are stupid and inadequate, and that they cannot understand and are never helpful.

Whatever the therapist's feelings, they resonate both with the therapist's own dynamics and with what is occurring to the patient. This is the process that in classic psychoanalysis is referred to as countertransference. In the early discussion, it was sometimes mentioned as though it were a monster to be exorcised or avoided. In fact, there is no therapy without countertransference; if the therapist is continuously alert to his own feelings, and especially his apparently irrational feelings, he will get accurate information about the relationship with the patient and what is going on in the patient's experience. Because the experience of a schizophrenic patient is so much more unpleasant than that of most neurotic patients, the countertransference experience of the therapist for a schizophrenic is more gruesome. In addition, there are the unpleasant experiences the patient stirs up in the therapist as a technique of conscious resistance, as in the paranoid patient.

If the therapist masters his initial qualms and begins the process of treatment, he will nonetheless get ample opportunity to experience pessimism and a sense of failure. Schizophrenic patients are masters at communicating their own despair about the world to the therapist in such a way that the therapist begins to despair of the work that he is doing.

The simplest apparent failure is the patient who seems not to respond at all. Hour after hour is spent with him, and the therapist gets no feedback and no evidence that the patient is getting better. The patient who does not respond at all for long periods of time is a vivid example of the special communication problem of schizophrenic patients. The patient hears you, is responding, and may be doing a great deal of psychotherapeutic work. He cannot communicate this to you clearly for fear that it will be used against him. Consequently, the therapist must scrutinize the patient for small cues and listen to other people in the patient's environment for evidence that the therapy is being effective. Even in the absence of discernible cues that the therapy is effective, the therapist must continue working day after day, week after week until the inevitable clinical improvement occurs. This seems like an extraordinary demand to the therapist until he has seen his first "intractable" patient improve. To persevere, the therapist must be able to fall back on his past experience, and/or on his supervisor's experience, and on his knowledge of the patient's fear of communicating.

The second apparent failure is the patient who responds, and seems to get better. The therapist feels the work is worthwhile: "Aha, they can get better, I can do this work!" While the therapist is feeling optimistic, the patient plateaus or even gets slightly worse. This is attributable to a number of things. One is the nature of psychotherapy in general: it is not like climbing a ramp, where you start at the bottom and go until you reach the top. It is like climbing the foothills leading to a mountain, where you go up, and you go down, but you do not go down as far, and you do not stay down as long, and you climb higher each time. There is an unevenness to the journey, because there is an unevenness to life experience, on the one hand, and an unevenness to one's inner emotional turmoils on the other. More specifically, in the earliest stages of psychotherapy, the schizophrenic patient may begin to make progress on the basis of the strong relationship that he or she has formed with the therapist. At last the patient has found a dependable human being. The therapist and the patient have understood some problems. The world seems surprisingly accessible to the patient, and he improves. The plateau represents the end of the therapeutic honeymoon, as the patient experiences doubts and fear or he is certain that you will turn out like everyone else in his life. This is simply material to be understood and worked through.

The third apparent failure is the 6-month catastrophe. The therapist begins working, the patient makes progress (the therapist, of course, feels good about it), and approximately 6 months into treatment there is a catastrophic regression. The same behavior or symptoms, apparently, as those that brought the patient into treatment recurs, for example, another suicidal gesture, or an acute psychotic episode. Whenever such things occur, the therapist will tend to feel "All of my time was wasted, I didn't accomplish anything." This is rarely the case if the patient has, in fact, been changing his behavior accompanied by insight into the relationship between his current behavior and feelings and his life history. In all likelihood, however, the conditions that were necessary to elicit this extreme behavior by the patient were of a much greater magnitude than those which precipitated the first incident. Often the disaster occurs when four or five or six reality events which have significant negative emotional meaning occur simultaneously. The patient could have handled any one, or maybe two or three of these events without resorting to such desperate measures, but with all of them happening in a very short period of time, the overload and strain become too much, and the patient resorts to a suicide attempt or a psychotic episode.

When such a disaster occurs, at any point in therapy, the patient will feel betrayed and inadequate; however, what he or she will talk about is the hopelessness of trying, the impossibility of the world, and his or her basic inadequacy. What the patient will not talk about is that he is angry with you for letting him down. In treatment he probably has moved to a point where, for the first time in his life, he really believed there was a chance that his life could change and be better, and now he feels betrayed.

The therapist will experience similar self-doubts and inadequacy, but the therapist who is not overwhelmed, who makes it
possible and permissible for the patient to deal with these feelings
consciously, and who actively investigates the conditions causing
the crisis helps the patient to weather this crisis, and future
crises—some even without the help of the therapist. It is important to let the patient "see" that he could have handled, and
has been handling, several of the pressures successfully, but that
too much happened too fast *this time*. (Of course, the therapist
should examine the extent to which the patient "arranged" the
pressures to occur.)

Being Consumed by the Patient's Dependency

Frequently the novice therapist becomes aware that he feels
as though the patient really represents a menace—an all-con-
suming, demanding individual whose dependency could never be
satisfied. Some therapists have this fear without any help, and
others are encouraged by their supervisors, who warn them of the
excessive dependency of their patients. Closely related to this is
the injunction, "Don't let this patient manipulate you."

The supervisor who warns the novice therapist of the schizophrenic patient's dependency always places it in the context that
meeting these needs will be bad for the patient. You are doing bad
therapy if you let the patient depend on you. You are doing bad
therapy if you let the patient manipulate you. By letting the
patient depend on you, you are preventing him from being able to
grow in self-responsibility and self-reliance. The novice therapist
feels guilty if he or she feels a patient is depending too much on or
has manipulated him or her.

The defenses against this are obvious: Do not take any very
demanding patients, put them on medication, schedule visits not
more than once a month, meet their dependency with physical
satisfaction in the form of a bottle of pills, and do your best to
transfer the actual contacts with the patient to some other professional or even paraprofessional. Or, rather than do therapy with
them, refer them to social education classes, self-assertiveness
classes, or social skills classes, where you give them training in

how they should do the right things and then attribute their continued failure to their lack of motivation.

It is rare for a supervisor to point out honestly that the only danger with these patients' dependency is that the demand may be too much for you to tolerate. As in so many other contexts, when you take a problem out of the moral dimension (I am a bad therapist because I indulge the patient's dependency) and deal with it in terms of consequences, the burden becomes more bearable and the consequences can be evaluated.

The schizophrenic patient indeed is very dependent. The needs of the patient are great because his dependency needs have not received as much legitimate gratification as people with less severe symptoms. That is why the symptoms of schizophrenic patients are so severe. If the therapist gratifies their needs to the extent that it is practical and realistic and bearable to him, he is often amazed at how far that gratification goes. It frequently is enough. Sometimes, of course, the patient is trying to prove that his dependency needs are so excessive that no one could have met them, either when he was a child or now. This is another effort on the part of the patient unconsciously to prove the parents were good by proving the patient was not.

As for the patient being able to manipulate the therapist, what is wrong with a patient who is terrified and feels no one is dependable, learning that he can do something to the therapist that will get the therapist to meet his needs? Rather than being destructive, it is frequently an element of safety in a dangerous world. The only problem with manipulation is the hostile patient who uses it as a form of sadism and to whom successful manipulation means the therapist is weak and therefore cannot be depended upon. One can recognize even disguised sadism, however; it hurts. It goes beyond what is bearable. It is a good clinical axiom that one never indulges either a sadist or a masochist. The sadistic manipulative patient can have this fact pointed out, and the issue can be talked about. But most manipulative schizophrenic individuals are not primarily sadistic. They are primarily afraid of other people and are looking for a little bit of security in a very frightening world. Even hustlers are frightened.

Therapists may also feel overwhelmed by the patient's dependency because of the therapist's own unmet dependency needs.

They may be angry at the patients because they are allowed such gratification. Psychotherapy with severely disturbed patients is not a mutual process, and it is important for the therapist's own dependency needs to be in the background. To do this, the therapist must satisfy his or her own dependency needs in his or her life outside the therapeutic situation.

Boredom

Sometimes the patient does not wear us out with dramatic problems or try to terrorize us or make us feel guilty. Instead, he says what he has said before. We hear it, and we feel bored. The patient may be talking quietly and defending against getting into new material. We go on from hour to hour, feeling more and more bored, and perhaps sleepy.

When the therapist is feeling bored, he has to assume that it is similar to boredom in the patient; that is, it is usually defensive, and is most frequently a defense against anger. Attention to one's own boredom will always reveal some therapeutic activity which could usefully be undertaken to get the therapy moving again. The patient may be depressed, or bored, or defending against anger, and needs to have these issues made explicit. Or the patient may be avoiding an issue of which the therapist has some vague awareness but would rather, at least momentarily, avoid also.

Activity and Countertransference

The question of how active or passive a therapist "should" be is a point of technique frequently discussed; however, it is often presented as a rule without either understanding the historical origins of the technical issue or a clear rationale for differential activity with different types of patients or with the same patient at different times.

Historically, the issue has roots in Freud's injunctions about therapist activity. These were designed for the neurotic patient, but they were also designed for Freud himself; that is, they were designed for a man whose early writings clearly show him to be capable of a great deal of activity and energetic effort to be of service to patients. These injunctions reflected his awareness that it was helpful to talk less and listen more than his natural inclinations, and provide a more neutral screen for the patient's transferences.

Unfortunately, the trainee therapist, medical or nonmedical, is not in the same position. Usually he is anxious about whether he is adequate or not and guilty about doing the wrong thing. Whatever he does has to be reviewed by supervisors who may act like punitive superegos, or to him they may be experienced as punitive superegos even when they are not. Consequently, the safest way seems the least active way. This defense against anxiety and guilt by means of passivity leads the novice therapist to take Freud's dicta not as a theoretically motivated corrective to overactivity, but as a way of life in which the therapist does as little as possible on the patient's behalf.

The willingness for the therapist to act becomes critical with severely disturbed patients. The patient himself is so afraid of dealing with life and of getting into his conflicts that he requires a more active therapist, in the sense of bringing up more subjects. Moreover, the patient is frequently incompetent in this world, and needs advice and information, as well as therapy. Self-destructive consequences of the patient's behavior must be brought into initial therapeutic focus by the therapist rather than the patient. The objection that an active therapist obscures the transference is less relevant when working with the schizophrenic patient because the transference is so dramatic, even if it is not communicated in words.

One example of the need for increased activity involves the missed therapy session. It is almost always a mistake just to wait for the next hour when working with a borderline or ambulatory schizophrenic patient. The patient is usually going through something when he misses a session, and you cannot depend on him to bring it up. Usually, as with any sudden increase in resistance, a missed session means that there is something that needs to be attended to. If you call, you and the patient may be able to interrupt what otherwise may become a disaster. It is our usual practice to call a borderline patient if he is more than 10 minutes late. If he is not available, we always leave a message. Strangely enough, the patient reacts as though the therapist had rejected him when he does not try to contact him after he has missed a session. This occurs even when the patient has never missed a session before, and cannot realistically anticipate what the therapist will do.

This injunction to the therapist is particularly important when he feels relieved that the patient has not appeared. There are many patients who are so adept at making us uncomfortable that we feel as though it would be nice if they went away. Such reactions on the part of the therapist are inevitable; but they always require self-investigation. When the wish that a patient would suddenly disappear occurs at a specific point in therapy with a specific patient, it usually is a reflection of something that is happening to that patient; he is communicating some concerns to the therapist in an unconscious manner and these are making the therapist feel uncomfortable.

In general, the discomfort of the therapist is never an accident. Indeed, all of the therapist's ruminations, fantasies, and feelings are usually in reaction to the patient. The novice therapist who is not sure that his reactions are those a therapist "should" have easily succumbs to the impulse to hide these reactions from a supervisor as well as from himself. It is always important to consider which part of the fantasy is from the therapist's own dynamics and which part of that fantasy is being generated from the relationship with the patient.

The sexual fantasies of the therapist are usually provoked by something the patient does. The hostile fantasies of the therapist are usually provoked by something the patient does. This does not justify the therapist's suddenly attacking the patient with an accusation, "You're trying to seduce me," or "You are angry with me." Rather, the therapist raises the question with himself as to what the patient is doing that provokes these fantasies, and whether it would be helpful to the patient to focus on them. Sometimes one only has to say, "I wonder why you are doing this?" Typically, the patient will explain it as "normal" or "usual." It is useful to point out that it is not "usual" or not usual in the therapy situation. Frequently, that will be enough to get the patient to explore the meanings or begin to talk about it in a way that will allow the therapist to explore the meaning. Sometimes the issues will have to be interpreted more directly, but as tactfully (i.e., noninsultingly) as possible.

Therapeutic Use of Countertransference

An anally incontinent and physically violent male patient was in treament with me (Karon) and I was disgusted by the patient's urinary and fecal incontinence. I was afraid of the patient's capacity for physical violence, since he was muscular and had broken the jaws of several attendants in the course of his varied hospitalizations. In addition, I did not like him.

It was something more than just being disgusted by his incontinence and afraid of physical danger. Those were perfectly rational responses. I did not like him, and it was more than a rational response.

I began to think about that, "Why don't I like him? He reminds me of those dirty little bastards I grew up with, who used to beat up other kids." Already it made sense not to be angry with the patient because he reminded me, on a transference basis, of "kids" I grew up with who were violent and picked on other "kids." My internal dialogue continued: "They used to pick on me, but because I soon became big, they picked on other kids even more. Those dirty little bastards." It then dawned on me that they usually were "little guys." It further dawned on me that maybe they were afraid. Maybe they were afraid because they were little and were proving that it was not them, but the other guy, who was in danger. The next time the patient threatened me with violence, as he periodically did to all members of the institutional staff, I told him, "Look, I know how scared you are. Why don't you use my strength to protect you?" and he calmed down.

The attendants thought this was very funny. As they said in private, "You know, he could tear you to pieces with one hand." But psychodynamically he felt protected. It was later learned that he first got into trouble as a child by beating up other children. He was sent to a series of treatment centers for progressively more seriously disturbed children because he beat up children at each treatment center. Thus, the countertransference reaction not only was not an impediment to therapy, but its appropriate analysis allowed the therapist to deal with his resentment of the patient, and, more importantly, even to uncover a central dynamic of the patient's difficulties and to dissolve a central resistance, since no therapist is willing to get bodily destroyed just to cure a patient.

Therapist Vulnerabilities and the
Patient's Successful Paranoia

Insofar as the therapist has weak spots, the patient will exploit them (and all therapists have weak spots). This is particularly true if the patient happens to be paranoid. Paranoid patients are geniuses at finding the weak spot and exploiting it: after all, their whole lives are organized around defending themselves in a very dangerous world.

It is impossible for a therapist to work with a truly paranoid individual without having him surprise you into acting grossly inappropriately. It is critical whether or not your guilt at having done something inappropriate so paralyzes you that you cannot continue the work successfully. The therapist, thus, should never be surprised when the patient says something that is upsetting or that throws the therapist off balance; patients will zero in on something the therapist feels he should not be upset by, or they may find a way to put the therapist in a quandary as to whether it is a bad idea or a good idea to be upset (because he would be perceived as phony or self-hating not to). For example, a borderline patient slips the word "Jew" meaning "bargain" into the conversation as a way of making a Jewish therapist uncomfortable. A Black therapist, or a therapist of any other minority, will get similar treatment from patients who do not share their minority status.

A patient brought up his homosexual conflicts in the following way: turning suddenly to the therapist, the patient put his arm around his shoulders and said, "You're homosexual just like me, aren't you?" Such behavior will freak out the therapist who is not sure where he stands, will even freak out the therapist who is an overt homosexual, and will certainly freak out the therapist who is rigidly afraid of examining homosexual impulses.

Luckily, in this case it was possible to say to the patient, "No, I'm not interested in fucking you, but I'm proud of you, because most people who have had homosexual experiences have difficulty talking about it, and we should talk about this in your hour." That evening in his therapy hour, the patient was able to talk about his homosexual experiences for the first time.

A more common way of bringing up such impulses (again intended to freak the therapist out) is when a patient suddenly says, "I really want to suck your cock."

The proper response is to interpret upward, that is, to say to the patient the socially acceptable equivalent of the communication: "You must admire me a great deal."

This has a therapeutic effect. Inevitably, what you will learn is that the patient does admire you, but is afraid of his positive feelings toward you. By expressing them as a homosexual impulse in its crudest form, he can express them in a way that is intended to get them rejected. This serves the purpose of resistance; that is, it interrupts the therapy.

Resistance by Proxy

The patient may be consciously or unconsciously alert to the possibility of using people outside the therapy situation to upset the equilibrium of the therapist and, hence, disrupt the therapy. He may seek an "ally" in the community, someone who will attempt to persuade the therapist not to be such a "cruel" person, to be more appreciative of the problem of the patient.

For example, the patient may talk with his physician about the anxiety and stress that he is experiencing in therapy with a non-medical therapist, knowing at some level it will elicit a reaction in the medically oriented nontherapist physician to the "incompetence" of the nonmedical therapist. The patient arranges unconsciously for his physician to tell him to stop seeing his therapist, and to see a "psychiatrist who will stop the hurting." Usually, the patient already knows his physician's opinion and, if he acts on his advice, will find some other way of being equally resistant to a medical therapist (unless, of course, he is able to manage the ultimate triumph of resistance, finding a psychiatrist who does not believe in psychotherapy, and will not ask the patient to understand himself).

Of course, the nonmedical therapist can be depended upon to feel angry and offended by the intrusion of the nontherapist physician into what the psychotherapist feels is his professional domain. The feelings are normal, but how one acts requires tact. There may also be irrational ambivalence based on a tendency in the nonmedical therapist to defer to the status of the physician and resentment over one's own tendency to defer. The nonmedical therapist must take an educative stance to both physician and patient, frustrating as that may be. The therapist must remember that the physician is probably genuinely concerned about the patient, but uninformed about the larger context of the issue the patient may have raised with him. It is useful to enlarge his understanding of the problem. He may also be uninformed about psychotherapy, and about the training of nonmedical psychotherapists. Professional images being what they are, it is useful to cite to physicians medical therapists whose views about treatment are similar to the nonmedical therapist. It is helpful if the physician can become an understanding ally reinforcing the treatment.

With the patient, it is useful to explain why the physician might differ from the therapist, including the limitations of medical training as it relates to psychotherapy. This is part of a generally useful procedure of helping the patient to understand legitimate differences of opinions even among "experts" on the basis of differences in training and experience. (The patient's parents all too often pretend to be experts about everything.)

Such discussions with the covert aim of sabotaging the therapy may occur with any number of people. In general, there is more communication with others. Often for the first time the therapy makes possible using people outside the therapy as well as outside the immediate family as sources of information. But the patient will, particularly early in treatment, use these helpful processes as forms of resistance, thus demonstrating (unconsciously) that healthy processes are self-defeating. The patient may present to a schoolteacher several distorted aspects of a discussion in therapy about child rearing. They may use an understanding gained in therapy to express hostility to a spouse or parent. There are any number of individuals with whom the schizophrenic patient may interact so as to arouse sufficient anxiety that out of concern they will call the therapist and attempt to convince the therapist to cease doing therapy in a meaningful way. The therapist is likely to be annoyed by the supposedly helpful call. There may be an impulse to "pull rank" on professionals of "lower status" or treat relatives as if they are merely interfering. In each instance, the therapist must be therapeutic, educative, and tactful—both with the caller and the patient.

The Struggle for Independence:
Normal Feelings Versus Unhelpful Defenses
of the Therapist

The phobic avoidance of dependency gratification early in therapy with a schizophrenic patient is a serious mistake, but discouraging the development of independence in the schizophrenic patient later in therapy is equally serious. Throughout therapy, independence is to be valued, but not required until the patient is capable of it.

Just as parents have difficulty letting their children grow up, therapists frequently have trouble letting their patients grow up and become independent of them. This may be experienced as a loss, or a loss of control, or as a rejection. Separation is a central problem of all human beings, including therapists. Unconscious handling of the problem of separation is both self-destructive and harmful to others. Schizophrenic patients frequently have had parents who were symbiotic or characterized by "dominating dependence," whereby the patient was controlled in order to meet the parent's dependency needs. They do not need a therapist with similar defenses. The therapist who is *consciously* aware of his own problems with separation, and the feelings it arouses in him, will be helpful to the patient.

Many therapists, even therapists who are helpful in the initial stages of therapy, find the maturing patient to be a threat to them. This can be manifested in a number of ways. It is obviously destructive to interpret the patient's struggle for independence as unhealthy.

One example is the therapist who says to the patient, "Why are you interpreting your own material? You're not an analyst," or some variation thereof, implying that the patient does not have the right to think about himself.

Of course, no one has a better right, even if he is mistaken. Patients will learn from their misunderstanding and absorb the perspective of the therapist, until, it is hoped, at the end of treatment they can examine and understand their own thoughts, feelings, and actions with useful insight, without the therapist. Letting patients share a greater and greater role in understanding and interpreting their own material certainly has its parallel in adolescence, when children still need parents but need them in smaller and smaller amounts.

Later manifestations of the problem of not being able to let go include insufficient attention to such practical matters as earning a living, living on one's own, finishing one's training, or taking a better job at a distance from the analyst or therapist. This last issue is of course a difficult one.

There are times in therapy when the therapy is most urgent, and a change in jobs is less pressing. There are other times when an appreciable improvement in jobs is a sufficient reality factor that it is worth interrupting the therapy or transferring therapists. The judgment must be made by the therapist and patient working together, but the therapist's difficulty in evaluating the options may come from the therapist's omnipotence—"Only I can help this patient, forever!"—a feeling that is never true.

But there is also the problem of therapists who give in to the first sign or request for independence on the part of the patient and terminate treatment too quickly. This problem frequently occurs with patients who have had difficulty establishing independence or difficulty acknowledging their need to be dependent. The therapist is the first person who has been willing to talk about dependence and independence with them. The patient, as a form of resistance, insists that the first assertion of his independence must be in relationship to the therapist. They propose to do this before they have done it in relationship to their own parents or spouse. This is the giveaway that it is resistance.

This is a difficult problem for a therapist to confront. Permitting premature separation serves the same function for the therapist that not keeping the last appointments does for the patient; that is, it prevents experiencing the unpleasant feelings connected with separation. The potential premature separation may be avoided by explaining to the patient the difference between the nature of his dependence on you and your concern for him, as compared with the dependence that he had on his parents and his parents' reluctance or fear of letting him grow up. You make it clear to the patient that you differ from the parents in the sense that you want to help him to be able to grow as a person, and that includes growing away from you. You present to the patient the fact that to enact the initial struggle of separation in relationship to you rather than the parents is going to result in cutting him off from being able to utilize you further. Yet you are someone whom the patient knows he has found helpful in furthering the process. Premature separation puts the patient in the position of having to rely on one or both parents for help and understanding in growing up, people who they already have demonstrable evidence are entrenched in holding them in a dependent relationship.

You let the patient know that the separation from you is inevitable and healthy, but that at the moment you believe it is premature. As long as major symptoms are still there, it is your duty to point them out to the patient, and to point out that such things do not go away spontaneously. You never go along with termination without countervailing effort when you feel the premature termination would be destructive to the patient. On the other hand, you are not a police officer. Patients are allowed to make decisions and mistakes and, as we shall describe later, even the patient who interrupts against advice may learn a great deal from the period of therapy and from the period between therapy. We prefer using the word "interruption" to "termination" with patients, allowing the possibility that, if life requires it, further help is available.

8

Special Issues in Psychotherapy, as Related to Schizophrenia

Certain issues are usual in the treatment of schizophrenic patients but not usual in the training of therapists; consequently, therapists frequently respond in ways that are either temporarily or permanently counterproductive. Therapy with schizophrenic patients frequently fails, not because the issue is uniquely schizophrenic or mishandled, but because more general, serious, and often dramatic human problems are not dealt with adequately. It is possible for some psychotherapists phobically to avoid these problems in dealing with neurotic patients; however, it is not possible to avoid these issues with borderline and schizophrenic patients.

Such fundamental problems as suicide, the inability to sleep or eat, the possibility of committing murder, or of being the victim of murder, are usually neglected in theoretical discussions of psychotherapy, and yet they are central to the treatment of schizophrenic patients. Patients who are very poor (as are most schizophrenic individuals), or who act out, or who are criminals or delinquents, or who use drugs or alcohol are not often thought to be suitable for psychodynamic psychotherapy of any sort; the therapist for schizophrenic patients cannot afford the luxury of avoiding these patients or of being ignorant of the appropriate handling of these problems. Ethnic subgroups such as Blacks and Hispanics may use specific resistances (defenses or coping mechanisms), or may arouse characteristic countertransference reactions with which the therapist is unfamiliar. Of course, such designations as Black, Hispanic, or Anglo are obviously imprecise, and knowledge of the relevant subcultural group may need to be specific in cultural heritage, socioeconomic status, geography, and generation from last migration.

In this chapter, we will review some of these issues as they apply to schizophrenic individuals. Of course, most of these problems (and our recommendations) are not confined to schizophrenic patients, but then neither are the schizophrenic patients uniquely schizophrenic after the first part of therapy. We will discuss the economically poor patient, the problem of homicide and suicide, patients who will not eat or cannot sleep, the problem of prejudices in both the patient and the therapist, alcoholism and drug abuse, and dealing with prisoners and criminal behavior.

The Economically Poor Patient

Schizophrenic patients are far more numerous in the lower socioeconomic classes, primarily because life in the lower socioeconomic class is much harder, not only for the patient, but for those family members on whose resources, emotional and otherwise, the patient would ordinarily depend. Of course, it is also true that psychopathology itself interferes with the economic status of the individual. The failure to understand how to treat economically poor patients has as much to do with the apparent failure of psychotherapy with schizophrenic patients as does a lack of knowledge of the psychopathology, or of appropriate technique.

Moreover, psychotherapists are typically far from excited at the prospect of working with the economically poor patient. Even such otherwise sophisticated authors as Hollingshead and Redlich (1958) are doubtful that psychoanalytic psychotherapy is of much value for poor patients. It is often assumed that the economically poor are not (and cannot be) psychologically minded, that reality problems preclude dynamic psychotherapy, and that poor patients cannot understand what psychotherapy is about.

That is not our experience. The above assumptions are true only when the patients are inappropriately treated; however, to treat poor patients appropriately in psychotherapy, therapists need to know about the special difficulties (resistances and counter-transferences) to be encountered in doing such treatment with poor patients and how to deal with these special difficulties.

In what ways are poor patients different? In brief, they are poor; reality problems are greater. We are not using the word "poor" to mean "in temporary financial distress." Primarily, we mean people who have been poor all their lives, whose parents were poor, and who have a high probability of remaining poor. It is thus a social as well as an economic condition. This definition of "poor" does not have sharp boundaries, but includes the un-employed, partially employed, and the lower-income members of the working society.

Poor patients tend to be less well educated, hence less verbally fluent and less knowledgeable about many matters, including what real psychotherapy is about. They are more likely to be accustomed to being treated in an authoritarian way, both in childhood and adult life. Hence, they tend to be more compliant, but they are also more distrustful and resentful of authorities, including so-called helping professionals. Either they do not freely voice their com-plaints or questions, or they tend to voice them in such a way that both the patient and the patient's complaints are rejected.

In what ways are the therapist's reactions to poor patients different? In brief, therapists tend to be more pessimistic, less interested, more fearful of the time commitment involved, more apprehensive about overdependency, and they tend to find it harder to identify with patients; hence, they also tend to believe the patients are not psychologically minded, or capable of being psychologically minded, or that they are in a situation in which increased insight would be of no value.

Ordinarily, if the therapist is attentive and reflective, the experience of doing therapy teaches him whatever he still needs to know to be helpful, especially if the patient is unusual or difficult. This feedback process may not happen in psychotherapy with poor patients because the special communication problems may prevent it; such problems may even prevent the therapist from being aware that there is a communication problem. In fact, the problem of communication with the poor patient is so central that the failure of the therapist to appreciate this difficulty may by itself account for negative treatment results.

All of these problems in treating the poor patient in psychotherapy, particularly the economically poor schizophrenic patient, and the consequent appropriate procedures to overcome them, will be discussed more fully below.

SOCIOECONOMIC COUNTERTRANSFERENCE FANTASIES

If defenses, motivations, or inhibitions central to the therapists's felt integration are threatened by working with a particular patient, the patient will not be treated (and, most typically, the "fault" will be viewed as lying in the patient). Thus, when working with unusual or difficult patients of any sort, it is important to consider one's own psychologic needs as they relate to attempting to treat such patients. There are some common countertransference difficulties in working with poor patients which can be described.

There are, after all, only therapists who come from two kinds of backgrounds: those from lower-class backgrounds who were socially upwardly mobile, and those who came from at least upper-middle-class backgrounds. Each group has difficulty working with poor patients. Obviously, there are no therapists from lower-class environments who were comfortable there.

The upwardly mobile therapist has escaped his or her childhood environment by means of education, impulse control, and hard work. The therapist's need to maintain his view of how miserable his life would have been had he not escaped (in order to justify to himself the hard work and scarifice that went into upward mobility) may interfere with doing psychotherapy with poor patients. In a sense, the patient may acquire the unconscious meaning of the therapist's "bad self," that is, the part of the therapist that wishes to be lazy, self-indulgent, and unsuccessful. (Of course, such impulses are common to everyone.) The projection of the therapist's rejected impulses can lead to an exaggerated view of the patient's weaknesses. The patient has not escaped, and usually cannot escape by the *same* techniques that the therapist did. The therapist cannot conceive of either living without escape, or of other ways of escaping.

The therapist from an upper-middle-class background frequently cannot conceive of how anyone can live in the circumstances in which the poor patient lives. The inequity between the therapist's life and the patient's life is dramatically apparent. This therapist may also feel guilty about the suffering he has never experienced. Or, he may feel inadequate at the thought that he could not cope if he had to live under such conditions. To relieve his guilt or inadequacy he may seize on behavioral characteristics of the poor patient which "justify" or "explain" the inequity. In a sense, the patient may acquire the unconscious meaning of this therapist's "bad self" too, that is, the therapist either as exploiter or as inadequate victim, immoral, and without social conscience. (Of course, these impulses are also common to everyone.) The projection of the therapist's rejected impulses may lead to an exaggerated view of the "badness" of the patient's behavior. The therapist may fail to see these traits as either results of or as attempts at adjustment to the patient's environment.

The therapist may not conceive of the possible, even necessary, function in a different milieu of behavior which would be maladaptive or incomprehensibly "bad" in the therapist's own milieu.

There is a less frequent reaction to the poor patient, and this reaction may occur to therapists of any socioeconomic background; it is to "romanticize" the poor patient. By "romanticizing" the poor, the therapist may feel that "they" are compensated for the inequities of life, or he may express his unconscious idealization of the child versus the parent (the rich one in the family). The freer expression of aggression (adaptive or neurotic) permitted in lower socioeconomic environments may lead to the therapist's subtly supporting such behavior by the patient without evaluating it in terms of the real consequences for the patient. Such inappropriate handling is a defense against the rage the therapist himself would feel if he lived in such circumstances, and it is a displacement of rage from his own emotionally and/or economically unsatisfying childhood circumstances.

Whatever the reason for romanticizing "the poor," it can lead to discouraging or not encouraging changes that would improve the patient's life, including changes in socioeconomic status. As always, the key mistake is the lack of emphasis on realistic consequences for the patient, evaluated from the patient's point of view, given the added knowledge of the therapist and the therapeutic dissolution of neurotic and psychotic distortions of reality. Indeed, even the well-intentioned therapist may romanticize the poor out of respect for the patient's individuality. But not to raise a possibility for benign change to the patient is never a service; the patient in real therapy is always free to reject what does not make sense or does not seem useful. These "romanticizations" are just other ways of not empathizing with the patient, and are no different from the countertransference difficulties to be dealt with in any psychotherapy.

It is understandably painful, however, for therapists to empathize with poor patients living under circumstances the therapist would not willingly (and perhaps could not) endure. The easiest way to avoid such painful fantasies is not to accept such patients, unconsciously to maneuver the patient into dropping out of treatment, or not to do real therapy but only aid with a misery-abatement plan or escape plan (i.e., only deal with "reality problems").

Like all fantasies of the therapist, the fantasies about the poor patient described above do not interfere with treatment if they are conscious and attended to, rather than unconscious and acted out or defended against by pseudotherapeutic maneuvers. This is consistent with Siassi's (1974) report that lower-class patients were more likely to drop out when seen by psychotherapists who have not been through personal analysis than when seen by psychotherapists who have had personal analysis; Siassi attributes this to greater awareness of and attention to transference and countertransference.

LENGTH OF TREATMENT AND DEPENDENCY

The reluctance, however, to examine closely the physical and psychologic realities of the poor patient's life, based on such unexamined countertransferences, is not what therapists talk about when voicing their reservations about working with poor patients. Usually therapists mention their concerns about the length of treatment and/or dependency. The following views are commonly stated: the poor patient will require such inordinate expenditures of time as to make therapy unfeasible and/or this therapy will require the therapist to do all the work; alternatively, the poor patient will not stay in therapy long enough to make any difference and/or the patient will not allow the therapist to do anything. Similar statements are made about schizophrenic patients. Paradoxically, both convictions are frequently voiced by the same therapists on different occasions.

Problems of overdependency or counterphobic independence and overly long treatment or overly brief treatment, however. are not really any different with poor patients than with any other patient. The poor patient is more likely to appear more extremely compliant or noncompliant than other patients, reflecting his feelings of having less power with respect to authority figures. These behaviors are not necessarily unsatisfiable overdependence or unmanageable resistance. Poor patients' demands and resistances often enrage and/or frighten prospective therapists. Therapists need to know how to understand the seemingly more extreme reactions of poor patients and how to respond to them.

Some poor patients do seem to expect or even demand perpetual treatment, which may not be indicated, and is not feasible in any agency. Such patients demand from a therapist the all-pervading acceptance and care that they feel vaguely entitled to and deprived of, but which is too threatening to connect consciously with their childhood and family, particularly the mother. It is less threatening to demand it from and be angry at a "nongiving" therapist. It also may have the function of proving (unconsciously) that the patient's parent was not defective, since the patient's demands are so excessive no one, including the therapist, can meet them. When described, it is obvious that these same problems occur in other patients, but they are not acted out so intensely.

The therapist should help the patient become aware of this by sharing his own understanding with the patient; of course, the interpretation should be made in a way that the patient can utilize—it must be understandable and sufficiently tactful that it cannot be misinterpreted as an accusation.

Agencies, however, often reinforce the staffs' displacement of concern about time and dependency by arbitrary rules imposing rigid procedures for ultrabrief "therapy" (not even meaningful crisis intervention) or simple-minded and single-minded behavioral goals that make little sense from the perspective of the patient's well-being or from the nature of psychotherapy and of symptoms. It is, of course, well known that the presenting symptom is usually the last event that pushed the patient into seeking help, not the sole or even the most important symptom. The poor patient is more likely either to accept such an arbitrary definition of the problem without overtly raising his or her objections, or else leave without explanation.

The relationships between time and psychotherapy are complex. One relationship is very simple, however. If an agency is only open from 8 to 5, poor patients will not be able to use it, unless they are unemployed or too disturbed to work.

Poor patients, even schizophrenic patients, can frequently be helped by crisis intervention or brief psychotherapy. Indeed, they may accept only crisis intervention, because, from their perspective, psychotherapy seems like a luxury, unless they are overwhelmed by their problems. Patients in crisis, however, can truly make good use of therapeutic time because of their high level of motivation for change and understanding during the crisis. It has become increasingly obvious that, for patients of any socioeconomic class, crisis intervention can be of real and lasting value (if appropriately carried out).

Surprisingly enough, we have found *repeated* crisis intervention can be as effective as continuous psychotherapy for schizophrenic patients who will accept help only on such a basis (Karon and VandenBos 1972). Since this is not well known, when the economically poor patient chooses not to continue treatment, even an effective therapist may inappropriately feel ineffective, as well as rejected. If the patient reappears with a new crisis, or several repeated crises for intervention at irregular intervals, the therapist may inappropriately conclude this proves his interventions were certainly useless.

Nonetheless, just because the patients may request short-term treatment does not mean that they are inappropriate for long-term treatment or will necessarily reject it once the therapist has explained why he makes such a recommendation. Poor patients are often psychologically minded and are eager to talk once they know the therapist is interested and that there is something they can gain by talking.

AUTHORITY AND COMMUNICATION

Economically poor patients have special difficulty in dealing with psychotherapists. They are intimidated by them, just as they are by all doctors and indeed, all authority figures. This leads to and perpetuates a problem in communication, in addition to the general communication problems of schizophrenic patients. As we said before, this is so serious a difficulty that psychotherapy will fail if it is not dealt with directly. All therapists use a language with which poor patients are not familiar, in part because of their own socioeconomic class, education, and broader knowledge of the world, but even more because of their technical training. The patients may also use a language (of their ethnic, socioeconomic, and geographic group) with which we are not familiar. Any such language barrier not only prevents both parties from giving or understanding meaningful information; it may even prevent us from asking meaningful questions.

What makes this communication problem more important with the lower-class patient is that he is more intimidated by us. He feels that if he does not understand us, or we do not understand him, he is at fault. Unfortunately, most human beings try to hide their inadequacies. He feels inadequate and does not want to reveal this inadequacy by telling us we did not understand him or asking us what we meant.

The feeling that one should not ask if one does not know what is happening, or correct an authority's misunderstanding of one, is obviously a transference problem, as well as a reality problem.

It is well known that lower-class parents are more apt to stress unquestioning obedience than middle-class parents. Parents do get angry and act as if the child is defective. Unfortunately, most authority figures (e.g., teachers, police officers, employers, etc.) in later life act similarly, and this transference reaction is so convenient for the authority figures that it will be encouraged. It may be comfortable, unconsciously gratifying to us, and in some ways even useful, to be a frightening authority figure. But it is not only inappropriate, it is incompatible with psychotherapy, except when it is discussed as a resistance.

Poor people do have a realistic basis for distrusting authorities. Frequently, authorities do (and have previously in the patients' lives) act in the best interest of some system, institution, or person other than the patient while claiming to be acting in the patient's best interest. Authorities do use information furnished by the patient against his best interest. For example, parole and probation officers may use information inadvertently revealed to convict clients of parole violations. Social agencies may make information available to collection agencies. Social agencies, schools, and hospitals may use information given with a supposition of trust to deny the client privileges, services, and financial support.

Thus, poor patients in one big city psychiatric hospital believed that if they had been previously admitted to that or any other psychiatric hospital, or had an alcohol or drug problem, they would not be given careful consideration for first-rate treatment (which in this case meant psychotherapy). They were right. They characteristically lied about these matters; if they trusted the hospital and did not lie, they were obviously punished by not being given adequate treatment.

A way of dealing with the communication problem is to tell the patient simply and straightforwardly that sometimes we talk in ways that are "funny" and hard to understand and that, in addition, *we* have difficulty understanding people. We tell the patient he must help us by telling us when he does not understand, and we will try to tell him when we cannot understand him. We let him know that people frequently think they understand each other or are being understood, when they are not. Here in psychotherapy it is important to be sure that we know what each of us is talking about.

The therapist makes it clear that he expects and, in fact, desires questions, thereby making the contrast with the parents and other authority figures more apparent and facilitating the discussion of previous experiences in communicating with authority figures. Of course, the patient will still transfer and still believe such things as, "I would have been told if I was supposed to know," or that to ask for information implies a criticism of the therapist (which will be resented), or that his asking will be viewed (and condemned) as presumptuous. But a clear statement early in therapy (and repeated) provides an opening wedge for the therapeutic work.

Another issue that must be directly addressed is trust/mistrust of the therapist, particularly since other authorities may not have been trustworthy. We specifically tell patients they do not have to believe anything we say; in fact, there is no reason why they should. We invite them to do what they will do anyway, distrust us; but, we encourage them to check us out. We might say, "Nothing is true just because I say it. Check me out. I personally distrust anyone who says, 'Never doubt me.' If they are telling the truth, they can stand being doubted. And I can stand being doubted."

Understanding us involves more than just a problem of language; we do have a set of concepts which justify our therapeutic procedures. The patient needs to know what we are doing and why, if he is to be a working participant in the therapy. Lower-class patients generally have little idea what to expect and no idea at all why cooperating with psychotherapy should be helpful.

Why should talking be of help? What does the therapist have to offer other than advice? (Implicit in the patient's views are that if they are good people they should not need advice, and that their options are limited all too often to unquestioned acceptance or secretive rejection.) Even more fundamental is conveying to the patient the knowledge that his specific symptoms are such that psychotherapy might be of use to him. Indeed, even the fact that his problems might be symptoms that could be helped rather than simply facts of existence is important and even startling information.

Sometimes, of course, the symptoms are such that they might be psychogenic, but we cannot be sure even after appropriate diagnostic procedures. Then, as with any patient, one is direct and says that the symptom may or may not be psychogenic, but a trial period of therapy is the best way to find out.

As long as the patient believes that what he experiences is a fact of life, there is no hope and no motivation for change; hence, we explain psychologic functioning and the therapeutic process.

EDUCATIVE COMMENTS

This does not mean we give an extended lecture. What we explain and when are always governed by what we think is relevant. If it is assumed that we are practicing a psychoanalytic therapy, the patient should be educated about the unconscious, repression, resistance, transference, free association, dreams, and any procedures with which we expect the patient to cooperate. By means of a few sentences at a time, as they become relevant, we teach the patient what therapy and psychologic functioning are all about. We do this, as we do all therapy, using bits of the patient's thoughts or behavior, to convey our meaning as vividly as possible to aid them in understanding themselves concretely, and to demonstrate dramatically psychologic principles.

It may be helpful to share some of the specific comments we might make to patients. When it becomes relevant to some specific behavior, or ideation, we have said such things as:

"You know, we can't fight an enemy we can't see. If we see it, it may scare us; but, we can handle it, particularly since you don't have to handle it alone. You have me on your side."

"There's a part of the mind we know nothing about that nonetheless pushes us around and causes problems, and we don't know why. Down there are all the memories, conflicts, and feelings that were too scary, or guilt-provoking, or made us too angry, or that we couldn't handle. It's sort of like a sewer, and we put things there that stink too much that we can't or don't want to see or handle. We all do it. And that's OK, if it works. But when we do things we don't want to do and can't stop, it usually involves something from the unconscious, and we have to find out what."

"What's in the unconscious is there for a reason—you couldn't handle it any other way at the time. Now things may be different, but the unconscious doesn't know. What is unconscious doesn't change. When it is conscious, you can change it, if you want to."

"Everybody in treatment starts doing things to get in the way of learning more about themselves, even though they want to learn. Even consciously we may find ourselves not wanting to find out. But unconsciously we all don't want to find out. That's why we shoved it in the unconscious to begin with. But, if we deal with the difficulties of looking at ourselves, we will always be dealing with the right thing. What makes it difficult to talk about things here, makes it difficult to think about them when you're away from here."

"Sometimes you're going to be angry at me, and think I'm rotten, mean, and out to hurt you, and sometimes you're going to think I'm a lot better than I am. Whatever you feel about me is important to our work, and you will find talking about it will help you learn about your life. Let me assure you I can take it, and I will only use it to help you understand what is going on. You and I can talk about anything. It's an essential part of what's going on here."

There is nothing special about these words. What is special is that the therapist talks to the patient in a way that is both factually correct and is as likely as possible to be understood. What we are emphasizing is that one of our goals in the early sessions of psychotherapy is to teach the patient about the process of therapy. This education is not the only goal or even the most central goal. But patients, particularly poor patients, need to have a rationale for understanding themselves and treatment if they are to be motivated to stay in treatment and if they are to be "partners" in treatment rather than weak, submissive recipients of advice. It should be obvious by this time that we do not assume the patient will necessarily believe the first or even the tenth time we say anything, but a basis for examining the discrepancies has been laid.

DIFFERENTIATING REALITY AND PSYCHOLOGIC PROBLEMS

When an economically poor patient discusses a "reality" problem, it often happens that the therapist either responds to it as *solely* a reality problem or *solely* a psychologic problem. Neither is optimally helpful, because neither one is truly realistic! One of the tasks of a therapist is to deal with the intertwining of reality problems and psychologic problems, a clinical skill seldom discussed in graduate school or medical school.

Indeed, reality problems are often taken to be a counter-indication for psychotherapy. Yet when Freud was asked whether he would treat someone whose reality situation was so bad that neurosis might be considered the best solution, his judgment was that he would still analyze the patient, "It is better to go down in a fair fight with destiny than to be a neurotic." It is our experience in the psychotherapy of the poor that the patient does not go down.

The therapist must be, first of all, that dependable person who is reliable no matter what difficulties the patient encounters or arranges in life, and who expects and accepts anxiety, rage, and any other feelings. But the therapist is also someone whose gaze is firmly fixed on reality, insofar as it is known to him. In other words, the task of the therapist is not only to accept and talk about any feelings or thoughts whatsoever, but also to help the patient clearly evaluate actions in the light of reality, that is, the consequences of his own action. Of course, the therapist must also introduce the possibility of psychodynamic factors, but with the acceptance of the patient's realistic and unrealistic feelings and the acceptance of the reality factors in the patient's problems, whatever discrepancies exist between "reality" and the patient's reaction tend to become clear, and the transference (or other psychodynamic) basis of the discrepancies can then be dealt with in a context that makes sense to the patient. Such a stance, which is necessary with all poor patients, is absolutely essential with schizophrenic patients.

In any event, the therapist should review (and hence direct the patient's attention to) the events that have actually occurred. The importance of conveying to the patient the attitude of always starting with the relevant information that one's own experience provides, and encouraging gathering relevant information (i.e., asking questions about what will happen and why) cannot be overstressed. By "gathering relevant information" we mean focusing the patient's attention on his own behavior and that of others. This approach stands in contrast to discussing merely the patient's interpretations and abstractions without checking against whatever information or observations might be available.

Consider, for example, the poor patient who presents in psychotherapy his difficulties in dealing with the Welfare Department. What are the reality and psychodynamic aspects of the dilemma?

First, the therapist must appreciate the realistic anxiety and anger resulting from such extraordinary dependence on a bureaucratic agency. Often, what seems to the agency to be a minor delay may mean the difference between real suffering and its alleviation. In addition, the poor patient has little knowledge of the internal functioning of the agency: what needs to happen, why, how long it should take, and what is likely to go wrong in the process. The patient, simply because of his or her socioeconomic status, probably does not fully understand the functioning of the agency, or of agencies in general.

The patient's handling of the current reality situation may be complicated by the patient's reservoir of anger based on a lifetime of varied frustrations. The patient expects that anyone he depends on will frustrate him, and that expressing his frustrations or anger will only lead to more frustration. It feels safer to displace the conflicts of dependence, frustration, and anger onto the agency as opposed to being aware of the original conflict, about being a particular child in a particular family. The patient's parents typically became angry and rejecting if the parents' motives were inquired into.

The therapist should share specific knowledge of the agency with which the patient is having difficulty, so that the patient and therapist can begin to sort out the difference between the patient's view of the situation and its reality. If the therapist does not know the agency, he does at least know agencies in general and can convey a sense of what the process may be about and why it is progressing as it is.

Only by direction of the patient's attention to what he knows (and to a lesser extent, what the therapist knows) can you make the patient aware of the critical difference between the events and his interpretation of them. Of course, at first the patient will simply be aware that the discrepancy is between his interpretations of events and yours. Eventually, he will learn that your interpretations of events and casual sequences lead to more predictable and/or more satisfactory consequences. He may account for this discrepancy by attributing it to your being a better person, but with your continued focus on the descriptions of actual events, gathering and seriously considering relevant information, and considering the possibility of transference or other psychologic distortions, the patient will eventually learn that such a way of approaching and understanding events leads to more realistic con-

sequences. The therapist must help the patient learn what constitutes relevant or irrelevant information in any particular situation, and, of course, begin the central, difficult, but most helpful
process of sorting out the reality and transference elements in
current difficulties. (Indeed, one could readily argue that that is in
essence what psychotherapy is all about.)

Often the patient's experience, even with the added experience of the therapist, is not sufficient to permit an immediate
understanding and solution. The therapist must teach the attitude
of being able to tolerate not knowing. The patient needs to learn to
live with uncertainty rather than leaping to premature closure and
that, in most instances, further observation of one's experience
will eventually clarify what is going on.

There are many areas of living that the patient knows far
better than the therapist. It is not the therapist's task to teach the
patient everything he needs to know to live. Only a fool would
presume to tell the patient how to deal with situations remote from
the therapist's experience. The therapist helps the patient take his
own judgment seriously, act on it, and learn from his action,
especially his mistakes.

For example, when a poor patient says, "I fight too much,"
the middle-class therapist is apt to advise the patient to talk out
any personal difficulties and to apply that to all situations. But, in
some situations, it is appropriate to fight, and it is the proper role
of the therapist to help the patient use his own feelings, judgments,
and coping abilities and to consider whether a given situation
could be dealt with differently.

The therapeutic task in this example is to help the patient to
assess his unique situation. It may be that he is provoking fights
when they are not in his best interest or that he is always looking
for a challenge; then one would help him to explore the psychologic
reasons for this aspect of his behavior. But there are many times
when the fighting is important, and the task of therapy is to help
the patient to assess more accurately when he should fight and when
he might wish to consider alternative ways of handling the situation. The therapeutic task is to help the patient be aware of the
complex feelings that are involved, including fear, the role his
fighting plays in handling and/or provoking internal stress, and its
relationship to his past.

In general, even when a patient has an appropriate coping strategy, he may feel it is inappropriate. It is important for him to learn that it is his guilt, feelings of inadequacy, or anxiety which is inappropriate rather than his coping strategy or understanding in such cases. (Usually there is someone in the patient's current life whose inappropriate negative judgment the patient is accepting on a transference basis.) Of course, it is important to learn that inappropriate strategies are inappropriate; however, therapists sometimes act as if only the latter task is important and ignore the former.

To take a dramatic example, consider the patient who says someone is going to kill him. One first directs the patient's attention to relevant information: Who wants to kill him? Why? Has there been any threat? Does the dangerous person own a gun? Has the supposed murderer ever killed or seriously injured anyone?

In some instances, the fear is realistic. A male delinquent talks about an ex-friend he has beaten severely in a quarrel over a girl; the ex-friend has made threats, carries a gun, and has physically injured people in the past. The patient's strategy of avoiding that city is not phobic.

In other instances, the fear is not realistic. A gas station attendant has short-changed a patient 5 cents, and the patient is afraid to ask for the change. "He'll murder me. He nearly did anyway." The patient needs to know murder was not at hand and is highly improbable under the circumstances. But the projection of her rage and the transference of her parents (who had actually made murder attempts on each other and on her) must be dealt with, because this feeling of being in danger of being murdered by a stranger over trivia can be guaranteed to recur, unless it is dealt with therapeutically. The patient will agree to discuss it, because this fear has recurred and/or will recur inevitably. Moreover, the therapist is well advised to deal with it before it is reexperienced as the stranger called "therapist" who is the assassin.

In still other instances the fear is unrealistic, but is a disguised representation of a realistic fear, handled unrealistically. Take the case of the patient whose husband does not have a gun, has not made a threat, and has never been violent, but the patient "knows" that he is going to kill her. It seemed likely that the husband was thinking of leaving her ("getting rid of her") which he had not directly said. Upon investigation, this turned out to be the case. She was dealing with this reality issue of separation psychotically as "he's going to murder me." This not only expressed her transference fears, i.e., separation equals death, but also served to avoid the reality problem of a husband who's tired of the trouble and expense of a psychotic wife. At some level, it was intended to get the therapist to reassure her, "It's not going to happen," when in fact, the husband would leave unless this delusion was seen as reflecting a reality problem, and the avoided issue dealt with. (Adjunctive interviews with the husband did in this case suffice to deal with his anxieties, and led him to tolerate the temporary discomfort of his marriage while his wife received further help. If it had not, it would be important to help her cope with the separation.)

These communication problems, reality problems, and the need to differentiate reality factors and psychodynamic factors (and respond to both) are particularly pertinent for the so-called schizophrenic patient. Schizophrenic patients are likely to assume that their difficulties happen only to them, are specifically directed at them, and something they are doing has caused these difficulties. Such beliefs typically have been encouraged by the patient's family (Lidz 1973). The families of most schizophrenic patients have, throughout life, systematically discouraged the use of people outside the family as sources of information and help; that is, those extrafamilial relationships and identifications that most of us use to correct the impact of ineffective hurtful identifications, misinformation, and other harmful consequences of the emotional limitations of our families of origins. Therefore, giving accurate information, teaching the patient to direct his attention to relevant knowledge and information, and to possible transference become even more critical.

It should never be forgotten, however, that even psychotic patients know a lot about their reality. It is just as important to get a psychotic patient to take his own knowledge, perception, and judgment seriously as it is to help him unravel his distortions of reality. No one completely distorts reality. The patient's family frequently has imposed their distortions on him, so that he does not trust his own judgment even when it is demonstrably correct.

SOME SPECIAL PRACTICAL CONSIDERATIONS

Sometimes a poor patient has urgent practical needs that he or she is incapable of dealing with for realistic or symptomatic reasons, and which require immediate action, e.g., no food for a baby, critical medical needs, no place to sleep. It then may be necessary for the therapist or some other staff member to help directly with that urgent practical problem. Similarly, the therapist must act for the patient who asks for and needs protection from his own impulses: "Lock me up so I can't kill (or hurt) someone." Such a patient is using the therapist or the institution as an ego-extension to bolster his own absolutely necessary defenses.

The rule of thumb is: never do for a patient what they are capable of doing for themselves. But what they are capable of doing is always a clinical judgment. As we noted earlier, in many instances a person looks incapable because he or she lacks information about reality or the nature of feelings, and for the therapist simply to give information in a single therapeutic interview (as described above) makes it possible for the patient to handle the situation; however, if at the end of the interview the individual still seems genuinely incapable of action, *and* the consequence of inaction is likely to be irreversible (e.g., fatal), the therapist must act.

Sometimes it is not primarily the patient's emotional disorder which is preventing action, but the nature of the agency or personnel of the agency (e.g., welfare, parole, police, prosecutors, etc.) from whom the patient is seeking assistance; the agency may be more responsive to a call from the (higher status) therapist, but such help should be temporary. Direct practical intervention does not mean we stop talking to the patient. Emphasis should be placed, as far as possible, on teaching the patient what needs to be done, how such crises can be avoided, and discovering what in the patient prevents him or her from taking such actions.

A further practical step, which was occasionally taken in the Michigan State Psychotherapy Project (Karon and VandenBos 1972), was to provide money for transportation and/or baby-sitting expenses (e.g., $5/session). This permitted the patients to remain in psychotherapy on a regular basis without undue realistic hardship (and hardship never facilitates treatment). The cost of such reimbursements are minimal as compared to the cost of staff time. We would recommend this option to be available whenever the therapist feels it would be helpful.

Homicide

Most schizophrenic patients are not dangerous to anyone. In general, our schizophrenic patients have been less violent than our nonschizophrenic patients; however, our schizophrenic patients have a higher likelihood of making threats that they are going to kill or injure someone. There is an occasional patient who is potentially or actually murderous: the patient may or may not also be schizophrenic.

Realistically, nothing catches the attention of therapists more centrally than the possibility that the patient may murder someone. Obviously, the therapist's greatest concern is that he will be the victim. Most frequently, however, the danger of homicide is not a question of acting out in the therapy, but of violent and dangerous acts against people in the outside world.

A therapist should always treat a threat of murder seriously; that is, pay serious attention to the threat, evaluate the probability that the murder will or will not be carried out, and, of course, under what circumstances, and do that which therapeutically will make the murder improbable.

To assess or treat murderers or potential murderers appropriately, it is necessary to understand how murderers differ from nonmurderers. Unfortunately, most "clinical" views of the dynamics of murder are not based on actual therapeutic experience with people who have committed murder, and the speculations of people who have neither committed murder nor treated someone who has committed murder, are most likely to run in the wrong direction. Even professionals are too much influenced by detective stories. Detective stories are written by people who enjoy their murderous fantasies and are able to cast them into an artistic form that others are able to enjoy. Such people would probably be least likely to commit murder. The usual misconception is that the murderer is someone who is consciously angry, nurtures his anger in secret, plots a devious way of murdering someone, or is characteristically assaultive and violent, and carries out an impulsive murder. But all of this is misleading.

Through psychotherapy with a number of murderers, it became clear that they were always people who could not tolerate conscious anger. This is the most important thing to know about murderers. This characteristic of murderers is true whether or not the murderer is psychotic. The generality of this finding has been confirmed by more rigorous research (McKie 1971). It is an old psychotherapeutic axiom that what you are aware of you can control; what is unconscious controls you. Therapists seem loath to apply this fundamental principle to the area of murder, but it is successful.

This is not to say that anybody who cannot consciously feel angry is a murderer. There are many other kinds of more tolerable symptoms that can be developed as a result of repressed rage.

Every murderer, however, is someone who cannot tolerate conscious anger. When the anger does break through, it spills over into immediate impulsive lethal action. Alternatively, some murderers never experience the anger at all. They may coolly and deliberately kill people, never feeling any conscious anger. As one rather monstrous human being said, "I can't understand how anyone could be so immoral as to hate. I couldn't hate anyone. I could dislike you a little. If I disliked you enough, of course, I would kill you. But I could never be so immoral as to hate you." This man who gave sanctimonious sermons earned his living by mugging. While this occupation is not plied by people who are known for their tender loving sentiments toward other human beings, even his partners could not stand the extent of his brutality. In the mugging for which he was in jail, the victim had been beaten and kicked by this man until his skull was fractured in five places, and there were injuries of equal severity over his whole body. Yet the injuries were limited because the other muggers had stopped him. We would be more comfortable with a man who could hate us.

McKie (1971) gave TATs to institutionalized murderers, half of whom had a history of being psychotic and half of whom had no such history, and compared them with control groups of other jailed criminals who had not committed murder. He used the TAT to assess their dynamics and confirmed what we had seen in psychotherapy. The murderers could not tolerate conscious anger. Moreover, in general, they were not physically aggressive, but when they did get physically aggressive, it was of murderous intensity.

Thus, the typical murderer is less likely to hit you if you get him angry, but if he does assault you, he is more likely to use a knife or gun or some other weapon that will make that assault final. He also found that murderers could not tolerate unpleasant affect in general, and, there had been a violent model in one of the parents of the murderer. At least for this sample of jailed murderers, the murderous impulse and actions tended to be connected with sexual jealousy. This undoubtedly relates to the fact that these are jailed murderers, and jailed murderers tend to be caught on the basis of motive.

A striking finding was that murderers were more different from nonmurderers in their handling of aggression than psychotics were different from nonpsychotic individuals. This is an instance of a general phenomenon. Whenever we understand a specific human problem, such as murder, its dynamics tend to be similar whether the patient is schizophrenic or not.

Whenever homicidal impulses or fantasies seem to be surfacing, the worst thing the therapist can do is to avoid the issue. The second worst thing is to panic. Therapists sometimes voice the fear that they will put ideas in the patient's head and thereby encourage the patient to act out if they discuss dangerous behavior with the patient. Actually, it is just the opposite. The more dangerous the potential action might be to others (or to the patient), the more important it is to talk about it. If the therapist can talk about it, the patient may be able to talk about it. If it can be talked about, it can be thought about; what can be thought about can be controlled.

In most cases that come to attention, the patient has not yet committed murder, and the therapist has to make the judgment as to whether this is a serious possibility. In assessing the danger, the therapist uses (1) what is obtainable about the present situation and the patient's plans, (2) aspects of the past history of the patient that might be relevant, and, (3) the patient's response during the therapeutic hour, including any change that occurs from the beginning to the end.

Some of the questions that one wants to answer, in addition to why the patient consciously wants to kill the intended victim, are how does he plan on doing it, how lethal is that method, and is the intended weapon available. A patient who plans on buying an exotic poison will have many intermediate steps and therefore time to rethink; a patient who carries a loaded gun need have very little loss of control to be lethal. A house with a loaded gun is obviously a greater risk than a house where the gun and the ammunition are kept in separate rooms. Of course, we directly advise patients to get rid of their guns or to unload their guns or to not carry their knives, if their living circumstances are such that that makes sense. If someone is a member of a violent gang of delinquents, it does not make sense for him to disarm himself, and he would not follow such "crazy" advice. But middle-class patients generally have no rational need for such readily available violence.

The most important factor in the social history is, has the patient ever killed someone before, or seriously injured them, and under what circumstances. Beyond this is whether he's ever senselessly killed an animal; it is a more frightening predictor if the animal was his own pet. It has also been noted that fire-setting behavior in childhood is related to murderous potential.

The important thing to assess in the current situation is the amount and nature of contact with the potential victim and what it will take to provoke murder. Thus, if the potential victim is the spouse and they live together, the odds of contact are obviously high. If the event necessary to precipitate murder is the wife having an affair and everything you know suggests she is unlikely to do this, the potential for murder would ordinarily be low. If, however, you know that the wife has been having an affair, and she is likely to flaunt this out of hostility, the potential for the murder is obviously high. It is equally high, even if the wife is not having an affair, if the patient believes she is, either because of his own projection, or because the wife expresses her hostility by implying she is having an affair when she is not.

One of the simple effective interventions that a therapist can make when dealing with a potential murder, whether his patient is the potential murderer or potential victim, is to suggest disengagement. People who are unconsciously bound on a collision course as murderer and victim, rarely, if ever, think of the possibility of separation, either from a momentary encounter or from a long-term relationship. People who have slated themselves for a part in a tragic drama feel compelled to maintain that tragic drama to its end and are startled to find out that there is an alternative, and that the therapist will not think badly of them if they do disengage. They feel as if it is not possible to survive, or to survive with honor, if they disengage. It is, therefore, very useful for the patient to learn that one can walk away from a momentary encounter or move out overnight or permanently, as seems advisable. This advice cannot be overemphasized.

The therapist must be educative and supportive. He should get across his general value that very little, if anything, deserves capital punishment, but, in particular, the patient deserves a chance to think through his or her life, and therefore, to live better than he or she has lived to this point, with or without the other person. The consequences of murder are tragic for the patient as well as for the victim. We cannot stand by and permit the patient to destroy his or her life.

The issue of disengagement is even more central in dealing with a potential victim. Dynamically, in some cases, the unconscious arrangement is to ensnare the other person in an unbearable relationship which can be terminated only by murder. In other cases, this is not even the unconscious intention, but it is nonetheless the effect of the patient's pathologic dependency. For example, one patient argued (with VandenBos) that she could not or would not leave the home because that would give her husband a legal right to the entire $2,000 equity on the house, despite the fact that she feared for her life. Her husband had threatened her life, had loaded guns in several rooms, had lost his temper every day for a week, and each time he became increasingly violent. His last outburst included choking her and threatening her with one of the guns. Nonetheless, she was reluctant to leave. Luckily, she was not more obdurate than her therapist. When she tried to leave with the children, her husband threatened to kill her for taking the children from him. Since he had never been violent to the children or threatened them, she left without them. A week later, her lawyer was able to get a court order for her husband to leave the house, and relinquish the children, with which the husband complied peacefully.

The most central therapeutic task with a potential murderer consists of getting the patient to be aware of his anger and of his wish to kill and helping the patient to be comfortable with such feelings in consciousness, and also to become aware that he has control of his actions: if he allows himself to feel angry, even murderous, he does not have to carry these actions out. One can then introduce the fact that the consequences for him of acting murderously are self-destructive, but there are no consequences for simply feeling angry. Do not tell a patient it is all right to "get angry." For many patients this means "doing something," like attacking someone. The important word is "feeling"; it is all right to "feel angry," but not to act angry. In general, the first step is to deal with the anger and its legitimacy as a feeling, and the difference between thoughts and actions. This differentiation, which is central in treating all schizophrenic patients, is also central in treating all potentially murderous patients, schizophrenic or not.

The therapist must discover and give legitimacy to the angry feelings in the present, helping the patient to accept these feelings consciously and also explore the childhood origins which resonate with the present situation, as well as where in childhood the patient learned to block these feelings from awareness. Both the intense murderous rage and its repression owe their origin to the helplessness of a child in coping with its feelings toward the parent. It is not an accident that the two plays which have intrigued people in our society for the longest period are those about Oedipus and Orestes, who killed their father and mother, respectively.

By giving a transference meaning to the murderous impulses, the therapist and patient are in a position to examine both the current cause and the childhood antecedents. This helps the patient to predict when these impulses are going to arise again. A one-sided approach is not usually apt to be sufficient.

The above guiding principles serve to orient the therapy whether the patient is totally unconscious of his anger (which is the most lethal), is struggling precariously with rage that threatens to break through, or is overwhelmed with murderous impulses.

In giving a transference meaning to the acting-out, you do not necessarily imply that the current rage is inappropriate. The patient may well be in a situation which would enrage anyone. Almost everyone has been in situations in which he or she would have killed someone, if he or she had had a loaded gun in his pocket at that moment. Luckily, most of us do not carry guns.

The conscious or unconscious wish to kill someone is universal, and the conscious wish is harmless. We explain about anger, that anytime you are hurt, you will feel angry, and in the unconscious this is the wish to kill, because the unconscious is not very civilized.

Many outpatients, at some point in treatment, at least make a general statement about wishing to kill someone. Usually, there is no danger. Whenever a patient says something like that, one certainly explores the thought. This is more to assess what it may mean as communication to the therapist at that moment, than because of a concern with real danger. But some outpatients begin talking in a deeply veiled manner about an active plan that they have to kill someone. In this type of situation the therapist needs to make a more active intervention, so as to render the person less of a threat to the third party.

The outpatient who is struggling with the fear of loss of control over murderous rage frequently does not understand why he or she is so angry. If you can place this struggle with the current situation in the context of their whole life and of childhood experiences, it is often reassuring. It allows a patient to have a handle on what is happening so that he does not have to fear acting out the past in the present.

An example is a psychotic 28-year-old single mother with a 5-year-old son. In the first 6 months of therapy, she periodically talked about how enraged she was with her young child. Typically the therapist (VandenBos) responded by talking about the normal angers that all parents feel toward their children for demanding things. After several months, however, the patient began to describe thoughts about killing her child, which took the form of detailed plans for suffocating her child during the night. Over several sessions she discussed this in greater and greater detail. The patient became increasingly fearful that she would actually do this. Imbedded in one session was her thought that the child was purposely provoking her, trying to make her angry. This material led into her own childhood anger toward her mother. She could recall some times purposely trying to hurt her mother by hiding things the mother needed, when the mother was in a hurry to leave her. Her childhood fear was that her mother would find out and would kill her for doing this. Moreover, at the present time, her child was in fact playing her off against her mother, the child's grandmother. As is so frequent with women who are still struggling with their hostility toward their mothers, no psychologic separation had been achieved, and she still lived with her mother. The grandmother was "giving" to the child in a number of ways in which the grandmother had never given to the patient. This situation gave rise to tremendous rage in the patient. She was jealous of her own child for being able to get what she did not get in her own childhood and could not get even now in adult life. She was also murderously enraged at the grandmother for giving to the grandchild now, and this included the childhood rage toward her mother for not "giving" then. As we began talking of this material—both how it was activated in the present and as it was experienced in childhood—her concerns and fears about injuring her child disappeared. The anxiety and rage that was being generated and reactivated was discussed actively and handled consciously, and she did not fear acting it out.

It is our experience that a proper therapeutic approach does change a potential or actual murderer into a nonmurderer. Some of the murderers we have treated have, before therapy, been people about whom we have had very strong negative feelings. They had no qualms about what they had done. The therapist really felt that these patients were monsters, that they really did not deserve therapy, given that it is in short supply, but thought it was the only way to protect society. Interestingly enough, as they got better, they began to feel guilty about their crimes, and they became likable to the therapist.

It is extremely important to explore the specific actions or contemplated actions to discover their dynamics. While the general discussion above of the handling of anger is relevant, any particular murderous act bears the impress of the patient's personality and has specific meaning. Let us illustrate the homicidal danger handled in therapy.

A prisoner convicted of petty larceny had committed two successful murders and was likely to continue murdering other innocent people, if not treated. He had been referred to me (Karon) as an emergency state hospital transfer. Inasmuch as he was listed as being in psychotherapy with another therapist, who was not there that day, I felt that such a transfer should be made only by his therapist unless a genuine emergency existed. The inmate had made a disturbance in the reformatory school and had been sent to detention, where his behavior seemed to become more and more bizarre. I examined him in his "detention" (solitary confinement) cell. He was extremely disturbed and obviously hallucinating. A 2-hour therapy session sufficed to restore sufficient control so that he could be returned safely to the regualr reformatory "cottage." It was essential to produce this much control in the session, since the confinement in a detention cell reenacted a specific trauma in his childhood: he had been locked in his room by his father for minor disobediences until he had written "I must not talk back," or whatever his offense was, not the 500 or 1,000 times that school boys are accustomed to when given as punishment, but until he had filled 500 pages, both sides. He had once broken a leg by jumping out of a window when he was confined in this manner.

It turned out that he had seen his therapist only a few times, and the therapist had no desire to continue the treatment. This was understandable.

While the crime of which he had been convicted was theft, he had committed two murders, although these were not provable. He described them in detail during the therapy, and also during a psychiatric examination under sodium pentothal by his first "therapist." This psychiatrist had tried to turn him in for the murders, but he discovered that the only way the patient could be convicted would be if he confessed. This was something the patient was unwilling to do except in the privacy of a psychotherapy hour.

The patient also claimed that he liked to walk down the street at night; if the street were deserted, he would go up to a stranger and ask for a match. When the stranger put his hand in his pocket, the patient would knee him, and beat him, and then walk away. "He deserved it. I wouldn't give a match to a stranger on a deserted street late at night. Anybody that does that is asking for it."

The patient was brighter than most reformatory inmates, and initially made a good impression on people. Because of his intelligence, he had been given a desirable job at the reformatory, working in the library. He had to be taken off this job because he was suspected of having started a fire, which he then helped to put out. In the reformatory school he proved persistently disruptive. In fact, he was in trouble for some infraction of the institution rules several times a week.

As might well be guessed, he was a genius at making people hate him. For the next two sessions, I was benign and acceptant toward him, despite his provocations. In the middle of the next session (the fourth session), while he was talking, he leaned over and jabbed me in the knee with a nail he had secreted.

I yelled. I was angry. I told him I ought to "throw him the hell out of my office," and "not out of the door" (my office was on the third floor of the reformatory), that he must really be crazy to do this to me, since I was the only friend he had in the reformatory.

After I had exploded at him, I pointed out that he had jabbed me in order to get me to hate him, that he must have been afraid I would not hate him if he had to go so far. I pointed out further that he probably did this to other people all the time and asked him what was so frightening about not being hated. He said he did not know. I then told him that it was to prove that the rest of the world was worse than his parents, so that he could continue to believe that his parents were good as compared to the rest of the world. I added that actually his parents were bad.

This proved to be an entrée to his central problems. He began to recognize his feelings that his mother did not love him and that his father was cruel. As he improved, he was able to face his hostility toward his parents and the fact that they left much to be desired, not only as parents but as human beings.

The first time he had injured an innocent person he was walking down a street. He had passed a scaffolding on which a man was painting, and as he passed he knocked out one of the supports. He then casually continued down the street. The scaffolding crumbled, and the man fell and broke his leg. It was only in therapy that the patient began to recall, when asked, what had happened before this incident, which was that he had just been beaten by his father and left the house. He had committed this act of wanton cruelty while experiencing no feelings about either the beating or the scaffolding incident.

Each of his two murders involved killing a man older than himself whom he had never met before the time he killed him. The reason his murders were "successful" was that there was no reasonable motive to link him to his victim in either case.

As he began to understand his murders and cruelty as derivatives of his murderous impulses toward his father, he began to develop emotionally. He increasingly became guilty about what he had done to other people. His relationships with other inmates improved. The changes in the patient were obvious to the institutional personnel. After approximately 6 months of psychotherapy, he was recommended for parole with continuing psychotherapy as a mandatory condition of parole.

While he did return to the reformatory at a later time for another theft, as far as could be determined he has not committed another murder.

If a patient seems murderous or close to murder at the beginning of the session, and as a result of dealing with the anger, with the antecedents of the murderous impulse, and the dynamics of the fantasy, there is a change in the patient so that the patient now seems in control and has alternatives other than murder available, one can feel comfortable about the situation. If the patient does not seem to be modified by the therapeutic hour, and if the therapist is not sure in his own mind whether the patient can be trusted until the next therapeutic hour, we have found an assessment by means of the TAT most useful. It is nice to be able to sleep at night.

Since the Thematic Apperception Test (TAT) indicators that predict homicidal danger are not well known, let us share our clinical experience. First, one looks for stories in which the hero commits murder. This does not mean stories in which the hero thinks of committing murder; such stories predict murderous thoughts. One must take Tomkins's (1947) concepts of level and distantiation seriously. Thoughts predict thoughts, and actions predict actions. The most dangerous story is one in which the central character or "hero," who is the same age and sex as the patient and under similar circumstances, actually commits a murder. Heroes who are different from your patient in age, sex, conditions, or time (year or century) when the action occurs, are less dangerous. Any even semi-murderous story is to be used clinically, of course, to help you specify the nature of the murderous impulses and the probability and circumstances under which the patient would become dangerous.

The other kind of dangerous TAT is one in which no anger occurs in any stories. This type of TAT will probably include lengthy discussions on duty, obligation, and "doing the right thing." While people may be injured by one party or another, the injury will frequently be described and discussed in terms of "punishment" and appropriate retribution for people misbehaving or not doing their duty. Another dangerous indication in the "no anger" TAT protocol would be violent accidents and other inexplicable events that harm people in the stories.

Recently the issue of the therapist's legal responsibility to the potential vicitm has been raised. A therapist whose patient threatened to kill someone notified the police and his supervisor of the threat, but not the potential victim. The patient quit therapy and later committed murder. The Court in California has held that the therapist was responsible to have notified the potential victim. This court decision concerns psychotherapists. Max Siegel (1976) has enunciated the more traditional position of psychotherapists that their relationship to the patient requires absolute confidentiality. He cites cases early in his experience in which there was an attempt to notify the authorities or the victim or both and the tragedy was not prevented. In other cases where confidentiality was maintained, the therapist was able to end the risk of murder.

The ethical issue is simple. You must do all that you can do to prevent the tragedy. The question of what you can do best to prevent the tragedy is a matter of judgment, depending on your skill and the situation. The optimal solution is to do what Siegel recommends, namely to use your skill as a therapist to change the patient in such a way that he is not a homicidal danger. Siegel, from his own experience, clearly has cases where that was possible and can cite cases where the attempt to do anything else only broke up the therapy and prevented the therapist from having any influence in preventing the murder.

We agree with Siegel that this is the optimal procedure wherever possible. For the therapist who is unsure of his therapeutic ability or whose patient seems bent on committing the murder despite the therapist's best efforts, there is one alternative that Siegel did not discuss. There is the alternative of hospitalizing the patient. After all, a legitimate reason for hospitalizing a patient is to prevent him from injuring someone else. One would, of course, explain this to the patient. This is done in terms of the irreversible impact on the patient's life and that it cannot be allowed, and that the hosptialization will give him time to think and talk about it in therapy.

Some patients will themselves use the hospital as a means of temporary self-control by asking, "Hospitalize me, I'm going to hurt somebody." We have known tragedies that were avoided when such a plea was heeded, and other tragedies that were not avoided because the plea was ignored.

Suicide

Nearly every psychotic or borderline psychotic patient, in the course of treatment, considers suicide as a solution. The most effective way to deal with this problem, that is, to prevent the suicide, is to treat the problem psychotherapeutically.

One is tempted to use organic therapies when suicidal danger is suspected, but, while electroconvulsive therapy (ECT) may end the immediate suicidal threat, its use disrupts psychotherapy and retards the patient's progress in later attempts at psychotherapy. Research (Avery and Winokur 1976) indicates that ECT may defer but not prevent suicide. Well-known patients whose suicidal impulses were "cured" by ECT are Ernest Hemingway and Sylvia Plath. Farberow, Shneidman, and Leonard's data (1961) on suicide among schizophrenic patients indicate that suicide often occurs after a symptomatic improvement by organic treatment and discharge from the hospital; indeed, the fear of a new course of ECT was a major precipitant of suicide.

Similarly, tranquilizers (or "antipsychotic" medication) may "take the edge off" the patient's problems, but, if they do, they will also, "take the edge off" the therapy sessions. Of course, everyone is now aware that tranquilizers are the most popular means of suicide in America.

Suicide may best be understood as an aggressive retaliatory act toward significant figures in the patient's present life or toward fantasies of significant figures in his past. The primary motivating fantasy includes the wish to hurt someone else and the belief that suicide will accomplish this end. The patient has an image of how sorry or guilty people will be if he dies. This fantasy is expressed in popular folklore as, "I'll eat some worms, and then I'll die, and then they'll be sorry." Anything which is conscious in every child must be in the unconscious of every adult.

Suicidal patients, much more frequently than others, have had a parent or close relative die or commit suicide when the patients were children (Moss and Hamilton 1956; Walton 1958). They have witnessed the distress, shame, and guilt among those left behind. This memory supports the fantasy that killing oneself is an effective way to hurt someone else. The essential other-related character of suicide is also consistent with the fact that most patients who do, in fact, kill themselves have repeatedly communicated this intention to those close to them during the months before suicide. It is also true that, while these plans were generally unheeded, the people to whom the patient had communicated his intention did feel guilty, ashamed, or disturbed after the death (Robins et al. 1959).

Similar to the present position is Alfred Adler (1914), and Kurt Adler's (1961) insightful and sensitive description of the dynamics of suicide in relation to the treatment of depression:

> A threat of suicide will usually terrorize his environment into compliance with his wishes. If this, too, fails, he may in his rage and in revenge go so far as to attempt or commit suicide. He expects the particular person involved to be shattered by this act, and suffer guilt for not having acceded to his wishes. In addition, he indulges in a romantic delusion, a beau geste, designed to point up the worthlessness of others, and to absolve himself of all criticism: *De mortuis nil, nisi bene.* He will no longer have to carry on the Sisyphus work of covering up his own responsibility for his failures, which he feels is in danger of being exposed, and of upholding his illusory superiority ideal in the service of his vanity.

A wide variety of other fantasies connected with suicide have been described in the literature—rebirth, introverted anger, reunion with a loved one, return to the womb, etc. (Bergler 1946; Friedlander 1940; Hendrick 1940; Jones 1951; Schmideberg 1948), but while important, they seem to be secondary. Only when these fantasies exist in conjunction with a fantasy of suicide as aggressive retaliation do they lead to an actual attempt at suicide.

The only alternative clinical formulation (Jensen and Petty 1958) which seems also tenable is the rescue fantasy—that is, that the victim arranges to be rescued and only dies when the rescuer fails in his mission. The victim projects his or her superego onto the rescuer, implicitly saying, "Do I deserve to live?" However, this is always a hostile projection, and implicit also is the statement, "If I die, you are my murderer."

If the patient makes you his superego, if he asks you implicitly or explicitly does he deserve to live or die, you should make it clear that you would decide for life.

The affect of hopelessness is frequently present, but it is not in itself a necessary or sufficient condition for suicide; however, its obverse—a strong hope of attaining an important goal through living—seems to preclude suicide.

The view that suicide is intended as an aggressive retaliation logically implies that the way to deal with suicidal patients is to attempt directly and dramaticaly to contradict or undercut this fantasy. In graphic and affect-laden terms, the therapist can describe how happy people will be, especially those closest to the patient, if the patient commits suicide. At worst, they will be unhappy for a relatively short time. The therapist should even indicate how untroubled the therapist will be if the patient kills himself.

Of course, this does not mean that the therapist should be cold and rejecting toward the patient while *alive*; the therapist indicates by his manner that he is interested in the patient, but that he is not interested in or troubled by dead patients. The senior author used to say that he, too, would be happy if the patient killed himself; this was obviously untrue and the patients did not believe it. We now simply state that we are interested only in live patients, have no interest in dead patients, and would merely get another patient. This is true. Moreover, if the patient has any sibling rivalry at all, the image of someone else in *his* therapy hour is not a pleasant prospect for him.

It may seem peculiar to make statements to the patient about how happy the survivors will be, when, in fact, suicide usually does produce suffering in the survivors. But the anguish of the survivors is never of the heroic proportions that occur in the patient's fantasies. Then, too, the individual whom the patient is most intent on hurting is often least affected by the death. The patient is angry because at some level he perceives the other as malevolent, but suicide does not effectively hurt anyone who is genuinely malevolent. The somewhat exaggerated words of the therapist are given credence by the realistic paradox that the more justified the anger, the less effective will suicide be as retaliation.

The effective principle seems to be the conjoint pressure, on the one hand, of the denial of the effectiveness of suicide as retaliation, and, on the other hand, of the arousal of hope by a warm, interested therapist who is willing to come to grips with any of the patient's problems, but who is available to the patient only if he is alive.

The therapist should communicate that the problem is solvable. After all, what do people commit suicide over? The loss of money, loss of a job, the loss of a lover, the loss of a spouse—we know that these are replaceable. People can live in poverty; people can find other jobs. While, to the patient, it seems as if there never will be another person to replace a lost lover or spouse, we know better, if the person stays alive; half the world is of the opposite sex.

We cannot, and must not, falsely say that we can solve this problem today, or that we have any magic, but that, in principle, this is a solvable problem in the long run, and we will talk until we do. That you can reasonably offer the patient, and it is a great deal.

In the following accounts of two suicidal patients, the denial of the effectiveness of suicide as aggression is obvious. Less obvious but equally important was the therapists's warmth, interest, and willingness to deal with anything, that is, his capacity for arousing hope. This capacity is more a matter of the therapist's manner of relating and of the atmosphere of the session than of specific words. A cold, rejecting therapist, who is unwilling to face, or incapable of facing, the intensity of the patient's suffering, would not deter suicide, no matter what technique he used.

A male borderline schizophrenic reformatory inmate, age 17, was referred because he had attempted suicide in the county jail shortly before being transferred to the reformatory. He had broken a light bulb, and used a piece of the glass to tear at his arm. Luckily, he was noticed immediately and overpowered, alive but with deep gashes running the length of his forearm. During a previous arrest and incarceration he had attempted suicide twice. Once he had been overpowered while using a piece of glass, and the other time he had jumped out of a fourth story window, but succeeded only in breaking a leg.

The results of projective tests agreed with his own statements: "I won't kill myself if I know what I'm doing, but when I get into one of those states, I don't know what I'll do." The projective tests indicated that he would not consciously set out to kill himself unless he had a psychotic "break," in which case he would again try to take his own life. The occurrence of such a "break," according to the tests, seemed certain under the rigors of incarceration.

He was immediately started in psychotherapy on a daily basis. We discussed the subject of suicide in direct and dramatic terms. "You know what your parents are going to say? They're going to laugh! That crazy bastard! At last he's killed himself. Hurray, let's go out and celebrate! Frankly, I'll probably go out and throw a beer party myself." The patient resented these statements, but also said wryly that he'd like to go to the beer party himself.

The fourth session centered mainly on his ambivalent feelings for his mother. Afterward, he became unruly in his "cottage" and was sent as punishment to "detention" (an isolation cell). The therapist (Karon) saw him the next day in the detention cell. The inmate was clad in his pajamas. Apparently there was nothing in the bare cell which could conceivably be used as a weapon.

As soon as the guards left, the patient said, "I'm sorry."

"For what?"

"I've let you down."

"What do you mean?"

"Look. After all your work, and I did this."

He took his hand from the right side of his neck and there were superficial cuts. He had concealed these from the guards. (An unsuccessful suicide attempt, in the ordinary course of events, would have meant additional days in detention and additional time added to his sentence.) He showed a piece of broken light bulb which he had managed to bring with him when he was sent to detention and which he had hidden on the sill on the top of the door frame.

"I didn't feel anything. I just watched myself pick it up and cut a little bit and then cut again and again. I'm sorry I let you down."

"But you didn't. I'm proud of you. You stopped yourself. Always before you had to be stopped by someone else. But this time you stopped yourself. I'm proud of you." No further suicidal attempts occurred during this patient's treatment.

In another case, a female outpatient, age 32, denied any suicidal ideas at the beginning of psychotherapy despite projective tests indicating a strong impulse to suicide which was not entirely ego-syntonic. Six weeks later when faced with an apparent break-up of her marriage, she telephoned the therapist (Karon) saying she was about to kill herself. This was immediately interpreted as retaliation: "There's only one reason anyone kills herself. It's to get even with someone else. But it won't really hurt your husband. It'll just solve his problems for him. No indecision, and it will save him the price of a divorce. As for your parents, they will be glad to get rid of you. And I'll just get another patient."

The patient became angry and insisted, "I am not trying to get even with anyone. I just feel hopeless. That's the stupidest inter-pretation I ever heard of. It has nothing to do with me."

Nonetheless, she did not kill herself. Further, she complained in her later therapy sessions, "It wasn't true. It has nothing to do with me. But now I can't kill myself. I used to think that if things got too bad I could always kill myself. But now you've taken it away from me. You've made it impossible." Projective tests ad-ministered 4 months later showed that her suicidal impulses at that time were minimal.

Sometimes the patient is ambiguous, and it is not clear to the therapist whether or not a suicidal danger exists. The therapist should never be afraid to raise the issue and to ask directly, "Are you thinking about killing yourself?" As with homicide, the in-timidated therapist is afraid he will "put ideas in the patient's head." In no case is this possible, unless the therapist is involved in an elaborate acting out with the patient. A direct question relieves anxiety. It is always the therapist's role to be on the side of clarity in the fuzzy world of the schizophrenic patient. The patient feels the world is too dangerous to see clearly. The therapist knows that the more clearly you see the world, the less dangerous it becomes.

Male suicide attempts are more likely to be lethal than female, and women are more likely to threaten suicide and not attempt it than are men. Individuals under 40 are more likely to threaten or make unsuccessful attempts, while individuals over 40 are more likely to die of suicide. Thus, the most dangerous suicide threat is made by a male patient over 40, and, in general, the individual to be least concerned about is the adolescent female.

If the patient says that he is going to kill himself, this should always be taken seriously. The patient who says this quietly and unemotionally is probably more dangerous than the one who is terrified of it, because the patient who has made peace with his suicide will report it unemotionally.

Of course in making the assessment of suicide potential, there are reality factors to be considered. One needs to ask: Does the patient have the means at hand? How lethal are the means that he or she envisions using? An overdose of aspirin allows much more leeway to change one's mind or be rescued than a bullet or an overdose of lithium carbonate. If the patient has these means at hand but is unsure he wants to kill himself, you suggest disposing of the danger by getting rid of the guns, flushing the pills down the toilet, or even switching to an electric razor. One wishes to make suicide inconvenient in order to protect the patient against a momentary impulsive act. Obviously, a patient who enlists you in protecting him against his impulses by giving you the suicide weapon should always get the reassurance he seeks. You will, of course, never give back a suicide weapon, anymore than you would give him back the means of a contemplated homicide. No gun is that valuable, and returning it would mean collusion in his death. That is the only meaning with which a therapist can be concerned.

George Atwood (1972), in a brilliant paper on suicide in psychotic depression, points out that the psychotic depressive patient who improves and then kills himself is not merely killing himself because he now has enough energy. Rather, such a patient has made a decision to kill himself; this decision seems a solution to his problems, leading to an improvement in his depressive symptoms. One can, he points out, differentially diagnose true improvement in psychotic depression from improvement on the basis of a commitment to kill oneself by the following three criteria: (1) The patient who is truly improving will have increased insight into his depression, whereas the patient who is about to kill himself will improve with no increase in insight. (2) The patient who is improving will talk more about the future as he improves, whereas the patient who is about to kill himself will not discuss the future because he doesn't have any. (3) The patient who is improving will become increasingly willing to discuss suicide, whereas the patient who has made a decision to carry it out will not be willing to discuss it. If all three of these indications are running in the same direction, the differential diagnosis is clear.

There are fail-safe techniques which are available to the therapist when dealing with acutely suicidal patients. It is, of course, legitimate to hospitalize a patient to keep him alive. Unfortunately, hospitals are not as safe as we would like. We have seen patients who were hospitalized on a locked ward specifically for suicidal danger and who found ways to escape, and committed suicide by throwing themselves onto the freeway in front of the hospital. This is not necessarily the fault of the hospital staff. Seriously suicidal patients can show great ingenuity; even patients in solitary confinement cells with no clothing and no furniture have found ways of concealing the means of their suicide. Nonetheless, a well-run hospital does have advantages in preventing suicide.

Similarly it is frequently possible simply to arrange for relatives or friends to "baby-sit" with the patient until the period of acute danger is over. The patient may feel reassured that he is not being left alone to cope with his impulses, and gratified that someone cares enough about him to take the trouble to stay with him. This provides more psychological protection than the friend or relative can actually provide physically.

For some patients, the availability of medication as a fail-safe that they themselves can employ is sometimes useful; however, medication is dangerous as a fail-safe, since it is also a convenient and attractive means of suicide. Moreover, it is unfortunately apt psychodynamically as a way of acting out the transference hostility, that is, dying by means of the therapist's "help."

When the patient is in acute danger, we offer our home phone number. This is perhaps the most important fail-safe. The fact that the therapist can really be reached when it is necessary, while it has led to some unnecessary phone calls, has also prevented suicide, in our experience. Our patients are instructed that if they do not get us, they should call back an hour later and to keep doing this until they do get us (as detailed in Chapter 6).

When in the course of therapy, we become aware of a potential for suicide, we deal with this therapeutically in that hour, not only assessing the immediate danger, but also interpreting as described above, and evaluating the impact of that hour at reducing the danger. If at the end of the therapeutic hour it is not clear whether a patient, schizophrenic or not, is suicidal, we continue with diagnostic procedures. The most useful diagnostic procedure for suicide, when the clinical picture is ambiguous, in our experience is the TAT.

While this is not widely known, it is clinically true that the TAT predicts suicide very well. The problem with many attempts (such as Bellak 1954) to use the TAT unsuccessfully is that "suicidal stories" are used to score many different kinds of stories which do not predict suicide. Broad-spectrum "suicide" scoring categories, which include stories about people who fantasize about suicide, dream about suicide, think about suicide, commit suicide on the plantet Zeron, or go from lightness to darkness (which according to some clinicians' intuitive judgment is a "symbol for suicide") will get you nowhere. Do not use any simple scoring technique, that is, a small set of broad-range categories that throws away most of the information. The way to use the TAT effectively is to use it clinically; that is, consider many different facets and their implications, or to use a specific functional scoring category designed for a clear theoretical concept (such as "pathogenesis," Meyer and Karon 1967), when one wants an accurate measure of just one concept.

What one looks for in the TAT in assessing suicidal danger are stories about heroes who commit suicide. Again, heroes of the same age and sex as the patient and under similar circumstances to the patient are the most lethal. As in our discussion of homicide, the more "distance," as described by Tomkins (1947), there is in the story the less dangerous the impulse, that is, distance in time, space, circumstances, age of the characters, or sex of the characters. Symbolic suicides do not predict suicide. It is analogous to symbolic sex, which tends to be found in the TATs of people with strong unsatisfied sexual drives. That which is ego-syntonic and acted upon does not get symbolized. The suicidal impulse which is not ego-syntonic is not dangerous. The dangerous patient is the patient who has made peace with his death. Let us repeat the important point. The dangerous story is a story in which a character of the same age and sex and under similar circumstances actually commits suicide. Stories about fantasies of suicide predict fantasies of suicide. Stories about thoughts about suicide predict thoughts about suicide.

A 20-card set is best. But if one has very limited time, a recommended subset would be Cards 1, 3BM, 6, 7, 10, 12M, 14, and 16. It is important that the most obviously suicidal card, card 14, be included, but not be the first card administered. The choice of these particular cards depends on the following usual meanings to the stories given: Card 1—Childhood as it really was; Card 3-BM—The most pressing present problem (works well with either sex); Cards 6 and 7—The patient's relation to his mother and father; Card 10—How the patient handles tenderness; Card 12M—What kind of transference the patient has; Card 14—The most obviously suicidal; and Card 16—Being blank is the most completely projective. Card 14 was designed to get at the speculative inner life of the individual, but if one is suicidal it seems obviously a man about to jump out the window; the patient does not feel self-conscious because it seems that the therapist has given him an unambiguous stimulus. With such a small set, one usually can make very accurate predictions. Of course, one can always get a fuller and more detailed picture of the human being from the TAT if one has time to give the full set. One advantage of the TAT is that it not only tells you about the present danger, but also gives you information about the circumstances under which this patient will and will not be dangerous.

The more disparate the stimulus value of the card is from suicide, the more dangerous an indication is a suicidal story. Suicidal stories early in a 20-card TAT are more dangerous, since earlier stories are usually a better predictor of overt behavior.

We would conclude our discussion of suicide with our finding that the best suicide prevention is effective psychotherapy.

Patients Who Will Not Eat

The psychotic patient who will not eat raises problems, including clinical, legal, and medical ones. If the noneating lasts long, it can be a threat to life. Understandably, heroic measures such as intravenous feeding and forced feeding have been used, but such procedures are somewhat traumatic for the patient. A slightly less traumatic medical intervention is to inject the patient with sodium pentothal or amytal; this frequently makes the patient temporarily cooperative; that is, long enough to eat one meal, but it seems to have no real long-term effect.

It is more effective, in the short and the long run, to deal with the eating problem psychotherapeutically. In our experience, the psychotherapeutic intervention is most apt to be effective if one takes the simple practical step of scheduling daily therapy sessions at mealtime (having one's own meal during the therapy session, and having both your meal and the patient's served together and be identical, or, if in a cafeteria, chosen from an identical set of alternatives).

Food, food preparation, and eating are vehicles of communication in any family, particularly in childhood, but in some families they replace other modes to a surprising extent. Food can have the significance of love, nurturance, and warmth, but these meanings in themselves do not usually cause people problems. As therapists working with noneating patients, we are more concerned with meanings of hatred, resentment, fear, and control which are communicated around and via food. Talking with the patient about food, meals, who prepares them (or used to), and what mealtime was like, in the context of a meal, is extremely effective.

Obviously, the memories and experiences with respect to food will vary from patient to patient. But it can be surmised that it was not likely that the symptom of not eating reflects much experience of food as a good thing, eating as one of the pleasures in life, and/or meals as social situations of shared enjoyment. On the other hand, most people who choose to be psychotherapists do have such positive views about eating. The identification with a therapist who obviously enjoys food, whether or not the patient does, has a corrective effect.

Any interpretation concerning eating or eating difficulties is more effective in an eating situation. Moreover, the patient typically feels envious of the gratification so readily and yet so distantly available.

The fear of being poisoned, which many noneating patients have, is related inevitably to feelings of anger and resentment by the mother which accompanied meals or feeding in childhood. If the patient is afraid of being poisoned, it is obvious that you are not if you eat the same food the patient would, and if you eat your meals with them. They may watch you strangely as you eat or be surprised when you return again the next day to "do it again." Sometimes fantasies of cannibalism or fellatio, or defenses against such fantasies are involved. Regardless of the specific emotional issue surrounding eating, this procedure of eating your meals with the patient can facilitate discussion and initial exploration of a conflict area that will quickly enable the patient to let himself eat.

For example, a continuously hallucinating, "hopeless" schizophrenic patient was neither sleeping nor eating. The staff of the hospital, which had classified him "hopeless," insisted on ECT, which in his case would have been even more of a tragedy than usual; the man was, in fact, a brilliant intellectual, as his career subsequent to psychotherapy amply demonstrated. On my (Karon) advice, he was removed from the hospital, and psychotherapy initiated. He was treated as an outpatient, with family and friends taking turns staying with him continuously during the early months of treatment.

Obviously, the practical problem of feeding him had to be attended to first. After his first session, the psychotherapy sessions were scheduled early in the morning (7 A.M.), before the rest of the workday, at a local all-night restaurant. The therapist ate his breakfast during the session. At first the patient objected: "They'll think I'm crazy."

"No, they'll think you're drunk."

Then he objected again, "I'll throw up!"

"Do you think you're the first drunk who has thrown up here tonight?"

The therapist discussed food, the fear of poisoning, and its possible origins while eating. The patient reported nausea at watching the therapist eat. By the third restaurant session, the patient took some coffee for himself. Then coffee and toast at the next session. Finally, he ate breakfast, but he objected: "I'm paying for therapy, and all I do is watch you eat. I've got a right to be listened to." At that point, we returned to the office for more traditional treatment.

The patient had been concerned with being poisoned; while he had what he termed an "ideal" mother, she had resented taking care of him. He had had severe food allergies as a child, which served as a basis for her insisting on foods he found unpleasant. She consistently taught him that food was dangerous, particularly new food, or food away from the house (an attitude she still maintains, although he has never reported severe symptoms to any food not prepared by his mother). Nonetheless, in his prepsychotic period he had never had a meal without some nausea. Needless to say, no meal had ever been a great pleasure.

Subsequent to analytic psychotherapy, not only was treatment successful in all the more important parts of life, but he became a gourmet and a wine connoisseur. Indeed, after a trip to France, he said with tears in his eyes, "There is no way for me to describe what French cooking can really be like."

Even in less seriously disturbed patients, such dynamics readily appeared. For example, one jail inmate had refused to eat for 5 days after having been locked up. During therapy sessions with him, over lunch, it was revealed that his mother would frequently refuse to prepare meals for the family because of the "misdeeds" of the children (such as their watching a TV show other than the one she wanted to see, although she never stated in advance what she wanted to watch). His father occasionally would refuse to eat meals prepared by his wife, and would storm out of the house over such things as his wife giving the first plate of food to one of the children (even though the father came to the table late). The children had long learned to express disappointment over school and anger at family members by skipping meals. This way of expressing anger was tolerated for a short time, but if continued long enough brought attention from the mother.

The patient had been arrested under unusual circumstances. He had expressed anger verbally at his mother, she had convinced him that this meant he needed psychiatric treatment, and he went willingly with her to a hospital and was admitted. (He really did need treatment, but not for the reasons his mother told him. He began psychotherapy, and the therapist was helping him to accept and understand his anger.) He was wanted for serious violent crimes, however, and the police found out that he was in the hospital. Since he was "not insane," he was arrested in the hospital and taken to jail.

He was angry at his mother for getting him to go into the hospital for expressing anger, and he was angry at the police for taking him away from treatment which was helping him. His refusal to eat did make both his mother and the police anxious. Therapeutic intervention solved not only their problem, but aided the patient too. A starving man is in no position to look out for his own best interest. Moreover, it helped to demonstrate to the patient how therapy worked, how apparently unconnected things were connected, and helped to channel the patient's anger and energy into less self-defeating behavior.

Although we have not worked with anoretic neurotic patients, such a procedure may also be helpful with them.

Eating in front of the patient is not a substitute for psychotherapy, but psychotherapy carried out over a meal is the best and fastest way to deal with the conflicts around eating for a noneating patient. We have found such a procedure effective even with catatonic patients who will not eat.

Patients Who Cannot Sleep

Patients who cannot sleep are frequent among schizophrenic patients, as well as among patients with milder disorders. While it is true that the absence of sleep for sufficiently long periods can generate psychotic-like thinking even in normal individuals, the absence of sleep is not the cause of psychosis and is not the patient's most central or urgent problem. Moreover, one does not die in any discernible period of time from not sleeping. Nonetheless, patients who cannot sleep usually try to panic the therapist into some kind of hasty action, or they use their sleep disturbance as a reason for not discussing other problems. This clinical issue is not one about which the therapist should panic.

Traditionally, therapists with a medical orientation have felt that it was only kind to give the patient with a sleep disturbance a sleeping pill. Sometimes tranquilizers are used for the same purpose. Indeed, it may be an act of kindness toward the ward staff or the family to provide such temporary assistance. Some patients do feel better after a night's sleep, but this is true most often in manic or depressed patients rather than schizophrenic patients. Among the problems with narcoleptics (sleep-inducing medication) are: (1) physiologic or psychologic addiction, (2) interference with psychotherapy, and (3) habituation—the effective period of use is less than 2 weeks (Institute of Medicine 1979). The most serious problem, however, with the use of barbituates or tranquilizers to induce sleep is that the therapist has handed the patient a readily available means of suicide which can be used impulsively by the nonhospitalized patient. Moreover, the common sleeping pills interact with alcohol so as to potentiate each other, creating the potential for real or psychologically motivated accidents, some of which will be lethal. Suicide by means provided by the therapist is particularly appealing to the patient's transference fantasies of aggressive retaliation.

Despite a great deal of later research on sleep, the conclusions arrived at clinically by Alfred Adler (1914, 1919) are still in essence valid for the range of sleep disturbances, including those in schizophrenia. First, human beings do not really need sleep. What they need is rest. Sleep has evolved as a mechanism for ensuring that animals rest. One does not do very much work when one is unconscious. If one can lie reasonably quiet for 8 hours, this is as efficient as 5 hours of deep sound sleep. After 5 hours of sound sleep, one can function adequately the next day.

According to Adler, the purpose of most sleep disturbances is unconsciously to prepare an alibi in advance. "How do you expect me to do well when I did not even get a decent night's sleep?" is the implicit meaning. The beauty of this as a neurotic symptom lies in the fact that if the patient does well, he can reassure himself, "Think how well I would have done if I'd got a good night's sleep." Unfortunately, like all neurotic symptoms, the patient pays a price for his infallibility—the probability of actual failure is greater. Also, the conscious suffering caused by the symptoms may be considerable.

This describes the sleep problems of schizophrenic patients in therapy after the initial psychotic period. During the initial florid psychosis, success in life is not a possibility. The patient insists that not being able to sleep is the problem. As with the neurotic, it provides an unconscious alibi for not being able to cope with either the real world or one's internal experiences.

Adler suggested that one could explain to people that they did not need to sleep, that one could interpret the unconscious alibi formation if that did not work, and he even suggested one practical tip: if you really need to induce sleep quickly, suggest that the patient pay careful attention to the thoughts he has when he is unable to sleep, and ask him to tell you about them, because they will be very valuable for the therapy. If anything will induce immediate sleep, it is this instruction.

It is our experience that you can always suggest to patients, including schizophrenic patients concerned about not sleeping, that this is something with which you can help them. This is often a way of building a working alliance with a schizophrenic patient. We find that it is best not to offer further explanation unless the patient comes back to the subject. To spend the hour talking about sleep just because the patient started by saying, "I can't get to sleep," is a waste of time if that is not really a major concern of the patient. It is sufficient to let the patient know that you can help if he or she wants it.

If the patient wants help, you explain, "It is not necessary for a human being to sleep. It is only necessary to rest. Eight hours of rest is as good as 5 hours of deep sleep. Now, then, when I say rest, I mean lying quietly all night, for 8 hours. I do not mean absolutely still; no one can do that. I mean with the usual tossing and turning. I do not mean read a book. I do not mean watching TV. The typical person who cannot sleep does not lie quietly. They typically get up, go to the bathroom, go back to bed, get up, have something to eat, go back to bed, get up, have a cigarette, go back to bed, get up, walk back and forth, and go back to bed. Indeed, they typically do 8 hours of hard work during the night, and the next day they feel like it."

The patient typically objects that it sounds boring. "It is boring. It is one of the most boring ways to spend a night I know, but the next day you will be able to function."

Surprisingly enough, roughly 70 percent of the people who complain of sleep disorders, including schizophrenic patients, will find that this advice is sufficient to deal with their problem. This change occurs after the patient tries the advice out and finds it works. Then sleep is just not the big "hassle" that it was before. It is easy to see why giving direct advice should solve the problem for the bulk of people who cannot sleep. If Adler's view is correct, the patient need only discover that sleep is not necessary for the lack of sleep to no longer serve as an alibi; hence its dynamics are undercut without interpretation.

For those patients for whom the advice does not suffice or only suffices temporarily, it is our usual procedure to proceed immediately to Adler's interpretation, using the example of not being able to sleep before an exam, where the unconscious alibi, made in advance, is easy to see. This simple interpretation suffices for more than half of the remaining patients.

For the remainder of patients, one has to explore the sleep disorder in more detail; however, we are now dealing with a very small group of patients. In exploring with patients what happens when they cannot sleep, it is useful to ask what thoughts came to their minds when they could not sleep, not only because it tends to bring about sleep, but because it helps find out what is going on. The schizophrenic patient may insist he can't sleep, or even try to rest, because, "I can't stand what runs through my mind. I can't stand it." To which the appropriate reply is, "Tell me about those thoughts."

The patient who persists in an intermittent sleeping problem after advice and superficial interpretation should be asked in a fair degree of detail about what he actually did in the afternoon or evening—whom he saw, what they did, what they talked about, etc. By contrasting the differences between nights when he did and did not sleep, one will get clues to the psychologic basis for the sleep disturbance. The patient will be reluctant to give you specific details. He is apt initially to slough off your questions by saying these two evenings were essentially the same, or there was nothing different, "just the usual thing," but the therapist needs to persist and get the actual detailed report of the differences.

The reader may wonder why we do not take into account the so-called "dream deprivation" studies, which suggest that dreaming and hence sleeping are in fact necessary. Aside from the fact we have questions about the assumptions, methodology, and conclusions of these researches, their findings are clinically irrelevant in this context, since the patient will in fact begin sleeping again if he rests.

In 25 years of clinical work, I (Karon) have had only one patient whose presenting complaint was a persisting inability to sleep. The problem resisted sleeping pills for many years, and took almost 6 months to resolve. The dynamics were idiosyncratic. The patient became aware that as he started to fall asleep he became anxious, which woke him up. Eventually, he became aware that what he was afraid of was that he would die if he fell asleep. Further work revealed that he felt that he deserved to die as punishment for his unconscious death wishes against his father. When that was brought into awareness in a meaningful way, the sleep disturbance disappeared and did not return as of a 3-year follow-up. Other than that, neither of the authors has had a patient who was able to persist in therapy with a sleep disorder for more than a month.

The attitude the therapist takes about the inability to sleep is, "it's really not very important." The therapist is concerned about dealing with it because the patient seems so concerned about it. Having said that it is really not very important whether you sleep or not, the therapist acts as though he means it, because he does mean it. Typically, the associative material that one gets when analyzing the sleep disturbance helps in unraveling other problems of greater importance in the patient's life than the sleep disturbance itself.

It is very rare for a patient's sleep disturbance not to be handled quickly. The patient is surprised and impressed that you can handle it, and handle it without medication. He is also grateful. One should not underestimate how troubled the patient is who cannot sleep and who feels that he must. It demonstrates that the therapist is someone who does know something and can be helpful with real problems.

In those unusual cases where the sleep disturbance persists, one should consider investigating the possibility of recently discovered, physically based sleep disturbances (Hauri 1977, Williams and Karacan 1978). However, such specialized diagnostic tests should be the last resort, not the first.

Prejudice, Ethnicity, and Sexism

Psychotherapy with a schizophrenic patient is likely to fail if issues concerning the subculture of the patient are ignored. Even at this late date, one must remind therapists that knowledge of the experiences typical of people of the ethnic group and socioeconomic status of the patient is as important as knowledge of other psychodynamic factors and of psychopathology. Schizophrenia is more prevalent among the members of any group against which there is prejudice. For a successful psychotherapeutic outcome, it is necessary to deal with how the experience of being the victim of prejudice affects life problems, possible realistic solutions, family structure, defense mechanisms and resistances to therapy, and countertransference problems.

In professional discussions of psychotherapy, ethnicity is frequently limited to discussion of Blacks and, increasingly, Hispanics, but literally thousands of ethnic distinctions could be usefully studied. Within the white population, for example, such subgroups as Estonian-Latvian, Finnish, and Polish subcultures have been found to have clearly distinctive features relevant to psychotherapy. Socioeconomic status, geographic area of residence, generation from last migration, and the individual's own view of his or her relation to the subculture are also all relevant. The South Boston Irish subculture is different from the rural Massachusetts Irish subculture. The Detroit ghetto Black is different from the Philadelphia ghetto Black, and the nonghetto Black in each city is different again, and each is different from the West Indian Black. The Los Angeles Chicano who has lived all his or her life in Los Angeles is culturally different from the Chicano migrant farm worker, etc. Indeed, the possible subcultural specificities are literally infinite. Luckily, it is not necessary for the psychotherapist to know everything about the subculture from which the patient comes, but everything he does know will be helpful.

What is necessary is to be aware of the possibility, indeed the certainty, that you do not know all of the relevant subculture, for even each family has its own subculture in some respects. Therapists are in trouble if they think they understand all they need to know of the patient's subculture and do not. Such therapists do

not permit their patients to teach them what they need to know.
This is no different from any other important aspect of the patient's
life.

Each ethnic subgroup living in the United States also shares
the American culture in all its diversity as well as ethnic specificities. The patient will expect that the therapist at least knows the
general American culture. Schizophrenic patients in particular do
not know that general culture very well, and they may not know
their own ethnic culture either.

Luckily, most of the problems of patients, schizophrenics or
otherwise, are basically human or generally American, but the
patients frequently do not know that. The feeling "we are different," presented publicly as "we are better," frequently masks, in
our patients, a belief that "we are inferior," based on their inadequate knowledge of the human condition or the general American
culture. Ethnic identification is useful if it helps build a sense of
identity, but unhelpful if it creates a sense of shame.

Therapists should be alert to the possibility both that what
they are considering pathology is really part of subcultural normality and that the therapist may be overlooking symptoms or
problems because they are being erroneously viewed as subcultural
normality. Not only the therapist but the patient may make such
mistakes, although less frequently. As always, the combined judgment of the therapist and patient, working together in therapy, is
inevitably better in the long run than either of them alone.

The therapist who is ethnically different from the patient may
be ignorant of some relevant issues and have difficulty understanding the culture. In addition, the patient may have difficulty
identifying with or relating to the presumably different therapist.
The patient may feel a need to conceal what he thinks are inferior
aspects of his subculture, as well as his reactions to discrimination
from outsiders (like the therapist). On the other hand, such a
therapist may be helpful in providing a broader perspective (such
as that the problem is not ethnically specific) and readily notice
ethnically shared perspectives or defenses.

The therapist who shares or partially shares the patient's
subculture has the advantage of understanding many issues easily
and automatically, but may share some of the patient's blind spots

(ethnically specific defenses). Moreover, the patient may project his own self-hatred or feelings of inferiority on the ethnically similar therapist.

Lack of knowledge of subcultural issues can lead a therapist not to provide access to treatment. For example, in the late 1950s, I (Karon) worked as a psychologist in a reformatory in a northern state where half the inmates were Black; my case load was approximately evenly divided between Black and white patients, as would be expected. I was startled to learn from one of the two Black staff members that I was the first psychologist or psychiatrist at that reformatory who had ever considered any of the Black inmates as "suitable" for psychotherapy.

A lack of relevant cultural knowlege can also lead to inappropriate treatment. For example, there exists in Arizona a traditional American Indian subculture where incest, as defined by the general American culture, is acceptable. (To consider native American subcultures homogeneous is a mistake no native American or anthropologist would make.) Therapists report that the incest experience does not seem to be traumatic when it is culturally defined as normal, and carried out only in the culturally appropriate fashion. Female patients from this subculture characteristically cannot get help from therapists unfamiliar with their culture because the therapists focus on the incest experience, assuming it is the most important trauma in the patients' lives, and ignore the patients' attempts to get help with more urgent issues. Only when the therapists take the patients' perspective seriously, and deal with the issues in order of urgency as experienced by the patient, are they helpful.

Of course, the patient who moves out of the traditional society and into the major American culture may then experience conflicts over the differential meaning of this same experience.

In any subculture, the individual's own view of his or her relation to the subculture, and the view the patient's family takes of their relation to the subculture, are also going to make a difference. It is not the job of the therapist either to make the patient accept his subculture or to separate him from it, but the patient must feel free to consider or to do either, or both. The therapist's role is to help the patient feel free to choose, feel free to change his or her mind, and effective in whatever he or she choose to do, in this area as in any other.

The dynamics and other psychologic processes of the prejudiced individual have been well summarized in Allport (1954). These dynamics apply to patients as well as other human beings. Particularly important psychodynamically is the mechanism of projection. In the words of one paranoid patient (whom we shall call "McCarthy," not his real name, of course):

"Most of what you say turns out to make sense, Doc, even though it sounds weird. But one thing you say doesn't make sense."

"What's that?"

"Every time I talk about hating niggers, you act like there's something sick about it."

"That's 'cause there's something sick about it."

"See what I mean. Look, I've been hating niggers all my life. I'm from South Philly. Everybody hates niggers. Why do you act like there's something sick about it."

"Because there's something sick about it."

"See what I mean. Just because I hate those black McCarthy's, you act like there's something sick about it."

"What did you say?"

"Just because I hate those black *McCarthy's*"

"Say it slower."

"Just 'cause I hate those black *McCarthy's*. . . . that's not what I meant to say."

"But it is what you meant to say."

He hated Blacks, he said, because they were dishonest, untrustworthy, violent, homosexual, and wanted to rape white women. He himself had led a life of crime, claimed he had stolen from everyone who trusted him except the therapist (Karon), had fantasies about several white women he would have liked to rape, and had developed severe symptoms as a defense against thinking about a homosexual partner (whom he had had relations with "just for the money" and who had been the only kind and dependable person in the patient's life). By dealing with his prejudices, one is led directly into many of his central problems.

*   *   *

For the victim, on the other hand, prejudice and discrimination have a three-level structure psychologically. The first level consists of actual external discrimination: physical persecution; economic discrimination (e.g., employment, housing, education); social discrimination; discriminatory social myths, sometimes presented as scientific theories (inferior intelligence, uneducability, laziness, dirtiness, dangerousness, criminality, hypersexuality, etc.); and patterned individual prejudice. All of this is part of the external reality with which the patient must cope.

From the standpoint of the victim of discrimination, it is simply one more way in which the world is difficult and painful. The more severe the discrimination the higher the rate of psychosis. The one apparent exception has been the cities of the North since the 1960s, where Black migrants from the South have a lower rate of psychosis than northern-born Blacks (unlike earlier generations). This is because southern-born migrant Blacks usually have improved their lives by moving North, whereas northern-born Blacks started out believing that they were relatively better off (than the South), and that things would improve; however, because of unpredicted population increases, migration of southern whites and of southern Blacks to the North, resegregation of integrated neighborhoods, the overcrowding of Black inner-city areas without concomitant increases in services, and the spread of whites to the outer suburbs from which Blacks have been excluded by both legal and extralegal procedures, this generation of northern Blacks has had to cope with a worsening situation for which they were not prepared.

There is ample evidence that being clearly aware of the difficult situation in which one is involved, and being able to feel legitimately angry at it, removes much of the psychologically destructive impact of even terrible pressures (Karon 1975). This is a task with which a therapist can certainly be helpful.

Moreover, the therapist can help the patient develop rational coping strategies. Often the patients, even psychotic patients, know more than the therapist about how to cope with their problems, once they feel free to think about these issues clearly. As always, when the resistance to discussing an issue in psychotherapy has been removed, the barrier to thinking about it clearly both within and outside of therapy are also removed.

One of the most debilitating effects of prejudice and discrimination is that a victim of prejudice frequently does not know with certainty whether something happens to him or her because of their ethnic identity or not. Prejudiced people frequently do not tell you. Consequently, the victim may overreact with anger to people who are not acting out of prejudice, and may rationalize his own shortcomings, or may feel guilty and worthless over failures that are in no way the result of personal shortcomings. After all, none of us is omniscient. Again, the therapist can be very helpful in permitting the patient to live with and tolerate the inevitable uncertainty. Schizophrenic individuals frequently feel that they must have certainty in situations in which there is no way of being rationally certain. The idea that uncertainty is an inevitable part of human life, and therefore tolerable, is new to most of our patients.

Affirmative action programs, and publicity about them, have had a paradoxical effect on some individuals. The legitimate feeling of worth when they are successful may be undercut by the feeling they did not "do it on their own." Individuals whose opportunities in life have not been affected by such programs, but who believe the publicity that all members of their ethnic group have it easy, experience increased feelings of personal worthlessness.

Insofar as the therapist is not part of the same prejudiced-against group, the patient is likely to have irrational (or rational) resentment, which they are certain the therapist would not tolerate. The therapist must make it easy to express even irrational resentment at the therapist, and then at other members of the out-group, if therapy is to be successful. Members of a group that suffers from prejudice often believe that all members of the out-group know about and approve of the patterns of discrimination in our society.

The therapist from the same ethnic subgroup may be seen by the patient as a traitor because of the therapist's professional identity, and again the therapist need only encourage the patient to express even irrational resentment for the therapy to be helpful.

Of course, every member of an ethnic subgroup resents being treated as though he were only a member of that subgroup. Even being treated kindly, but not individually, is humiliating. No one wants to be Ralph Ellison's "invisible man." This certainly is a mistake no therapist should make.

Involvement in personal and social remedies to the real external problem of discrimination is a movement toward health, but beneath this external reality problem is the second level, the fact that most people who suffer from prejudice partially internalize the prejudice, so that they themselves feel prejudiced against people like themselves. One may even use involvement in the external problem to distract oneself from the fact that the prejudice is not only in the ouside world, it is also inside one's own head. (Of course, as with any inappropriate or symptomatic thought or feeling, we do not advocate thought control, but rather understanding of the origin of the inappropriate thought or feeling, and conscious reevaluation of actions motivated by such feelings.)

Even awareness of the prejudice in one's own mind is not enough. Below that is the third level, the fact that the prejudice was not learned directly from the society at large or from the outsiders. Rather, the prejudice was learned very early in childhood from the reactions of the people closest to one, the members of one's own family. Learning under such circumstances is inevitable and most painful. Patients will often use their understanding of their own prejudice as proof of their own worthlessness, and refuse to consider its origin in the problems of their parents.

Therapeutic consideration of all three levels of prejudice is helpful and usually necessary in the treatment of any patient, including schizophrenics, from a group that has suffered from prejudice. Of course, one does not deal with any more of the structure in any one session than seems useful at that moment. As usual, the rule is that you communicate what you think the patient can make use of at that moment.

Sexual Prejudice

The same three-level structure of prejudice applies, of course, to sexism—the prejudice against women. There is the reality problem, the prejudiced feelings and ideology, and the discriminatory actions, both individual and institutional, with which women must cope. The effort to change those discriminatory practices is obviously important, both for society and for the individual making the effort. Again, the therapist is on the side of seeing reality clearly, tolerating uncertainty, and developing coping strategies. Among the reality problems is the fact that the two-career family often means the husband has one career, and the wife two. Mothering may be devalued, as if the bad things that happen to children are caused by mothers, but none of the good things, or that mothering is an activity not worth a competent individual's time. As with other prejudices, the prejudice against women can be found in women. Focusing only on the external problem is not enough in therapy; one must confront one's own prejudice. The prejudice against women, particularly the patient's daughters, must be dealt with in both male and female patients.

For schizophrenic patients, it is most usual for the patient to idealize the opposite sex and dislike his or her own sex, although strong prejudices against the opposite sex or both sexes are not uncommon. It is essential to help the patient understand that people are more human beings than men or women, that strengths and weaknesses are not sex-specific, and reasonable expectations of reciprocal relations can be derived from one's own inner experience.

Striving for equality is always healthy, but the striving for reversal—becoming the oppressor and making the man in one's life (husband or son) the woman one does not wish to be—is a coping strategy that is destructive to the female patient, her spouse, and her offspring. There is a dilemma in trying to avoid both the problems caused by sex role stereotyping and those caused by a blurring of sexual identity. One solution is to suggest that children (and patients) need a clear sense of gender identity. By gender identity, we mean knowing clearly that one is a boy (man) or girl (woman), and that it is a good thing to be a man or a woman. It is important for the patient to know that being an adult woman includes being intelligent, independent, and mature. The content of the sex role can be highly varied. One can even honestly let children know that sex roles are in a process of change and redefinition. Children are rarely hurt by the truth.

Just as one can ignore one's own prejudice by focusing on the outside problem, other people's prejudice, so both of these can be used to distract one's attention from the fact that the prejudice against women has been learned from one's parents. Even more destructive than the father's male chauvinism is the mother's rejection of her daughter for being female. The daughter thinks, "After all she is a woman, and if she thinks I'm bad, I must be bad."

The woman who feels there is something wrong with her because she is a woman, or who wants the privileges, preferred status, or the love of her parents which boys seem to get in her family, may symbolize this in her dreams or symptoms as "penis-envy" (just as male patients may symbolize their wish to be a woman as "breast-envy" or "vagina-envy"). She may unconsiously attempt to resolve this by having a male child, that is, giving birth to herself as a boy. When she has a daughter, she may then react as if the daughter is a disappointment. Since all children initially accept their mother's judgment, the little girl searches for why she is such a disappointment. The discovery of the anatomic differences combined with the mother's apparent preference for boys leads to an obvious explanation, and the use of "penis-envy" as a symbol, as well as the problem itself, has been transmitted to another generation.

THE BLACK PATIENT

Since schizophrenia is disproportionately frequent among the poor, the unemployed, the undereducated, the migrant, the poorly housed, and those who are discriminated against, it is disproportionately frequent among Blacks. Discrimination against Blacks has restricted access to quality mental health care—psychotherapy. The vast majority of mental health professionals are white; it was only in the mid-1970s that serious efforts were begun to recruit minority group members into the mental health professions. Even well-intentioned white therapists may be so unfamiliar with Black individuals that they are unable to recognize suitability for psychotherapy among Black patients.

We will not attempt to characterize the Black subcultures of the United States or the problems which are more frequent in those cultures. Any proper psychotherapeutic approach will discover these matters as they impinge on the patient. What we are concerned with are those aspects of the subculture which prevent psychotherapy at all, or which may interrupt the process of psychotherapy; these latter prevent the therapist from getting enough information early enough to be able to deal with the problem appropriately.

It is fashionable, in some quarters, to say Black people, or Black schizophrenic individuals, just do not need or respond to psychoanalytic therapy. It is fashionable, in other quarters, to say that only the effects of white discrimination need to be dealt with in psychotherapy, and that the encouragement of Black identity and social action are the only remedial steps that are necessary, denying explicitly that Blacks are affected by the dynamics of their specific individual family experiences, or that they have unconscious fantasies and defenses, errors at least as great as ignoring the realities of discrimination and their impact. With schizophrenic, as with other patients, one needs to deal with discrimination against Blacks as a reality and to help the Black patient cope with this. But one also must deal with their individual fantasies and defenses.

No Black American has ever completely escaped the effects of discrimination and prejudice. The patient who says being Black has never been a problem and that he has never been discriminated against is lying either to you or to himself.

The handling of anger is the most central special dynamic problem of Black patients (Grier and Cobbs 1968; Karon 1975). This anger is related to the unfair pressures to which Black people are subjected directly and indirectly by whites. Consequently, a special resistance for a Black patient dealing with a white therapist is the white face of the therapist, which arouses anger because of all the white people who have gone out of their way to hurt him or her. The therapist expects this. He must deal with it explicitly, and make it explicit to the patient—make it clear that he expects the patient to be angry at him for having a white face, and that it is understandable, given the unnecessary pain to which the patient has been subjected as a result of being Black. Only if the therapist accepts as justifiable the anger of the Black patient toward the therapist because he is white, and the necessary anger at other white people who have hurt the patient, can the therapist then deal with what must be dealt with in the long run, namely, that the deepest and most painful hurts have come from people who have Black faces, that is, as with all human beings, from one's own family.

Black people know by the time they are 3 years old that they are Black and that being Black is "bad." This does not come directly from the outer society. It is learned within the family. Unfortunately, the prejudice of the white society against Blacks is partially internalized by the parents (in part because of the reactions of their own parents), and the child may notice that the lighter-skinned sibling may be preferred. This teaches the child that being Black is a bad thing at an age so early that it is difficult to unlearn. It is very helpful to a Black patient to have a therapist who can help him or her unravel these early painful experiences.

Usually, it is not possible to discuss this prejudice within the family until after one has dealt with the prejudice outside the family, namely the prejudice and discrimination of whites against Blacks, and the justified anger it arouses. The therapist can certainly help patients feel their anger and know it is appropriate even if their evaluation of the instigating circumstances was in error, since there was no way of their knowing that. Indeed, even the need to evaluate the instigation is cause for justifiable rage.

The therapist can also help with ways to express anger in terms of effectiveness and probable consequences. Patients are not likely, without help, to consider the possibility that finishing school might be a more effective way to "get even" than dropping out. Suggesting that succeeding might be a good way to fight back is very helpful for some patients: "You have to make a choice between letting the system defeat you, or are you going to win."

The past decade has witnessed the emergence of Black pride. It has at times been called "Black Power," "Black History," "pan-Africanism," even "Black Separatism," but its essence has reflected the inevitable development of an increased sense of identity and healthy self-determination. Recent research (Kirk 1976) has shown that Blacks who are consciously concerned with Black identity are less likely to commit suicide. This demonstrates that this era of Black pride has unquestionably been valuable and important, but the aspect of separatism has also created new problems—for example, Blacks' increasing ignorance of whites. Thus, a Black patient in psychotherapy cannot discuss fellatio because "white people don't do that sort of thing," or he considers the universal (in our society, at least) phenomenon of adolescent rebellion to be specifically Black and indicative of the inadequacy of Black parents; or a Black psychologist talks to Black graduate students as though it were a strictly Black phenomenon that the victims of Black homicides are largely relatives or close friends of the murderer (when this is true of homicide in all American ethnic groups).

The ghetto Black is most apt to have the least first-hand knowledge of how much of their lives is typically American as opposed to specifically Black. Educated Blacks who did not grow up in the ghetto may have a different problem. They often feel guilty about not having suffered enough, or even that some part of each of them feels good about not having suffered, or feel guilty about feeling better than less fortunate Blacks. Often such a patient will be dogmatically ideologic about Black pride, without the enhanced self-esteem one would expect, because of the guilt just under the surface.

Most of the problems of Black patients, like those of all minorities, are not specifically Black—they are specifically human or American. It is helpful for the patient to find that out.

Black identity itself may arise as a problem in therapy with a white therapist. The Black patient who relates to a white therapist, likes him or her, and identifies with him, may feel as if he has given in to his own self-hatred as Black. Consequently, the patient feels guilty and may withdraw, attack, or disguise his or her affection for the therapist in some socially unacceptable form, such as homosexuality or some other "perverse" fantasy. Whatever one's value system with respect to homosexual behavior, it is clear that when patients express homosexual feelings for their therapist, it is always because they wish to express affection in a way they expect the therapist to find repulsive, because some part of their own conscience is repulsed by it. The purpose is to disrupt the therapy.

The Black therapist will find the Black patient projecting self-hatred onto the therapist, "putting down" the therapist's ability, training, etc., implicitly or explicitly comparing the therapist unfavorably with a fantasy of the white comparison. The Black therapist may have a problem with countertransference (resentment) unless the therapist realizes this projection primarily serves the purpose of resistance, as well as being a defense utilized by the patient in his ordinary life, that needs psychotherapeutic attention.

The Black individual and family are subjected to special pressures because of discrimination, and then they react as any set of human beings would under such pressures. Thus, households headed by a mother do not represent a carry-over from the cultural tradition of slavery, as some writers have maintained, but an adaptation to current discrimination. Blacks have ideas similar to whites about what a household ought to be, but economic realities in the form of jobs or welfare have often permitted Black women more stable or better earning power than Black men. Given the general American expectations of roles, this often led Black women to experience their men as exploitative, and Black men to experience their women as emasculating, a set of psychologic pressures under which the relationship could not survive. The therapist can help patients evaluate the actual people they are involved with now in terms of reality, as well as increasing their understanding of their families of origin, in terms of the pressures to which their families were adapting.

Most Americans, Black or white, find that a large family is a hindrance to upward mobility. The Black ghetto family with eight, nine, ten, or more children is not rare. Contraceptive advice is needed to avoid misery, and yet some Black groups have called this genocide, an attempt by whites to destroy Blacks. Interestingly enough, Black sociologists have pointed out that those Black leaders most vociferous on this issue almost always have small families themselves, indicating that they themselves practice birth control, and that the voices are almost exclusively male. Recently, Black women have become more vocal on this issue, and the "birth control equals genocide" equation has been appropriately called into question. This misuse, or nonuse, of contraceptives, however, is more often based on lack of information, religious beliefs, or psychodynamic factors—a real man or woman doesn't use such things—than on ideology. The therapist should not hesitate to be helpful by discussing this problem factually, and, if necessary, psychodynamically.

"Affirmative Action" programs do make success easier for Black Americans who achieve beyond a certain level of education and professional qualifications, but the bulk of Black Americans, particularly the poor and the uneducated, still feel the brunt of discrimination in employment and do not have the same chance of success as other Americans.

HISPANIC-AMERICANS

There are professionals who argue in all seriousness that Hispanic-Americans are incapable of being treated by insight therapy and should be treated by suggestion (Kiev 1968). Such a view is nonsense. It is a particularly pernicious view for schizophrenia, since the incidence of this illness among the socioeconomically poor and for those who are discriminated against is elevated. As with any subculture, a knowledge of the cultural differences that will pose special difficulties in psychotherapy is essential.

We personally are less familiar with Hispanic patients than with Black patients because of the geographical location of our practice, nor do we speak Spanish. Therapists who speak Spanish have an advantage in dealing with Hispanics, unless the patient speaks English fluently. We will, however, offer comments about aspects of some Hispanic patients, as they appear relevant to successful treatment.

It is essential not to treat Hispanics as though they are all alike. It is also essential to respect the people with whom you work. It is important for the different subgroups of Hispanics to be recognized as distinct. The assumption that one Hispanic ethnic group understands another better than a non-Hispanic is mistaken. Rivalry, socioeconomic circumstances, and cultural traditions of different Hispanic-Americans are different; some rivalries may be bitter.

There are three major groups of Hispanics in the United States: Chicanos (Mexican), Cubans, and Puerto Ricans. Other than speaking Spanish fluently, therapists from one of these three groups do not necessarily relate more easily to patients from the other two groups than do Anglo-Americans. Most of our knowledge has to do with Chicano and Puerto Rican patients, the two most numerous Hispanic-American groups. While culturally different,

there are certain similarities in terms of psychotherapeutic considerations. Each generation since immigration increases the degree of similarity of cultural values and beliefs with the current
general American values.

The family serves as a mechanism for solving problems in a
way that is more integral to the personality functioning, as well as
to the social and economic functioning, of these Hispanic-Americans than of other ethnic groups. Since it is a more viable defense,
it also occurs as a resistance in psychotherapy (following the
general rule that what is a resistance in psychotherapy is nothing
more or less than the defenses a person uses to cope in life). For an
Hispanic-American to give up a relationship with a cousin may be
as difficult as for an Anglo-American to give up a relationship with
a brother or sister. If therapists do not realize this, they will again
and again be puzzled at the difficulty that their patients have in
handling familial relations. One must expect intense ambivalent
feelings to a wider range of family members in dealing with Hispanic
patients and to expect that giving up even a distant relative could
be a major psychologic struggle.

How central the family is to their adjustment is demonstrated
by Toch's (1975) data on suicide in prison. Suicide in prison is far
more frequent among Puerto Rican Americans than among Black or
white Americans. This is also true of Chicanos. Imprisonment
interferes with the relationship between the Hispanic-American
and his family. So, too, may psychiatric hospitalization. If, in
addition, a further impairment of this relationship occurs—for
example, the family decides to move away or in some other way
becomes further estranged from the prisoner or patient—the Hispanic becomes a serious risk for immediate suicide.

This dependence upon the family has served the Hispanic well
in the face of very real discrimination, deprivation, and misuse,
both in their country of origin and in the United States. Unfortunately, the dependence upon the family has led the Hispanic-
American not to use other alternatives, e.g., the agencies of
government. In some cases they tend to be "invisible" politically,
certainly not as visible as their numbers in the population would
lead one to expect them to be. This is now in the process of change,
but for many groups of Hispanics, particularly the Mexican-Ameri-

can and the Puerto Rican, the effective use of government agencies and institutions is still a skill that requires more widespread dissemination.

The Chicanos (Mexican-Americans) were imported into this country to do the least desirable agricultural work. They were economically exploited in this country and they accepted it, because they were even more severly exploited economically in Mexico. The importation of Mexican-Americans was largely based on the realization that they did not have the tradition of owning their own land in Mexico, and their loyalty to their family would prevent them from saving enough money to buy land. Therefore, it was hoped they would constitute a permanent agricultural laborer class, unlike other groups of immigrants who, in the American tradition, always eventually tried to become independent farmers. Unlike other immigrants, they were encouraged to keep their Spanish language and not to assimilate. Consequently, many Mexican-Americans are in rural areas, they tend to be undereducated and they, in general, have little knowledge of the utility of psychotherapy.

There are urban Chicano cultures, however, such as in Los Angeles, Chicago, and other cities, where the Chicano culture has assimilated to the urban American subculture in an idiosyncratic manner. In working with Chicano patients, one should try to learn as much as possible both from the patients and from external sources about the local Chicano subculture. In both urban and rural Chicano communities, there may be many undocumented aliens who are realistically fearful of authorities. This aspect of community life may prevent Chicanos from being willing to use psychotherapeutic services, and it may be responsible for their guarded attitude when talking in therapy.

Puerto Ricans are in a different situation. They are legally American citizens and have been encouraged to accept American ways. Nonetheless, they have a Spanish-speaking culture, tend to be poor, are discriminated against as foreigners, and are mainly found in large cities on the Eastern seaboard. They are more likely to be familiar with bureaucracies than the Chicano, and they are also likely to have all the "bad habits" of the slum dwelling urban family where a certain amount of character pathology helps one survive. Both Mexicans and Puerto Ricans tend to be poor and always to have been poor.

Cuban refugees, on the other hand, are frequently better educated and from the propertied classes, because they are fleeing a communist revolution. Consequently, programs aimed at all Hispanic-Americans which treat Cubans and Puerto Ricans as similar people, or who hire only Cubans (because they are better educated), are doomed to failure. Probably the Cuban and Puerto Rican subgroups have more trouble in understanding each other than they do when dealing with an Anglo-American. For a member of a traditionally cultured and educated group in a country with widespread poverty, it is important for one's peace of mind to be able to believe the poor are poor because they deserve to be. From the standpoint of someone born in poverty who wishes things were changed, it seems axiomatic that the rich are probably evil.

Alcohol and Other Drugs

It is not possible to treat schizophrenic patients without confronting the issue of the patient's use of alcohol and other drugs. Alcoholic hallucinosis, except for differential diagnosis, is not a major problem, and patients suffering from this are rarely treated as schizophrenic. But schizophrenic individuals who abuse alcohol are a frequent problem. Nearly everyone in our society uses alcohol, and alcohol abuse is more socially acceptable than schizophrenic symptoms. The situation with other drugs is more complex, as discussed below.

Use of alcohol and other drugs, however, is frequently the focus of the patient's attention or the family's. Drinking or drug-taking may be used to divert attention from other more serious problems. The patient may use them to earn a label that justifies erratic behavior, or the patient may use them as self-medication to control behavior or symptoms.

While we are impressed with the help Alcoholics Anonymous is able to provide for many people, schizophrenic individuals are rarely able to make use of such a group. The majority of our nonschizophrenic alcoholic patients had already tried Alcoholics Anonymous before seeing us, and they had failed. A few of the nonschizophrenic alcoholic patients we have seen were concurrently attending Alcoholics Anonymous. Such a situation adds some therapeutic problems but has proved workable, with the primary resistance being the citation of AA tenets that seem inconsistent with psychodynamic exploration.

ALCOHOL

There are three kinds of problems that result from alcohol abuse. The first is when you do things that interfere with relationships with your family or friends. The second is when your drinking interferes with work. The third is when you drink so much that it has physical consequences. Even when these consequences are not major aspects of the patient's symptoms, however, alcohol can serve as a defense against therapy.

Alcohol and other drugs are used as resistance in two ways. The patient may take a drink or drug before the treatment hour. This will diminish his or her anxiety during the hour and the emotional reactivity on which the therapeutic benefit of the hour depends. Or, the patient may talk about alcohol or drugs to the exclusion of other issues. Both of these resistances can be discussed when they occur.

The most important thing to remember in dealing with people, including schizophrenic individuals, who have a drinking problem is not to make the alcohol itself the center of the treatment. This does not mean that you ignore it. The question is always what the person does. No one does anything drunk that he or she does not wish to do when sober. The man who beats up his wife when he is drunk does not have a drinking problem. He has a problem with beating up his wife. The man who cannot hold a job because he gets drunk does not have a drinking problem. He has a problem of not being able to hold a job. This is the attitude the therapist must take: You are responsible for what you do. If your behavior is not what you think it should be or want it to be, we have to understand why you do it; drinking is not a sufficient explanation.

Sometimes what the patient does when drunk is perfectly acceptable from a rational standpoint, like having a sexual relationship. But the patient's conscience, based on the childhood dicta of their family, does not tolerate it. Clinging to childhood puritanical standards does not prevent the behavior, it only requires being drunk or drugged in order to do what other people can do without alcohol. Our attitude as therapists has to be that you do drunk what you want to do sober, and the reasonableness and unreasonableness of behavior must be judged always in the light of its consequences.

Some patients drink in order to prevent themselves from doing bad things. Even though they may do hurtful things while drunk, e.g., beat someone up, they report that they would literally kill someone if they did not drink. They see the alcohol as a means of incapacitating themselves, or, at least, of deadening the pain that instigates them to engage in this behavior that they do not consciously want to engage in. Such people, of course, can be helped greatly by psychotherapy. We must teach them that there is an easier and better way for self-control, namely by insight and understanding in the long run, and utilizing the relationship with the therapist in the short run.

This attitude that the patient, not his drinking, is responsible for what he does should be imparted to the relatives too. This is particularly relevant when the patient is not the supposed alcoholic, but the spouse or the child of an alcoholic. For them it is a neurotic defense to say, "He is a wonderful man (or she is a wonderful woman) except when he (or she) drinks." The patient must learn that people whose behavior is unacceptable are people whose behavior is unacceptable, whether or not they have been drinking. It is neither better nor worse to beat someone up when you are drunk than when you are sober. "Rotten bastards" are unlikable, regardless of whether they drink.

The alcoholic husband of a patient would frequently get drunk, urinate on himself, and collapse at parties, or leave the house so drunk that his wife was afraid he would kill himself while driving. This alcoholic behavior was a small part of the array of chronic problems in the patient's life. I (Karon) was initially concerned with the wife's being able to tolerate such a terrible situation, so that psychotherapy could begin to help unravel her situation. She would eventually have to evaluate what was good and bad about her marriage, how much it was possible to improve it as she changed, and whether with that improvement, it was worth maintaining. I, therefore, insisted that she could not really control her husband's drinking. Reluctantly she agreed. Given that, it was suggested that she could not be responsible for what she could not control. She was not responsible for what he did. If he got drunk at a party and collapsed, it was he collapsing, and she did not have to apologize for him. If he urinated on himself because he was drunk when friends were present, it was he who urinated on himself, not she. If he was going to drive drunk, she was advised to tell him that she wished he would not, because she was afraid that he would hurt himself, but that she could not stop him. Taking such an attitude, it seemed to the therapist, would make the situation of living with this alcoholic man tolerable. When the wife consistently took this attitude, however, the man's drinking altered dramatically. He stopped getting drunk. He even became a social drinker. This, of course, did not solve the real problems in their marriage, but it did lead him finally to seek therapy.

Alcohol is a superego suppressant. In our experience, there are two areas in which the patient who uses alcohol symptomatically would most often feel guilty if he or she did not drink: "I should not feel this angry," or "I should not want love and approval this much." Superego restrictions are lessened when drunk, and the anger or the dependency may be expressed. The difference between the behavior of the patient when drunk and sober indicates which of the two areas it will be most fruitful to address first.

The patient who is "concerned" about his or her alcoholism may present their problem as simply "a drinking problem," and become obsessed about the guilt over getting drunk. But the guilt belongs somewhere else. The therapist must get the patient to think about where it might belong. While such guilt may be appropriate for behavior while drunk, it is more often appropriate to the impulses, wishes, or fantasies that occurred to the patient before drinking, and it may have roots in childhood. The alcohol may be used to block awareness of what the patient was feeling or thinking.

The guilt may be real, given childhood parental standards, but it is not being generated by the drinking. The alcoholic will attempt to use insights, such as that he or she is really guilty about something else, as a justification for continuing excessive drinking. The therapist must disrupt the process; the purpose of insight is to enable change, not to rationalize symptoms.

The patient as a child may have ingratiated himself with a parent by guilt. He or she misbehaved, mother or father was angry, the child was "guilty," and all was forgiven until the next infraction. If he was not "guilty," he was punished, rejected, and saw himself as bad. It is important in the therapy to let the patient know that just feeling guilty is not enough, one must understand and change.

An alcoholic patient frequently has had an alcoholic parent, whom the patient has usually resented. The patient's own alcoholism seems to be another example of unconsciously preserving the parent-image, by becoming worse. If, as is usual, one parent is nonalcoholic, that parent is frequently "long-suffering" and overburdened, and the patient's adult guilt may be over childhood resentment of the nonalcoholic parent.

When the patient tells the therapist what was happening before he or she started drinking that day and what happened afterward, it is often useful to present a fairly lengthy interpretation, pointing out what unacceptable feeling the patient was struggling to keep out of awareness before getting drunk and how it was expressed in what the patient did while drunk. Then the therapist attempts to indicate the appropriateness of the feeling and to interpret in light of the patient's life, as best one can, why or how the patient came to the conclusion that it was inappropriate. In other words, take away the defensive denial, acknowledge and normalize the feelings, and interpret how he came to believe that he should not experience those feelings.

The dependency need may be masked as a sexual need in both men and women. To be dependent is not "masculine," to be alcoholic is. If one makes a heterosexual overture or has a fight, one may be "bad" according to childhood dictates, but one is "masculine." Closeness to others of the same sex, may be "homosexual," according to the childish superego, but it is all right if one is drunk. Indeed, homosexual behavior may be "taboo," but if one is drunk, such actual behavior "doesn't count." Women as well as men frequently express dependency in the form of sexuality (heterosexual or homosexual), but may be so guilty about sexuality that it can be acceptable only while drunk. Women, too, may feel anxious about their sexual identity, allay that anxiety by casual heterosexual activity, but require alcohol to deal with their guilt about sexual activity. Sometimes alcoholic sexual activity in women is a disguised expression of anger at the men in their lives, or at their parents.

Our concern with drinking is always with consequences. We are neither pro-drinking nor anti-drinking per se. Where the destructive consequences are interpersonal or occupational, the consequences, not the drinking behavior, are the focus of attention. If, however, a patient suffers physiologic damage from drinking and continues to drink, or is drinking at a level certain to cause such damage and knows it, we have to raise the issue of the patient's self-destructiveness.

Patients may not know the physiologic consequences of their drinking patterns, however. At the time of publication of this book, our best knowledge suggests that the equivalent of a half pint of whiskey (80 proof), a fifth of wine (12%), or a six pack of beer consumed every day will produce physical damage to the body within 5 to 7 years. It is generally believed that the body can easily tolerate one-third of this dosage. (Indeed, available research suggests that mild to moderate drinking is associated with greater longevity than total abstinence, but this may be a result of the associated life-styles, rather than the alcohol itself.)

Forgetting may be a principal aim of drinking. Thus, an 18-year-old borderline schizophrenic patient who had been getting "falling-down" drunk three to seven times per week since the age of fifteen, was referred because of his drinking problem. Several weeks after therapy began, his drinking pattern altered dramatically, so that he got drunk only on Saturday night (which was "normal" among his friends). When asked about the change, he explained: "I was trying to forget. Now my life depends on remembering. And alcohol doesn't help you remember."

In another case, a 28-year-old man was referred because of his 6-year history of excessive drinking. The therapist (VandenBos) asked early in the first session: "Why do you drink so much?"

"To stop hurting."

"What hurts so much?"

"Remembering."

"Remembering what?"

"I ruined her life and I can't forget it." On a date with his fiancée 6 years earlier, they had been kidnapped by three men. With a knife at his throat, he was forced to watch each of the men rape his fiancée. Later, he and the girl were not able to discuss this with each other or with anyone else. Within a month, they ended their engagement. He began drinking until drunk nightly. Several months later she attempted suicide, and finally he lost contact with her (but fantasized worse and worse things happening to her). He felt he had ruined her life, caused the rape, failed to act like a man and prevent the rape, and was a monster for rejecting her. All of her subsequent problems were his sole fault and responsibility. Only much later in therapy did he connect these feelings with the same set of feelings about his mother who had said to him, "I only stayed with him (the husband) for your sake." He had adopted his father's defense; his father had been an alcoholic.

He did not drink at work, however. His job was so demanding that he reported being "too busy to think." But each evening he got drunk. If he saw a couple together, or a parent and child, or had a sexual thought, he would remember, and feel guilt, anxiety, and pain. Then he would consume four or five drinks in 30 minutes, after which he would not remember or hurt.

DRUGS AND LONELINESS

Everything we have said about alcohol can be carried over to other drugs. The drug of choice is largely dependent on generational and subcultural patterns. One function of drugs is to deal with loneliness. Americans, in general, tend to be lonely, and patients tend to be particularly lonely. The use of drugs other than alcohol creates a convincing illusion of relatedness. This is not widely known, but it is one of the real satisfactions of almost all drugs, and it is what makes them so appealing to the schizophrenic patient as well as to other patients.

The illusion of relatedness, without the work and anxiety of developing a real relationship, has enormous appeal. Patients will insist that the people who take drugs with them or supply them with drugs are really their "friends" and that they think alike and commune with each other. Inevitably, the fact that the understanding was an illusion will in time become apparent to the therapist, and sometimes to the patient.

Indeed, the supplier of drugs is usually not only someone with whom there is not a close mutual understanding, but he is often someone with sadistic tendencies. The more dangerous the drug, the more sadistic typically is the supplier. The user almost always denies the sadistic element in his "friend," but continually reports getting hurt inexplicably. Even patients who have come close to dying from overdoses or from being given the wrong drug or impure drugs will refer to the person who supplied them with the nearly lethal dose as their friend, who "really likes" them and "understands" them.

HALLUCINOGENS

The use of hallucinogens is often very attractive to people who already hallucinate and want to know why. It is not unusual to discover that the patient with frequent hallucinatory "drug" experiences began hallucinating before ever taking a drug. Anyone who is treating schizophrenic patients on a routine basis needs to be aware of this possibility. Borderline patients are usually in touch with reality, but at times become very frightened and regress. Typically, they are also frightened by the regressive phenomenon itself. Such patients struggle to put order in their world. They will be told about drugs, try them, and experience what they usually experience, but be relieved that they now have an explanation.

The hallucinogens have been explored and extolled as routes to self-understanding. It has been the experience of most psychotherapists that this also is an illusion. In our experience, nothing can be accomplished with the hallucinogens that cannot be accomplished better without them. Indeed, when people gain insights under a hallucinogen, they have difficulty making a bridge between those insights and the rest of their lives. It is a frequent outcome that evn valid insights are repressed, and a rigid set of defenses reinstituted.

When the hallucinogens first became popular, starting with Aldous Huxley's (1954) *The Doors of Perception,* they were extolled as harmless. Unfortunately, one need only go to the emergency room of a hospital near any large university and stay there for a

week to know that the harmlessness of the hallucinogens is doubtful. Clinically, it seems as if people who would not otherwise have
psychotic breaks do have psychotic breaks under the influence of
hallucinogens, and people who would have had psychotic breaks
with a good prognosis for spontaneous recovery seem to take
much longer before recovering. While it has been disputed, there
seems to be ample clinical evidence for the occurrence of "flash-
backs," that is, the recurrence at a later time of hallucinogenic-like
experiences without further ingestion of the hallucinogen. While
the original hallucinogenic experience is frequently pleasurable,
the "flashback" is almost always unpleasant.

If borderline patients in a fragile condition are using hallucinogens regularly and in high dosages, it should be pointed
out to them that they are contributing to the possibility that they
will go crazy and remain crazy a long time. Such drug-taking
should be interpreted as self-destructive.

Very few professionals would consider the hallucinogens
harmless drugs today, and it is the therapist's responsibility to
share this information with the patient. Again, if the patient does
not follow his advice, it does not mean that he is criminal, but the
information should be shared.

PCP

The use of PCP, originally developed as an animal tranquilizer,
is increasing, particularly among adolescents. Its low cost, in
comparison to other street drugs, is related to the increase in its
use. It is sold under a variety of names, including "angel dust" and
THC. (There is no real THC available on the streets, due to its cost
and chemical properties.) Because PCP is easily available and
inexpensive, it is taken occasionally by schizophrenic patients.

Its effects vary. Unlike other drugs, PCP causes auditory
hallucinations, and violent outbursts are common. The latter may
be of concern to law enforcement officers and hospital personnel.
When violent behavior appears to be due to PCP, it is useful to
decrease stimulation immediately; for example, by moving the
patient into a dimly lit room with minimal noise and intrusion (as
opposed to the usual brightly lit confusion of an emergency room)
or wrapping the patient in blankets or a mattress. For details on the

diagnosis and medical and psychological handling of PCP abuse, see McAdams, Linder, Lerner, and Burns (1980).

When the patient is not now using PCP, but we suspect that he may have used it in the past, use of this drug is to be discussed in the same manner as the use of other drugs.

MARIJUANA

The use of marijuana is rapidly becoming an accepted American custom, exceeded only in its popularity and respectability by alcohol. Nonetheless, the research evidence is neither as reassuring as its devotees maintain, nor as frightening as its opponents have maintained. Obviously, it is now well known that "pot" does not cause genetic damage and is not physiologically addictive. It does not lead to violent crimes or necessarily to harder drugs.

If patients ask about pot, we share our view that we really do not know, because careful research has begun relatively recently. In 10 years we will know. Clinically, we feel one should treat marijuana the same way one treats alcohol, evaluating its use by its consequences. If it has no negative consequences for the individual, it is all right. If it has negative consequences, it is not all right. By negative consequences, we mean what they do or what they experience, but what they do is explained by what they wanted to do, not by the fact that they were on pot.

Perhaps a special word is needed about negative emotional experiences. Just as it was popular in the 1930s to expand imaginatively the fictive dangers of smoking pot, it is now fashionable to maintain that nobody ever has a negative reaction to smoking pot and that if they do they must in some way be defective. This moralism causes patients to be ashamed of having a negative reaction and not describing it to their friends or to their therapist. From time to time, patients will report a depression after smoking pot. If a drug that is supposed to make you feel good makes you feel bad, there is really not much point in taking that drug. This view should be shared with the patient.

In rare cases, real psychotic symptoms get triggered by smoking pot. These patients may have smoked with no apparent harmful effects for some time but then manifest such a reaction. The patient tries to deny that the reaction could be from pot. Our advice would be the same as it would be for someone who had a severe psychotic reaction when drunk. "For you, pot isn't a good idea." Strangely enough, when such cases of psychotic reactions to marijuana are reported in the American literature, they always have a paranoid flavor; when they are reported in the French psychiatric journals, they are always manic-depressive.

A 20-year-old patient, who had smoked pot with friends a number of times without harmful consequences, was at a party, smoking with her friends, when she suddenly realized that they were plotting to kill her. Quickly, she made an excuse to leave, packed her belongings, got on a train, and went home to her family. When she got out of the train and was met by her family, she realized that they, too, were plotting to kill her. Since she had already begun psychotherapy with less serious symptoms, she suspected that this might be a symptom and called the therapist (Karon) long distance. "I don't want to be locked up."

She was told, "Then don't tell anybody about it, and come back here immediately. Luckily, time is on your side. You will dry out." She asked what that meant, and was told, "It's a term we use with alcoholics. As time goes by the drug will work its way out of your body, and if this is due to the drug, it will disappear."

She returned, saw the therapist for two successive sessions, and the psychotic paranoid reaction disappeared. Three weeks later, as she talked about pot and repeated the attitudes of her drug culture friends, she said, "You know, nobody ever has a bad reaction to pot."

The therapist was startled. "What about your reaction 3 weeks ago?"

She said, "What are you talking about?" She had repressed the unfashionable memory of her "weakness," that is, her negative reaction to pot. This makes us skeptical of research based solely on the memories of pot smokers who believe that pot is harmless, as a certain guide to its actual effects.

Marijuana is known to potentiate LSD, and at high dosages research subjects cannot distinguish THC (the active ingredient in marijuana) from LSD, so that the reservations one has about the hallucinogens may apply to high-dosage use of marijuana. In a review of cross-cultural studies of schizophrenia, Victor Sanua

(1969) reports that in Egypt hashish produces "a clinical picture of schizophrenia." Of course, the typical Arabic user of cannabis is smoking a much more potent form of the drug than Americans, and smoking it all day long. It seems clear that if the pot is strong enough and at high enough dosages there can be a marked incidence of psychotic reactions.

The question becomes whether or not there are negative reactions to marijuana at the low dosage usual for American smokers. VandenBos was a psychological consultant at a drug education center for 5 years. In that time he came to know a number of relatively normal regular marijuana users. Ninety percent of them reported that they had had at least one, and in some cases more, "bad trips" on marijuana that were very intense and very frightening, and these occurred most typically with a potent batch of marijuana, often ingested orally in brownies and pancakes.

Recent findings from the West Indies suggest chronic marijuana use there is harmless. Until research findings become clear, we recommend deciding on an individual basis.

UPPERS AND DOWNERS

The use of uppers, primarily amphetamine sulfate (Benzedrine), dextroamphetamine sulfate (Dexedrine), and methamphetamine hydrochloride (Methedrine), can be a problem. The source of such drugs is frequently a prescription. It is well known in the street culture that methamphetamine is dangerous, but that does not prevent our patients from taking it. The amphetamine psychosis, which all of these drugs in sufficient dosage are capable of producing, is very dramatic, very bizarre, and often very aggressive. All the horrible reactions attributed to marijuana in the lurid literature of the 1930s are occasionally carried out during an amphetamine psychosis. Fortunately these reactions will disappear as the drug disappears from the patient's body.

In the realm of downers, the most popular are the barbiturates. These are usually prescribed as sleeping pills. We have already indicated our view that sleeping pills are not necessary as an adjunct to treatment and that sleep disturbances are to be handled by advice and psychotherapy. In some cases, the prescribing physician is careless and prescribes a dosage that is addictive. In other cases, the patient may get prescriptions from more than one physician. In still other cases, the patient is able to buy the medication on the streets or borrow it from friends. The problems with barbiturates are that they potentiate with alcohol (so that a nonlethal dose may become lethal) and they are physically addictive. Often patients are not told this when barbiturates are given them for sleep. A nonmedical therapist should always consult with a physician on the handling of the withdrawal from barbiturates. From a purely physical standpoint, the withdrawal symptoms of the barbiturates are perhaps as serious as any withdrawal symptoms with which we are called upon to deal. Withdrawal should be handled with careful medical attention.

HARD DRUGS

Strangely enough, the so-called hard drugs represent the least common drug problems in schizophrenic patients. They are far less frequent than alcohol, hallucinogens, pot, and uppers and downers, but schizophrenic individuals may well take substances that are weird. For example, one patient had cupboards full of nutmeg and would ingest half a can of nutmeg in a cup of hot water several times a day. Such ingestion of nutmeg is psychologically destructive. It is not ordinarily discussed because even small quantities of nutmeg have so many unpleasant side-effects that one has to be psychotic to keep taking it.

Heroin is addictive. It was developed as a cure for morphine addiction, which was developed as a cure for opium addiction. Methadone, which is a cure for heroin addiction, is also addictive, but it is not covered by the narcotics law, and therefore its legal use by prescription has led to a decrease in the ancillary crimes which heroin addicts commit in order to buy their supply. Unfortunately, it does not improve the patient's interpersonal relationships.

One of the characteristics of heroin addicts which is not well known is that they are struggling with enormous rage. This first became clear when a VA hospital submitted several TATs to be interpreted blindly by Karon for training purposes. He did not know anything about the patients other than age, sex, and that they were veterans. All the protocols were of people struggling with intense sadism. It turned out that each protocol was of a heroin addict. The physical effects of heroin, after all, are those of a sedative and analgesic, as well as euphoric. The individual loses sex drive and is quieted down. If one thinks of any drug dependence as self-medication, one may ask what kind of person so badly needs to be quieted down?

It is characteristic of heroin addicts that they "mess up" their friends and relatives. This is usually explained on the basis of the addiction being so great that they will do anything to get their fix; however, it seems clear that the motivation for stealing the family television set may have to do with the need to hurt their relatives and friends.

Treatment at SYNANON, devised by heroin addicts for heroin addicts, is essentially sadistic. Professional psychotherapists would never have considered a treatment that sadistic, but it seems helpful with some heroin addicts because, whether they are on the receiving or punishing end, the sadism is satisfied. It is axiomatic at SYNANON that the heroin addict is a liar, a cheat, totally untrustworthy, and mean. Only someone who really believes that that is true would tolerate that kind of treatment program. Recent publicity suggests, however, that the sadism may not always be sublimated.

It is now known that the withdrawal symptoms from heroin are not the massive physical agony that used to be portrayed so heroically in the movies. They are, in fact, unpleasant but bearable, if the motivation is strong enough. Of course, if there is no source of gratification in life other than heroin, if one's sexual desires and the pleasure of sexual activity are minimal, if one needs be sadistic and have a rationale for that sadism, if one's chief pleasure is outwitting the cops to prove that you are somebody, or being top dog rather than bottom dog in the dealing game, then it is very difficult to see how one can live without heroin.

It is our belief that the best single measure that could be taken to eliminate heroin addicts would be to legalize heroin by prescription, as in the British system. In our experience most heroin addicts have been created by other heroin addicts. The easiest way to get the money for your own supply is to exploit your friends. Since such a change in the law—legalizing heroin—would take the profit out of it, such a change is unlikely, for there is an industry that would disappear, and whose lobbyists are well known to be influential.

Cocaine, patients will tell you, is not addictive. They are right about this. You do not have to worry about addiction in the physical sense. Psychologic addiction may be noted. While patients may minimize the danger, it has been known for a long time that it is not totally harmless, ever since Freud's friend, Wilhelm Fleischel von Marxow, who was given cocaine to help him lose his morphine habit, died of cocaine.

Nonetheless, cocaine use is not generally a serious problem for schizophrenic patients because it is very expensive. Consequently, it is rarely used by schizophrenic individuals, and when it is, the experimentation is usually brief. It is just too expensive, compared to other illegal medications, to serve the patient's psychologic needs.

Patients who use drugs will tell their therapist that it is very important to have accurate knowledge of their particular drug and not to confuse one drug with another. This makes therapists uncomfortable, and that is exactly the intent. The fact of the matter is that when most drug users wish to use a drug, they will take any substances at hand and regularly mix them up. It is a mistake for therapists to get too worried about what specific illegal drug the patient is taking and its characteristics as opposed to the characteristics of another drug. If the therapy is successful, drug use will decrease or disappear from the patient's life.

Prisoners and Other Criminals

Many schizophrenic individuals get in trouble with the law for actions which clearly constitute criminal behavior, and a significant minority of imprisoned criminals are schizophrenic. In both of these situations, there is a very good chance that the schizophrenic person will not be treated. Police departments frequently do not prosecute obvious "mental cases," but they usually do not refer them for treatment either. Prisons often lack adequate mental health treatment services. This is because of the frequently voiced opinion that criminals and delinquents, whether incarcerated or free, do not suffer from psychodynamic problems and do not re-spond to psychotherapy. It is sometimes fashionable to add the corollary that rehabilitation of criminals does not work. The fact is that in those few cases in which meaningful rehabilitation has been tried, it does work, but our society rarely has made a commitment to rehabilitation. In a real rehabilitative attempt, psychotherapy would have to play a major role.

A. S. Neill, the well-known author of *Summerhill* (1960) reports that the person who taught him the most about the treatment of children ran a therapeutic reformatory in England. When the director died, the therapeutic reformatory ceased to exist. Within the psychoanalytic movement, such people as August Aichorn (1935) have shown dramatically useful results, but always the follow-up has been negligible. When the originator dies, the pro-gram dies with him.

It is clear in our experience that criminals and delinquents largely suffer from neurotic or psychotic problems. In many instances, the crime itself is simply a symptom. Thus, a man in his 20s, the night before his marriage, walks with his best friend past a policeman. One block later he says, "Let's go joy-riding," steals a car, and drives past the same policeman, who arrests them. This is clearly a crime, but it is also clearly a symptom. Of course, actions and not just feelings or physical states, are symptoms.

A man who had difficulty in dealing with his anger, particu-larly with his wife, had been taught as a child that men should not beat up their wives, but he was not taught how to deal with the realistic anger that can occur between husbands and wives. His wife, he said, was beautiful but "she is a real bitch." On one occasion she impulsively bought $2,000 worth of furniture, despite their having no money; another example involved their agreeing not to have a second child for at least two years because money was tight, and, without telling him, she stopped taking birth-control pills and became pregnant. He would frequently be furious with her, but he would not beat her. Rather, he would go to a bar, have a couple of drinks, take offense at something another man said, and beat the man so seriously that the victim usually had to go to the emergency room of a hospital. The patient would be arrested. This always happened after provocative incidents with his wife.

Even such an obviously psychodynamic case as the following is sometimes treated by the police as a routine criminal matter. A 20-year-old man, who did not live with his parents, visited them at least once a week. When they argued with him, the patient got enraged. He wanted to kill his father and he did not want to. So he went into the parents' bedroom, got the shotgun kept there, and threatened to kill himself. The parents then called the police. The police always attempted to get him to lay down the gun; sometimes he fired the gun into the ceiling. This sequence of events happened regularly. On one occasion, he shot out a window, and in shock threw the gun down and surrendered. He was then charged, not in relation to the family incident, but with endangering the life of a police officer.

Sometimes when a patient's behavior is antisocial or criminal, professionals may label them "sociopathic" or "character disorders" without recognizing that the dynamics of the patient's behavior are simply neurotic or psychotic. We have no objection to these descriptive labels as long as they do not prevent the investigation of the neurotic or psychotic mechanism underlying the patient's antisocial behavior, as well as other symptoms. A therapist who does not help the patient to see the relationship between psychologic factors and what the patient is doing will not be effective.

In our judgment, at least a quarter of convicted criminals are convicted for actions which are clearly simply symptoms. It is also our experience that only a very small minority of criminals can be explained away as primarily rational (the best way he could make a living) or sociologic (this is the way everybody in my neighborhood lives) criminals. In most cases where the crime has a more rational or sociologic element, the person is still basically a neurotic or psychotic individual, whose symptoms would prevent him from changing a criminal way of life.

In one study, made by Karon in the 1950s, 40 consecutive admissions to a reformatory for male adolescent first offenders were examined. All of them had committed crimes serious enough to be sent to jail. Surprisingly, every one of the 40 consecutive inmates had been diagnosed as emotionally disturbed before being in trouble with the law. Usually the school had referred them to a child guidance center, where diagnoses (elaborate pieces of paper) were prepared, but no real treatment offered. In some cases, medication was offered, which the patients found did not help, and which the patients reported they would not take if it had helped, because it made them less aggressive and their status with their peers depended on their aggressiveness. Moreover, they could not have afforded the medication without stealing even if it had helped and if they had been willing to take it. In essence, no treatment was offered.

VandenBos, in talking with 64 male jail inmates ranging in age from 18 to 30 in therapy groups, found in the 1970s that virtually all of them reported they had had contact with a mental health professional before the age of 18. The most usual pattern involved a teacher suggesting that there was a problem about which the parents should seek help, and this most typically oc- curred when the inmate was between the age of five and nine. It is interesting to note that half of the inmates indicated that they had seen a professional whom they had expected to see again, but their parents did not take them back. It seemed that the lower-class family had had contact with a psychologist, psychiatrist, or social worker who, unfortunately, did not understand social class dif- ferences and did not make sense to the parents. The relevance of what the therapist wanted to talk about as compared to what the parents were concerned about was never made clear. The parents may have felt guilty or frightened or ignorant, but they pulled their child out of treatment, because it seems they did not under- stand why it would make any difference.

The child continued to be a problem for the parents, or he became one. By adolescence, the parents were fed up. The child had been a nuisance for a long time, and they saw him as just bad, ornery, or stubborn. When there were further problems, the parents had to make a choice about where to turn for help: the previously unhelpful child guidance center or the Juvenile Court. Lower-class parents are more likely to take the child, at this point, to Juvenile Court; the Juvenile Court is more likely to view the "problem" as solely the child's. By the time the child is 18, he is seen by the parents, the court, and often themselves as a hard core delinquent or an adult criminal. (Most convicted criminals are male.) The child adopts the view held by his parents and the legal system. He does not think of going to a mental health professional to understand himself and change his behavior.

TREATING THE SO-CALLED SOCIOPATH

We feel there are three important technical considerations for treating so-called sociopathic patients that are not well known:

(1) Such patients have a need to prove that they themselves are evil, and that all people will treat them badly so that they can maintain the fantasy that, as compared to everyone else at least, their mother and/or father really were good (Fairbairn 1954). This mechanism must be pointed out, especially when the patient maneuvers the therapist into either disliking or apparently mistreating him.

(2) Male delinquent patients are terrified by their own passivity; therefore they cannot accept being made passive, e.g., being made to lie down on a couch. Similarly, they do not dare to relate to a therapist who seems to be passive.

The female delinquent has a related problem with men. She tends to equate sadism with masculinity, is drawn to men who are sadistic, yet complains that all men are "bastards." If you choose sadistic men because you think they are masculine, you may not get a masculine man, but you will get hurt. If the therapist listens carefully, he will almost always find that there were men who were not cruel, but the female patient dropped them quickly because they were not "masculine" enough. A passive male therapist may also be avoided by such patients.

(3) Despite our orientation toward dealing with underlying fantasies, we have found it necessary with most sociopathic patients to tell them the differences in how lower-class and middle-class people act, in the way they think, in the way they dress, and what they get out of life. These patients typically are unaware of all the distinctions, but are able to see the consistencies when they are pointed out. They find it just as exciting as you and I did, when we first learned of it in Introductory Sociology. The patient becomes aware that it is an advantage in our society to be middle class in at least some respects, if one can, and painful not to be.

They also become aware of the ways in which they prevent themselves from becoming middle class. One can then analyze the psychotic and neurotic barriers that prevent them from doing what they now want to do.

Thus, for example, I (Karon) have said to a male patient, "Tell me, would you talk to me if I had a duck's ass haircut and a leather jacket?"

The patient said, "Of course not."

"Would you hire me as a bank president?"

"Are you crazy?"

"Would you hire me as a teller in a bank?"

"Of course not."

"Would you hire me as a sweeper?"

"Maybe."

It then becomes clear to the patient that there are things that he could do to influence how people relate to him.

In dealing with criminal offenders of any age or status, it is essential that the therapist not be moralistic. The crime must be viewed through the eyes of the criminal. This does not mean that any reasonable therapist would condone murder. But the therapist does allow the patient to disagree. With most criminals, crime is apparently a way of making a living, and the therapist explores this with the patient. It is the negative consequences for the patient which will make the patient reform. Thus, patients who say they will not commit a crime because it is wrong, it is a sin, it is immoral, or just because it is a crime are all unlikely ever to reform. The patient who discovers that it takes more work to steal money than to earn it is very likely to reform. The patient who comes to realize that his criminal behavior is the symptom of stress, anxiety, guilt, or anger in relationship to his family and that these problems can be solved, is more likely to cease his criminal behavior. The therapist deals with symptoms, including criminal behavior, in terms of his total view of their seriousness. Thus, a homicidal patient who does not murder anymore, but continues to be a shoplifter, is a considerable therapeutic success.

In discussing social class differences (or any other issue), it is important to try to be accurate. Therapists can tell patients that middle-class males get less sexual gratification as teenagers than lower-class males do, on the average. But lower-class persons, male or female, are already old in their thirties, whereas middle-class individuals are just beginning. It is not uncommon for a delinquent to say, "Hey, I could have the best of both worlds."

If one never deals with the psychodynamics, one would expect to have very poor results in changing criminal behavior, and indeed, that is the usual finding. What distorts the picture about rehabilitation is that there often are staff members listed on the table of organization as psychiatrists, psychologists, or counselors who have neither the training nor the time and inclination to provide real psychotherapy. Psychologists, psychiatrists, and social workers who only write reports and psychiatrists who prescribe medication to inmates are not doing psychotherapy. A prison counselor whose main job is to check in the prison laundry is not doing counseling. It is absurd to point to such names on the table of organization and say we have tried rehabilitation and it does not work.

At best, jail rehabilitation programs gear themselves to the things which are the easiest to provide and which are useful, but which do not treat the patient and the patient's behavior in the total context of his life. Most good rehabilitiation programs provide education, job training, and job counseling, but not psychotherapy. Far too often when a patient does have some kind of counseling, the counseling is aimed at educating the patient about the self-defeating aspects of alcohol or drug use, again a useful thing, but done only in light of conscious awareness on the part of the patient and without a view toward the psychodynamic aspects of the situation.

The issue of psychodynamic rehabilitation was well described by a psychotic patient, who was referred after a suicide attempt. Initially, he said that he was praying 12 times a day, and he didn't see why he had to talk to a psychologist too. Nonetheless, he began at my (Karon) insistence. After a course of therapy, he not only lost his psychotic symptoms, he also lost his so-called sociopathic ones. Despite the fact that his therapist was not at all a religious man, and the patient expressed negative feelings about his own religion, he indicated that he believed in God more strongly as a result of the therapy. The puzzled therapist asked him why. He said,

"I was praying 12 times a day, and you were here. Reformatories don't have people like you. I know. I've been jailed eight times. If they had had somebody like you the first time, I wouldn't have had to go to jail eight times." Unfortunately, the patient was correct.

CRISES OF INCARCERATION

When working with incarcerated prisoners, there will be two early crisis points. The first is the initial jailing in a short-term jail or police holding facility. The therapist is involved at this point either because the inmate is in crisis or to do an initial evaluation. It is always advisable to tell the inmate why you are there and how little influence and what type of influence you have on his disposition. Because the final disposition of his case is not known, the prisoner fears what will happen to him, and this resonates with what has happened at other times when he was awaiting punishment. The inmate attempts to convince the therapist of his innocence and elicit the therapist's aid in getting him acquitted; this frustrates many therapists, but, this is a realistic maneuver. Not all "manipulations," however, are realistic, and the therapist can help to explore these counterproductive maneuvers in the context of the patient's early life.

Prior to trial and conviction, inmates rarely work on problems of long-term nature. Their focus at that point is crisis-evoked symptoms, including psychotic breaks. Such symptoms relate to the meaning of incarceration as punishment and the loss of choices and relationships.

After the inmate's case has been settled, the second crisis point occurs when the reality of the enduring loss of freedom hits. The beginning of the full sentence is usually coupled with a transfer to a new facility. The inmate loses whatever support systems he has built up in the initial jail, along with having to deal with the loss of his freedom. This crisis will resolve in 2 to 4 weeks, but the therapist can influence the kind of resolution.

It is possible to avoid much of the destructive effect of incarceration by directly asking inmates which of the limited options available in prison they prefer (Toch 1975). Some prisoners want physical security above everything, some want activity, others quiet, some want interactions, and others to be left alone. Toch has formalized these options in a questionnaire readily utilizable on a routine basis.

It is well known that when prisoners who have been incarcerated for 2 years or more are within several months of being released, they have a higher incidence of disruptive behavior, emotional upset, or escape attempts. The typical assumption is that this "release anxiety" is simply related to feeling out of touch with the routines of everyday life. While this is true, even more is going on emotionally. As the inmate gets close to release, he reexperiences anger about being incarcerated, he fears he will express it, and he attempts to deny it, only to project it onto the other inmates: "They're trying to make me mess up." The inmate's dependency has been gratified during incarceration, and the institution provides an external superego. Having to assume greater responsibility for oneself provokes anxiety, despite the protest that the patient is looking forward to freedom. In addition, long dormant issues in the inmate's interpersonal life resurface.

For example, one female prisoner spent 3 years in jail with virtually no contact with her family and was comfortable with this. As she neared release, she began to experience intense anxiety. Much of her worry related to what would be her father's reaction to her after her release. Would he be there to greet her? Would she act appropriately? Would he reject her? This was puzzling because virtually all of the members of her family had been in prison at some point, and there was little stigma in the family attached to having been in jail, but it had greater meaning to this patient as it reenacted an earlier separation and reunion.

When she was 12 years old she had almost died in an automobile accident; her father had been driving. A 6-month hospitalization followed, and her father never visited her because he was "too busy working." While she supposedly had been close to her father prior to the accident, he did not even acknowledge that she existed when she was released from the hospital. The parents had divorced while she was hospitalized; neither parent wanted her or her sister. The father was living with another woman and caring for her children, a double defeat for the patient, who was sent to live with an aunt until the patient married at 16.

She had experienced fury at this continued rejection. No one in the family was willing to acknowledge those feelings or was capable of helping her deal with her murderous fantasies toward her father. As she neared release from prison, she longed for acceptance and love from her family, particularly her father, but also reexperienced her rage, and was terrified she would "let it out" and be rejected forever.

PRISON HOMOSEXUALITY

The single most psychologically disturbing element of correctional institutions is the peculiar form of homosexuality practiced therein. According to the prison culture, a man who uses another man sexually, particularly by beating him up, is a "wolf" or "man," as long as his participation consists of only using his penis. The individual who uses his mouth or anus, even if he is literally raped, is considered a "fairy." Strangely enough, the professionals often accept this ideology.

This pattern of sadistic homosexuality is rampant in most institutions, and the custodial officers recognize that they cannot protect an inmate from the other inmates except by solitary confinement. Many authorities have recognized that conjugal visits are not only a humanitarian measure, but they will also decrease this most serious problem of prison, jail, or reformatory management. On the other hand, it is fashionable among many professionals to say that prison homosexuality is not homosexuality, that it is an adjustment to being in jail, and that one need not examine it too carefully. Indeed, the attitude of many career prison workers is to know that it exists, but not to want to talk about it. Many years ago Albert Ellis (1959), in a symposium on sexual problems of criminal offenders, suggested that much of the pressure would be lessened if inmates were allowed to masturbate. The paper was not included in the symposium when it was published.

It is useful to indoctrinate prisoners by giving a talk to them as a group, as follows: "Anybody who wants sex with another man bad enough to beat him up for it is a fairy. Somebody who only uses his prick still thinks of playing the other role, always. And anybody can be beaten badly enough to do anything. It doesn't mean a thing."

This latter statement is very effective with the sadistic homosexuals, who all too often enjoy a position of status within the inmate population. Frequently, they will seek out help, and in private say, "How did you know about that, Doc? I never told anybody."

The patterns of homosexuality in long-stay prisons with older inmates are not as violent as they are in institutions for adolescents. Usually in long-stay prisons if an inmate fights back a couple of times, even if he gets beaten, the other inmates will no longer attempt to rape him. With adolescents, the attempt to fight back is more apt to lead to repeated rape, until the individual who is not an effective fighter simply accepts his status as a homosexual object for the stronger inmate. Occasionally, an inmate who enjoys homosexuality has committed crimes in order to be incarcerated.

The homosexual pattern in reformatories, jails, and prisons often leads to a life of violence. Homosexual activity, other than being raped, like any sexual gratification, is pleasurable. The fashionable view that prison homosexuality is not homosexuality would lead one to believe that such feelings would disappear once the individual was free to engage in other kinds of sexual activity. The fact is such thoughts and feelings remain after release. The ex-prisoner feels anxious and guilty about such thoughts and handles them in a characteristic way by becoming aggressive. Within the delinquent and criminal subcultures, the way to prove you are a man is to be sadistic. Many violent crimes or acts of violence are committed on the basis of the need to prove that one is not a "fairy."

In particular, a large percentage of rape-murders are committed by men who have been previously incarcerated. The motivation is always to prove that they are not "fairies." How much more heterosexual can you be than to want sex with a woman so bad that you are willing to rape her, or even rape and murder her? This kind of violent crime could be greatly reduced by a more reasonable handling of the problem of homosexuality in prisons.

9

Early Clinical Formulations and Case Histories

The Number Four as an Example of the Use of Symbols in Schizophrenia

Bertram P. Karon

Jung was among the first to study schizophrenic patients psycho-analytically, and the importance of the number four within the framework of Jungian theory is well known (Jacobi 1949; Jung 1920, 1953, 1954, and see, in particular, *Mysterium Coniunctionis* Jung 1956, pp. 164–321). Jung points to the quaternity of the four mental functions (the two pairs of opposite functions: thinking versus feeling, and sensation versus intuition) which play such a central role in his theories. He also documents in detail the attractiveness and power attributed in many different cultures and periods to the manifestations of this archetype. Such manifestations are: the number four itself, the quaternio, the square, the circle divided into four parts, and the four-armed cross (for example, the Christian cross). According to Jung, this is an archetype of almost unequaled potency, importance, and interest, and, like all archetypes, it is put forth by Jung as evidence of the racial unconscious, inasmuch as it is postulated to exist in all cultures.

An alternative view with respect to universal symbolism, and one to which the present author subscribes, is that certain human problems are universal because of the biological nature and common experience of human beings. Where there are simple and readily available objects and ideas which are peculiarly apt for the expression of certain emotional themes, and where these objects and ideas are widespread over the earth's surface, their use as symbols of these emotional themes will be similarly widespread. For example, snakes (or ideas of snakes) are to be found in almost all parts of the world. Snakes are somewhat penis-shaped, capable of rigidity and extensibility, alive (that is, outside the control of the ego), and dangerous. Is it then surprising to find that an un-educated village girl in India employs the snake in her dreams as an unmistakable penis symbol (Alexander 1956) just as surely as any neurotic in western society (Abraham 1953)? (See also French's excellent 1954 discussion of water symbolism.)

This view of universal symbolism, which obviates the ne-cessity for postulating a "racial unconscious," follows directly from Ferenczi's description of the ontogenetic development of symbolism (1950c). Although such a view is not identical with Freud's (1900) original formulations, it is compatible with the symbolic interpre-tations he presented. These interpretations, while more mundane and restricted to the psychosexual sphere than those of Jung, have also proved more capable of experimental verification (Bettelheim and Hartmann 1951; Farber and Fisher 1943). Of course, despite generally found symbolic meanings, certainty as to the meaning any particular individual attaches to a symbol can be attained only by an intensive study of that individual.

In Freud's view of symbolism (1900/1950, p. 164), the symbol serves a specific disguise function. Its function is not only to express the unconscious, but at the same time to preserve the meaning of what is being expressed from reaching consciousness. It is this dual function which accounts for the use of the symbol. This disguise-function has been disputed not only by the Jungians, but by others who see the symbol as simply a primitive language without any disguise-function necessarily involved, for example,

Fromm (1951) and Hall (1953a; 1953b, pp. 99–100); however, the Freudian position once more seems to have experimental verification (Clark and Sensibar 1955). Rosen (1953, pp. 3–4), in developing "direct analysis," a psychoanalytic therapy of psychosis, extended this insight of Freud's to the symbols of the psychotic. As part of the direct analytic technique, direct interpretations are made of unconscious content, to undo the disguise-function of the psychotic delusions. A correct interpretation renders the patient's previous psychotic resolution ineffective, and makes possible a healthier resolution with the help of the therapist. Therefore, a knowledge of symbolism is a valuable tool for the direct analytic therapist.

The number three, according to Freud (1961/1943, p. 146), is "in a class by itself" as a penis symbol. It takes on this commonly found significance from the universal biologic fact that the male genitalia have three parts. But what of the number four? Freud presents no interpretation for this symbol and I found no reference to it elsewhere except in Jung.

In Jacobi's (1955) lectures on number symbolism at the Jung Institute, odd numbers were described as masculine, and even numbers as feminine. Three was described as the first "real number." Its meanings include such diverse referents as "the child," masculinity, and activity. Four was described as "three plus one," the quaternity which in turn is the "root and source of changing nature."

Jung himself (1954, p. 17) describes the meanings of the quaternity as completion, wholeness, the totality of the four mental functions, and "the container and organizer of all opposites . . . the possibility of order in wholeness." It may represent a totality with the four elements unintegrated within it, or it may represent integrated totality, unity, integration, and the self. Along with the closely related symbol of the circle, it is the "hallmark of the individuation process" (Jung 1954, p. 321), that process which is the aim, according to Jung, not only of psychotherapy but of all mental life; and the archetype of the quaternity refers both to the past and the future. Such a meaning would account for its compellingness as a symbol. Jung is unequivocal about the fact that this meaning is not dependent on experience but is inherited as part of the racial unconscious: ". . . for the latter [the quaternity] is not a human invention at all but a fact which existed long before consciousness . . ." (Jung 1954, p. 227).

It was, therefore, with great interest that the author noticed that the number four played a large part in the systematic delusions of a paranoid schizophrenic patient. The patient considered himself God, the "infinity being." He was arranging the world so that "everything be best." ("Best," it turned out, meant breast. "The mystics told me about the connection," he said, "many years ago, but I don't think about such things any more.")

The patient divided mankind into four parts: "the poor and bad" and "the good and best"; the same four-part division was applied to inanimate objects and to ideas. He made it clear that he wanted to deal only with the last two and have nothing to do with the first two of these subdivisions. He never differentiated the poor from the bad or the good from the best; nevertheless, he resisted the idea that there were only two subdivisions and insisted on four.

There were four sexes: male, female, male-female, and female-male. Each of these could be subdivided into four more subsexes labeled the same as the major sexes. In fact each of these 16 could again be subdivided into four more, again with the same labels, making 64 "if you want to be technical." There were also four dimensions: space, time, space-time, and time-space.

There were also four divisions of the world: mankind, animal, vegetable, and mineral. There were four ways men could be inspired to do good things: for themselves, for all people, for the world (including animal, vegetable, and mineral), and for him (God).

There were four earthly punishments he (God) could inflict on men: pain, suffering, obstruction, and social limitation; plus four degrees of damnation: eternal damned, accursed damned, worse damned, and temporary damned. There were four times: infinity past, infinity present, infinity future, and infinity eternal. There were four activities: thinking, believing, knowing, doing. In fact, the patient would insist that anything could, and should, be looked at from the standpoint of the four dimensions. Two phrases which recurred in his delusional monologues (in which he was "making the world best") were "four ways infinity from every present point in time" and "four ways infinity best."

The four activities (thinking, believing, knowing, doing) did indeed sound very Jungian; perhaps one should give the patient credit for tapping the collective unconscious instead of seeking a concealed psychodynamic problem. Thinking and believing might very well be the patient's equivalent of Jung's thinking and feeling. Similarly, knowing might be the equivalent of intuition. But doing hardly seems the equivalent of Jung's sensation, so Jung was abandoned as a source of enlightenment in favor of the patient himself.

The patient explained that, as God, he was also, of course, the greatest of philosophers. All of modern philosophic thinking would be impossible without his great discovery, which was none other than the "fourth dimension" (by this, he meant a fourth dimension to everything). You cannot, he would say, really think about anything unless you think in four dimensions. In three dimensions you can't find anything. People who "think in threes" are lost; they cannot do anything.

"If I say anything three times, it comes out all rotten. If I add a fourth, it comes out best." One day he was talking about childhood games, and devised a compulsive ritual which he explained as, "Step three times, then turn it into four."

One day he gave the author a lecture on numerology. When he was asked what the number four meant, he replied, "That's difficult. A square. A way of action. Perfect. Saturn number. Heavy—holding down. Perfect is turning threes into fours."

In this last sentence, the mystery was solved: "four" meant simply "not three." But why not two or five rather than four? In the patient's "lecture" on numerology, two was described only as "a feminine number," representing the breasts, and apparently the dangerous aspect of them. (After having reacted with fear to the approach of a woman with a well-endowed bosom, he explained his reaction as, "She came near me with her breast and I had a pain in my side; she was ruining me.")

The number one was also unacceptable, since it symbolized the same thing for the patient that three did. Five, on the other hand, was described cryptically as simply an "activity number"; it was perfectly acceptable. An alternative expression, and one apparently synonymous with "four ways infinity best" is "four, five infinity best." The patient got upset if four was changed to a lower number; he did not object to its being changed to a five. His reactions to other numbers depended on the special significance of the particular number: He, himself, never used anything but threes, fours—including 16 (four times four), 64 (four times four times four), and 256 (four to the fourth power)—and fives in his delusions. The lower numbers (one and two) are also avoided because someone might add something to change them into threes; four is the least number for which this cannot be done (and with abstract ideas no one can take away an element). Further, the patient can easily change any three into a four by the addition of another element, as when he added to the three more obvious times—infinity past, infinity present, and infinity future—a fourth, infinity eternal.

There remain only two more steps in establishing the thesis that the number four represented the denial of the penis (and of sexuality in general) for this patient: first, to show that three is for him a penis symbol, and, second, to relate the denial of the penis (and of sexuality in general) to his pathology.

In his "lecture" on numerology, his explanation of the number three was: "Success. Jupiter [it developed that Jupiter was the god, not the planet] has threes." Jupiter, it became clear from the rest of his material, represented the patient's father. Whenever Jupiter appeared in hallucinations, he appeared as three gods—either as three Jupiters, or as one Jupiter accompanied by two lesser gods. The clinching evidence for the significance of the number three for this case came one day when the patient was sitting contemplating three pencils which he held in one hand. The writer took the middle one, and the patient yelled in distress, "Give me back my penis."

As to whether this denial of masculinity makes sense, the patient hid his penis with his hand when talking to people. In the middle of a fairly friendly conversation when he was responding freely, the writer asked him what the number four meant, why everything had to come in fours. He immediately stopped talking and put his hand over his penis. He would make no further response to the question.

Hiding the penis represented both an attempt to hide the existence of the penis and to protect it from castration (of which he was afraid, partly because of his own desire for castration).

He referred to himself as a middle-aged woman, or woman-man. He said he was not a homosexual, but a lesbian. He then said that all sex was bad, it was not "best," he would not have anything to do with it. When urinating, he squatted like a woman; he did not stand. During one visit from his mother, the first thing he said was, "Gloria Vanderbilt [a mother symbol] is stabbing me in the back," accompanying the statement with a wiping motion from his anus. After she left, he said he was a lesbian. When the interpretation was offered to him that he thought his mother would love him if he were a woman, he replied that his mother was perfect, but that she liked young girls like Gloria Vanderbilt. Another time he brought up his mother's preference for young girls and was asked whether she was a lesbian. "No," he said, "she's a different kind of thing. She's a homosexual and I'm a lesbian."

"Are you a lesbian?"

"No," he said.

"Why?"

"You'll get mad."

"Why?"

"I'm going to learn; Greer Garson will teach me. Greer Garson and me will be lesbians. We will go and get some young girls together. Greer Garson has a penis which she hides."

"Do you have a penis?"

"No . . . I mean, yes."

The question was repeated a couple of times, and each time he first said, "No," hesitated, and then said, "Yes."

When talking to his mother he generally referred to himself as a woman and to her as a man. Still, he could not accept his desire to be a woman for fear of the castration involved—although he wished for it. He was terrified and wished to escape to a realm where there were no penises (and hence no sexuality). He was afraid of being touched by either sex. Interestingly enough, whenever Hera—who represented his mother—occurred in his hallucinations, there were always four Heras—four goddesses.

*   *   *

In brief, he felt that his mother resented his being a man, that this accounted for her hostility. Denying that he had a penis ("turning threes into fours") was one of his persistent symptomatic attempts to gain what he felt he lacked—the unconditional, unreserved love of his mother as symbolized by the good breast ("makes the world best").

This significance of the number four was derived entirely from the consistency of the observations; the meaning adduced for this symbol was not presented to the patient until after the paper was complete. Nevertheless, it has been maintained (Rosen 1953, pp. 3–4) that the best evidence for the correctness of an interpretation presented to a psychotic patient is a marked change in the pathology. In addition to Jungian concepts, the possibility that the number four referred to the four members of the patient's immediate family, or to traumatic events occurrng at the age of 4 years had been explored, without therapeutic benefit. It is worthwhile noting, therefore, that this interpretation did, in fact, have a marked effect: the number four, with which the patient had been concerned continuously for years, disappeared from his delusional system when it was interpreted as a denial of his penis and of sexuality in general.

Patients are always capable of teaching us what we wish to know about the unconscious, if only we are willing to listen. The problems which this patient symbolized by the number four are certainly common enough to suggest what the significance of this symbol may be for other human beings, normal and pathologic. In conclusion, the question may be raised whether it is a coincidence that the theory of Carl Jung, which originated in the denial of the importance which Freud ascribed to sexuality (Jung 1915, pp. 19–44, 67–95), should take as its cornerstone the symbol four.

Acknowledgements

The writer wishes to express his appreciation to Per Ostman for corroborating the clinical observations; to Robert Firestone, Anton S. Morton, Jack Rosberg, and Alden E. Wessman for helpful suggestions; and to John N. Rosen, under whose supervision the patient was treated.

A Contribution to the Understanding of Postpartum Psychosis

Jack Rosberg and Bertram P. Karon

Approximately 9 percent of all psychotic reactions in women develop in connection with pregnancy, according to Pasquarelli's (1952) review of the literature. Depsite the physiologic changes associated with pregnancy, he finds that "nearly all writers have agreed that psychological factors are of prime importance in the etiology of puerperal mental disorders." Unfortunately, there is no such agreement as to the nature of these psychologic factors. As Pasquarelli points out in a footnote, "The discussion of psycho-analytic concepts . . . is unfortunately brief because of a lack of specifically pertinent literature."

Physical discomfort, the meaning attached to being a mother, and sexual guilt are mentioned in Boyd's (1942) description of the psychologic roots of puerperal disorders. The physical discomforts that he lists include pains and sleeplessness during pregnancy, exertion during the delivery, and exhaustion following it. According to Boyd, being a mother may mean the end of carefree youth, it may mean being irrevocably tied to a husband who is disliked, and/or it may mean having to compete for the husband's love (sibling rivalry). In discussing sexual guilt, he states that when such feelings are strong (especially when incestuous fantasies are involved), pregnancy may be seen as the punishment for sexual activities. Frigidity as an indicator of susceptibility to psychosis is mentioned by Boyd; Pasquarelli, on the other hand, doubts its prognostic value in view of its high incidence in the general population.

Pasquarelli mentions, as etiologic factors, the anxious expectation of delivery as a great physical ordeal, leading to mutilation or death, and the factor of economic insecurity as indicated by the increased incidence of pregnancy disorders during the depression of the 1930s.

Both Boyd and Pasquarelli state in general terms that psychotic reactions are determined by the previous personalities of the patients and that one must be careful to distinguish cases where a previous psychosis is merely complicated by the pregnancy from those in which the pregnancy is a major etiologic factor.

These discussions seem somewhat unsatisfactory. In the first place, most of the problems which are mentioned are such as to reach their maximum intensity before—not after—the childbirth; yet only 15 percent of the psychotic reactions to pregnancy occur before delivery. Thus, the great majority of pregnancy psychoses remain inadequately explained.

Moreover, the factors mentioned are most likely to lead to gradually increasing anxiety and guilt reactions than to an acute psychotic break. Davidson (1936) reported that patients in whom psychoses developed during pregnancy did indeed show gradually increasing mood swings, insomnia, headache, and mild anxiety, but he found a considerably different picture in postpartum cases: sudden onset, mostly with excitement, which was sometimes precipitated by the patient's return from the hospital. Again, one can find no adequate explanation in the literature.

Finally, the discussions of psychologic factors by the writers surveyed seem superficial. Although fantasies are mentioned (incest, sibling rivalry), they are not thoroughly explored.

Fortunately, the psychoanalytic treatment of psychosis provides an ideal technique for the investigation of underlying fantasies, because of the intensity and depth of therapy necessary with psychotic patients. In the course of the treatment of a schizophrenic woman, a postpartum case, certain fantasies were discovered which, the writers believe, shed a new light on the postpartum psychoses.

The patient, a woman in her thirties, had been unsuccessfully treated in several institutions. Her treatments included both insulin and electric shock therapies.

At the time the treatment began, she was extremely aggressive, so much so that she was kept in restraint in bed during the first part of the therapy. Far from objecting, she preferred this treatment "because getting up makes me dizzy" (i.e., makes her lose control). At that time the patient was grossly overweight (approximately 55 pounds more than her normal figure). Most of this weight had been gained in the latter part of her institutionalization before the beginning of the direct analysis.

The reason for her illness, she said, was that "my husband made me pregnant." Pregnancy, she referred to, as "going through the mill." "The mill is responsible for my illness." At other times, she would deny any relationship between intercourse, pregnancy, and children; she would then say that children came by an arrangement "with the state." During the "pregnancy," she was nauseated but never vomited, according to her account.

As the analysis progressed, it became clear that her husband had, in many ways, replaced her mother in her emotional life. Their relationship to her might best be described as dominating dependence, whereby the mother, and later the husband, dominated her so that she would gratify their own dependency needs. Her mother had forced the patient to assume the mothering role to the patient's own siblings, and finally to the mother herself, on innumerable occasions. The transfer of this attitude to the husband is exemplified by the patient's description of the role of the ideal wife: "A good wife calls her husband at his place of business at least six times a day to make sure that things are going well and that she's available in case anything comes up. Also, she tells him what to eat, and how much to eat, and also when to change his underwear and his outside apparel. If she doesn't do this, she can't be considered a good wife."

This replacement of the mother by the husband was most graphically demonstrated when the patient was finally able to face the fact that her feelings of guilt about sex were derived from her mother. She then identified the voice she heard saying "Shame, shame," whenever she masturbated, as that of her mother. At this point her mother's voice disappeared, only to be replaced by her husband's voice saying, "Hermit."

"Hermit" was a word of reproach used by her husband to her during their courtship when she seemed uninterested in getting married. She said that she did not know what he meant by it, and asked people for many years thereafter what the word meant, since her husband would not tell her.

The change in the hallucinatory reproach not only mirrored the earlier temporal replacement of mother by husband, but also reflected a change from guilt about sex per se as opposed to sex in which she did not gratify the demands of the husband (mother).

The reverse process, replacing the husband with the mother, was shown during the periods when she attributed pregnancy and children to "the state." The state, it turned out, represented the impersonal controlling mother. This same impersonal controlling mother was represented in her delusions by the cathedral of Notre Dame, with herself as the cathedral's hunchback whose only security lay within the structure's impersonal confines.

Sexual relations were described by her as "the woman sucks with the vagina or mouth" (fellatio). She sometimes referred to her vagina as a "vagina-mouth." "A woman has two mouths: an oral mouth and a vagina-mouth." She insisted that she had "on doctor's advice" had intercourse "Russian style"; that is, she had put the testicles as well as the penis in her vagina. No matter how much she got she could never get filled. She referred to the testicles as "the two Ts" which also seemed to mean teats. Semen, she said, was like milk. After intercourse she was full of "semen and milk."

"Being through the mill," her expression for pregnancy, referred to the "mill" where flour was made; flour was white like semen and milk. Pregnancy, she said, was being "filled up with semen and blood and milk." The swelling had the significance of becoming "more and more full." "It's the only time I was completely full." In other words, a pregnancy represented the final solution to the oral problems of her life. These may be summarized as having to give (be a mother) instead of receiving (mothered), which is the need of every child. The husband (who replaced the mother) was at last giving, instead of taking, during intercourse, but he could never give enough. When, however, she had actually been pregnant, this signified, on the level of fantasy, that she was getting "fuller and fuller" of milk. The satisfaction she longed for was at hand; but just when she was satisfied, the child would be born, and she would be empty again. During the period in her psychosis in which she had gained the excess weight, she had eaten prodigiously and was so fat "that I couldn't move." She said she had been trying to fill the emptiness, but she had never been satisfied.

"When I went to school, I was hungry. My mother wouldn't feed me. So when my husband badgered me to marry him I accepted, thinking he would provide me with the things I needed, food and a home. When it turned out that he couldn't, I became pathological. The mill, or pregnancy as you called it, also did this and I got lockjaw." When the therapist interpreted the lockjaw as punishment for wanting to suck the penis or paternal breast, the patient got very angry, and denied the interpretation, saying it was "a movie version." She added that the therapist was "as draining" as her mother, husband, and sisters, who, she said, made constant demands upon her. If only she could avoid these relationships and rest, she could "fill up again."

A good deal of the delusional material dealt with scars. She felt that she had scars all over her body, including her face. Almost all of these were hallucinatory. One scar which did exist, and which she talked about considerably, was a scar in the vaginal region caused by childbirth. The hallucinatory scars on her face seemed related to a sense of shame. In addition, these scars, with the other hallucinatory scars, were proliferated representations of the vaginal scar, which she felt was very ugly. When she said that this scar was "growing," she was asked if she felt the vagina was growing. She said yes, and indicated that she felt the vagina itself was very ugly, like the scar.

The "ugliness of the vagina" was related to her feelings of guilt about her sex (about being female), which, upon analysis, seemed to be predicated upon two fantasies: first, her mother needed a man and it was wrong, therefore, to be a woman; second, it was wrong for her to want so badly to be fed by the mother-husband as to have a second mouth—the vagina-mouth.

Thus, when the oral catastrophe of childbirth had befallen her, the earlier explanations for her mother's mistreatment of her were reactivated to explain the fantasied loss (that is, the loss of all the "food" that had been filling her).

The attempt at a psychotic solution to this oral problem may be seen in her description of her "two mothers, the person on the outside who calls herself mother and the mother inside of me that is warm, loving, and affectionate." Was it any wonder, then, that she should cling so tenaciously to a psychosis which included the inside mother, when recognizing the external mother seemed the only alternative?

To recapitulate the fantasy connected with childbirth: being pregnant signified being filled with milk—the final solution to all the patient's deep oral problems—and the childbirth represented a catastrophic loss of this gratification. The prevalence, as a severe oral trauma, of such fantasies of childbirth seems likely, because of their potency in precipitating psychotic reactions; the preponderance of oral content has long been reported in the literature on psychosis (Fenichel 1945, pp. 387–451).

Moreover, Seidenberg and Harris (1949) have noted the relative absence of nausea and vomiting before delivery in women who later developed postpartum psychoses, as in the case discussed here. This may be understood when one considers vomiting as representing an undoing of the pregnancy in oral symbolic terms (cf., Grace and Graham 1952). The woman heading for a postpartum psychosis has no wish to undo the pregnancy; it is the delivery which is the trauma. The observation that the return from the hospital is often the precipitating factor becomes understandable, inasmuch as the hospital represents a temporary gratification of oral dependency needs. The problem becomes acute when the patient is deprived of even this gratification.

At this point, several objections may be raised to the implication that such fantasies as are discussed here form the basic factor in postpartum disorders: (1) that this is, after all, a single case; (2) that the case is that of a severe schizophrenic, whereas postpartum psychoses more frequently show manic-depressive than schizophrenic symptoms; and (3) that such fantasies might be present in previously pathologic individuals but certainly not in normal persons or even in neurotic individuals.

As to the first objection, a single case thoroughly understood is of far more scientific value than any number of cases superficially presented, and the other objections are based on the assumption that the fantasy pattern suggested here is special and limited— where the fact is that evidence can be cited pointing to the existence of this fantasy both in normal and pathologic individuals. Further, there is value in setting forth a hypothesis, even when the initial clues are few, for only when a hypothesis exists, as a guiding thread in the scientific literature, can further empirical data be assembled.

Such fantasies as those under discussion operate largely on an unconscious level, but the unconscious can be unearthed, and the existence or nonexistence of specific fantasies can be determined through the direct analysis of psychotic patients and the conventional psychoanalysis of neurotic patients.

Interestingly enough, analysts (for example, Silverberg 1952; Klein 1948) have reported dreams and fantasy productions of neurotic patients which are highly suggestive in terms of the present postpartum hypothesis. They report material that indicates that intercourse was viewed as being fed at the breast. It is a short step from such a view of intercourse to viewing pregnancy as being filled with milk.

Moreover, Michel-Hutmacher (1955) reported that in response to the question of what they believed was inside their bodies, children up to the age of 7 said that the body was a bag filled with food. From 7 to 9 anatomic details began to appear, but, only around the age of 10, were correct answers given. Apparently then, the notion that anything that fills the body is food not only can be found in normal persons, but is present *in consciousness* up to the age of 7.

Finally, consideration of a case of postpartum *neurosis* reported in the literature will serve to eliminate the possibility that this fantasy is peculiar to schizophrenic reactions. The case was reported by Freud (1892), when he was just beginning his discoveries. He treated the patient by means of suggestive hypnosis which was, surprisingly enough, successful. The patient, a young and normal-appearing woman, happily married and mother of one child, found herself repeating, with her second baby, certain extraordinary difficulties she had had with her first one. These had to do with her inability to nurse. As long as she tried to nurse her newborn baby, she was unable to eat, vomited, became agitated when food was brought to her bedside, and was reduced to a state of extreme depression and exhaustion. Her family doctors brought in Freud, and he tried hypnosis. The very first night he gave ordinary reassurances and commands: "Do not be afraid. You will make an excellent nurse and the baby will thrive. Your stomach is perfectly quiet, your appetite is excellent, you are looking forward to your next meal . . ." and so on. This worked temporarily, but at noon of the following day all the mother's symptoms had returned. That night Freud hypnotized her again and this time "acted with greater energy and confidence. I told the patient that five minutes after my departure she would break out against her family with some acrimony: What had happened to her dinner? *Did they mean to let her starve? How could she feed the baby if she had nothing to eat herself?* and so on." (Italics are the writers'.)

Note that this second suggestion was markedly different in character from the first. The first hypnotic suggestion had consisted merely of directions to suppress symptomatology, and its effects were temporary. The second suggestion was closer to an interpretation: the patient was directed to express oral needs rather than to suppress symptoms. Surprisingly enough, this peculiar character of the second suggestion, which, the writers believe, accounts for its effectiveness, is nowhere discussed by Freud.

From then on, the mother had no trouble. "Her husband thought it rather queer, however, that after my departure the evening before she had clamored violently for food and had remonstrated with her mother in a way quite unlike herself. But since then, he added, everything had gone all right."

The symptoms returned with a third child, but again were relieved by Freud. Unfortunately, he was not concerned explicitly with psychosexual development at that time and so has left no hint as to whether the same kind of interpretive suggestion was responsible for the second "cure."

Freud—in 1892—then confines his theoretical discussion to a consideration of the hysterias in general in terms of the operation of an "antithetic idea," which, he says, is inhibited, dissociated, and "often" unconscious, and which puts "itself into effect through the agency of the somatic innervations" despite the conscious intentions of the patient.

He continues, "I therefore consider that I am justified in describing my patient as an *hysterique d'occasion* since she was able, as a result of fortuitous cause, to produce a complex of symptoms so supremely characteristic of hysteria. It may be assumed that in this instance the fortuitous cause was the patient's excited state before the first confinement or her exhaustion after it. A first confinement is, after all, the greatest shock to which the female organism is subject, and as a result of it a woman will as a rule produce any neurotic symptoms that may be latent in her disposition."

From the vantage point of 1956, one may believe that Freud's 1892 discussion can be expanded to include the rather important description of the "antithetic idea" in terms of the later development of Freudian theory and of the present authors' own investigations. The remarkable effectiveness of the direct suggestion would seem to be the result of its interpretive character. This interpretive suggestion consisted of directions to act out the oral problems which the writers have reconstructed in their own schizophrenic patient. When Freud's patient was able to comply, the symptoms disappeared.

To sum up, the deficiencies in our present knowledge of postpartum psychosis seems to be caused by the inadequate consideration that has been given to the fantasy structures that underlie the traumatic impact of childbirth.

Through the psychoanalytic therapy of a schizophrenic woman with a postpartum psychosis, certain fantasies came to light which shed new light on the problem. Pregnancy had the significance to her of the final gratification of unresolved oral fantasies. The patient felt that the increase in girth was caused by the body's filling up with semen, which was equated with milk. The delivery was then viewed as a sudden catastrophic loss of this gratification.

Such unconscious fantasies seem to account for many of the unexplained characteristics of postpartum disorders.

The Mother-Child Relationship in a Case of Paranoid Schizophrenia

Bertram P. Karon and Jack Rosberg

"My mother is crazy. She made me crazy to save herself. She made me crazy to keep from going crazy herself."

Those writers, who, like the present authors, feel that their experience in the therapy of psychosis indicates a psychogenic basis for the disorder, have generally traced this basis to the relationship of the child to his mother from the earliest days of childhood on (Arieti 1955; Fromm-Reichmann 1950; Rosen 1953; Sullivan 1953). The notion that the child is, in a sense, the symptom of the mother, is not new; however, the descriptions that are to be found in the literature tend to lack specificity. We therefore feel it is of value to trace in some detail the interrelationship between the emotional pressures from the mother and the resultant symptoms in one patient with whom it has been possible not only to reconstruct the relationship from the therapy but also to observe the patient and his mother interact spontaneously over a period of many months. Striking was the finding that the symptoms did not seem to be the result of isolated traumatic incidents, but of continuing pathologic interpersonal pressures which prevented the problems of childhood from being resolved. Even today these same pressures can be observed in the involuntary reactions of mother and child when they spontaneously interact.

The patient, a male paranoid schizophrenic, began his psychoanalytic therapy when he was 32 years of age. His first institutionalization occurred at the age of 16. Subsequently, the patient had been in and out of various institutions, not because of remissions but because of successful escapes. During this time he was actively hallucinating even in those periods in which he was able to function in society.

At the time the treatment began, the patient had a completely developed delusional system in which he was God and was the object of many plots. The patient continuously talked in a loud, high, and feverish voice. Concomitantly, he made magic signs with his hands. The talking and magic signs would continue during all waking hours. These were in response to auditory, visual, and somesthetic hallucinations which he suffered continuously.

The first part of the treatment was carried out while the patient and his mother were living in a private house. One therapist lived in the house and other therapists were in contact with the patient during the course of the day.

Superficially, the mother does not impress most people as either disturbed or particularly unpleasant. It is only in viewing the interaction of the mother with the patient and with other members of her family that her pathologic state becomes manifest.

The lack of feeling in the mother was first demonstrated the day the patient arrived. At dinner there were four people: the mother, the patient, and two therapists. During this meal, the sole interest of the mother was that the patient act with decorum; she continually blocked his attempts to verbalize his fears—an attitude totally inappropriate to the situation in which the patient was making his first contact with the people who were to treat him.

The deep emotional involvement of the mother with the child was shown in the way in which she referred to him in talking to the therapists and to people in the treatment milieu. She seemed very proud of her brilliant, crazy son, and accepted not only his real accomplishments but also several of his delusional claims to brilliance. For example, the patient had, at one time, written a "book" which he had submitted unsuccessfully to several publishers. He claimed it was his PhD thesis in philosophy. He had written it while a special student at a midwestern university. It embodied certain essential parts of his delusional system. Although it was obvious to all the professional people concerned that this was delusional material, the mother insisted that this was a great philosophical work which showed the genius of her son, and she grew irate with the therapist when he began dealing with this as delusional material.

It seemed that she treated her son's accomplishments as if they were her own. She seemed to be fulfilling her own life through the efforts and achievements of the child; yet as we shall see, he could never be too successful, for then he would become independent of her. This may explain the fact that she did not differentiate those accomplishments which were delusional from those in which the patient had real ability.

The patient had been a child-prodigy; and much of the behavior of the mother seemed aimed at perpetuating that kind of relationship—a brilliant crazy son, like one who is a child prodigy, is one whose products would be admired, but whose enforced dependence on the parent can be exploited.

For example, she showed with great pride the poetry the patient had written as a child. For a child of that age, the work would have been considered promising, but, judged by any standard other than the age of the child, the poetry was worthless. The mother seemed oblivious of this fact. This might have been attributed to a simple overevaluation of her child's productions, except for the fact that repeated experiences with the mother in which she overvalued trivial or nonexistent accomplishments led one of the therapists to amazement when he found that the patient actually did have a real talent—since the mother had not differentiated the real talent from the nonexistent ones—and had shown him examples of the nonexistent talents first.

This is a good example of how the mother's conscious and unconscious motives interacted. Consciously, she was attempting to impress people with the accomplishments of her son; unconsciously, she was convincing them of his worthlessness by presenting the worthless productions first and the worthwhile productions later or not at all. The mother manifested no insight into the process.

The impress of such pressures was described by the patient at a period in the therapy when his delusional system had broken down: "Nobody thinks I'm worthwhile. My mother is the only person who thinks I'm worthwhile, she is always telling people I am worthwhile." But as exemplified above, the way she told people that he was "worthwhile" was such as to convince them of his worthlessness. His awareness of her real feeling came out when the therapist refused steadfastly to accept this valuation of the patient. Insistently he said: "Nobody thinks I'm worthwhile. And if you don't believe me ask the best people, like my mother." (It became clear from the analysis that the word "best" referred, in his delusional system, to the breast.)

The patient had one real talent—art. In this area he showed considerable ability. In the opinion of the therapist (Karon), the patient showed a great deal of talent as a draftsman, but very little feeling for color. When the therapist suggested that the patient was a better draftsman than colorist, that he seemed to enjoy charcoal drawing more than painting, the patient agreed saying, "Michelangelo told me I'd never be better at colors than him, but that I beat him in drawing." Nevertheless, during the brief periods when the patient was willing to use his talents, he labored mostly on oil paintings. This seemed to be because of the higher prestige he felt was attached to oils, and because of certain anal problems.

"What's the connection between shitting and painting?" he asked the therapist one day. "I don't understand it. They say there's a connection."

The therapist offered the interpretation that the child offers his feces to the mother as a present, and then when he finds that she doesn't like it, he may instead smear brown and black substances on a canvas and present it to her. (In fact, the lack of color sense in his paintings seemed to result from a predominance of brown and brown-black hues.)

These paintings, however, were not only an offering to his mother, but one she had demanded from him. When he was a child, she used to go into his room at night and go through his notebooks, taking out any paintings or poems she felt were complete. He used to cry and plead that they were his, but this never dissuaded her.

Within the first weeks of therapy, the mother complained to the therapist that the patient "always took and never gave; it's about time he started giving a little;" a complaint which again seemed totally incongruous to the situation of a sick child just beginning treatment. Moreover, the mother revealed at a later time in a conversation with the patient that "you were always a good child. Remember how you used to bring me gifts? When you get better you can do this again." There seemed to be a constant demand upon the patient from his childhood on, which he had attempted to fill at the expense of his own needs, but the needs of the mother were insatiable.

These overriding needs to take (be fed) were exemplified one day when the therapist observed her cracking a pile of nuts. These nuts, which grew wild in the area, were hard, tasteless, and not very meaty. She said, "After the rain all the nuts had fallen to the ground and the squirrels had stacked them in little piles and I came along and took them all." She chuckled and continued cracking.

The mother informed the therapist with a great deal of pride that she had breast-fed the child; having read considerably in psychoanalytic literature, she said to the patient at breakfast one day: "Didn't I have enough milk? Didn't I give you enough to drink?" To which the patient replied: "The cow gave her calf milk and then kicked it. She shouldn't do that. It's something that happened hundreds of times in the history of the world." When, in therapy sessions, the therapist reminded the patient of this statement, he steadfastly denied that it had anything to do with him: "It's just something that happened. The cow gave her calf milk and kicked him. It has nothing to do with me."

During the early weeks of therapy, the patient who at first had refused to drink milk finally told the therapist that "the Athenian girls are laughing at me. They say their breasts are poisoned." When the therapist assured him that he (the therapist) was stronger than the Athenian girls and that his milk was not poisoned, the patient asked for and received a large glass of milk which he drank, asked for a second which he also drank, and showed no distaste for milk thereafter.

The "poisoned milk" seemed to be caused not by any characteristic of the milk itself, but by the fact that the mother had resented any demands upon her to feed the infant, so that immediately after feeding she became angry. The child then felt the impact of her hostility, and was hurt.

This early problem was reflected in the patient's psychopathology in still another fashion when he was sitting down one day and was approached by a woman with a rather well-endowed bosom. He made frantic wiping gestures from his side. Afterward he told the therapist that "she approached me with her breast and I got hurt in the side."

The inability of the mother to feed was shown by the fact that after raising two children and after many years of married life, her cooking was barely palatable. As the patient told the therapist: "Why do you say things about my mother? I have a perfect mother."

"Does she give you good food?"

"No. It's terrible. She can't cook. She could never cook. You eat her cooking, too. How do you stand it?"

The therapist agreed that the food was pretty terrible.

Nevertheless, the essence of the oral problem was not in the food itself but in the feeling conveyed to the patient through the medium of food. This was shown by the hallucination of the pyramids which tormented him at one period, so much so that he finally brought himself to take what he considered the desperate step of asking the therapist, "You say you can help me. What do the pyramids mean?"

He was instructed to tell the therapist everything he knew about pyramids.

"There are many of them. They are from a long time ago in the history of the world. The history is not in mankind but in the stones. They are made of stone and have four sides."

"Do you know anything more about them?"

"There is a dead man buried inside of them."

The therapist interpreted the pyramids as representing the breasts, and the stoniness as representing the fact that the patient's mother's breasts had been hard and cold like stone, because there was no love. "A long time ago in the history of the world," it was pointed out, was what the patient said whenever he talked about his childhood. "The history is not in mankind but in the stone," was interpreted as the patient not remembering these things, but that they could be reconstructed from his hallucinations. The four sides, it was pointed out, referred to the patient's characteristic use of the number four to refer to a magical denial of his penis (three) and of sexuality in general because he felt these to be incompatible with his mother's love. The dead man was interpreted as the patient trapped inside his insanity which was like the stone breasts of his mother—cold, unrewarding, but the only breasts he knew.

"Why are there many of them?"

"Because it refers to things that happened again and again when you were a child."

The patient was asked to repeat the interpretations, which he did, changing only the significance of the dead man, which he said represented the penis which was dead. The therapist accepted the change, and the patient left the session tremendously impressed and excited by the interview—expressing the idea that maybe he could get better by talking to the therapist—an attitude sharply in contrast to his usual rejection and hatred of both the therapist and the therapy. Moreover, the hallucinations of the pyramids completely disappeared.

The feeling relationship between mother and child was further delineated when the patient explained to the therapist what love and hate were: "Love is when you go away from me, and hate is when you come near me." This relationship to people was interpreted as based on the patient's being able to fantasize an ideal image of his mother as loving him when she was not present, but when she was near him he could feel her hatred. This same relationship was in fact observed by the therapists in the patient's interaction with the mother in the treatment milieu. No matter how steadfastly he would defend his mother-image to the therapist, during meals and other periods when the mother was in close interaction with him, his hostility and resentment toward her would break through. As he said at one meal, "She's mean. Her meanness is like shit. She is always shitting. This is a shithouse."

Such an invocation of anal factors is not to be ignored. In fact, the mother showed many typical anal retentive traits. Focusing upon those which had a major impact upon the patient, we may note her insistent inquiries as to whether he had washed his hair, or hands, or showered, saying he smelled bad. "He smells like a pig" (despite the fact that the patient in reality was quite clean in his habits). Here we see the pattern of conscious concern for the patient's welfare, i.e., that he be clean, joined with unconscious hostility to make him feel that he is bad, worthless, and is in fact himself feces, which is what he seemed to be in her unconscious.

At the time she told the therapist that the patient had been breast-fed, she also mentioned that he had been completely toilet-trained before the end of the first year. Here again, we see her intolerance for feces, and her satisfaction of her own needs for cleanliness with little real regard for the needs of the infant.

"You don't understand me and my mother. You're a warm, a hot person. Me and my mother, we're cold people. And you can't understand us. My mother doesn't hate me. There was no emotion. She was just cold."

Just how strong the resultant fears of his own feces were in this patient was shown in the fact that periodically the patient would fast insofar as the therapists would allow it, even after his fears of being poisoned had been resolved. These fasts were not terminated until the patient explained that if he could stop eating he would "not have to shit." The therapist demonstrated that the patient's feces were not harmful by accompanying him to the while he was defecating, essentially demonstrating that the therapist did not find the feces repulsive. Further, the interpretation was offered: "Look how clever your mother was. She knew you had to shit every day in your life. And if she could make you feel guilty about it, she could be sure that you would be unhappy at least once every day."

(The schizophrenic patient maintains an ideal mother-image, the corollary to which is that he himself is worthless, since the ideal mother rejected him. The therapist, therefore, attacks this image, often going to extreme lengths. Under such provocation, the patient is often able to face his own hostility for the first time by expressing it as a "defense of the mother," e.g., saying, "She didn't intend to do it; she hurt me because she couldn't help herself.")

The importance of these anal pressures to the patient was shown when he was asked to talk about his envy of his younger brother. He immediately mentioned anality:

"There's no envy about shit."

"Do you remember anything about shit?"

"My brother shit in the bathtub when he was five years old and my mother cleaned it up."

"If you had shit in the bathtub at that age, what would have happened?"

"I don't know."

"Would your mother clean it up?"

"No."

"Would you be punished?"

"Yes."

"How would they have punished you?"

"I don't know. But it would be awful."

Thus we see that this patient's feeling that his brother was loved more than he (which we find in nearly all patients) was in fact based on preferential treatment. Moreover, at the time the brother was born (when the patient was 4 years old), the patient suffered from whooping cough and was tended by the mother personally while he was confined to bed. Suddenly the mother left him to have the second child and did not come near him for almost two months—a minor eternity to a sick 4-year-old. No wonder he felt that his mother loved the younger brother more.

Paradoxically, by her preoccupation with him, the mother seemed to show that the patient was actually her favorite; in fact, she maintained this to one of the therapists. This may be understood when it is realized that the patient, who had been crippled emotionally by the mother, was crippled in such a way as to fulfill her pathologic needs; insofar as he did so, he was naturally the favorite. The other child who was not needed for such pathologic purposes, was allowed a more nearly normal life. His problems are much less severe; still, she had produced in him a neurotically overdependent character-structure.

Observation of the mother's relationship with the male members of her family revealed that she dominated and in many respects emasculated them. One of the sources of her hostility to the therapist, who lived in the same treatment house with her, was his unwillingness to participate in the housework. This contrasted sharply with the attitudes of her second husband who, for example, washed every dish at every meal whenever he visited the treatment house. She once told the patient: "Remember how you used to help me with the dishes? When you get better you can come and do my dishes for me again."

When, during the first few weeks of therapy, the mother inquired about another patient, "Will she go back with her family?" she was informed that patients are not considered cured if they have to go back and be dependent upon their family, that they must be able to start a new life and find their own friends. This casual comment provoked marked signs of anxiety in her.

Quite striking in terms of its dynamics was the contrast between the patient's version of an incident in his childhood and the way his mother related it. When the patient started his analysis, he steadfastly maintained under repeated questioning that he could remember nothing about his childhood or his family, and anyway "my mother was nice, my father was nice, my family was nice, and nothing happened in my childhood." One day, however, the patient was talking aloud delusionally in an English stage accent.

When asked where he had learned that accent he said from his grandfather. Upon further inquiry, he said that his grandfather had been very rich and was born in England and used to visit. It was his paternal grandfather. He then produced a memory of his grandfather having taken him in to New York to buy a Little Lord

Fauntleroy outfit. He had cried and refused, because he didn't want to be a sissy. Because of this they didn't get the suit and his grandfather was very angry with him.

"Was there anyone with you?"

"Yes."

"Who?"

"My mother."

"What did she do?"

"She wanted me to get the suit."

"Why didn't she stand up for you?"

"My grandfather was rich."

"Wouldn't a good mother have stood up for you?"

"No, my grandfather had money."

"Was your father there?"

"Yes."

"What did he do?"

"He didn't do anything that I remember."

Here we see the patient forced into being a "sissy" and crying because of it. The version of the same incident which the mother told the therapist was that the patient had resented it once when he was bought a hat. They had, she said, bought him a velvet suit and then when they bought him a man's hat to go with it, he started to cry. When asked if it wasn't the suit that be objected to, the mother said, "No, it was the hat. He started to cry when he was told it was a man's hat."

In this version, the masculinity rather than the effeminacy was the cause of the upset. This corresponded to the mother's wish that the son be emasculated lest he threaten her with the specter of her being a woman (mother).

The patient had at first denied that he was a man, and maintained that he was a woman; at times he denied that he had a penis, referred to himself as a lesbian and to his mother as a homosexual. When he claimed that he was a woman, the therapist asked him whether he thought his mother would love him if he were a girl. The patient said: "My mother loves little girls like that, but I don't see what this has to do with me."

Other factors leading the patient to a homosexual solution were, of course, his desire to find oral gratification from a masculine breast (the penis) if no feminine one could be attained, as well as an escape from the fear of castration engendered by oedipal feelings. The latter represents the classic view of homosexuality, but we find even this presented in the case material in a somewhat different fashion than is described in the literature.

The most patent expression of oedipal feelings came one day when the patient heard his mother in the next room. He called: "Come in here, mother, I want to fuck you." The mother came in from the next room and said, "What is it, ——, is there anything I can do for you?" The patient changed the subject. Interestingly enough the mother acted as if she wasn't quite sure what he had said although she seemed pleased; however, the physical surroundings were such that is was practically impossible for her not to have heard the patient's words quite clearly.

The oedipal theme came through even more clearly when the patient suddenly reported a dream. He was at another treatment house talking to a middle-aged female patient, who showed no great interest in him. After trying unsuccessfully several times to attract her interest by interrupting a game of Scrabble which she was playing by herself (this maneuver only aroused her hostility), he suddenly announced: "I had a dream about you before I came here. (In fact, the patient had met her only since his arrival.) I thought it was ——'s wife, but now I see it was you. I fucked you and my penis came off." When he returned to his own house, he immediately ran up to his mother and said, "Mother, I had a dream. I dreamt I fucked —— (the female patient) and my penis came off." Here we see the mechanism noted by Ferenczi (1953, p. 349), whereby the person the patient is eager to tell his dream to is the one whom it concerns. The middle-aged woman whose identity keeps changing would lead us to suspect the mother in any case. In talking about this and related delusional material with the therapist, the patient finally said, "It's not that I wanted to fuck my mother, it's that there is an agreement that I have to do it. I don't want to do it because there is a fixture on the cunt which will hurt my penis and it will come off. I don't want to do it, but there is an agreement and I have to." This agreement seems to be his representation of the pressures from the mother.

Underlying this castration fear is not only the feeling that she will take his penis after he has been forced to have intercourse with her, but also there is a wish to be castrated so that the demands of the mother that he give up his sexual products will not have to be met. This comes out in his repeated use of the number four in his delusions, as well as in the delusion that his brain is injured. On analysis, the number four proved to represent a magical denial of the number three ("Perfection is turning threes into fours"), and three was clearly revealed by the patient's associations as a penis symbol.

The significance of the delusion that he was brain-injured was revealed in the first dream the patient had during the analysis (after about 6 months of therapy). He carefully dictated to the therapist: "I was walking along the street in a city (probably Philadelphia). I looked down to the left down one street and saw about one-third down there a tall office building being taken down. It was 20 stories high and the facade was left. I was afraid it would fall down on the street because it had no backing. I looked more carefully and I saw that there was a scaffolding and workers were carefully removing the planks so that there was no fear of the office building falling down, either hurting me or hurting the crowd. There was about this time the thought or vision of a plank but there was no connection.

"I walked along the street and met a woman, middle-aged, grey hair, a middle sized woman, very nice. The people in the street told me spiritually to fuck the woman, or to have intercourse with the woman; we have to be diplomatic or facetious about it. Sexual relations are the words I use. I was doubtful about it for the first time, but the ladies on the street told me it was best, or rather good, that I should do it. So I, following directions, as I had for 16 years, when I was crazy, following other people's directions, agreed to do it and went with the lady. We looked for a place where we could have sexual relations and she took me to a house on the opposite side of the city street. The house was about five stories high, an old building, going into the house we found a whole lot of booths, small rooms, whorehouse I suppose it was. In the business, that is. We went up about three or four, four or five floors and then when I got up to the fifth floor, I sat down at a table and another lady gave me a notebook. It was a notebook of Eisenhower's about me, and there was no greatness thought on it. It was about 50 pages, brown cover. There was a methodical objective about me, I don't know what it was. I read about two-eighths of the book. I came across four pages of outline drawings of my head. On each of them there were numbers, four or five numbers, on the fourth drawing there was on the right cheek, no, on the left (the right of the drawing), a note 'saggital (sic) nerve of the occipital lobe is cut,' severed you had better put down. In remembrance it may be 'sanguinary' (sic). After that I woke up. I thought to read the rest of the notebook but I didn't. The lady wasn't fucked in the dream."

The patient reported that he had had the feeling of brain injury the night before and it had continued until he woke up after the dream and "cleared it off" with magic signs. Here we see the sequence of the patient about to have intercourse with a female who represented the mother. Instead of this he gets a notebook which says that there is brain damage. The specific meaning of the brain damage as castration was revealed by the patient's associations.

"You said it was the saggital or saguinary nerve that was cut."

"Yes . . . no . . . it was more . . . it was the saggitary, that's it, the saggitary nerve."

"What does saggitary mean?"

"I don't know. It's just a word the physiologists use."

"There's no such nerve. Have you ever heard the word saggitary anywhere else?"

"No."

"Can you think of anything that sounds like saggitary?"

"Nothing at all."

"Are you sure?"

"Yes."

"Have you ever heard of Sagittarius?"

"Yes. That's in astrology which I studied for many years."

"What do you remember about Sagittarius?"

"Nothing. What month is it?"

"What does Sagittarius carry?"

"A bow and arrow."

"And what is an arrow?"

"A penis."

"Who told you that?"

"I don't know. No one."

Thus we see that the individual avoids intercourse with the mother by wishing for castration. Since the incestuous relationship is not conceptualized as a desirable lustful experience but as an onerous and dangerous task in which he is obliged against his will to give up his products to his mother, such a wish to be relieved of the obligation seems a natural resolution—for with a penis it is both dangerous to have intercourse and dangerous not to comply with the demands of the mother.

Finally, we may ask what it was that determined the actual outbreak of the overt psychotic symptoms. When the patient was 12, his father had died from what may have been an accident. Certain circumstances, however, strongly point to the possibility of suicide. The patient was never told how his father died "to spare his feelings." Once more we see a consciously benevolent attitude masking an unconscious malevolent attitude—what better way to ensure guilt feelings over death wishes toward the father than to keep the manner of death mysterious?

The father had been a weak, ineffectual character, nevertheless loving as compared with the mother and hence a sustaining force in the patient's life. When he learned that his father was dying, the patient had his first hallucination, according to his recall. He prayed to God to save his father's life, and a voice told him his father would be spared. The next day the father died.

The mother traced the illness of the patient to the death of the father. Her insistent repetition of the more or less classic interpretation of death wishes toward the father when there was nothing in the behavior or conversation of the patient which related to these feelings aroused the suspicion of the therapist. Literally hundreds of times the mother said to the patient with no provocation, "Did you think you killed your father? You didn't kill your father. Nobody blames you for killing your father."

The mother described the family situation before the death of the father and, in fact, during the patient's whole childhood as having been "happy." Eventually, however, the patient revealed that 6 months before the death of the father, the mother had left, saying she wanted a divorce and then had returned later "because she needed money." Eventually the patient was able to recall the "civil war" inside him when he felt he had to choose between his mother and his father, and he chose his father. And then his father died, and he felt his mother had killed him and would kill the patient too if he ever got her mad. The psychosis at first took the form of an interest in spiritualism, and the hallucinations (or spiritual world) represented the fact that there was no death, that it really didn't matter whether one was alive or dead. The patient was able to hide the fact that he was actively hallucinating for several years. Apparently, with the reassurance that the hallucinations gave him that death was unreal, he was able to deal with his mother, but no delusional system really works, and eventually it did not suffice; he then complained about the conspiracy against him in which his mother was involved. He was first institutionalized at that time.

The close involvement of the mother's adjustment with the psychosis of the patient was exemplified by the fact that the hostility of the mother to the therapist who carried out the bulk of the analysis varied directly with the patient's improvement: whenever the patient took a turn for the worse, her hostility decreased; whenever the patient began to improve, the hostility increased. The mother showed no insight into this process—the hostility was always attributed to other sources, and consciously she was going to great lengths in order to ensure the cure of her son; however, her underlying feelings were revealed transparently in a casual remark to another therapist: "I'm so busy now I don't have time to worry about myself, but when he gets better I'll have a nervous breakdown," and the patient revealed his understanding of the relationship when he said one day, "My mother is crazy. She made me crazy to save herself. She made me crazy to keep from going crazy herself."

In summary, we have examined the interaction of a schizophrenogenic mother and her child and have found the following dynamic constellation:

The mother is an immature person whose immaturity is a result of the deprivations she herself suffered in the course of her emotional development. There is a paucity of abilities on her part. She fulfills her own life through the efforts and achievements of the child; yet he cannot achieve too much without raising the specter of escaping her. Therefore she must present the twin demands—produce great things for me, but don't be too successful at it.

Her immaturity is reflected in her lack of warmth, and her inability to accept herself as either a woman or a mother. Her inability to accept herself as a woman, makes it impossible for her to accept masculinity in the men in her life, including her children; and when projected into a situation of mature responsibility in which she has to give (be a mother), she faces this responsibility with increasing hostility, anxiety, and resentment which inhibits the growth of the child.

Her self-evaluation is negative; this is projected onto the child. The good traits of the child are accepted as her own. The child necessarily accepts the projected bad qualities in order to maintain the ideal image of the mother. This is especially true with respect to attitudes toward feces. The mother feels like feces and projects this feeling on to the child, who accepts this negative evaluation. This exchange of her own bad traits for the child's good possessions seems to be the mechanism whereby the mother staves off a psychotic breakdown in her own personality.

The Oedipus Complex in an Apparently Deteriorated Case of Schizophrenia

Jack Rosberg and Bertram P. Karon

The existence in psychotic patients of classic oedipal problems as described by Freud is unmistakable. The authors feel that any observer who comes in close contact over a prolonged period of time with psychotic individuals cannot fail to see evidence of such fantasies; however, the meaning, as we see it, of such fantasies seems to be somewhat different from the classic interpretation and more in keeping with Freud's 1931 statement, in a different context, that ". . . it seems that we shall have to retract the universality of the dictum that the Oedipus complex is the nucleus of neurosis . . ." (Freud 1931/1950, p. 253).

The significances which we have found in psychotic patients for such fantasies were most clearly presented to us by an apparently deteriorated and almost unreachable patient. The patient had a long history of slowly developing problems. He had been sent to many schools for disturbed children, each school eventually finding him too difficult to handle and sending him on to a school for the more severely disturbed. Eventually, he entered a conventional outpatient analysis at the age of 17. After a short period, his analyst gave up, saying the patient was psychotic. He was sent to a psychiatric institution, where he was unsuccessfully treated by standard procedures, including electric shock and insulin treatments. After physical therapies had proved unsuccessful, psychologic therapies, including several psychoanalytic approaches, were attempted at several different institutions. These also failed to remit the psychosis.

At this point, the authors began treatment. The patient, a young man of muscular build, was approximately 26 years old at the time. At this point, he showed little responsiveness to his environment and had lost all control over his bodily functions. It was necessary in the treatment milieu to care for him in every respect—feed him, clothe him, bathe him, care for all his physical needs. This was complicated by the fact that the patient was given to periodic outbursts of violence. These were accompanied by a relative improvement in contact to the point where he would utter one or two intelligible words. The most frequent of these were "room," "dear," "drink, drink," "the work," and "get out."

There were marked signs of physiologic dysfunction. The patient's hands were generally cold, his fingernails blue, and his skin showed goose pimples even in the hottest weather. His digestive processes were sluggish, as evidenced by the odor of decaying food which emanated from his mouth, resulting from not a mouth but a stomach condition. It will be noted that all of the physiologic disturbances manifested by the patient are components of the normal terror syndrome—vasoconstriction, slowed digestive processes, and lack of control over excretory functions. With respect to the last, however, he would at times manifest an extreme control over his bowels, with no movement occurring for weeks at a time.

Interestingly enough, in his bursts of aggression, he might lash out with equal vehemence at the people in the treatment milieu, at thin air, or even at himself. This was a considerable problem inasmuch as his physical strength had enabled him to break the jaws of two attendants at one institution.

The nights were fraught with terror for this patient; his sleep was light and the people who cared for him were awakened nightly by his terror-stricken screams, which were apparently in response to his hallucinations.

Because of the patient's strength and potential violence, it was necessary to keep him in restraints a good deal of the time.

At the time the authors began working with the patient, Karon spent 8 continuous hours with him. During this period, nothing the patient did or said was intelligible to the therapist: nothing the therapist said seemed to have the slightest impact. As a last resort, the therapist sat the patient in front of a TV set, hoping that the screen would hold the patient's attention, but it did not. The therapist sat down next to the patient, placed his arm around the patient's shoulders and said, "What a nice baby you are." The therapist hoped that the physical contact might reach the patient at some preverbal level. He continued this for a half hour. The patient showed little apparent awareness of even this contact.

In all future sessions, the two authors worked together. This had several advantages. Physical restraints could be discarded without danger to the therapists; the patient could be induced to move around, which seemed to "loosen" the psychosis; the emotional intensity of the therapy session could be maintained at a fairly high pitch for longer periods of time (by alternating therapists), and the therapist not working at the moment with the patient could pick up cues that were missed by the therapist who was intensely involved with him. Moreover, it is of prime significance that what restraint and control were necessary were imposed directly by the therapists and not by artificial restraints. The import of this will be discussed later in some detail.

It might be argued on the basis of classic techniques that the use of two therapists would lessen the therapeutic relationship by "diluting" the transference. The original object relationship, it might be pointed out, consisted of one person—the mother; however, it is our experience with psychotic patients that the needs of the patient for mothering are so intense that he readily forms a transference to several people. Moreover, it is questionable what meaning can be assigned to the concept of "diluting" the tranference unless a therapeutically usable transference exists. In this patient, although transference needs were present, they were therapeutically unusable because of his massive psychotic defenses. It was only by the combined efforts of both therapists that these massive defenses were penetrated and a workable transference established.

Incidentally, the apparently apathetic, deteriorated, unresponsive appearance of such patients is at least in part an active defense. It is a successful defense insofar as it exhausts any therapist who attempts to breach it, but by the continued persistent efforts of two therapists who alternated in a continued long-term high-pressure session, this patient's apparently almost insuperable defenses began to give way.

Each day the therapists devoted several hours to intensive continued work with the patient. A single question based on his fragmentary utterances, such as "What happened in the room?" might be repeated to the patient innumerable times day after day until the patient seemed to tire and respond. The lack of mechanical restraint and the willingness of the therapists to deal with the patient's aggression directly gave him a feeling both of freedom and of security. He had the assurance that nothing he could do could place him in jeopardy, that he could always depend on the therapists to control those urges in himself of which he was afraid. That this control would be exerted directly by the therapists enhanced the personal relationship and helped to build the therapists into the omnipotent benevolent parent figures which the sick patient typically has never had but which he wished for so desperately.

The first meaningful material that emerged for this patient (after about a week of such therapy) did not deal directly with the oedipal fantasies, but with a homosexual episode. In response to the question, "What made you crazy?" the patient finally said he was sick because of what he and his brother did. On further questioning, he stated that they had performed fellatio* upon each other. The patient then became angry with no apparent cause. Rosberg asked him why he was mad at his brother. The patient

*The discussions of sexual material were, for the most part, carried on in the Anglo-Saxon terms that were most characteristic of the patient's own speech. Less printable in 1958 than technical language, this form of discourse is much more meaningful emotionally and much more effective communicatively.

responded saying that his brother had performed fellatio upon him first (that is, the brother taking the oral role and the patient taking the genital role), instead of letting the patient take the oral role first.

On the following day, the first oedipal fantasy appeared. One of the words which the patient had from time to time muttered aloud was "the room." Again and again the therapists had repeated the question, "What happened in the room?" Finally, the patient responded that he had seen "them making love, being affectionate, knowing each other." In response to further questioning, he said that he was "in the room. The door was stuck." He couldn't get out, and he was scared. When asked who was on top, the man or the woman, the patient said, "The woman."

[And which one did you wish was dead, the one on the top or the one on the bottom?] "The one on the bottom."

Here we see a classic primal scene with oedipal feelings expressed, whether it be reality or fantasy. The child saw the mother and father having intercourse, and he wished the father were dead.

On the following day we explored this material further. The active defense of the apparent inability to concentrate was demonstrated by the fact that the patient would talk coherently until the threatening material was approached and then he would get dreamy and fragmentary. He finally admitted that he had been in the room and had watched them have intercourse.

[Who were they?] "The big." [The big who?] "The parents." [Who was on the top?] "The lovely wife." [Who was on the bottom?]

The patient would not answer this question. After repeated interrogation, the patient muttered something about "the brother," but was unwilling to elucidate.

Tiring of this tack, the therapist returned to asking what happened in the room, and when the patient said he saw them having intercourse, the therapist asked him how he felt about that.

"I have to give them a shot." [Both of them?] "One of them." [Which one?] "The lovely wife."

He then drifted off. The therapist brought him back again and again to the room situation. On one of these occasions he was asked how he felt and he said, "Western."

[What does that mean?] "The cow."

Again he became incoherent. After several more attempts by the therapist to bring him back to the room situation, the patient suddenly said, "Ouch." He seemed to be holding his testicles with his right hand, which was in his pocket. He then said he wanted his mother to play with it, but she might hurt it.

[Did they say they'd cut them off?] "Yes."

He was then asked who it was that said they would cut off his testicles, and he replied, "She."

[Did your mother say she would do it?] "She didn't mean it."

Here we may note that the castration threat seems to come from the mother and not the father. This is typical of castration fears as we have encountered them in psychotic patients.

The pattern was much more clearly demonstrated in a later therapy session. After describing an incestuous fantasy concerning his sister, who, he said, resembled his mother, the patient was plied with classic interpretations. For half an hour or more Rosberg, to test the theory, attempted to get the patient to react to interpretations that his incestuous wishes led to a fear of castration by the father. These repeated and intensive interpretations produced no sign of anxiety or of recognition. Finally, after an unsuccessful leading question, the therapists allowed the patient an opening for describing the mother as the castrator.

[If your father had a knife, what would he do to you for incest?] "I'm not sure."

Karon interrupted at this point and asked whether it was his mother or his father who would take the knife to him for having intercourse with his sister.

"My mother." [What would she do to you?] "Cut it off." [Cut what off?]

The patient said that it was his penis that would be cut off. It was possible at this point for the therapists to gain insight into the dynamics of this fantasy by pursuing their line of inquiry. They asked the patient why his mother would cut off his penis for incest.

"So that she could get a platter regularly."

The patient was asked whether he meant that his mother could use his penis "to feed her whenever she wanted." "That's right, so that she could get a platter all the time."

Thus, the patient told us that the reason he felt that his mother would castrate him was not as punishment for incest, but because she wished to appropriate a source of food.

Intercourse is viewed by the patient as a feeding experience with the penis doing the feeding and the vagina being a mouth (which makes accountable the patient's earlier use of the word "cow" in the primal scene).

Penises, he said, go into vaginas, and, "A penis is like a breast. Breasts give milk."

The patient told of another incident in which his sister had "dropped her pants" and showed him her vagina. He said she was trying to seduce him because, "She wanted me to feed her. She was like my mother."

One of the most effective questions employed by the therapists proved to be, "What's the worst thing that ever happened to you?"

On one occasion when this question was asked, the patient responded by saying that his mother had taken "it" off and "put it in the drawer."

[What?] "Her bathing suit."

The patient said that she had sat down on "the desk" and spread her legs and showed him her vagina and that he was scared. "She was always taking things away from me." He continued that he was afraid "she wanted me to feed her" and he couldn't. The patient was asked whether this was an "illusion" or reality, and, after some hesitation, the patient replied: "I think it really happened once."

On another occasion in response to the inquiry, "What's the worst thing that ever happened to you?" the patient replied:

"It hurts in the stomach." [What hurts?] "Being hollowed out."

It was clear at this point that the basic problem was one of being fed, filled up, as opposed to having to feed, to give up one's products, to be hollowed out. A demand is felt from the mother that he feed (have intercourse with) her, which conflicts with his own never-fulfilled need to be fed. He characterized vaginas as being "sadistic," and once described his mother's vagina as being "like a food chopper."

His reaction is shown in the therapy session in which the therapists brought up the subject of intercourse. The patient was asked whether he preferred having intercourse with an anus or a vagina. He said he preferred anal intercourse. He was then asked whether he preferred intercourse with a man's anus or a woman's anus. He said he preferred a man's anus.

[Why?] "Because you can get a drink." [From what?]
"From the penis," the patient said.

[Where?] (After a pause) "In the arm."

This reply puzzled the therapists. Eventually, the therapists got the idea that he meant a magic vagina which he formed with his fingers while he talked. When he was asked if this was the case, the patient said that it was. The therapists decided to put this to a further test at a later time, which they did by having Rosberg form a circle with his fingers and ask the patient:

[What is this?] "A zero."

The patient was asked whether it was a vagina, and he replied that it was not. The therapist then made the opening long and narrow, and again asked the patient whether it was a vagina. When the patient again said it was not a vagina, the therapist asked him to make it into a vagina. The patient reached out and reshaped the therapist's fingers until they were a replica of his own hand.

This wish to have a vagina, which was manifested by the magic vagina on his hand, came out clearly at another time when the patient said that he envied his sister. When asked why he envied his sister he replied that he envied her because she had a vagina. When asked why he envied her vagina he said, "Because it is beautiful and the old guy likes it."

On another occasion when he said that he wanted a vagina, he was asked why he wanted it and replied, "So that I can get my groceries through it."

His wish for a vagina implied a wish for castration; not only would he have another "mouth" to be fed through, but the possibility of his being called upon to act as a feeder would be eliminated, or, as he stated, no one could make him urinate in their mouths.

His visual hallucinations consisted of innumerable repetitions of two themes. The first of these consisted of his mother or sister making such "seductive" and terrifying demands that he "feed her." The second consisted of a series of related "room" fantasies. These "room" fantasies were related by the patient in response to the question, "What happened in the room?"

By far the most frequent answer related to the primal scene, which was apparently also the most frequent hallucination. The patient described this primal scene in detail in a therapy session, saying that they (his parents) were standing up and that his mother was bending over (more ferarum). He demonstrated the position. He said that he saw his father's penis go in, but he didn't see it come out, and "I felt bad."

In later therapy session, he commented on the primal scene, "I want to go home, but they don't want me."

At times when the patient was asked, "What happened in the room?" he would describe other scenes. In each of them, however, there were two people in the room. Sometimes they were his mother and a stranger having intercourse; sometimes they were his father and a stranger having homosexual intercourse; sometimes they were his father and his brother having homosexual intercourse; once it was his mother and brother without specifying their activities. Although the most frequent event referred to was the mother and father having intercourse, the most disturbing was the session during which he said that the two people in the room were his mother and sister. During this session, the therapists had asked him insistently again and again, "What happened in the room?"

The patient was at first mute, then as the questioning continued unabated, he became very angry. He rose from the chair in which he was sitting, but since each of the therapists held one of his arms he was unable to throw a punch. He nevertheless kicked out in front of him (luckily, neither therapist was directly in front of him) with sufficient force to split the table that was in the therapy room. When this burst of violence produced no effect on the therapists (who simply held his arms and repeated the question), the patient sat down and began to cry. The therapists repeated their question, "Who was in the room?" and the patient sobbed that his oldest sister was in the room on the bed with his mother. In the further elucidation of this, the patient explained that his mother was feeding his sister. As the patient talked, it became clear that, inasmuch as he viewed intercourse—both heterosexual and homosexual—as a feeding situation, all of the "room" fantasies, including the primal scene, dealt with a single theme: "Two people are in the room, including at least one from whom I expect food. Someone else is being fed and I am not wanted."

In summary, a severely regressed case of schizophrenia produced classic oedipal material, including a classic primal scene, during the process of a developing therapeutic relationship. Upon further elucidation, the material seemed to show dynamics which differ somewhat from the classic interpretations of the oedipal situation.

The patient interprets intercourse as an oral situation, equating the vagina with the mouth and the penis with the breast. His own needs to be fed and mothered were not met by the mother; rather he sees her as making demands on him to "feed" her. Thus, incest is seen as a feeding situation whereby he is forced to feed his mother against his will. Her demands seem so all-engulfing as to swallow up the penis itself, i.e., the mother and not the father is seen as the castrator. Underlying the castration fear is not only these insistently felt demands from the mother but, also, the wish to be castrated so that such demands can no longer be made. In place of the organ through which he can be drained, he wishes for a vagina through which he can be fed. Such a wish means turning from females to males for "feeding." The primal scenes seem to have been experienced as the mother's devouring needs being met by the father, and neither of them caring about the needs of the child.

The Homosexual Urges in Schizophrenia*

Bertram P. Karon and Jack Rosberg

Freud, in his classic study of the Schreber case (1911/1950, pp. 316–357), described paranoid symptoms as a defense against homosexual urges. But it is the experience of the authors that every schizophrenic patient has a paranoid-like delusional system, the only differences being the degree to which the system works and the degree to which the patient is able to communicate his system (see also Rosen 1953). This would lead us to believe that homosexual urges and the defenses they engender play a significant part in the pathology of schizophrenic patients.

Such is indeed the case, and one of the major hurdles in the therapy of psychosis is the handling of such homosexual problems. (As Freud pointed out [1937/1950, pp. 316–357], the handling of these problems represents one of the most difficult obstacles in the

*This paper was completed while Dr. Karon was on a Public Health Service Research Fellowship at Princeton University granted by the National Institute of Mental Health.

analysis of neurotic patients as well.) A prerequisite for the adequate handling of such problems is an adequate understanding of their source.

The classic view of homosexual impulses is that, although "innate" bisexual factors and oral and anal fixations may be involved, essentially they represent an avoidance of castration anxiety through the choice of a woman with a penis (a man), thus denying the possibility of castration. They also represent an avoidance of competition with the father for the mother (incest), and thus, protection against the father's reprisal. Of course, for women the protection is against the mother's reprisal.

In our experience, such oedipal interpretations produce no noticeable change in schizophrenic patients. Instead, we find that psychotic patients present us with alternative etiologic factors. When these alternative factors are dealt with, the patient responds and marked changes occur in the pathologic state.

According to leading psychoanalytic writers of the past two decades, (Fenichel 1945, pp. 415–452, and Bellak 1948, provide excellent reviews of the literature) the roots of schizophrenia may be traced back to the experiences of patients from their earliest infancy onward. They are the unfortunate victims of a pattern of malevolent mothering, which consists of a series of subtle and unsubtle rejections whose net effect is to leave them with a feeling of not being wanted, of being worthless and unlovable.

To be unlovable means that the parents may abandon you—a threat which to the child means the end of life itself. To deal with this overwhelming threat to survival, the child may do one of several things. One may deny the fact of rejection and create an "ideal mother image." It is not unusual in our experience to be told by a schizophrenic patient that he had a perfect mother. Of course, we may find that the patient makes a distinction between "my mother inside of me who is warm and loving and kind" and "that person outside of me who calls herself mother" (Rosberg and Karon 1959).

On the other hand, the patient may not differentiate the real mother from this ideal image and may chide the therapist that "I have a perfect mother" and, after he has begun to face some of the traumatic events in his life that "you don't know how to cure me. Instead of talking about those nasty things, if you really wanted to cure me, you would build the illusion that I had a perfect mother. Then I wouldn't feel the way I do about her and then I wouldn't act the way I do, and then she wouldn't act the way she does." Thus the patient attributes the rejection to his own feelings of hostility. On the other hand, he may try to become his own mother. One psychotic patient would cook large quantities of food if no one stopped him whenever he could get into a kitchen. Whether or not he could get to the kitchen, he insistently offered food or coffee to anyone who visited the treatment home in which he lived. This patient related a dream in which he rose through a mist or fog to a cloud. He looked at the cloud and inside it he saw himself feeding the birds. The patient's associations clearly showed he was resolving his own oral problems by becoming the mother and feeding the birds the way he should have been fed. His struggle to achieve a position where his satisfactions do not depend on anyone else was reflected when he told the therapist, "I often think of the possibility of a person who has breasts, a penis, and a vagina, all in the same person." (The role of genital organs in resolving oral problems will be discussed later.) Another patient told us solemnly that, "It is a scientific fact that if you eat only your own shit and drink only your own urine you will never get sick. It's a scientific fact."

Still another defense against rejection is to try and find its cause. We have already mentioned the patient who felt that his own hostile feelings were the cause of his rejection by the mother and his attempt to create the ideal mother image as a way of reducing these feelings. Unfortunately, the more ideal the mother is, the more worthless must the child feel if he is rejected. And since the rejection is, in general, based on the mother's problems rather than on any characteristic of the child (Karon and Rosberg 1958a), none of his measures of restitution will change the fact that he is rejected.

Nevertheless, the child goes on trying to find out what it is in him that accounts for his mother's rejection. If he attributes his rejection to some characteristic of his which it is in his power to change, the child will, of course, change it; however, his mother will continue to reject him, and the child must then seek some other answer.

Evidently (he reasons) the difficulty is in some characteristic which he cannot change, and, baffled, he faces this supreme challenge. There must be a way to change, and he leaps to the possibility of a magical solution. Signs, rituals, formulas—there must be a way. None of these works, but they have at least been comforting. "If they had worked, mother would have loved me, and perhaps there is still a chance if I persist long enough. It isn't that mother doesn't want to love me, but that I'm unlovable, so I'll try harder."

Thus he will claim that he has "perfect intelligence" or that he is "God." "Nobody thinks I'm worthwhile; maybe if I were God, they'd have to love me."

Among those characteristics which the child cannot change is his sex. The child learns that there is a type of person different from him, and he may hit upon this as the "real problem." If only he were the other sex, his mother would love him.

One adult male patient told us after he said he was a girl that, "My mother likes little girls like that." Later in the same day he described himself as a middle-aged woman and said that he was a lesbian and he was going to go out and find some little girl to "make love to." Here we see again a patient plainly putting himself in the role that he had fantasied his mother taking.

Seizing upon sex as the characteristic which has to be changed may be stimulated by direct pressures from the parents, especially from the mother. The patient who reported the "feeding" dream also reported in a different therapy session with a great deal of bitterness that he had been told by his mother that she would have preferred a girl when he was born. Similarly, a female patient reported that her mother loved her "step-sons more than her own daughters."

But there is still another answer to being rejected, and that is to find someone who will not reject you—to find another mother. In this search for another mother, the child necessarily turns to the most convenient available person. For most children, this is the father. Preschizophrenic children learn to look to the father for the love they cannot get from the mother.

The fact that the child in his desperation turns to the father does not necessarily mean that the father satisfies the child's need.

In fact, the schizophrenic solution is evidence to the contrary. In general, the schizophrenic patient tries not one but all of the mentioned possible solutions to the problem of rejection, none of which are successful.

The unconscious equation of the penis with the breast which we find in psychotic patients represents the equation of the father as the source of emotional nourishment with the source of physical nourishment. "My father has the milk." Equating the penis with the breast is only a short step from equating the vagina with the mouth and viewing intercourse as being fed at the breast.

"Intercourse is when the woman sucks on the penis with the vagina or mouth. Penises give semen or milk."

In some cases there may be carry-over, not only of the pleasant aspects of the breast but also the unpleasant. For example, one patient mentioned an hallucination concerning "two Negroes." In discussing this, the patient told of a homosexual episode with a Black attendant at one hospital. "It wasn't homosexual, it wasn't cocksucking. The voices told me to suck his cock, but I just took it in my mouth. But I didn't suck." On further exploration this seemed to represent his wish to be fed from a male breast (penis), and at the same time his fear of injury from the maternal breast carried over even to his homosexual fantasies.

In terms of the unconscious equation of the penis with the breast and the vagina with the mouth, the child may react to a primal scene (or primal scene fantasies) not in genital terms, but in terms of his own oral needs. He sees the mother who has left his need for food unsatisfied, now appropriating the new breast—the father's penis.

One patient described seeing the primal scene and added, "I want to go home but they don't want me," that is, neither the mother nor the father now cares what happens to him.

The mother who rejects the child not only denies the satisfactions necessary for survival but makes demands in terms of her own needs which do not take into account the child's inability to fulfill them. It is as if unconsciously the mother says to the child, "Mother me!"—a demand the child is in no position to fulfill. Concerning this demand, patients describe with considerable emotion their dread of "being hollowed out or emptied." This fantasy, which involves both oral and anal factors, they describe as the worst thing that ever happened to them. Apparently, the prototype of "being emptied" is the experience of gradually becoming hungry, of the food in the stomach apparently "draining away" with the passage of time if one is not fed again. During toilet training this fantasy of being emptied gains a new meaning as the same mother who would not fulfill his oral needs now seemingly "robs" the child of his products. The male genital version of the same fantasy sees the mother as again "draining" the child by robbing him of his products—but this time through the penis.

As one patient told us, the worst thing that ever happened to him was "when she took it off."

"What?"

"Her bathing suit. She sat down on the desk and spread her legs and showed me her twat." He said he was unhappy because she was always taking things away from him and he was afraid she wanted him to "feed" her.

It seems as if the fear of being drained is the most significant underlying factor in the development of homosexual urges in schizophrenic patients. Such a fear of being drained through the penis leads the patient to view homosexual relations as the only kind of relations which are reciprocal and hence not draining.

When, for example, a patient (Rosberg and Karon 1958) was asked whether he preferred intercourse with an anus or a vagina, he replied:

"Ass."

"Man's ass or woman's ass?"

"Man's ass."

"Why?"

"Because you can get a drink."

"From what?"

"From the prick."

The same patient told the therapists about homosexual episodes (or fantasies) dating back to the age of eight, when he claimed that he had had relations with his brother, and had gotten mad that the brother had "sucked me off first." It was clear that these homosexual relations represented the patient's attempts to overcome parental rejection by "feeding" and "being fed": the so-called passive role was the preferred one and the active role taken only in order to reciprocate.

This view of sex as a feeding situation and the wish for reciprocation was shown by a male paranoid schizophrenic who asked the girl who was taking care of the treatment home in which he lived whether, "I can fuck you. Then I'll kuck you. Then I'll suck you." ("Kucking" was the patient's word for anal intercourse.) He had told the therapist that he preferred "kucking" because "then you could pretend it was a man."

The therapist suggested that all the patient was really interested in was "sucking."

"That's right. But I've got to say the others."

The same patient described the fantasy of the devouring vagina, that is, a vagina which devours not only the sexual products, but the penis itself, when he said, "You've got it all wrong. It's not that I want to fuck my mother. It's that there is an agreement that I have to do it. I don't want to do it because there is a fixture on the cunt which will hurt my penis, and it will come off. I don't want to do it, but there is an agreement and I have to."

The patient who said that he preferred homosexual intercourse because he could get a "drink" from the penis, also described vaginas as "sadistic" and described his mother's vagina as a "food chopper." He said he was afraid that the vagina would eat up his penis, and described a primal scene in which he said he saw his father's penis go in but he didn't see it come out, and he was frightened by this.

In another session the same patient told about his fear that his mother would cut off his penis "so that she could get a platter regularly."

"So that she could use your tool to feed her whenever she wanted?"

"That's right—so that she could get a platter all the time."

In place of this organ which could be used to drain, i.e., make the patient feed someone else, the patients express wishes to have vaginas so that they themselves can be fed. If they could be a woman, they would have a vagina, and then they would be fed, they fantasy, rather than having to feed. Thus, one patient admitted that some of his actions consisted of attempts to produce a magic "vagina" through which "I could get my groceries."

At this point, we feel it is important to call attention to the fact that frequently the relationship between incest and castration is not that the patient is afraid of incest because he will be castrated for it, but rather that he wishes for castration so that he can avoid incest—which he equates with draining—and which he perceives as a threat to his very survival. The psychoanalytic idea that every irrational fear masks a wish is as applicable to the area of castration as to any other area of psychopathology. As one patient told us, in describing his wish to be rid of his penis: "No one can make you piss in their mouths."

It is from these deepest roots of the fantasy of draining, the wish for the vagina, and the wish for a resolution of the original mother-child relationship that we have found the homosexual urge to originate. When these factors are not taken into account, the homosexual urges block the progress of the therapy; when these factors are dealt with, homosexual urges are no more of a therapeutic problem than any of the other symptoms of schizophrenia.

10

Psychotherapy with Schizophrenic Patients: An Empirical Investigation

It is not unusual to hear the statement that psychotherapy in general, and psychoanalytic therapy in particular, have little to offer the so-called schizophrenic patient, but we now have rigorous data showing that even a small amount of psychoanalytic therapy— an average of 70 sessions over a 20-month period—produces changes that medication cannot produce. Patients who received psychotherapy as compared to those receiving medication showed less thought disorder (that is, they were more able to think logically when they wanted to), spent much less time in the hospital, and were able to live their lives more like human beings in a wide variety of ways. Furthermore, these effects became more marked the longer the patients were followed, and psychotherapy proved to be less costly in the long run.

A Review of the Literature

Before 1960, there were no studies of psychotherapy with schizophrenic patients that made any serious attempts at combining a control group of matched or randomized patients treated by different methods and a systematic comparable evaluation of out-

This chapter was written in conjunction with Paul O'Grady.

371

come for all patients. Since 1960, there have been six major studies in which there has been an attempt to use appropriate control groups to assess the effectiveness of psychotherapy with schizophrenic patients (Feinsilver and Gunderson 1975). These studies include: the Pennsylvania study (Bookhammer et al. 1966); the Wisconsin project (Rogers et al. 1967); the California project (May 1968); the Massachusetts project (Grinspoon et al. 1972); the Illinois project (Paul and Lentz 1977); and the Michigan State University project—which this chapter describes.

THE PENNSYLVANIA STUDY

This was the first attempt systematically to compare a sample of schizophrenic patients receiving a specific form of psychotherapy with a sample of schizophrenic patients receiving routine hospital treatment. The form of treatment was "direct analysis" (Rosen 1953), a form of psychoanalytic psychotherapy. As described, it is a dramatic, intensive technique intended to establish a strong parental transference and employing interpretations of unconscious content to foster the transference, interfere with the psychotic defenses, and bring the basic issues of early development into consciousness and into the therapist-patient relationship so that a sounder reintegration can occur. In addition to the therapy hours, patients are given considerable individual attention in humane surroundings by cooperative attendants. Unfortunately, the technique, as practiced in the study (Brody 1959), was fundamentally different. There was more emphasis on intimidation and producing compliant behavior than on making the unconscious conscious, as earlier formulations had suggested. The primary affect involvement of the therapist was described as being with the audience rather than with the patient.

While a number of books (e.g., Brody 1959; Scheflen 1961; etc.) were written on the basis of the project, the data representing the comparison of the treatment with the control patients were only briefly and separately reported (Bookhammer et al. 1966). Ultimately, two different "comparison" samples were chosen—a matched, concurrently selected sample and a retrospectively selected "random" control group. A clinical team rated patients as "improved" or "unimproved" and did so after a 5-year follow-up. The reason for the brevity of the outcome report seems to be the lack of significant difference.

The crudity of the criterion, the impact on young, first-admission patients of the psychotropic drugs that the control groups received, and, most important, the discrepancy between the techniques described in earlier writings and those employed on the project all contributed to obscuring the scientific implications. Nonetheless, a tentative conclusion can be arrived at that this technique, as used in the project, does not seem to have dramatic effectiveness. The importance of the study is that it is a first attempt at rigorous evaluation of psychotherapy with schizophrenic patients.

THE WISCONSIN PROJECT

In this project, an attempt was made to assess the elements of therapeutic relationships as well as outcome (Rogers et al. 1967). The relationships between the client-centered therapy "relationship elements" (warmth, empathy, and genuineness) and treatment outcome were explored. The researchers were building on a body of research, frequently ignored, that had already demonstrated client-centered therapy to be of value to neurotic patients (e.g., Rogers 1951); however, the project was daring in that not only had these techniques not been investigated with respect to schizophrenic patients, they had actually not been employed with such patients, and the experienced therapists were requiring themselves to develop a new expertise as well as to evaluate it.

It was not merely a test of client-centered therapy, however. There was an attempt to recruit a group of therapists who represented diverse therapeutic orientations, but this was only partially successful. While there was considerable variation in orientation, the client-centered point of view was overrepresented (Gendlin and Rogers 1967, p. 33).

The design involved the selection of a stratified sample of 16 "more chronic" schizophrenic patients, 16 "more acute" schizophrenic patients, and 16 "normals" functioning outside of the hospital. Subjects, within each "severity" category, were selected in pairs, being matched according to socioeconomic status, age, and sex. For these matched pairs, assignment was made to psychotherapy or hospital control by flip of a coin.

The hospital control subjects received the usual hospital treatment including medication, milieu therapy, and in some cases group therapy. The experimental subjects were seen in twice-a-week treatment for up to 2½ years. Patients were evaluated by a variety of instruments, ratings of behavior and symptoms, and interviews. The evaluations were made at 3- or 6-month intervals, depending on the instrument. In addition, the therapy sessions were recorded on tape and rated using the Rogerian process (relationship) scales. In addition to the therapist warmth, genuineness, and empathy scales, a new variable—"experiencing" (by the patient)—was evaluated because it seemed meaningful.

Overall findings were not impressive. On most measures, the differences between experimental and control patients were not significant. Two significant findings were that those who received psychotherapy showed a decreased need to "deny" experience, and greater appropriateness on the TAT. The psychotherapy patients also had a better rate of release, and spent less time in the hospital in the year after treatment. While these differences reached only the 0.10 level of significance, it is striking. In the year after the termination of therapy, psychotherapy patients spent an average of 117 days in the hospital, and control patients spent an average of 219 days there. That even a difference of this magnitude falls short of statistical significance illustrates the weakness of small-sample research.

The most interesting findings had to do with the relationship between therapists and patients. Schizophrenic patients initially saw their therapist as low on the Rogerian "relationship variables," regardless of the level of the therapist on the "relationship variables" as seen by independent raters. Only slowly over therapy did they perceive somewhat more "warmth, empathy, and genuineness" in their therapist. Level of patient "experiencing" was positively related to the patient's perception of these "relationship" conditions. The level of both patient "experiencing" and perceived "relationship conditions" was positively associated with many objective measures of outcome. Higher levels of these process measures were associated with a significant decrease in schizophrenic pathology and symptoms, and with a better record of remaining out of the hospital. Poor therapeutic "relationship" and "experiencing" were associated with worse outcome and longer stays in the hospital.

This is the first major study that has shown with a control group that psychotherapy has an effect on the outcome. Moreover, it demonstrates that the quality of the therapeutic relationship with a schizophrenic patient impacts directly on the outcome of treatment. It also documents the pessimism with which such patients approach the therapeutic situation, and the necessity for the therapist to be active in creating a therapeutic alliance, although that was not the terminology used by Rogers et al. (1967) in describing this fact.

The differences between the control group and the experimental group were contaminated and minimized by the fact that some of the control-group patients did receive "group therapy," and some of the experimental patients did receive medication. These contaminants were not controlled, or documented and quantified, thus tending to obscure the differences between patients receiving psychotherapy and those receiving medication as the primary mode of treatment.

These researchers performed a valuable service in making clear the complexity of doing meaningful research with any degree of rigor, and the complexity of the psychotherapeutic relationship. They, for the first time, attempt either to control or study the quality (i.e., to use different language, pay attention to "quality control") of the psychotherapy. They make clear the difficult problem of balancing rigorous design with keeping the research relevant to the phenomena supposedly studied. They also document the unpredicted difficulties added by members of the hospital staff who ought to have been neutral with respect to the outcome of the research, but clearly were not. That is a finding which will be replicated by any psychotherapeutically oriented researcher who attempts research in a medication-oriented setting. These researchers made clear the importance of evaluating patients at regular chronologic intervals, but also the realistic difficulty of carrying out such a design.

THE CALIFORNIA STUDY

May and his associates at Camarillo State Hospital attempted a controlled study of five methods of treating schizophrenic patients (May 1968). These treatment methods were (1) psychotherapy without medication, (2) psychotherapy with medication, (3) medication alone, (4) ECT, and (5) milieu therapy. Forty-one psychiatrists and residents having between 6 months and 6 years of "experience" were used as therapists. To control the personality factors, each psychiatrist practiced each of the five methods.

Patients were reported to be assigned randomly to the five treatments and those treated were only first-admission, clearly schizophrenic patients between the ages of 16 and 45, without organicity, and who were in the "middle third" of severity. This eliminated the very sick as well as the not very sick. Somehow this led to a largely lower middle-class white population of above-average intelligence, surprising for patients supposedly selected representatively from a state hospital schizophrenic population. Two-hundred-twenty-eight patients were used. On the average, patients in psychotherapy were seen twice a week until discharged or declared a treatment failure. Total time in psychotherapy ranged from 7 to 87 hours, with a mean of 49 hours. Superficially, the study seems very rigorous.

The therapists in May's study were not only inexperienced in general, but particularly inexperienced in administering psychotherapy with schizophrenic patients. They ranged considerably in their aptitude, personality type, and experience in living. All therapists were required to practice all five methods, without special recompense, despite any reservations about them (and some physicians seemed to have reservations about each form of treatment). Although the therapists are reported to have volunteered, one of the investigators in discussing our research design suggested that it was not necessary to pay psychiatric residents to work on the project, just require them to participate in order to finish their residency "like we did."

The psychotherapy provided was supervised by what was initially reported as highly experienced and prestigious psychoanalysts; however, most of them had little experience in treating schizophrenic patients. Some of the supervisors literally had no other experience with schizophrenic patients than they had received in their own residency (Wexler 1975). The quality and frequency of supervision also varied. The "quality control" of the psychotherapy provided on May's study thus must be questioned.

A battery of objective psychologic instruments was used to evaluate outcome. In addition, hospitalization data were collected, ward behavior was rated, and an independent research team rated improvement from the ward records. Cost data were also collected as a major feature of the research. Patients who refused the pretreatment testing were included in the study, even though they were not included in the data analyses of outcomes on tests they had refused initially, as well as on tests refused at outcome. The post-treatment evaluations were conducted on the day of discharge, rather than at a regular time interval from the inception of treatment. This procedure introduced a bias against the psychotherapy group. Since discharge meant termination of psychotherapy, as continued psychotherapy with the same therapist or any therapist was not a part of the research design, the day of discharge was traumatic for patients receiving psychotherapy, particularly if the relationship had been meaningful and helpful.

The authors' conclusions were that medication was the treatment of choice, that improvement on their criteria up to day of discharge showed an advantage to patients receiving medication over those not receiving medication, and that all other differences were trivial. Their book and most of their subsequent discussions in the literature have been based on the predischarge functioning and day-of-discharge evaluations. Unfortunately, as is well known, medication is particularly effective in improving ward adjustment, but ward adjustment is not highly correlated with real-world functioning. Much of the discussion of these authors is devoted to money spent on treatment and the argument that medication is cost-effective in the short run, i.e., while in the hospital.

They do note greater insight in patients receiving psychotherapy, but minimize the importance of such differences. Whenever they admit some benefit from psychotherapy, it is as frosting on the cake, an adjunct to the prime treatment—medication.

For a long time they did not publish follow-up data, although they had gathered it. In their published follow-up, reporting only hospitalization data (May et al. 1976), the differences after release from the initial hospitalization are generally not statistically significant. It should be recalled that this is a study with large numbers of subjects so that even small real differences should be statistically significant, but by 4 years from initial hospitalization less than half their sample is included in the data. Variability must have been high, since differences in mean hospitalization as high as 200 versus 600 days are not statistically significant.

They avoided the difficulties encountered by the Wisconsin group and our own project in dealing with hospital personnel covertly inimical to the project. "The principal investigator took charge of the admission service and had veto power on the research wards . . . The most sophisticated design will get you nowhere if the head nurse and the ward physicians are not on your side, and even then it helps to have muscle in the administrative hierarchy" (May 1974). The efficiency of such authority is obvious, but one has to wonder whether their staff would have dared not to find what they thought the man in charge wanted them to find.

THE MASSACHUSETTS STUDY

Grinspoon, Ewalt, and Shader (1972) rigorously evaluated the efficacy of medication in the treatment of schizophrenic patients and did an admirable job. Twenty experimental subjects were selected from among forty-one single males who had been hospitalized for over 3 years in Boston State Hospital. Random design was attempted, but "experimental" patients who refused, or whose families refused to change hospitals were reassigned to the control group. The control group remained in the state hospital on phenothiazines. The experimental patients were transferred to a new and unfamiliar setting—the Massachusetts Mental Health Center. All patients started on placebos in the new setting. Thirteen weeks later half of these patients (n = 10) were randomly selected to receive phenothiazine and the other half continued to receive the placebo. Medication was clearly more effective than placebos in terms of ward adjustment measures.

In evaluating psychotherapy, the control group was not so carefully matched. The experimental patients were all nominally in individual psychotherapy, twice a week for over 2 years with analytically oriented senior staff members supposedly favorable toward the psychotherapy of schizophrenic patients, but members of the treatment staff have expressed skepticism that the patients were really involved in a psychotherapeutic process. Only one patient was reported to develop a "therapeutic alliance" with his therapist. In other words, only one patient felt the therapist and he were on the same side.

This study is often cited as evidence that even experienced therapists are ineffective with schizophrenic patients, but while all of the psychotherapists were senior staff and "experienced," many were not experienced with schizophrenic individuals, particularly chronic schizophrenic patients, nor were they experienced with the resistances characteristic of low socioeconomic patients and the ethnic subcultures (e.g., the lower socioeconomic Boston Irish and Boston Italian subcultures). One-third of the therapists "found themselves for the first time in their life in a long-term therapy relationship with a resistant patient." Although distinguished (and presumably experienced), all participated without pay. They were asked and felt they could not refuse. It is stated that half of them reported this was not a problem. Presumably it was for the other half. Those experienced with chronic schizophrenic patients felt that twice a week was not sufficient time to work in their accustomed manner.

The easiest control would have been for each therapist to treat two patients blindly, one receiving placebo and the other medication. The next best procedure would have been rigorously to randomize assignment of therapists as well as assignment of patients to medication or placebo conditions. Neither of these procedures would have posed serious practical difficulties, and their omission is therefore notable. But the real problem was probably the lack of quality control of the psychotherapy.

An examination of the patients suggests that they were habituated to Boston State Hospital. As Braginsky, Braginsky, and Ring (1969) have noted, a chronic hospital population develops a way of life with satisfactions. These satisfactions were disrupted by transfer to the middle-class Mental Health Research Center. Moreover, at least eleven of the 20 patients selected for therapy had a history of ECT or insulin comas (five are reported as having had ECT alone, two had insulin comas alone, and four had both), and hence were probably brain-damaged. Psychotherapists experienced with treating schizophrenic patients have doubts about attempting psychotherapy with patients who have had ECT or insulin comas previously. It is not that treatment is impossible; it is just that treatment has been made much less effective. No serious study of psychotherapy would include such patients, particularly when there was such a small number of patients.

The measures of improvement emphasized were behavioral ratings by nurses, ward residents, patient's families, and the therapists. These ratings showed slight improvement for the patients receiving medication as compared to those receiving placebos, or to themselves when not on medication. No appreciable effect of psychotherapy was credited.

It is reported, however, that more of the psychotherapy patients (68 percent versus 37 percent) were able to live outside the hospital, a finding the authors do not value. The investigators, however, thought that the patients' lives outside the hospital were not good enough to warrant being considered better than they were when they were living in a hospital. Noteworthy is the absence of direct measures of the thought disorder, and of rigorous comprehensive blind clinical evaluations.

There was also a study of acutely ill patients, but there was neither a medication-only group, nor an untreated group for comparison. Again, it is clear that the study was designed to investigate medications; however, even if there had been a control group, the usual problem of quality control arises—the psychotherapists were inexperienced residents, and the supervisors were the "ineffective" therapists from the first study.

ILLINOIS PROJECT

Finally, the Illinois Project (Paul and Lentz 1977), while not a study of individual psychotherapy, evaluates psychosocial treatment and has relevant implications. Chronic "hard-core" hospitalized schizophrenic patients were randomly assigned (28 per group) to routine treatment (medication within a state hospital) or one of two psychosocial treatments (milieu therapy, or social learning treatment). To keep the wards full, additional patients were assigned as patients were discharged. The psychosocial treatments are specified in detail. The milieu treatment seems to have been much more active than that employed in the California Study.

The major findings were: (1) Both psychosocial treatments had an effect in initially improving the patients and maintaining them. (2) The social learning treatment was more effective in the long run than either milieu treatment or medication. (3) The major advantages were in release rates (social learning, almost 95 percent; milieu, about 67 percent; and medication control/comparison, around 45 percent). Regardless of treatment condition, patients out of the hospital functioned equally well (or badly) and had comparable rehospitalization rates, but it must be emphasized that almost twice as many social-learning patients were released as compared to patients treated with medication. The psychosocial treatments also showed advantages in terms of ward adjustment; however, no measure of the thought disorder was obtained. (4) The social learning and milieu treatments were "cost-effective" as compared to the medication controls. The per-case operational costs were 16.9 percent and 15.8 percent less than routine treatment with medication. When the additional treatment capacity of the social-learning staff (because of discharges) is taken into account, the savings become 32.6 percent. Both treatment approaches saved strikingly more than routine hospital care in terms of reduced need for continuous hospitalization. (Nonetheless, a later administrative decision terminated the programs as part of an "economy" drive, and returned patients to treatment by medication.) (5) When a randomized placebo design of patients on psychosocial wards was used, it was found that medication was of *no* additional value. (6) The milieu therapy was initially successful but foundered when sanctions (e.g., isolation) for violence were reduced, and the staff seemed unable to handle violence. Promoting interaction was not therapeutic when patients did not feel physically secure.

Thus, chronic hospitalized schizophrenic patients benefit from planned meaningful human intervention to a greater extent than to medication, and this is reflected in the ability to live outside the hospital. It casts doubt on the "proven" worth of medication as the treatment of choice, and it illustrates the tendency for administrative decisions to be made on political rather than evidential bases. The popularity, not of the "medical" model, but more narrowly the "medication" model, as a justification for treatment to be determined by medically trained, but psychologically naive, institutionally designated "psychiatrists" is called into question.

The Michigan State Project

In the early 1950s, the prevailing opinion in the fields of psychiatry and psychology was that schizophrenia was a chronic incurable disorder of unknown, but genetic and physiologic origin. Some therapists, however, were reporting successes in treating such patients, notably Fromm-Reichmann and Sullivan and their students. Rosen's work drew attention because it suggested that the painstakingly slow progress reported by Fromm-Reichmann might be accelerated. At the time, I (Karon) read Rosen's book (1953), listened to him lecture, considered working with him, and consulted two noted psychoanalysts about Dr. Rosen's work. One indicated he considered Rosen to have brilliant insights about the oral period, "If I were a young man, I'd work with him for a year myself." The other indicated the reverse: "He's a psychopath; and you can't believe a word he says!"

I decided to work with Rosen for a year to find out what was and was not useful. During that year and the subsequent one, the clinical papers coauthored with Rosberg were written. The patients dealt with were all chronic schizophrenic and had been previously treated at the best treatment centers in America for periods ranging from 10 to 20 years. Improvement as a result of intensive, theoretically relevant therapeutic work had to be taken seriously, because it was discrepant with the previous course of their illness for years, not only at other treatment centers, but even in that setting. That the most seriously ill of such patients responded to a determined effort at treatment (cf. Rosberg and Karon 1958) was a scientifically relevant observation. While the treatment in that case was so time-consuming as to be economically infeasible on a large scale, it provided a relevant basis for believing that the observed improvement was not a random event or a spontaneous recovery.

A reformatory for male adolescent delinquents provided clinical experience in resolving acute schizophrenic reactions and a semicontrolled comparison. Inmates who had schizophrenic breaks were transferred to a state hospital, where they typically spent 2 years before being returned to the reformatory. The hospital time might or might not be considered part of their reformatory sentence. Once a short period of psychotherapy without medication had been instituted as routine, no transfers were necessary, except for one patient previously given ECT, who was consequently considered unsuitable for psychotherapy. One week of five sessions sufficed to restore self-control. The first week was followed up by weekly sessions while the patient functioned on normal assignments within the reformatory. After I left the facility, these procedures were discontinued, transfers again became necessary, and remissions were as slow as before.

These experiences led to the conviction that a powerful understandable treatment was available. Hopefully, it was teachable. The first step in evaluating the possibility of generalizing these procedures was to supervise people of different temperaments to see if they could also be effective. They were.

It now became clear that systematic research was indicated. The Michigan State Psychotherapy project was conceived to determine whether acute schizophrenic reactions could be rapidly resolved by intensive psychotherapy, in which the therapist plays an active role, arouses intense affects, and handles certain central phantasies in a prescribed nonclassic fashion. "Rapid," as used, implied 1 month of intensive 5-day-per-week psychotherapy. The acute schizophrenic reaction may be said to be resolved when the patient's acute symptoms have remitted to the point where he is able to carry on his day-to-day activities without hospitalization, while continuing to receive outpatient psychotherapy.

If 4 weeks does not suffice, how long would it take? Moreover, it was an empirical question as to whether or not such patients, after the resolution of their acute symptoms, would continue to make progress with once-a-week psychotherapy, as had been the case with the reformatory patients.

Of course, more than one therapist needed to be studied. Could this form of psychotherapy be readily taught? Could relatively inexperienced therapists also produce striking therapeutic changes? The routine clinical use of phenothiazines and available research seemed to converge on the finding that medication was of use. Predictions were even being made that with phenothiazines there would be no schizophrenic patients in the hospital by 1970.

At this point, it was clear that the baseline against which psychotherapy had to be compared was the "new" routine treatment that was readily usable on a large scale—medication, and it was not clear whether the adjunctive use of medication facilitated or interfered with psychotherapy.

The original Michigan State Psychotherapy project proposal also included a comparison group of schizophrenic patients treated by paraprofessionals, but this innovation was discouraged by NIMH (the National Institute of Mental Health) as too dangerous an experiment.

The "final" proposal was turned down with a recommendation that it be resubmitted with changes. Two major changes, one helpful and one not so helpful, were required by NIMH. The unhelpful change reflected the then current (and still problematic) lack of attention to *relevant* training for psychotherapy for schizophrenic patients. The "final" proposal had called for 1 year of training of the psychiatric residents and psychology interns in the psychotherapy of schizophrenic patients, including for each trainee the treatment of one patient under supervision, but not to be included in the rigorous evaluations. The supervisors were to treat cases to be rigorously evaluated against controls, with the cases being observed by the trainees and discussed as part of the training. Further, it was felt that only if the supervisors' cases were demonstrably better than the controls would it make any sense to carry the project further. This was in keeping with the belief of everyone connected with the project that therapeutic competence cannot be established by credentials, but only by the results of their work as shown by the progress of the patients.

The "funded" project, however, eliminated the year's training, and required the trainees to be given clinical responsibility almost immediately. Nonetheless, the first two patients in each therapy group were assigned to the supervisors and their treatment observed for training purposes. Fortunately, this imposed change did not ruin the project.

The second imposed change was more helpful. It was pointed out that schizophrenia is traditionally defined as centrally involving a thought disorder, yet no direct measurements of the thought disorder were being made. After reviewing the available literature, the Drasgow-Feldman Visual-Verbal Test, the Porteus Mazes, and the WAIS were included as most likely to be relevant.

The design called for the selection of clearly schizophrenic patients to be assigned on the basis of a random number table to one of three treatments: (1) psychotherapy without medication, (2) psychotherapy with adjunctive medication, and (3) routine hospital treatment consisting primarily of phenothiazines.

Details of Design and Implementation

PATIENT SELECTION

All admissions to the wards of Detroit Psychiatric Institute (DPI) were reviewed for possible inclusion in the project. The initial intention was to select acutely ill but clearly schizophrenic patients. The criteria were: (1) unquestionably schizophrenic; (2) onset of blatant psychotic symptoms within 3 months prior to admission; (3) first admission; (4) no history of ECT or insulin shock treatment; (5) no organic brain damage; and (6) no history of alcoholism or drug addiction.

The selection and assignment of patients in our study was made by independent research personnel not connected with treatment. Evaluation for selection was solely in terms of meeting the selection criteria. Selection was made by the same criteria and the same research personnel throughout. Patients were not selected by status-oriented regular hospital staff, or with an eye to whose patient they might become. Our intent to obtain acutely ill but clearly schizophrenic patients (with no organic pathologic condition or previous hospitalization) required more adequate case histories and more thorough medical examinations before selection than the routine hospital procedure required. Suitable patients were selected in sets of three patients with comparable severity of illness. Patients were not assigned to treatment groups until there were three patients who had completed preliminary medical and diagnostic examination (so that the "set" could then be randomly assigned). If a patient was discharged before the assessment was complete, that patient was replaced as a potential project patient by another patient who was still hospitalized.

Approximately 15,000 patients per year who appeared schizophrenic were seen in the emergency room. Two-thirds of those patients were treated with tranquilizers and discharged without hospitalization at all. The admission rate to the wards was approximately 5,000 per year. Hence, in any given week, a pool of about 100 potential research patients would be reviewed using the initial criteria; however, roughly two-thirds of these were discharged within 2 weeks (e.g., before extensive medical and diagnostic examinations could be completed). Thus, the actual pool of potential research subjects was about 35 per week. Only one set of three patients was selected in a given week. In some weeks no "sets" were selected. All of the patients were selected within a 4-month period.

Suitable patients were selected in sets of three, and randomly assigned to the three groups: hospital comparison, psychotherapy without medication, and psychotherapy with medication. Assignment between experienced and inexperienced therapists and among inexperienced therapists was on a rotation basis. Supervisors did not select which patient they would work with. Since we believe that psychotherapy must be learned, it seemed necessary that the cases chosen in the first weeks be assigned to the supervisors, so that their work could be observed by the inexperienced therapists, via closed-circuit TV, and discussed. Because of the schedules and commitments of the inexperienced therapists, it was necessary that they begin to be assigned by the third "set" of patients. Hence, the supervisors treated the psychotherapy patients selected in the first two sets and in the last two sets of patients chronologically. Any differences in patient characteristics reflect possible week-to-week fluctuation in admissions (although they were well within the bounds to be expected from random variation).

In this project, 36 patients were studied. We felt the small number was necessary in order to be careful about gathering data on the patients, including careful, detailed, and blind rigorous outcome evaluations, as well as obtain greater than usual "quality control" of the psychotherapy provided. Many of the characteristics of schizophrenic populations become clear only after repeated follow-ups. We were familiar with the less careful assessment of patients that large samples unfortunately necessitate. Accuracy of inference from a sample is obviously affected not only by the number of cases, but even more by any systematic (planned or unintentional) bias in selecting these cases. The infamous *Literary Digest* poll included millions of cases.

The patients were primarily poor, inner-city, and Black. They tended not to trust authorities, particularly white authorities. The selection of patients took place about 12 months before the Detroit riot of 1967. In their world, information is to be divulged to authorities only if it cannot be used to punish the informant or his friends. They do not expect help simply for being emotionally ill; they are hospitalized primarily because they have disturbed or frightened someone else. Bizarre behavior and emotional suffering are accepted by the patients and their families as part of a painful world rather than as illness to be alleviated. Hence, they tend to have been ill for a long time (by middle-class standards) before hospitalization. According to an independent study conducted in the same city (Dunham 1965), the median time between onset of blatant psychotic symptoms and the first presentation to treatment was 34.5 months! The emphasis on the patients being clearly schizophrenic, and the attempt to get a rigorous baseline of independent measurements, led paradoxically to selection of a more severely impaired chronic population, resistant to treatment. The utility of a randomized control group in psychotherapy research is illustrated by the fact that the patients were more severely and chronically ill than we had intended or were aware of initially, but this difference applied equally to treatment and control groups. In the initial phase of the project, the treatment staff was disappointed in the apparently slow response to treatment as compared to previous experiences with "acute" patients. It was only after the 6-month data were gathered, and the control group found to be functioning even less well, that we became aware we were dealing with a more chronic population than we had intended.

Some patients had had previous hospitalization which neither the patient nor the relatives had revealed. Initial screening revealed no previous psychiatric hospitalization among project patients, but, by the end of the project, we had established that at least one-third of the patients had been previously hospitalized (group A = 4, group B = 2, group C = 5). Of those previously hospitalized, length of previous hospitalization ranged from 7 to 72 days, with a mean of 23.7 days. The patients and their families reasoned (correctly) that a previous history of hospitalization leads to worse treatment not only by hospitals, but by employers, social agencies, and people in general. The severity of illness of these patients is also shown by their pretreatment scores on the Drasgow-Feldman Visual-Verbal Test, 29 of the 35 patients initially scored at or below the norms for chronic schizophrenic individuals (i.e., patients hospitalized continually for 3 or more years).

Despite the attempt at careful medical screening, medical problems were also not ruled out. Four dramatic instances occurred.

Two patients died of embolisms (both diagnosed as catatonic). The first of these died before randomization had occurred, so that a new patient was selected, and that set of three randomized. The other patient lapsed into silence and died after therapy began. She was not replaced for two reasons: a new patient would not have been randomly assigned, and the student therapist who had tried to treat her was so traumatized by the death that he refused to treat another psychotic patient. Additional information on this last patient (which had been suppressed by patient and family) became known just before her death: she was a long-standing drug addict, had been hospitalized as well as jailed for several years, and had undergone a long course of ECT. Any one of these factors would have made her ineligible for inclusion in the project. If she had not died, we would have continued to treat her, but data on her treatment would have been excluded from the analyses.

Another patient (a female, in group A, treated by Karon) was eventually diagnosed as suffering from multiple sclerosis as well as schizophrenia. This patient had been cleared by both the neurology and internal medicine services before being selected for the project. She manifested a gait impairment. It was only after psychotherapy had progressively changed her thought disorder, reality testing, and ability to relate to others, while the motor symptoms worsened, that the diagnosis of multiple sclerosis was possible. The fact that the two sets of symptoms followed independent courses led us to include her in all data analyses as properly schizophrenic, as well as motorically impaired on a neurologic basis. This patient is *included* in the data, although analyses excluding this patient were run, and the findings were not materially altered.

Still another patient (a male, in group A, treated by a trainee), whose social history stated, "No history of drug addiction," began to talk about seeing moving colored animals. Such organic sounding material led to his referral for an EEG, which showed what were described as abnormal results, but not clearly pathologic. The unusual EEG was attributed to the probable effects of medication; however, the patient was not on medication. A second EEG seemed indicated, but was no clearer than the first.

Meanwhile, inquiries to the patient's girl friend, family, and finally the patient revealed that for many years he had taken seconal, dexedrine, and nutmeg in daily irregular large doses sufficient to produce brain damage.

Originally, the patient and the family had denied his drug history. On the first routine reexamination (after 6 months), they still denied his history. It was only after 10 months of treatment that the patient and family developed sufficient trust in the therapist to reveal the drug history and impairment. This patient was *excluded* from the data analyses, beginning with the 12-month data, in light of the inappropriate selection for the project.

Three of the initially selected patients are not *included* in the final analyses: the patient who died, the patient just described who produced material suggesting an organic pathologic condition, and a third patient because of staff interference with the treatment (described below). Analyses including the two living (but "excluded") patients have been run; their inclusion does not materially alter the findings.

A change of ward chief and of ward residents led to the staff interference. In general, violent acting-out on this ward increased after the change of ward chief, including one murder of a patient by a patient, an almost unheard of event.

The experimental patient was hospitalized; the new ward chief insisted to the therapist that the therapist could not give this patient pass privileges. The ward notes on the patient disappeared. During this time, a new resident was talking to the patient, and told him that he had the right to change doctors, and should choose him. The resident took the patient for a walk outside the hospital, and told him he would do the same again the next day. All of this occurred without the therapist's knowledge. The patient was seen by his project therapist a half-hour after returning to the ward. The patient said he was going to walk off the ward tomorrow, and he was going to change doctors. The therapist, thinking he was setting limits, said the patient could not leave the ward, and that he could not change doctors until he left the hospital. The ward chief had earlier asked the project therapist to set limits on the patient because "no one else can control him." (The locked ward was so insecure that a patient hospitalized on that ward because she was acutely suicidal had been able to walk out and kill herself by jumping onto the freeway in front of the hospital a week earlier.)

The patient, enraged at the apparent withdrawal of privileges just granted, hit the therapist and broke his nose. The reaction of the ward staff was positive to the patient. Unlike usual procedures in this hospital after an assaultive incident, the patient was not placed in restraints. According to the ward chief, "No one is able to do that." According to attendants who had placed him in restraints previously, "Of course it can be done."

Within a week he got a pass from the ward chief (against the therapist's advice). The patient's late return was not remarked upon, which was unusual. Ordinary procedure was to inform the police when patients were more than an hour late. When the patient did not return from another pass, he was discharged. Threats and minor assaults to his wife and girl friend were dismissed by the ward chief as irrelevant. The therapist, of course, disagreed, considering assaults and threatened assaults to be a serious symptom. The therapist was told that the patient was doing so well now that treatment should not be continued because it was not necessary. The patient left town. Within a day after returning, he was brought in by the police after assaulting someone severely, and was immediately transferred to the state hospital before the therapist or the research staff arrived at the hospital that day, because "he's obviously too dangerous for anyone to work with." The hospital staff well knew the project staff would have had a different opinion.

Distribution of patients by age, sex, race, education, and initial vocabulary IQ are summarized in Table 1.

THE TREATMENTS

The patients were randomly assigned to one of three treatments. Psychotherapy was provided under two conditions, one group did not use medication and the other group did. The comparison group was treated primarily with medication. Further details are given below.

Group A used a psychoanalytic psychotherapy as described earlier in the book, *without* medication. In this group, psychotherapy sessions were held 5 days a week until discharge (if discharge was in 2 to 8 weeks) and, for the most part, once per week thereafter. Four patients were treated by an experienced therapist (Karon), while the remaining eight patients were treated by five inexperienced therapists (three graduate students in clinical psychology and two residents in psychiatry) under his supervision.

Three patients in this nonmedication group received medication upon the demand of the ward staff as an alternative to mechanical restraints. Medication for these patients was rare and typically for very brief periods of time (in no case more than 2 weeks during 20 months of treatment) and in response to the distress of the ward staff. Our willingness to cooperate with the ward staff when their tolerance had reached its limit enabled them to cooperate with us in tolerating the additional trouble of non-medicated patients in general.

Two of these cases, however, do *not* appear in the final data. Deleting the third patient would only increase the apparent effectiveness of psychotherapy; we chose the conservative approach of including him. One of the medicated patients had to be deleted from the study because of evidence of an organic pathologic condition, as mentioned earlier. One had to be deleted because of staff interference with the treatment (of which the medication turned out to be the least). *It would be inappropriate to claim that this group was contaminated by the utilization of medication.*

Group B utilized an "ego-analytic" psychotherapy, *using adjunctive medication* (phenothiazines). The dosages were between 50 and 200 mg of chlorpromazine (Thorazine)—or its equivalent—two or three times a day, and generally they were decreased or eliminated at discharge. In this group, psychotherapy was initiated three times per week, for at least 20 sessions, and eventually

TABLE 1.
Patient Characteristics of Final Sample (n = 33)

Characteristic	Group A		Group B		Pooled Experimentals	Hospital Comparisons
	Supervisor	Trainees	Supervisor	Trainees		
Sex						
Male	1	2	1	6	10	5
Female	2	4	3	2	11	7
Race						
Black	2	6	3	5	16	9
White	1	0	1	3	5	3
Education						
Grades 1 to 5	0	1	0	0	1	1
Grades 6 to 9	0	2	0	3	5	1
High School (incomplete)	2	0	2	2	6	5
High School (complete)	1	3	2	2	8	4

TABLE 1. (*Continued*)

Patient Characteristics of Final Sample (*n* = 33)

Characteristic	Group A		Group B		Pooled Experimentals	Hospital Comparisons
	Supervisor	Trainees	Supervisor	Trainees		
University (incomplete)	0	0	0	1	1	1
IQ (Thorndike-Gallup)						
0 to 80	0	3	1	5	9	2
80 to 90	2	2	2	0	6	7
90 to 110	1	0	1	3	5	3
110 to 120	0	1	0	0	1	0
120 +	0	0	0	0	0	0
Previous Hospitalization as Known at End of Project						
None	1	4	4	6	15	7
0 to 14 Days	0	1	0	1	2	2
15 to 28 Days	1	1	0	1	3	1
29 to 42 Days	0	0	0	0	0	2
43 + Days	1	0	0	0	1	0

reduced in frequency to one session per week. Four patients were treated by an experienced therapist (Thomas Tierney), while the remaining eight patients were treated by five inexperienced therapists (two graduate students in clinical psychology and three residents in psychiatry) under his supervision.

Dr. Tierney has summarized his treatment philosophy as follows: "Schizophrenic reactions constitute a very wide range of psychological disorders resulting in disordered thinking, exemplified by loose associations, delusions and sometimes hallucinations. The psychotic reaction is a response used as a defense against something more frightening, such as fantasied retaliation for id impulses of murderous rage or uninhibited sexual acting out. The patient therefore tries to protect himself by using archaic defenses which are inefficient and break down because they are socially intolerable. Projection, denial, and withdrawal promote regression and are basic components of regression creating a vicious spiral into psychosis. There is a break with reality of major proportions, but when individual defenses are identified, some are seen to function in a healthy manner. The psychotic therefore acts in a crazy way, which is recognized by the healthy ego functions of the patient and other observers.

"There is a preponderance of evidence in schizophrenic patients of distorted object relations typified by a maternal rejection, inconsistency or lack of love. These distortions of object relations seem to be the hub about which the psychosis revolve. Maternal rejection is the focus of family conflict. This focus can be a multitude of factors such as the mother's own psychosis or other illness, a psychotic or psychopathic father, poverty, illness, etc., ad infinitum.

"The therapist has the multiple-facet role of providing a stable, consistent and accepting relationship. Honesty with himself and the patient is important in order for the therapist to be consistent. The positive object relationship between the patient and therapist is a basis for reality testing. Healthy defenses can be encouraged while costly and inefficient ones are observed realistically. Fear is diminished when the patient is able to use the therapist's ego in support of his own healthy ego functions, such as the therapist not being frightened of the patient's projections, hallucinations, and other fear provoking self accusations. The patient is encouraged to deal realistically with his environment.

"Therapy therefore is not just supportive, but helps the patient to gain insight and to utilize and encourage the healthy aspect of his personality. Narcissistic preoccupation is evaluated and fantasy is interpreted in the light of its preventing attainment of normal gratification. The patient is encouraged to become independent of the therapist by discussing his feelings about the therapist and his forthcoming termination."

It is evident that the approach of Dr. Tierney, while somewhat different, is not really discordant with the approaches of the authors. He was convinced on the basis of his own experience that psychotherapy for schizophrenic patients was not only effective, but was economically feasible on a routine basis, with the existing resources in the hospital. He had been recommended by the hospital's director of research as someone known to his colleagues as clinically effective with schizophrenic patients. He had completed his residency in that hospital with that patient population and had continued to be available to the hospital and this patient population for over 10 years. He was also committed to training others to do the same kind of work with schizophrenic individuals that he himself did. Unfortunately, his untimely death, the result of a heart attack shortly after the completion of the project, was a loss to the profession. As a result, this book does not include as full a clinical description of his views as would otherwise have been possible.

In reporting *some details about groups A and B*, several factors should be noted concerning these groups of "experimental" patients. All project therapists, both supervisors and trainees, were white, reflecting the ethnic composition of the hospital's professional staff and of the graduate students and medical students in clinical training at that time. This was a bias we were aware of and would have preferred to address, but minority therapists were unavailable in those training programs. Fortunately, the situation has since changed. In general, this should be a bias against psychotherapy, particularly in the 1960s, and indeed, was. The Detroit riot occurred during the 12-month evaluations. Black patients felt guilty about having a close relationship with a white person.

Heterogeneity of professions among both supervisors and students was intentional, and intended to minimize professional jealousies as a contaminating factor. It was successful for project personnel, but unsuccessful in reducing interprofessional jealousy on the part of nonproject hospital personnel.

"Experienced therapist," as used here, means approximately 10 years of experience (not merely doing psychotherapy, but specifically treating schizophrenic patients) and familiarity with patients of the relevant ethnic subculture. As is evident from Table 1, this means predominantly the Detroit Black subculture. Our sample of experienced therapists was small (two). It was crucial to know that the phenomenon we were studying was the one we wanted to study, and, as any statistician would agree, that superseded, and must supersede, all other considerations of research design. We felt it was critical to be sure that the experienced therapists had relevant experience in doing psychotherapy with patients such as those served by the hospital, and known to their professional colleagues to be clinically effective. We did not want "experts" whose reputation was based on their writings and lectures rather than on the demonstrated improvement of their patients. Experience treating neurotic patients by psychotherapy is only partially relevant to understanding and successfully treating schizophrenic patients. Experience in the treatment of physical/medical problems is even less relevant. Knowledge of the characteristics and consequent specific resistances of people of a given socioeconomic, ethnic, and subcultural background is at least as important as knowledge of the specific psychopathology being treated. The two supervisors in our study were better acquainted with poor and Black patients than are most psychotherapists. Dr. Thomas Tierney, as mentioned, had worked with that patient population over a 10-year period. Not only was he familiar with these patients, but he had a real commitment to understanding and helping such patients, a point which cannot be overemphasized, since poor patients are not typically "popular" with professionals. After the completion of the clinical phase of our study, he became director of resident training. Karon, the other supervisor, had earlier investigated the effects of discrimination on Blacks (1958), had worked with lower-class and Black individuals in other cities, and was particularly experienced in treating schizophrenic patients.

Our interest was whether or not adequately and relevantly trained (experienced or supervised) therapists were of value. We were not interested in whether the average therapist, inadequately trained and inexperienced in specifically treating schizophrenic individuals and/or treating people of lower socioeconomic level by psychotherapy, was helpful. Hence, an integral aspect of the project involved the training of the "inexperienced" therapists. The psychology interns and psychiatric residents had 3 months to 1 year of general practicum or residency experience before the project. In addition to reading material, the inexperienced thera-. pists watched, via closed-circuit TV, the beginning of the treatment of two patients by the supervisor in their group, before they themselves began to work with project patients. The inexperienced therapists' sessions, particularly the early ones, were watched by the supervisor and the other inexperienced therapists in that treatment group, and discussed. In the later phases of the study, more conventional supervision sessions were held.

Learning a complex skill is difficult. In the early phases of training, a great deal of attention was required. Psychotherapy of any kind is a difficult and time-consuming skill to learn and to apply. Moreover, it is the nature of schizophrenic resistances, as compared to those of other patients, that the patient gives the therapist almost no feedback to reassure the therapist that the treatment is helpful. The novice therapist (with this kind of patient) has a greater need for emotional support from a knowledgeable and provenly effective supervisor. Hence, we had two highly experienced supervisors, and trainees who wanted to learn to do such treatment. Trainees were genuine volunteers, and chose their supervisor as someone whose training they valued. The number of patients per trainee varied from one to three. The number of patients each trainee undertook was determined by their schedule and, secondarily, by their willingness. The extra difficulty and time invested in learning psychotherapy well were recognized in our study by paying the trainee therapists for their additional time. There were complications resulting from these payments, however. In the middle of the project (before the 12-month evaluations), NIMH required that these payments be suspended, on the basis that psychiatric residents were not permitted to "moonlight" by the American Board of Neurology and Psychiatry. After obtaining agreement from the residents to continue working without pay, and their having done so for several months, Dr. Tierney discovered that the Board rules had been changed, and we were able to convince a reluctant NIMH that the payments to residents should be reinstituted. Nonetheless, the effect on therapist motivation may have impaired the effectiveness of their work during this period.

Psychotherapy was maintained whether the patient was on an inpatient or outpatient basis, and the same therapist treated the patient on an inpatient and outpatient basis. While few hospitals follow such procedures, any reasonable theoretical rationale for psychotherapy readily yields the importance of the continuity of relationship (transference) in the treatment. In our view, whether a patient is in or out of the hospital has mainly to do with what kind of housing, controls, and physical care they require. It should not lead to a discontinuity of either the conceptualization of the patient's difficulties or the basic treatment process. The usual procedure in most hospitals of separate professionals on the inpatient and outpatient unit has no therapeutic rationale, but is an administrative measure taken without regard to the therapeutic process supposedly being administered. This is not a problem unique to mental hospitals (Duff and Hollingshead 1968).

Most frequently psychotherapy is offered to patients from 9 A.M. to 5 P.M., Monday through Friday, particularly at low-cost services. Again, this is an administrative decision that does not take into account the treatment process. Upper middle-class patients, professionals, and full-time housewives can reschedule their lives, but working-class and lower-class patients are employed in jobs where they cannot control the hours of work. They lose money if they take time off, and, more importantly, will be fired if the absence from work is repeated. It was agreed by all project therapists that outpatient therapy hours would be scheduled so as not to interfere with the patient's work, since undermining the patient's work adjustment is antitherapeutic. This is basic common sense, but unfortunately rare in mental health service planning.

Because personnel in automobile factories work 6 days a week during peak season (when patients are under pressure from overwork) this agreement meant Sunday psychotherapy hours in many instances. The annual lay-off period, during automobile model changes, when patients are under pressure from not working (which they interpret as evidence of personal inadequacy) and from too much contact with their families, posed no such scheduling problems.

In order to make attendance economically feasible, payment for transportation and baby-sitting expenses were available, five dollars per session. It is hard for middle-class professionals to understand that transportation and child-care are really economic burdens. When one is not sure he or she has enough money to feed oneself and one's children, any extra expenses can seem a luxury. Taking therapies are particularly apt to be considered nonessential by such an individual. There was a great deal of variation in the acceptance of this expense money. Only about one third of the sessions were accompanied by acceptance of such expense reimbursement. The same patient might accept reimbursement on one occasion and not the next.

Psychotherapy in groups A and B was intended to be sufficiently infrequent that its economic feasibility on a large scale could be considered. Nonetheless, at the beginning of therapy, sessions were frequent. It is important in the treatment of schizophrenic patients initially to treat them so frequently and so intensively that the therapist becomes established as a reality (and transference) object. Eventually, all patients were reduced to once-per-week treatment; however, individual therapists in both groups were allowed flexibility in utilizing additional sessions, while encouraged to minimize them. Despite efforts by the psychotherapists to induce the patients to continue outpatient therapy on a regular basis, patients frequently stopped seeing their therapists for weeks, in some cases for months, when outside of the hospital. Despite the flexibility allowed to the individual therapists, the average number of sessions per patient was comparable in both psychotherapy groups, and averaged about 70 sessions over a 20-month period.

Group C, the hospital comparison, utilized phenothiazines as the primary treatment. This is "treatment" as currently practiced at "good" public institutions and considered to be the treatment of choice by the majority of the staff of the hospital. The patient/resident ratio was eight to one. Psychiatric residents, under close supervision of senior staff psychiatrists familiar with this patient population, were permitted by the research design to adjust medication and dosage level for each patient individually in terms of their and their supervisor's clinical judgment of the optimal dosage for the patient at that time. We did not attempt to hold medication at a fixed arbitrary level, but allowed it to vary in accordance with good, and routine, clinical practice. Dosage levels typically were approximately 400 mg of chlorpromazine (or its equivalent), varying at different times in treatment from a high of 1,400 mg daily to a low of 100 mg. The dose was decreased somewhat at discharge, but was recommended by the physician for indefinite use. Interviews were used primarily to adjust medication levels, assess whether discharge or transfer was most appropriate, and provide minimal support.

If, after a few weeks, the patients in group C did not respond to the point of discharge, they were transferred to a state hospital, where treatment by medication was continued but with a higher patient/physician ratio (30 to 50 to one). This is still a low patient/staff ratio for a state hospital and sufficient for adequate drug treatment. All other services were, in fact, better staffed than DPI. The transfer practice between DPI and the state hospital was routine and "usual practice." In light of the regular relationship between the hospitals, the transfer of the patient and his records occurred simultaneously in one day. Medication was uninterrupted. The state hospital was better equipped with auxiliary services (occupational therapy, vocational rehabilitation services, recreational therapy, social services, etc.). DPI was organized as a 2-week stay hospital, and fully developed auxiliary services did not seem as imperative. The availability of the project psychotherapists made retention in DPI necessary if psychotherapy were to continue on an inpatient basis for groups A and B. Thus, psychotherapy patients were relatively deprived in the availability of auxiliary services.

Treatment (medication) continuity was maintained in group C; however, patient-physician continuity was not maintained, either when the patient changed institutions or inpatient/outpatient status. Most institutions which emphasize medication as the primary treatment modality do not typically maintain continuity of physicians, since it is not generally believed to be central to the efficacy of the treatment.

These procedures were followed with the comparison group because it seemed the most appropriate control group—patients treated with care but in the "usual" way. The control group was not intended to be a no-treatment control. Additional hours of individual psychotherapy can only be justified if they produce greater change than currently available mass treatment (i.e., medication).

OUTCOME MEASURES

Patients were evaluated at fixed intervals after the inception of treatment, irrespective of whether they were in or out of the hospital, or were cooperating with or resisting the treatment. Our intervals were 6 months, 12 months, and 20 months (end of treatment phase). This would seem to be a logical treatment evaluation. Some studies evaluating psychotherapy have used evaluations on the day of discharge; however, such a procedure results in a highly variable and noncomparable interval between evaluations. In addition, the day of discharge is a traumatic time for psychotherapy patients, particularly if the relationship with the therapist has been meaningful. Hence, we utilized a fixed interval evaluation schedule.

Each examination included a battery of intellectual tests, projective tests, and a clinical status interview. Hospitalization data were, of course, maintained. Intellectual tests were the Thorndike-Gallup Vocabulary Test (TGV), the Porteus Mazes (PM), Wechsler Adult Intelligence Scale (WAIS), and the Feldman-Drasgow Visual-Verbal Test (VVT). The patients were also administered a Rorschach and TAT. A clinical status interview was conducted by an experienced psychoanalytic psychiatrist who was familiar with the hospital's patient population, and recorded on tape. The Rorschach protocols, TAT protocols, and Clinical Status Interviews were reduced to quantitative data, using a scaling technique detailed later.

Each evaluation was carried out by personnel not otherwise connected with treatment or ward operations, and who did not know to which treatment group the patients belonged, except as the patient might spontaneously reveal it. Since a good clinical status interview is not likely to leave the interviewer "blind," these interviews were recorded on tape, and references to treatment deleted from the tapes before being rated "blindly" with regard to clinical status. Discharge was not entirely "blind," but was determined by ward chiefs who were not members of the project treatment staff or the research team.

Patients were reimbursed for their time and travel expenses when they returned for examinations subsequent to the initial one. This helped to account for the fact that *all* patients were evaluated at the end of the treatment phase of the project.

The TGV is a twenty-item multiple-choice vocabulary test, which has been found to correlate highly with full-scale Wechsler and Stanford-Binet scores (Miner 1957), but which is easier to take than the longer tests. It should be least affected by pathology aside from test-taking set. Since the same form was used in all administrations, practice effects might be expected.

The PM measures a function best described as "foresight" or "planfulness" (or its absence). Porteus (1959) makes the point that below-normal variation is meaningful, but that above-normal variation is trivial in meaning. The PM has alternate forms. The Vineland series was used for initial testing, and at 20 months; the Extension series was used at 6 months; and the Supplement series at 12 months. Rabin and King (1958) reported that the PM reflected patient improvement with successful treatment of schizophrenics.

The WAIS measures a variety of intellectual functions as well as test-taking set. It has a good parallel form in the Wechsler-Bellevue II (WB II). The WAIS was used for the pretreatment and the 12 months retest, and the WB II was used for the 6-month and 20 month evaluations. The WAIS was selected because previous research indicates it too, reflected patient improvement with sucessful treatment of schizophrenic patients (Rabin and King 1958).

The VVT is a concept-formation task in the Hanfmann, Kasanin, Vigotsky, Goldstein, Cameron tradition, but one which yields a quantitative score. It is reported to be uncorrelated with IQ in normal subjects, but specifically vulnerable to the schizophrenic thought disorder. According to Feldman and Drasgow (1951), there is no overlap in scores between normal individuals and hospitalized schizophrenic patients. Because of the length of the VVT (42 items), and because of the repeated testing, the odd-numbered and even-numbered items were used as two alternate forms. The test is scored in terms of total number of errors; on each item, one can get a score of 0, 1, or 2 errors. Thus, on the "half test" form, the score could range from 0 to 42. The odd-numbered items were used pretreatment and at 12 months, the even-numbered items at 6 months and 20 months. (Because analysis of covariance procedures, rather than difference scores, were to be used in the data analysis, strictly parallel forms of the test, in the statistical sense, were not necessary.)

The means and standard deviations of the VVT data are given in Table 2. Of course, the means should be doubled to be comparable to Feldman and Drasgow's norms, which are based on the full test. The standard deviations for the full scale will be slightly less than twice the tabled standard deviations, but not less than 1.4. The exact value is given by $\sigma\sqrt{2\ (1 + r)}$, where r is the odd/even correlation.

The apparent difference between the means of the odd and even items in Table 2 might suggest that the two forms were different. It must be remembered that the forms were administered at different times. The odd-item form was administered before treatment, when all patients were seriously disturbed, and at 12 months, during the Detroit riots, which occurred in the vicinity of the hospital. The differences between the mean VVT scores at different testing paralleled those on other criteria, so that they seem to represent real differences in the patients, not differences between the forms. Moreover, doubling the score of the patient on either form seemed to place him consistently in the range of Feldman and Drasgow's norms consistent with his clinical status.

TABLE 2.

Means and Standard Deviations of VVT Data for Each Occasion of Testing (Error Scores)

Testing Period	Mean	SD
Original (odd items)	23.7	11.7
6-month (even items)	16.5	9.0
12-month (odd items)	16.7	10.7
20-month (even items)	14.1	7.2

Despite the careful work by Feldman and Drasgow, this test has been neglected. This project allowed us to examine the concurrent and predictive validity of this measure of schizophrenic thought disorder. The concurrent correlation between the VVT and current functioning as measured by the Clinical Status Interview ratings described below (the measure with the greatest face validity), and the predictive correlation between the VVT and days hospitalized during the six months subsequent to the testing, are presented in Table 3. All correlations are significant beyond the .05 level. If the full test (instead of half the items) were used, the correlations would be even higher. Thus, the VVT seems to substantiate Feldman and Drasgow's claims that it is a sensitive measure of the schizophrenic thought disorder and that thought disorder is a central aspect of schizophrenic pathology, meaningfully related to concurrent clinical status and to prognosis. It is noteworthy that thought disorder, as measured by the VVT, is closely related to the ability to function outside the hospital on a long-term basis.

Discharge from the hospital was the responsibility of the ward chief (who was not a member of the research project). His decision was made on the basis of: the nursing reports of ward behavior, the therapist's recommendation, and the ward chief's own evaluation. The ward chief's concern was primarily to alleviate the shortage of beds on the ward by discharging any patient as early as such a decision could be made responsibly. The project therapist might recommend discharge or retention, but the final decision was made by the ward chief. In general, the effect of the therapist's recommendation was to delay discharge. The ward chiefs were *not* biased in favor of the project. If anything, they were biased against the project, the "outside" investigator, and the use of nonmedical psychotherapists.

The most immediate measure of the effectiveness of the treatment for psychotic patients is the ability of the patient to live outside of the hospital, as measured by length of hospitalization. Hospitalization data were routinely collected from DPI, various State Hospitals, and other area general hospitals with psychiatric units. In addition, at each evaluation, the patients were questioned regarding hospitalization as a double check. Hospitalization data were collected for the 2 years beyond the end of the treatment

TABLE 3.

Correlations Between VVT Number of Errors and Days Hospitalized and Clinical Status Ratings Within One Week of VVT Testing for 33 Schizophrenic Patients

	Original VVT	6 Months VVT	12 Months VVT	20 Months VVT
Days hospitalized subsequently[a]	0.51**	0.37**	0.39*	0.36*
Clinical status ratings	−0.50**	−0.58**	−0.38*	−0.36*

[a]For original VVT: Hospitalization during first 6 months
For 6-month VVT: Hospitalization between 6 and 12 months
For 12-month VVT: Hospitalization between 12 and 20 months
For 20-month VVT: Hospitalization after treatment phase of project (20 months to 44 months)
*p < 0.05
**p < 0.01

phase of the project. In other words, hospitalization data were gathered for a total of 44 months. This criterion is confounded by such uncontrollable factors as the fluctuation in the number of available hospital beds, the complexity of environmental demands on the patient, and the willingness of the patient's work and social environment to tolerate varying degrees of bizarre behavior.

A more uncontaminated, as well as a more refined measure, of day-to-day functioning can be obtained for research purposes in a thorough Clinical Status Interview (CSI) of such patients by an experienced clinician. Such interviews were conducted by an experienced psychoanalytic psychiatrist who was not involved with or informed about the treatment of the patients. The interviews were recorded on tape, and any references to type of treatment were deleted. Two advanced graduate students in clinical psychology blindly rated the degree of emotional health from the CSI tapes. The ratings were "global" and quantified by means of a scaling procedure.

While there are obvious specificities, nonetheless, an unidimensional concept of "mental health" may be meaningfully employed. Menninger, Mayman, and Pruyser (1963), for example, have criticized the value of the standard psychiatric nosology and suggested that, despite the obvious multiplicity of symptoms, most of the meaningful variation in mental illness can be summarized in terms of an undimensional construct. This assumption may be justified on the basis of data presented by Luborsky (1962), who found that the first principal component of a factor analysis of ratings with respect to 14 specific aspects of psychopathology accounted for 60 percent of the variance. Thus, one dimension meaningfully accounted for a great deal of the variation in emotional health, despite the fact that the additive arithmetic of factor analysis cannot take account of the substitutive nature of alternate symptoms. A sophisticated judge, however, cannot only take into account the relative severity of alternative symptoms, but also the implications of environmental context. Thus, while ability to hold a job is a central criterion of adjustment, a patient who has a job waiting for him may not be necessarily better adjusted than a patient who is having difficulty in obtaining work *de novo*. Similarly, an increase in the severity of a symptom like manifest anxiety which, everything else being equal, would indicate a worse adjustment, might mean movement toward health if it represents the results of the patient's abandoning a more pathologic defense, for example, the disappearance of hallucinations. The scaling procedure utilized allows such factors to be weighted clinically.

Both the raters and the interviewing psychiatrist were instructed to pay attention to the following characteristics: ability to take care of self, ability to work, sexual adjustment, social adjustment, absence of hallucinations and delusions, degree of freedom from anxiety and depression, amount of affect, variety and spontaneity of affect, satisfaction with life and self, achievement of capabilities, and benign versus malignant effect on others.

More subtle personality changes are assumed by clinicians to be reflected in projective tests, such as the Rorschach and TAT. Hence, these projectives were administered. The Rorschach protocols were recorded by hand. The 20-card TAT protocols were recorded on tape and later transcribed by a typist. Another pair of advanced graduate students in clinical and personality psychology rated emotional health from the projective tests. Ratings were carried out separately for the Rorschach and for the TAT; that is, the two raters first rated the TATs, and then the Rorschach protocols. Usually, while the raters rated the protocols independently, they were permitted to clarify the content of the protocol prior to the rating and to discuss the ratings afterward. The raters were told not to use "lack of repression," or "free id material," as an indication of either health or pathology, inasmuch as it has differing significance in the context of different treatments. In addition to the criteria used for rating the CSI, the following additional criteria were also utilized for the projective tests: length of protocol, variety of material or absence of stereotypy, presence of benign fantasies and helping nurturant parent figures, self-confidence, reality-testing, and direct representation of problems.

All raters were instructed to rate "mental health" because pretesting had indicated that "mental health" is judged more consistently than "mental illness." It seems as if there is no clear baseline of "health" from which to measure "illness," but that in rating "health" the baseline seems to be something like "no functioning at all." As an anchoring point, the raters were instructed to read "Winn, a happy man," a unique case history, complete with projective protocols, of an unusually healthy man occurring in nature, that is, without psychotherapy (Wessman and Ricks 1966).

QUANTIFICATION OF CLINICAL MATERIAL

The raters were asked to compare clinical materials from a pair of patients at a time. The raters were instructed not to use a formal weighting system for the specific criteria of emotional health provided, but to use such criteria clinically to arrive at a global, relative judgment of emotional health. After reading or listening to a pair of protocols, a rater made a judgment of the ratio of the emotional health of one person to the health of the other. This judgment was recorded on a 20-centimeter line. The rater judged who was the healthier of the two patients and placed that patient at the point farthest to the right of the line. The point farthest to the left represented an absence of mental health, or the zero point; that is, the length of the line represents the health of the healthier individual. The second decision involved taking the less healthy member of the pair and deciding, by placing a mark at some point along the line, what proportion of the first person's health the other person had. In order to get consistent judgments, according to previous research (Carter 1966), it is necessary to require that the healthier person be the length of the line, so the observation is always a proportion, between zero and one, with the healthier person being the denominator and the less healthy person the numerator. Such a judgment is a ratio score, using the healthier individual as the standard.

If all possible pairs had been compared, there would have been $(36 \times 35)/2$ comparisons, or 630 judgments for each rater on each type of material. To reduce the work, it was decided to select $2(n - 1)$ comparisons or 70 judgments. Previous work on psychophysical stimuli had suggested that stimuli close to each other provided the most stable judgments; however, it was necessary to order the stimuli (patients' protocols) before such adjacent judgments could be taken. Therefore, a comparison stimulus (person) was chosen, and all other stimuli were judged against that person, that is, using the constant stimulus method. These first $n - 1$

judgments were used to order the stimuli, and then adjacent pairs were determined to be presented to the judges for ratings. The tentative scaling was not discussed with the raters, and the pairs were randomized before presentation to the raters. The raters reported that it was easier to make the judgments using a constant stimulus when rating the interview recordings, but that the adjacent comparisons were easier to rate when dealing with transcribed projective protocols.

Calculation of the Scale Values

In order to illustrate the calculations involved in determining the scale values, suppose there are three patients—A, B, and C. A is compared with B, found to be 0.60, and B is rated to be 0.80 of C. If these ratios are meaningful, we can then predict that A will be $0.80 \times 0.60 = 0.48$ of C. When the rater actually does compare A with C, we get a check on whether these ratings form an unidimensional ratio scale. This check can be performed simultaneously over the whole matrix of data as described below.

The judgments of a single rater may be organized into a matrix with each stimulus being represented by a row and a column as shown in Table 4, which shows all possible comparisons of three stimuli. Each entry consists of the column stimulus divided by the row stimulus. In the matrix, there are missing entries wherever the numerator would have been larger than the denominator. The missing entry is obtained by taking the reciprocal of the comparison. If A and B are compared, A is seen as 0.60 of B. In the

TABLE 4.
A Matrix of Judgments

Stimulus	A	B	C
A	$\dfrac{A}{A}$	$\dfrac{B}{A}$	$\dfrac{C}{A}$
B	$\dfrac{A}{B}$	$\dfrac{B}{B}$	$\dfrac{C}{B}$
C	$\dfrac{A}{C}$	$\dfrac{B}{C}$	$\dfrac{C}{C}$

matrix, A over B is recorded as 0.60. In the same matrix, B over A is missing and is determined by computing the reciprocal of A over B, that is, the reciprocal of 0.60 or 1.67. (The diagonal entries are by definition 1.00.) A complete matrix is shown in Table 5.

Further computations can be simplified by transforming to logarithms. The logarithm of a ratio equals the logarithm of the numerator minus the logarithm of the denominator; that is, log A/B equals log A–log B. The matrix of ratios now becomes a matrix of differences, which makes the solution for the scale values arithmetically simple. Moreover, the logarithms of the judgments tend to have more nearly equal errors of measurement for extreme and nonextreme judgments than the raw judgments and tend to be more linearly related to other variables, as will be discussed below.

Those who are familiar with psychologic scaling techniques for precisely quantifying subjective judgments will recognize that the data analysis to be described is similar to that for Thurstone's well-known case V of the Method of Paired Comparisons (Guilford 1954, pp. 154–178; Mosteller 1951). In Thurstone's case V, the entries in the matrix are obtained by taking the normal deviate corresponding to the percentage of times one stimulus is seen as greater than another in a large number of trials. In the present technique, the entries in the matrix are obtained by taking the logarithm of the ratio obtained from a single judgment. Beyond that point, the computations are identical.

This computational procedure and its logic may be best understood by examining Tables 6 and 7. In Table 6, the logs of the ratios are substituted for the ratios in Table 4. It will be recalled that the log of a ratio is numerically identical with the difference between the logarithms of the numerator and of the denominator. As seen in Table 6, if the entries in a column are averaged, the log scale value of that column stimulus can be determined as a devia-

TABLE 5.

An Illustrative Complete Matrix

Stimulus	A	B	C
A	1.00	1.67	2.08
B	0.60	1.00	1.25
C	0.48	0.80	1.00

TABLE 6.

Matrix of Logarithms of Judgments

Stimulus	A	B	C
A	log A − log A	log B − log A	log C − log A
B	log A − log B	log B − log B	log C − log B
C	log A − log C	log B − log C	log C − log C
Sum	$3 \log A$ $-(\log A + \log B + \log C)$	$3 \log B$ $-(\log A + \log B + \log C)$	$3 \log C$ $-(\log A + \log B + \log C)$
Average	$\log A$ $-\left(\dfrac{\log A + \log B + \log C}{3}\right)$	$\log B$ $-\left(\dfrac{\log A + \log B + \log C}{3}\right)$	$\log C$ $-\left(\dfrac{\log A + \log B + \log C}{3}\right)$

Note: If the average log scale value $\left(\dfrac{\log A + \log B + \log C}{3}\right)$ is defined as equal to 0, the column averages simplify to log A, log B, and log C, respectively.

411

TABLE 7.

Logarithms Corresponding to the Entries in Table 6

Stimulus	A	B	C
A	0	0.22185	0.31876
B	9.77815 − 10 (=−0.22185)	0	0.09691
C	9.68124 − 10 (=−0.31876)	9.90309 − 10 (=−0.09691)	0
Sum	− 0.54061	0.12494	0.41567
Log scale value (column average)	− 0.18020	0.04165	0.13856
Antilog scale value	0.66	1.11	1.38

tion from the average log scale value of all the stimuli. Since the zero point of the log scale (i.e., the unit of measurement of the original scale) is arbitrary, one may set the mean log scale value at zero, in which case the result simplifies to the log scale value being the average of the column. This is a least-squares solution for a complete data matrix (all possible pairs compared), and is algebraically identical (but not experimentally identical) with Mosteller's (1951) derivation for Thurstone's case V. Numerically, this is illustrated by Table 7, in which the logs of the entries in Table 5 are entered, and the scale values computed.

Complete comparison of all possible pairs requires $n(n-1)/2$ comparisons, where n is the number of stimuli; however, $n-1$ comparisons are sufficient to determine the scale, and $2(n-1)$ comparisons, as used in this study, provide sufficient data to test internal consistency.

A more general least-squares solution, for both complete and incomplete data matrices, may readily be calculated as follows. For any one stimulus j, a least-squares solution for L_j (the logarithm of the scale value of j) is given by the following equation:

$$L_j = \frac{1}{N_i{}^*} \sum_{i^*} D_{ji}{}^* + \frac{1}{N_i{}^*} \sum_{i^*} L_i \qquad (1)$$

where D_{ji} is the logarithm of an observed ratio of stimulus j to stimulus i, that is, D_{ji} is an empirical estimate of $L_j - L_i$; and i^* is a value for i for which the comparison D_{ji} was observed. It should be noted that for these purposes, if D_{ji} was observed, D_{ij} is considered to have been observed, since it is determined by the same judgment and equals $-D_{ji}$.

A little algebra will readily generate the solution for the complete data matrix from equation 1. In any incomplete matrix in which a whole column (and row, obviously) is determined, the value for the stimulus is determinate; that is, as with the complete data matrix, the mean of the column of log observations is the log scale value, if the mean log scale value is set at zero. If, however, the column is not complete, the solution seems indeterminate at first glance. One may compute an iterative solution, however, using any trial values of L_j to compute the first approximations. The solution rapidly converges. In the empirical examples in our study, 4 to 12 iterations sufficed. To make the procedure more explicit:

1. Sum the columns of observations (after transforming to logarithms).
2. Divide by the number of observations in that column.
3. Sum the trial values of L_j for all stimuli with which that stimulus j (the column stimulus) was compared.
4. Divide by the number of observations (same number as in step 2).
5. Add the results of steps 2 and 4 to obtain the next estimate of L_j.
6. Do this for all stimuli (i.e., all columns of the matrix).
7. Repeat steps 3 through 6, using the new values of L_j.
8. Stop when the values of L_j do not change appreciably.

One may use any trial values of the L_j to begin with, such as all $L_j = 0$. Some iterations can be saved by using better initial trial values determined by using $n - 1$ of the comparisons. But no matter what the trial values, the solution will converge.

It should be noted that one of the scale values is arbitrary (as in paired-comparison scaling) so that one may set the average L_j or the value of one particular L_j as equal to zero to suit one's convenience. In most incomplete date matrices, it tends to be labor-saving to set one of the L_j equal to zero.

These computations yield the logarithm of the scale values. Intrarater reliability for the logarithmic data may be estimated by a method similar to that described by Gulliksen and Tukey (1957) for assessing the reliability of the Thurstone paired-comparison technique. The total sum of squares (the sum of the squares of the observations over half the matrix, either above or below the diagonal) may be divided by the total degrees of freedom (the number of independent observations) to determine T, an estimate of the total variance.

Using the scale values computed by the scaling method, one can derive a theoretical value of what each observation should be, if the scale values were correct and if the scaling method worked exactly. If one subtracts the theoretical value of an observation from its empirically observed counterpart, one obtains an error or discrepancy. By squaring these errors and summing over half of the matrix (either above or below the diagonal), one obtains the discrepancy sum of squares. Thus, the total sum of squares can be divided into two parts: the discrepancy sum of squares and the sum of squares accounted for by the scale values.

The total degrees of freedom may be secondarily partitioned. Since n − 1 scale values were computed from the data, n − 1 degrees of freedom were used in calculating the scale values. The total degrees of freedom (the number of independent observations) minus the number of scale values determined from the data (n − 1) yields the degrees of freedom for the error or discrepancy variance.

The discrepancy sum of squares divided by the discrepancy degrees of freedom yields D, the discrepancy variance. Internal consistency, Rss may now be computed as follows:

$$Rss = \frac{T - D}{T} \tag{2}$$

It should be noted that all failures of the scaling model, inaccuracies of judgment, unreliability of the judge, and lack of unidimensionality increase D and decrease Rss.

Interjudge reliability and validity may be determined using the ordinary product-moment correlation between the log scale values of two raters or between the log scale values and an external criterion, which is the procedure we used.

This scaling procedure may be contrasted with other scaling procedures. The simplest kind of rating procedure, the method of absolute judgments, has two drawbacks: it requires the judge to have an internalized scale with end points and units before judgment can be made meaningfully, and the judgment itself is experienced as very difficult by the judge. The technique described here, however, requires the judge to have neither an explicit end point nor unit, but simply to be able to compare one human being's functioning with another's, using one of the persons as the unit. This concrete judgment is experienced by the judge as much simpler. Moreover, internal consistency and degree of unidimensionality may be examined empirically, when judgments are made on pair-wise comparisons.

Thurstone's paired-comparison technique, while requiring only a "Which is greater?" judgment, has the fatal drawback that it requires each pair of stimuli to be compared by a large number of judges (50 or more) or by the same judge a large number of times, but if clinically sophisticated judges are required, one cannot for practical purposes obtain a large number of them, nor will one sophisticated judge cooperate in making the same judgment a great many times.

Reliability. Rss measures internal consistency and unidimensionality, as well as accuracy of judgment. On the original (pretreatment) evaluations, the first rater using the clinical status interview had an internal consistency of 0.83, while the second rater had the surprisingly low internal consistency of 0.37. The two TAT raters had an internal consistency of 0.86 and 0.81, while on the Rorschach they had 0.96 and 0.92.

One advantage of the Rss coefficient is that it immediately reveals whether a judge's ratings are consistent and unidimensional. If Rss is not satisfactory, one can search for and remedy the cause of the inconsistency.

The low internal consistency of one rater led us to question his data. This rater was physically blind, and had to depend on someone else to transcribe and label his judgments. An error or errors of transcription seemed likely. Since scale values can be determined from $n - 1$ judgments, and since the raters carried out two sets of $n - 1$ judgments, scale values were determined from his first set of judgments and from his second set of judgments independently. He was asked if the rankings of these scale values were reasonable. Those determined from the first $n - 1$ were meaningful to him. Those determined from the second $n - 1$ were meaningless to him, so he was asked to redo those judgments. After redoing them, his internal consistency was 0.79.

The traditional mode of assessing reliability in rating situations is by correlating the scale values between the two raters, and this was the next step.

Scatter plots of the logarithms of the scale values seemed to be more nearly linear in their relationship to each other and to external criteria than the scale values. More generally, the use of log scale values, rather than antilogs, for statistical analyses seems indicated by these data.

The interjudge reliability between the clinical status raters was 0.82, when the initial judgments were used, despite the low internal consistency of one rater. The interjudge reliability on the TAT and Rorschach was 0.94 and 0.95, respectively. Both of these latter figures are considerably higher than would normally be expected on a rating task. The first correlation of 0.82 might be expected to go even higher if the intrajudge reliability of the first rater were raised. Indeed, this was the case; when the second half of the ratings was redone by the rater who had the original low internal consistency, the resulting interjudge reliability was found to be 0.87.

But even when Rss was low, the least-squares scale values still yielded high inter-rater reliability. Examination of the validity coefficeints based on the average of two raters, revealed that they were essentially unchanged, and high. The correlation of the CSI ratings with the Rorschach rating was 0.44 with the low Rss ratings and 0.41 with the high Rss ratings; the correlation with the TAT was 0.55 and 0.57; with the PM 0.57 and 0.60; with the WAIS 0.43 and 0.40; and with days hospitalized in the next 6 months -0.71 and -0.71.

Thus, these scale values seem to be robust with respect to inconsistent or nonunidimensional judgments. They seem to represent a meaningful one-dimensional projection of the available data. Since Rss for each scale was 0.78 or better for the second testings, and since low Rss does not seem to make much difference in inter-rater reliability or validity, it was not calculated for subsequent testing.

Inter-rater reliability for all testings is summarized in Table 8.

TABLE 8.

Inter-rater Reliability for CSI, ROR, and TAT at Pretreatment,
6 Months, 12 Months, and 20 Months

Time	CSI	ROR	TAT
Pretreatment	0.87	0.95	0.94
6 Months	0.82	0.81	0.87
12 Months	0.82	0.77	0.59
20 Months	0.66	0.90	0.79

TABLE 9.

Validity of the Clinical Status Interview Ratings

Measure Correlated with CSI	Pretreatment CSI	6 Month CSI	12 Month CSI	20 Month CSI
Concurrent VVT (errors)	−0.50	−0.57	−0.38	−0.37
Concurrent WAIS	0.43	0.46	0.50	0.57
Concurrent PM	0.57	0.35	0.54	0.38
Days hospitalized in next period[a]	−0.71	−0.64	−0.65	−0.29

[a]For pretreatment, CSI uses DH 0-6; for 6 month, CSI uses DH 6-12; for 12 month, CSI uses DH 12-20; for 20 month, CSI uses DH 20-44.

Validity. Ratings from each of the three clinical measures were found to be valid both concurrently and predictively (Karon and O'Grady 1970); however, the highest validity coefficients were consistently achieved by the ratings made from the Clinical Status Interview, which is also the measure with the highest face validity. This is in keeping with clinical experience. Most clinicians who have to use only one technique of evaluation would choose the interview. None of the research findings concerning the Rorschach or TAT measures were statistically significant, and therefore we draw no conclusions about them.

The validity coefficients for the CSI ratings are summarized in Table 9. Concurrent validities were determined by the correlation with the thought disorder measures (VVT, WAIS, and PM), and predictive validities from the correlations with days hospitalized in the subsequent 6-month period for the first two evaluations, the subsequent 8-month period for the third, and the subsequent 2 years for the fourth. The lower correlation for this last period is in part a result of the distribution of days hospitalized; 18 (14 of whom received psychotherapy) out of 33 patients were never rehospitalized.

PROCEDURES FOR DATA ANALYSIS

Patients who could not or would not take intellectual tests *initially* were assigned maximal error scores. On the TGV, the "chance" score (four out of twenty items) was assigned. For the

PM, the "score" was the midpoint of the interval from zero to the lowest attainable score. On the WAIS and WB II, a scale score of zero was assigned for each subtest not taken, rather than prorating the IQ on the basis of the tests taken. This was done because the WAIS/WB II was being used not as a measure of general intelligence, but of intellectual impairment resulting from psychosis. A total sum of scaled scores of zero (zero on all subtests) was then given an IQ by extending the Wechsler transformation equation (or tables, which are equivalent) in the manual. In each case, this resulted in an IQ of 34. On the VVT, the maximum error score, 42, was utilized.

On the TGV, only two patients received such chance scores initially. One patient was in group A and the other in group B, both treated by trainees. On the PM, there were four such patients initially. Two patients were in group A and two in group B, all treated by trainees. On the WAIS initially, there were seven: group A, three (two treated by trainees); group B, three (all treated by trainees); group C, one. On the VVT initially, there were six: group A, two (treated by trainees); group B, three (treated by trainees); and group C, one.

A dichotomous variable ("take" versus "not-take" initially) was introduced for *each* test to examine statistically whether or not the assigned scores were appropriate. "Appropriate," as used here, is in the sense of predicting 20-month (or 12-month or 6-month scores). If the assigned initial scores were seriously inappropriate, this dichotomous variable would be statistically significant and was used to correct the score. At 6 months, this was necessary for the TGV and WB II. At 12 months, it was not necessary for any variable. At 20 months, such correction was needed for the TGV and WB II.

This procedure of assigning scores was *only used for the initial test data* (pretherapy) in order to determine the regression line, and not for the outcome data. The only alternatives to such a procedure are: (1) to eliminate all patients who, before treatment, are too sick to take the tests (This is the procedure which is all too common in schizophrenia research. Its defects are obvious.); or (2) to use a regression line for those who took the test with a single separately determined point for those who did not. This latter alternative is mathematically identical to the procedure used in our study when the "take/not take" correction is statistically significant, but using a theoretically meaningful point on the regression line leads to less sampling error in determining the regression when that correction is not statistically significant, and the statistical test of the "take/not take" correction provides an indication of whether the most theoretically reasonable score is, in fact, appropriate.

If a given patient refused a given test at later evaluations (at 6, 12, or 20 months), he was not included in the analysis for that test for that evaluation.

At 6 months, one patient did not take the TGV, a control. Three refused the PM: one in group B treated by a trainee; and two in group C. Two patients refused the WB II: one treated by a trainee in group A; and one control. Two refused the VVT: one treated by a trainee in group A; and one control. At 12 months, two patients consistently refused to be tested, one hospital control and one patient in group A (treated by a trainee). Consequently, only hospitalization data were included on these patients.

Importantly, it should be noted that all patients took all objective and projective tests at 20 months (end of treatment phase).

The data were analyzed by analyses of covariance. The present design meets with Campbell's (1970) stringent criteria (namely, that the subjects were drawn from the same pool and randomly assigned) for the appropriate use of analysis of covariance. The analyses of covariance used initial score as a covariate (i.e., holding initial score constant). The use of analysis of covariance with initial scores as the covariate rather than difference scores between test and retest may not be a familiar procedure to the reader. While generally the results of the analyses of covariance and of difference scores will be the same, the covariance procedure, first of all, has smaller error variance than difference scores, and hence is more sensitive. Secondly, it does not require that the groups be matched initially. As Edwards (1954) has pointed out, if two or more groups differ on initial scores, the analysis of difference scores may yield (or not yield) significant findings spuriously, because of regression toward the mean. In this case, while samples A, B, and C were randomized, they were not precisely matched. Moreover, when the supervisors' cases are treated separately, the match is even less perfect. Also, the tests do not have to be exactly parallel, in the statistical sense (i.e., equal mean, variance, and correlation with all criteria). Thus, the two forms of the VVT are not exactly parallel. Finally, the analysis of covariance allows one to correct for the effects of other covariates besides initial score, if they are meaningfully related to the dependent variable. The analysis of covariance does assume linear regressions, and in some situations this may produce more distortion of the analysis than the use of difference scores; however, if the nonlinear regression is a well-behaved function, the nonlinearity can be taken into account. This was done for age. As previous research indicated, age should be transformed to a log scale and a second-degree equation examined (Karon 1964a).

Before computing the analysis of covariance, the following possible contaminating factors were also examined and taken into account if the partial regression coefficients were significantly related to the later score: "take versus not take" test initially, age, sex, education, race, marital status, previous hospitalization, social class, religion, initial TGV, initial PM, initial WAIS, initial VVT, initial CSI ratings, initial ROR ratings, and initial TAT ratings. In other words, each of these variables might possibly be related to change in criterion score. If this were so, and if the samples are not identical on the variable, that variable might give rise to spurious findings.

Therefore, using a computer, the effects of all of these covariates (possibly contaminating factors) were examined simultaneously. Most of them had no statistically significant effect. The covariate having the least effect was deleted first. More precisely, the partial correlations of all these covariates with each criterion score were initially examined simultaneously within groups and within therapists. The least statistically significant covariate was then deleted and the partial correlations recomputed. Variables were removed one at a time because the deletion of one variable might increase the significance of one of the remaining variables. Covariates other than initial score were thus eliminated one at a time until all remaining covariates were significant at the 5 percent level. In addition, in view of the well-known instability of regression coefficients, even when determined from relatively large samples (and the present samples were necessarily small), a further

restriction of meaningfulness was placed on the regression coefficients. If a measure of initial sickness was, according to the
partial correlation, correlated negatively rather than positively
with later illness, and if the first-order correlation was positive, the
negative partial correlation was considered dubious and rounded to
zero. The partial regressions were then recomputed for the remaining significant covariates.

The analyses of covariance were then computed, holding the
initial score on each particular test or rating constant, and correct-
ing for any other significant covariates.

At 20 months, in addition to initial score on the same measure, the following background variables had significant partial
regressions and therefore were held constant: for the TGV—social
class; for the WB II—marital status, log age squared, and education; for the VVT—initial CSI, initial WAIS, initial WAIS "take/not
take," and social class; for the CSI—sex and social class; and for 20-
month hospitalization—initial PM and sex. Corrections were not
necessary on other measures.

At 12 months, the following background variables were held
constant: for the TGV—race; for the PM—initial Rorschach; for
the VVT—initial CSI, initial WAIS, "take/not take" initial WAIS,
and social class; and for hospitalization in the first 12 months—
initial PM and sex. Corrections were not necessary on other
measures.

At 6 months, the following background variables were held
constant: for the TGV—"take/not take" TGV initially; for the
WB II—social class and "take/not take" WAIS initially; for
hospitalization—sex and PM; for the CSI—social class; and for the
TAT—social class and education. Corrections were not necessary
for the other measures.

The Findings

THE VIEW AT 6 MONTHS

The corrected 6-month data are presented in Table 10. Patients in groups A and B are separated into those treated by supervisors and those treated by students. It is important to note that
this table includes the organic patient whom we later deleted; since

TABLE 10.
Six-month Outcome Data

Groups	n	TGV	PM	WAIS	VVT	Raw Data: Days in Hospital	Corrected Data: Days in Hospital	CSI[a]	ROR[a]	TAT[a]
Hospital comparison	11[b]	9.9	10.1	81.9	15.3	60.0[b]	72.9[b]	0.93	0.98	1.01
Pooled psychotherapy	23	8.6	11.3	85.6	15.9	56.0	49.4	0.92	0.98	1.05
Supervisor A	4	10.5	12.0	85.9	10.7	41.3	51.7	1.00	1.03	1.00
Group A trainees	7	7.9	11.2	80.5	20.8	101.3	70.3	0.68	0.87[c]	1.12[c]
Supervisor B	4	10.0	11.5	100.6	12.3	21.8	58.7	0.96	1.13	1.05
Group B trainees	8	7.6	11.0	82.3	16.1	40.9	25.0	1.06	0.97	1.01
		n.s.	n.s.	p=0.03	p<0.01	n.s.	p<0.02	p<0.05	n.s.	n.s.

[a]Scaled clinical ratings have an arbitrary zero point for each evaluation, and are only comparable between groups at the same evaluation. Comparisons between evaluations are not comparable.

[b]One hospital comparison patient refused all testing; this patient is only included in the hospitalization data, for which the n is thus 12.

[c]Based on six patients (one refused projective testing).

423

we found out about the drug history and organic involvement at a later time when more comprehensive and recent data were available on all patients, we did not reanalyze the "old" data deleting this patient because of costs and the availability of later data. These 6-month data represent what our findings would have been if the project had ended after 6 months, as unfortunately is all too frequent in psychotherapy and drug research. The patient whose treatment was later interfered with is appropriately still included. It also should be noted that these findings are conservative in the sense that the only patient who did not return for the 6-month evaluation was a patient in group C, who was functioning outside the hospital only by virtue of being treated as less than human by her mother.

All groups showed improvement over their pretreatment functioning; however, there are significant group differences. The WB II differences are significant at the 0.03 level. Even more significant are the differences on the VVT ($p = 0.002$), which is the most direct measure of the schizophrenic thought disorder. The differences in hospitalization among the groups without considering the effects of differences among the samples (significant covariates) are not statistically significant ($p = 0.10$); however, when the hospitalization data are corrected for the significant covariates, the group differences are significant at the 0.02 level. The CSI ratings are also significant among the groups beyond the 0.05 level.

The analysis of covariance appears to alter the hospitalization data considerably. This was examined to be certain the corrections were meaningful. The two factors being corrected for were sex of patient and initial PM score. Overall, holding treatment group and therapist constant, female patients averaged 39.73 fewer days in the hospital than male patients. Each increment of 1 year in the PM performance lessened the average length of hospitalization by 11.06 days. Inasmuch as the five samples did not have the same sex ratio (see Table 1) or PM scores, the analysis of covariance led to meaningful corrections. Investigation of the ward procedures as well as family attitudes revealed that sex really was a large determinant of length of hospitalization. Female patients were considered for release earlier, because potential for violence was generally less of a problem. More importantly, families were ready to take female patients back without qualms, but wives, parents, and children were likely to insist that male patients not be discharged until they were ready to return to work.

If one were to compare the pooled psychotherapy groups without regard for experience level or use of medication, one would conclude, 6 months after the beginning of treatment, that psychotherapy contributed little or nothing. Such a finding is frequently reported, and such studies frequently cover a 6-month period of time, utilizing inexperienced therapists. If one were to include only the two groups of inexperienced therapists, the differences favor the hospital control group, and medication seems to account for all of the improvement. This is strikingly similar in design and findings to the California findings.

The major finding at 6 months is that patients of experienced therapists show significantly more improvement than the control group, or the groups treated by inexperienced therapists. The role of medication for the patients of these experienced therapists seems minimal. The patients of the supervisors, as compared to the hospital comparisons, show an improvement in the thought disorder on both the WAIS and the VVT, and a reduction in days hospitalized, both with and without correction. A study using only patients of experienced therapists would conclude that, even in a period as short as 6 months, psychotherapy is of demonstrable value to schizophrenic patients as compared to medication alone. Moreover, adjunctive medication contributes little.

The medicated patients of the trainees show no difference in the thought disorder from medication alone, show some advantage on the CSI, and a dramatic reduction in hospitalization, corrected or uncorrected. It is interesting that the patients of the trainees in group B show a reduction in hospitalization, as compared to the control group, just as do the group B patients under the supervisor; however, the patients of the group B trainees do not achieve an improvement in the thought disorder, whereas the patients of the supervisor do.

The unmedicated patients of the trainees seem to be worse on the VVT, markedly worse on the CSI, and spend more time in the hospital than the controls. When the hospitalization data are corrected, they become comparable to the medication-alone group. This difference is not solely attributable to the organic patient, but reflects the fact that doing psychotherapy without medication takes longer to learn. (Later analyses will reveal a long-run benefit for these patients not revealed in the short-run data.)

THE 12-MONTH PERSPECTIVE

The 12-month data are presented in Table 11. It should be noted that, beginning with this evaluation and data analysis, the organic patient is excluded because sufficient information had become available. Of the 34 remaining patients, three refused all tests and interviews, and hence are included only in the hospitalization data. It must be remembered that the Detroit riots occurred while these data were being gathered. The hospital was located in the riot zone. Patients were realistically frightened, and just as their neighbors were, they were angry at whites, in a time of confrontation; they were also conflicted and guilty about their relationship to their white therapists.

Nonetheless, there were differences among the groups. There were significant differences in the VVT, CSI ratings, and hospitalization data.

Whether making available an average of 60 sessions in the first year of psychoanalytic psychotherapy made a difference can be answered by examining the comparison between the hospital controls and the pooled psychotherapy group, in Table 11. Beginning with the criterion which is the most clear-cut measure of improvement for a schizophrenic population—hospitalization, the "control" patients spent an average of 116.7 days in the hospital during the first year. The pooled psychotherapy group only spent 71.0 days, after correction. This difference is significant, and obviously favors the psychotherapy group. The difference between the "raw" and "corrected" hospitalization data is meaningful and followed the same pattern as the 6-month data. The best measure of the level of overall functioning is the CSI. The control group had an average rating of 0.92, while the pooled psychotherapy group averaged 1.07. This difference is significant, again favoring psychotherapy. The most striking difference is on the Visual-Verbal test, which was specifically designed to reflect the schizophrenic thought disorder. The average corrected number of errors by the control group is 19.8 and the experimental groups average 13.4. This difference is significant beyond the 0.001 level.

TABLE 11.

Twelve-month Outcome Data

Group	n	Raw Data: Days in Hospital	Corrected Data: Days in Hospital	TGV	PM	VVT	WAIS	CSI	ROR	TAT
Hospital comparison	12[a]	93.0	116.7	8.7	9.4	19.8	85.3	0.92	1.07	1.00
Pooled psychotherapy	22	77.6	71.0	8.7	8.6	13.4	86.7	1.07	1.05	1.01
		n.s.	$p<0.03$	n.s.	n.s.	$p<0.001$	n.s.	$p<0.05$	n.s.	n.s.
Supervisor A	4[b]	67.0	84.6	7.7	7.8	7.0	84.7	1.06	0.97	0.93
Group A trainees	6[c]	162.0	126.0	11.1	9.6	12.2	89.0	1.10	1.06	1.08
Supervisor B	4	28.8	91.6	10.6	11.90	14.0	90.3	1.14	1.17	1.05
Group B trainees	8	43.9	12.6	6.7	7.8	18.0	84.2	1.02	1.02	1.00
		n.s.	$p<0.01$	n.s.	n.s.	$p<0.01$	n.s.	n.s.	n.s.	n.s.

[a]One control patient refused all tests and interviews and is *not* included, except for the hospitalization data.
[b]One experimental patient refused all tests and interviews and is *not* included, except for the hospitalization data.
[c]The organic patient and dead patient are excluded; in addition, one of the remaining six patients refused all tests and interviews and is *not* included, except for the hospitalization data.

427

Thus, the pooled psychotherapy patients are hospitalized for a shorter length of time (over 1½ months during the first year), exhibit less thought disorder as measured by the VVT, and are seen in the diagnostic interview as functioning in a healthier manner than those persons in the hospital control group.

The five-group analysis allows comparison of level of experience, use of medication, and their interactional effect, to which the 6-month data and previous research had already alerted us. These data are also presented in Table 11. There are significant differences in hospitalization and thought disorder related to experience and to the use of medication.

The patients of the experienced therapists showed "balanced" improvement, that is, hospitalization is strongly decreased and the schizophrenic thought disorder is dramatically improved as compared to the Hospital Comparison patients. This is an extension of the finding at 6 months.

The patients of the trainees, however, did not show balanced improvement. The patients of group A trainees (without medication) were actually hospitalized longer than the Comparison group, but showed a striking improvement in the thought disorder. The patients of B trainees (with medication) were hospitalized for a dramatically shorter period of time than the hospital controls, but the thought disorder remained essentially equivalent to that of the comparison group. These results reflect the reactions of inexperienced therapists to the therapeutic modality they are using. When medication is used adjunctively, behavioral control, and hence release from the hospital, is easier to obtain, and the inexperienced therapist will focus on what he seems to be able to effect. These therapists were "seduced" by the apparent effectiveness of the medication, and did not pay careful attention psychotherapeutically to the thought disorder, as did their supervisor, and as he recommended they do. The group A trainees were "forced" to deal with the thought disorder psychotherapeutically. Only by doing this could they get their patients to a point at which discharge was feasible. They were able to effect a change in the thought disorder in less than a year of treatment, but it required a hospitalization longer than that of the control group.

This might well have been the final evaluation, and these our final conclusions. The original design called for 24 months of treatment, and rigorous evaluation at 6 months, 1 year, 2 years (end of treatment), and annually up to 5 years post-treatment (or a total of 7 years from the beginning of treatment). At 18 months into the project, we were informed that NIMH would not fund beyond 24 months. Given the time for initial preparation and the staggered beginning of treatment, that would not have permitted an end of treatment evaluation. Rebudgeting and replanning was undertaken; the hospital returned part of the overhead payments to us to help out. Therapy was terminated at 20 months, and complete evaluations carried out within the month after termination, so that by 28 months after the beginning of the project all treatment and evaluations were complete.

THE FINAL PICTURE: END OF TREATMENT EVALUATION DATA

While evaluations and data analyses were conducted after 6 months and 12 months, the most important question is what the patients were like at the end of treatment. The conclusions of the earlier evaluations become more clear in the final (20 months) evaluation. The results are presented in Table 12. The measures of the effectiveness of psychotherapy may be divided into four groups: (a) length of hospitalization, (b) clinical evaluation of functioning (CSI), (c) direct measures of the thought disorder, and (d) projective tests.

The first question is whether making an average of 70 sessions of psychoanalytic psychotherapy available over 20 months made a difference. This can be answered by comparing the pooled psychotherapy groups (A and B) with the hospital comparison (group C). The data are summarized in the top portion of Table 12.

The most obvious criterion of the effectiveness of treatment is length of hospitalization. *Both* the corrected and uncorrected differences are significant beyond the 0.05 level, and the magnitude of the difference is sizable. The psychotherapy group spent 31 to 51 percent less time in the hospital (35 to 75 days) than the comparison group, depending on whether the raw or corrected data are used. This represents a real difference in the patients' lives, use of hospital facilities, and hence, cost.

TABLE 12.

Twenty-month Outcome Data:
Average Hospitalization and Corrected Hospitalization, Intellectual Tests Scores, Projective Ratings, and Clinical Status Interview Ratings

Group	n	Raw Data: Days in Hospital	Corrected Data: Days in Hospital	CSI	VVT (errors)	WAIS	PM	TGV	TAT	ROR
Control	12[a]	113.5	146.4	0.89	17.5	89.1	10.8	7.9	0.98	1.02
Experimental	21	78.4	71.8	1.00	12.9	97.4	12.9	9.0	1.02	1.03
		$p<0.05$	$p<0.03$	$p<0.02$	$p<0.005$	$p<0.005$	$p<0.05$	$p=0.07$	n.s.	n.s.
Supervisor A	3	44.7	38.7	1.11	9.1	95.1	13.5	10.7	1.13	1.14
A trainees	6	165.9	139.8	1.28	10.2	105.8	13.5	9.2	1.05	1.03
Supervisor B	4	32.0	122.0	1.05	12.0	93.9	12.2	9.9	0.94	1.11
B trainees	8	48.5	8.1	0.89	16.9	93.7	12.7	7.5	0.99	0.94
		$p<0.05$	$p<0.05$	$p<0.005$	$p<0.001$	$p=0.06$	n.s.	n.s.	n.s.	n.s.

[a]For CSI only, n = 10.

430

The most comprehensive criterion of overall functioning is the blindly rated clinical status evaluations. The difference is significant, and favors the psychotherapy patients. It is conservative in that it was impossible to interview two "control" patients (who, however, had already taken the other tests). One of these had been hospitalized continuously for the 20 months of the project. The other patient was functioning outside the hospital under medication in an almost childlike state in which his mother was directing his behavior; he had not held a job in 3 months.

On the direct measures of the thought disorder, the pooled psychotherapy group was also functioning significantl, better than the hospital comparisons on three (VVT, WAIS, PM) of the four measures. The VVT, the measure which had been specifically designed to reflect the schizophrenic thought disorder, and which should be most sensitive to what Eugen Bleuler (1911) called the primary symptoms of schizphrenia, was most striking. On the projective tests, however, the results were not significant.

On five of the eight measures, psychoanalytic psychotherapy for schizophrenic patients made an appreciable difference as compared to medication alone. The psychotherapy patients spent less time in the hospital, showed better overall functioning, and less thought disorder than those patients receiving "routine" treatment. In addition, it should be noted that these results are conservative in that the evaluation was made at the termination of treatment, which is a crisis for psychotherapy patients.

A more detailed and meaningful examination of the findings is possible by a five-group analysis, as before, separating not only groups A, B, and C, but also separating the patients treated by the supervisors and the trainees within groups A and B. These data are also contained in Table 12. The hospitalization data, CSI ratings, and VVT scores are significant. The overall F tests indicate whether more than chance differences exist among the five groups. The relative means, despite the small n, suggest what these differences might be. While the authors feel that such inspection readily reveals the meaningful comparisons, for those readers who prefer a rigorous multiple comparison procedure, Dunnett's *t* statistic (Dunnett 1955) for comparing a number of samples with a control, was applied to the three variables whose F was significant; despite the small n's there are clearly significant differences. The results are summarized in Table 13.

TABLE 13.

Comparison of Each Experimental Group with the Hospital "Comparison"
Group by Dunnett's t Statistic

Measure	Supervisor A	A Trainees	Supervisor B	B Trainees
Hospitalization (raw)	$p < 0.05$	$p < 0.05*$	$p < 0.05$	$p < 0.05$
Hospitalization (corrected)	n.s.	n.s.	n.s.	$p < 0.05$
CSI	$p < 0.05$	$p < 0.01$	$p = 0.07$	n.s.
VVT	$p < 0.02$	$p < 0.01$	$p < 0.05$	n.s.

*Indicates significantly longer hospitalization than the comparison group, while all other differences in the table refer to shorter hospitalization or better functioning than the hospital comparisons (group C).

The findings noted at 6 and 12 months concerning the patients of the experienced therapists are even more clear and extensive at 20 months. The patients of experienced therapists manifested a "balanced" improvement across all outcome measures. They were hospitalized less than the controls, were functioning better than the controls, and showed greater improvement in the thought disorder on a variety of instruments. Clearly, appropriately trained and relevantly experienced psychotherapists are effective in the psychotherapy of schizophrenic patients.

The trainees providing psychotherapy to schizophrenic patients were also helpful, but to a lesser extent. Continuing to be evident is the "imbalance" across criteria of improvement, and the large difference that the adjunctive use of medication makes in the nature of the help such inexperienced therapists can provide.

The unmedicated patients of A trainees are comparable in length of hospitalization to the medicated hospital controls. Patients of group A trainees have slightly longer hospitalization in the uncorrected data and slightly shorter in the corrected data, but there are striking differences between these two groups in terms of level of functioning and thought disorder. By the end of treatment, the unmedicated patients of the group A trainees represent the best functioning group of patients in the project, as determined by the CSI ratings, and the improvement in the thought disorder is major as reflected in VVT and WAIS performance.

The patients of group B trainees (with medication) were hospitalized an amazingly short period of time; however, their level of overall functioning, as rated from the CSI, is identical to that of the medication-only group. Furthermore, the level of their thought disorder is essentially parallel to that of the hospital controls.

It should be noted that while trainees tend to produce "unbalanced" effects compared to the experienced therapists, on *no* criterion do the patients of inexperienced therapists do worse than those patients treated by medication alone. The difference between A and B trainees is on which criteria their patients do better than the patients treated with medication alone. Thus, patients who receive psychotherapy, even from inexperienced therapists, with appropriate supervision and motivation will do as well as those receiving medication on all criteria, and will do better on some.

There is an apparent inconsistency between the 12-month data (Table 11) and the 20-month data (Table 12). The first apparent difference is related to the "raw" hospitalization data for supervisor A. At 12 months, it was 67.0 days and at 20 months it is 44.7 days. The difference is caused by the deletion of the patient whose treatment was massively interfered with. There had been earlier interferences with his treatment, but not sufficient to warrant removal from the project until after the 12-month evaluation. We did not recalculate the 12-month data without this patient because of the cost and because of the availability of later, and hence more comprehensive, data.

The second apparent inconsistency related to the changes between the "raw" hospitalization data and the corrected hospitalization data for supervisor B and the B trainees. As was mentioned when discussing the 6-month data, sex of patient and initial PM scores were significantly related to length of hospitalization. These relationships were examined and found meaningful, as described earlier. Inasmuch as the five samples did not have the same sex ratio or PM score distributions, the analysis of covariance led to meaningful correction. Only the data for supervisor B and B trainees change to any great extent.

In the raw data, the patients of supervisor B show only 32.0 days hospitalized, but show 122.0 days hospitalized in the corrected data. The patients of the B trainees had 48.5 days of hospitalization in the raw data and 8.1 hospital days in the corrected data. For the B supervisor, this is a sizable difference; however, it must be remembered that being female was related to very short hospitalization over the entire sample, and three of his four patients were female. Hence, a correction toward lengthier hospitalization was necessary. The PM correction also affected patients in the same direction.

Thus, we looked at these data to see if the change was meaningful and reflective of reality, rather than an artifact. Since it seemed to be, we publish the data, along with the raw data in case the reader does not agree with us.

This statistical procedure only alters this one variable, and only affects the subcomparison between supervisor B and the B trainees. The difference does not alter any major conclusion, and does not reflect an inappropriate statistical operation.

The difference in the nature of the treatment provided by the inexperienced therapists and its interaction with medication first became apparent in the 12-month data and is amplified in the 20-month data. In the 12-month data, the evidence for a greater decrease in thought disorder for the patients treated without medication by trainees first appeared. At 20 months, this improvement is still apparent in the VVT, but appears to have radiated to the CSI ratings.

The measure designed specifically to reflect the schizophrenic thought disorder, the VVT, nonetheless yielded the most striking differences among the five groups ($p < 0.001$). Patients of the supervisor and trainees in group A, receiving psychoanalytic therapy without medication, not only show more improvement in the thought disorder than group C (receiving medication alone), but also more improvement in the thought disorder than both subgroups (supervisor and trainees, respectively) of group B, receiving medication as well as psychoanalytic therapy. As can readily be determined from Table 12, the mean VVT error scores for *all* the patients in group A (without medication, combining supervisors and trainees) is now only 9.8, for group B (combining supervisor and trainees), the *overall* mean is 15.3, and for the hospital comparison 17.5. All three groups are improved over their pretreatment means, but those patients treated without medication show the most dramatic improvement. Medication, thus, seems not to facilitate as great a change in thought disorder. This is not to say that the changes in the thought disorder produced by medication alone are not greater than would occur with no treatment at all. This was not tested in our study, although the literature suggests that at least in the short run such benefit probably occurs, but it is not comparable to the changes produced by psychotherapy, and while psychotherapy in addition to medication does produce greater improvement in the thought disorder, it does not have the same potency as psychotherapy without medication.

This diminished effect on the thought disorder of psychotherapy, when accompanied by medication, may in part be a function of the diminished affective reactions of the patient on medication. While diminished affective reactions, particularly of fear and anger, may be useful in maintaining behavioral control, it may be an interference with one aspect of what is specifically therapeutic in psychotherapy (e.g., Alexander and French 1946; Krystal 1975). As we have mentioned earlier in the book, the apparent lack of affect of schizophrenic patients is really a chronic terror state, which overrides other affects. Because of its chronicity, the patient may not even have it labeled as "fear." ("You're wrong, Doctor. I am not afraid. I just can't live outside a hospital. I can't survive, and I can't feel anything, and I mustn't talk.")

One of the therapeutic actions of medication is to reduce the massiveness of that anxiety. This, in some cases, may provide the appearance of increased affect. The adjunctive use of medication at the beginning of treatment may be necessary for some patients and/or therapists, but the importance of decreasing medication is underlined by our finding. While it is usual to hear lip service paid to the idea of decreasing medication, in practice, medication is usually maintained forever for schizophrenic patients (at least insofar as people other than the patient make the decision).

But to understand our findings and to understand the conditions that lead to other views, we must consider the impact of the use of medication on inexperienced therapists (as well as their patients). The use of medication with schizophrenic patients not only reduces anxiety for the patients, but also reduces the therapist's anxiety. The inexperienced and uncertain therapist has a "treatment" which makes an obvious difference in a short period of time. Maxwell Jones has described this well; in his pioneer therapeutic community, psychiatrists prescribed less and less medication the longer they were there. This was not related to changes in the kinds of patients treated, but to decreases in the professional's own anxiety (Jones 1953).

Psychotherapy, particularly with schizophrenic patients, arouses anxiety in the novice therapist because of the issues with which it deals; it also arouses feelings of inadequacy because it is an incompletely mastered complex skill, because these patients are so difficult, and because the feedback from these patients rarely indicates that they appreciate or are being helped by the therapist.

Is it any wonder that so many therapists get seduced by the medication and the immediate behavioral improvement it provides? This may have unfortunate long-term consequences for their professional development. Never having to master their anxiety about having to handle difficult situations psychotherapeutically, they never learn the potency of psychotherapeutic work. They never learn really to do psychotherapy with such patients. Consequently, they may carry throughout their professional careers the belief that what they offer to patients in psychotherapy is barely useful (and, unfortunately, they may well be correct—for they have never mastered their anxiety and never learned their supposed professional skills). This may lead to obsessive defenses—a ritualized approach to psychotherapy or an obsessive search for the "ideal" drug.

It would be a mistake to cite our position as objecting to all uses of medication. Medication is better than no treatment at all, and it may even be better than treatment provided by inappropriately trained and unmotivated therapists. As an adjunct to psychotherapy, it may be helpful to some psychotherapists in the beginning of treatment, or as an adjunct to weather a particularly upsetting crisis. Whether or not, and to what extent, medication is employed will always be a clinical decision based on the importance to the therapist at a given time of change in behavioral control versus change in the thought disorder.

As is pointed out in Gunderson's (1977) review of the literature, research in the 1970s is consistent with our conclusions. While a replication of our study of individual psychoanalytic therapy has not been completed to date, other researchers investigating the interaction of psychosocial treatment (group therapy, Soteria house, family therapy, active milieus, specifically designed behavior modification, etc.) with medication have reported their finding that drugs can be deleterious to the effectiveness of psychosocial treatment (Goldstein et al. 1975; Paul and Lentz 1977; Rappaport et al. 1980). "The (reviewed) results do, however, suggest that a variety of psychosocial residential treatments may obviate the need for drugs, or actually render them harmful" (Gunderson 1977).

AN ADDED BIT OF DATA: THE 2-YEAR FOLLOW-UP

Follow-up hospitalization data were collected 2 years after the termination of the treatment phase of the project, not only from the public hospitals where patients had been previously hospitalized, but also from private and possibly relevant psychiatric hospitals in the metropolitan area. Luckily, these patients tended to confine their geographic mobility to the Detroit area, and hence were not likely to be hospitalized outside this metropolitan region. The follow-up findings with respect to hospitalization are presented in Table 14.

If we follow our earlier comparisons, the first comparison is between the pooled psychotherapy group and the hospital controls. The psychotherapy patients had an average of 56.4 days of hospitalization, and the "controls" had 99.8 days. Patients who had received psychotherapy spent roughly half as much time in the hospital during the follow-up 2 years as did those who had received primarily medication therapy. Indeed, patients who did *not* receive psychotherapy had a two-to-one chance of being rehospitalized. That probability was exactly *reversed* for the patients receiving psychotherapy; they had a two-to-one probability of *not* being rehospitalized.

When the data are examined in five groups, the findings are also clearly significant and elaborate our earlier findings. In both psychotherapy groups, patients of experienced therapists do better in the long run than those of the inexperienced therapists. Moreover, the patients of experienced therapists have spent *much* less time in the hospital than the comparisons (group C). There does not seem to be a large *differential* impact on long-term hospitalization between the patients of the two experienced therapists (despite differences in technique and adjunctive use of medication).

TABLE 14.

Two-year Follow-up of Hospitalization—Plus a Recap of Earlier Related Findings

Group	n	Rehospitalization Rate (20–44 months)		Mean Days Hospitalized During 2 Years after end of treatment[a] (20–44 months)	20-month VVT (errors)	Recapped Data	
		Number Never Rehospitalized	Number Rehospitalized			Raw 0–20 Months Days Hospitalized	Total 0–44 Months Days Hospitalized
Comparison	12	4	8	99.8	17.5	113.5	213.3
Pooled E	21	14	7	56.4	12.9	78.4	134.8
Significance level two-group comparison				$p < 0.05$	$p < 0.005$	$p < 0.05$	$p < 0.05$
Supervisor A	3	3	0	0.0	9.1	44.7	44.7
A trainees	6	4	2	40.8	10.2	165.9	206.7
Supervisor B	4	3	1	10.8	12.0	32.0	42.8
B trainees	8	4	4	112.3	16.9	48.5	160.8
Significance level five-group comparison				$p < 0.05$	$p < 0.001$	$p < 0.05$	$p < 0.05$

[a]The follow-up hospitalization data were not significantly correlated with any of the initial covariates; hence, no statistical corrections were necessary.

438

Differential utilization of medication, however, appears to be more critical when the treatment is conducted by inexperienced therapists. It will be recalled that the inexperienced therapists not using medication (group A) produced a striking change in the thought disorder during the treatment phase of the project, but their effectiveness in reducing the length of hospitalization during that period had been at best comparable to drug treatment. On the other hand, the inexperienced therapists using medication (group B) had produced a dramatic reduction of the length of hospitalization during the treatment period, but had not produced more change in the thought disorder than medication alone.

In the follow-up data, this effect on hospitalization is reversed. Patients of the inexperienced therapists *not* using medication (group A) show a marked long-term reduction in hospitalization as compared to group C, in which the patients of the inexperienced therapists using medication (group B) were hospitalized essentially as long as the comparison group.

Also presented in Table 14 is the 20-month VVT data for the five groups, as well as hospitalization data during the treatment phase of the project and *total* hospitalization data covering the treatment phase and follow-up period. The long-term follow-up hospitalization data seem to reflect the change in the thought disorder during therapy (cf. the 20-month VVT data which are the 20-month outcome that most closely parallels long-term hospitalization, much more so than the hospitalization during the treatment phase). These findings suggest that the immediate change in the thought disorder is more closely related to the long-run ability to function outside of the hospital than are the short-term behavioral criteria (e.g., docility) usually related to ward adjustment and to hospital discharge. This is in keeping with Bleuler's (1911) classic observations that the thought disorder is a primary symptom, and others are secondary. It is also in keeping with recent psychiatric research by Cancro (1968, 1969), which found the severity of the thought disorder to be highly predictive of prognosis.

Despite the fact that the rigorous attempts at research on psychotherapy with schizophrenic patients are often cited as discrepant with the findings reported here, a striking similarity emerges. In our follow-up data, the patients receiving psychotherapy were hospitalized less than those on medication alone.

Furthermore, those patients who received psychotherapy with medication were the intermediate group in long-term hospitalization.

This is consistent with the much overlooked findings of both the Wisconsin and Massachusetts studies. In the Wisconsin project, psychotherapy patients spent an average of 117 days in the hospital during the year after termination of therapy, while the control (medication) patients spent an average of 219 days in the hospital in the same period. In the Massachusetts study, 68 percent of the psychotherapy patients were able to live outside of the hospital, whereas only 37 percent of the control (medication only) patients were able to do so.

ANOTHER VIEW OF THE DATA

To this point, we have presented a five-group breakdown, because the data seem so meaningfully different when derived from the patients of the experienced and inexperienced therapists; however, most research on the interaction effects of psychotherapy and medication using a three-group breakdown consists of medication alone, psychotherapy alone, and psychotherapy plus medication. In other words, it is a breakdown by type of treatment condition which ignores the level of experience of the therapist.

One can easily determine the three-group comparison from Tables 12 and 14. We have pooled the data in the more "traditional" manner, and present it in Table 15 for the convenience of the reader. The results are impressive. Even though two-thirds of the patients are treated by inexperienced therapists, on every outcome criterion other than initial hospitalization during the treatment phase, and the projective ratings, the three groups now order as follows: patients who received psychotherapy alone did best, patients who received psychotherapy with medication did next best, and the medication-alone group did least well, despite the fact that the latter compare favorably with other groups of patients treated with medication only in the literature (e.g., May 1968; May et al. 1976).

The findings parallel many of the conclusions we have already made. Psychotherapy alone (while experience of the therapist is

TABLE 15.
Review of Project Data in the "Traditional" Medication Alone, Psychotherapy Alone, and Psychotherapy Plus Medication Format

Treatment	n	Days Hospitalized				Rehospitalization Rate During Follow-up (%)	20-month Outcome Data						
		0-20 Months		Raw Follow-up: 20-44 Months	Total[a]: 0-44 Months		CSI	VVT (errors)	WAIS	PM	TGV	TAT	ROR
		Raw Score: 0-20 Months	Corrected Score:										
Medication alone	12	113.5	146.4	99.8	256.2	67	0.89	17.5	89.1	10.8	7.9	0.98	1.02
Psychotherapy alone	9	125.5	106.1	27.2	133.3	22	1.22	9.8	102.2	13.5	9.7	1.08	1.07
Psychotherapy plus medication	12	43.0	46.1	78.5	124.6	42	0.94	15.3	93.8	12.5	8.3	0.97	1.00

[a]Using *corrected* days hospitalized for the 0-20 month period and *raw* days hospitalized for the 20-44 month period.

441

ignored) takes longer to have an impact, but the long-term consequences are a lower rehospitalization rate and lower long-term
hospitalization. In fact, the longer initial hospitalization is more
than offset within 4 years by the lower rehospitalization in the long
run. The psychotherapy-alone group demonstrates far greater
improvement in overall level of functioning (CSI), and far greater
improvement in the thought disorder (VVT). Their average WAIS
IQ is now 102.2; what one would expect in testing a normal
population.

The psychotherapy *with* medication group also demonstrates
greater improvement than the medication-alone group. The patients who received psychotherapy plus medication show a dramatic reduction in initial hospitalization, and a slight reduction in
follow-up hospitalization and rehospitalization rate as compared to
the medication-alone group. The follow-up hospitalization and
rehospitalization rate of the psychotherapy *plus* medication is
greater than that of the psychotherapy-alone group, and total
days of hospitalization over 4 years of the two groups are comparable. The psychotherapy *plus* medication group shows only a
slight advantage over the medication-alone group on the CSI, VVT,
WAIS, and PM. This is in line with our earlier discussion of the
possible interfering effect of medication as an adjunct to psychotherapy, either because of its direct effect on the patient, or
because of its effect on the therapist.

The medication-alone group is certainly improved over its
pretreatment level, but compared to the other treatment groups, it
does not look impressive.

A Comparison of the Benefits and Costs
of Psychotherapy for Schizophrenics

Our data demonstrate that making available even a minimal
amount of psychoanalytic psychotherapy (an average of approximately 70 sessions over a 20-month period) as compared to medication dramatically decreased the thought disorder, improved
overall functioning, and appreciably shortened hospitalization both
in the short and in the long run. The differences in clinical status
and ability to think logically found between people classified as

schizophrenic who received psychotherapy and those who did not are mirrored by increased ability to be economically self-sufficient.

While these benefits are obvious, the necessarily concomitant economic consequences were not spelled out. The purely economic perspective may be restricted, but it is usually the critical perspective in public policy decisions and therefore needs to be made explicit. The most important economic criteria for consideration are: (a) the direct cost of treatment, (b) the cost of other governmental assistance for individuals who are not capable of independent existence, and (c) the loss in earning capacity and the consequent decrease in tax revenue. People in a hospital do not hold jobs; people outside a hospital can hold jobs, *if* their level of functioning permits.

We will address only the first of these criteria, although the amounts involved in the second and third criteria are far more sizable and must be kept in mind in formulating public policy. It has not been possible to obtain detailed information concerning nontreatment government economic costs and long-term earning for our patients; however, even a cursory scrutiny reveals that 75 percent of the patients treated by medication alone received welfare benefits in the first 20 months of treatment as compared to 33 percent of their randomly assigned comparisons who received psychotherapy. (It is a routine part of predischarge planning by the Social Service staff at most hospitals to arrange for welfare benefits for patients who need them to survive outside the hospital.)

For the first criterion (direct cost of treatment), however, it is possible to be more precise. For our project, there were two primary cost factors: cost of hospitalization and cost of psychotherapy services not ordinarily provided (and training costs). The following discussion is conservative. It assumes that psychotherapy could not be provided without increases in staff. This was our assumption, not being members of the staff of Detroit Psychiatric Institute, the hospital at which the clinical work was carried out. As was pointed out by Dr. Tierney, one of the experienced supervisors on the project and a psychiatrist already on the staff of the hospital, this assumption was dubious. He maintained that, in his considered opinion, such treatment (and training) could be made routinely available at that hospital at no increase in cost, requiring only reallocation of staff time and the motivation to provide such treatment.

Two methods of determining cost are presented. The only differences between the two determinations are in the initial hospitalization data and the resulting figures for the cost of initial hospitalization. Both the "raw" or actual hospitalization data and the statistically "corrected" hospitalization data are presented. We believe the latter data are the most appropriate to consider.

The determination of the cost of additional services (psychotherapy) received by these patients was calculated using the 1971–1972 per hour cost figures of psychology interns ($6/hour), psychiatric residents ($8/hour), psychologic consultants ($25/hour), and psychiatric consultants ($35/hour). In our project, for both supervisors and trainees, there were an equal number of therapists from each profession. Hospitalization costs are based on the 1971–1972 average patient-day cost in DPI; this figure was $70.00. (Our first publication of these data (Karon and VandenBos 1975) used a lower figure initially supplied to us by the hospital, which was later discovered by the State Auditor General's office to be in error. This latter corrected audit figure is used in this book.) The cost reported here is cost to the hospital, not the fee charged the patient, third-party payers, or the government.

The costs of treatment for the control group and the "pooled" experimental groups are presented in Table 16.

The first noteworthy difference between the two groups is in terms of length of hospitalization during the treatment phase. The experimental patients receiving psychotherapy were hospitalized for less time than the control patients not receiving psychotherapy. The difference is 35.1 days for the uncorrected data and 74.6 days for the corrected data. In terms of the savings resulting from providing psychotherapy routinely, hospitalization costs were either $2,459 or $5,222 less per patient for the experimental group than for the control group—from 31 to 51 percent savings!

It did cost something, however, to provide psychotherapy to these patients. Hence, a "cost of additional psychotherapy" figure was added to the treatment cost of the experimental group, assuming that such services could not be absorbed in the current budget. Averaging over all experimental patients, whether their

TABLE 16.

Average Treatment Cost Data for Control and Pooled Experimental Groups

Group	n	Days Hospitalized (0–20 months)	Initial Hospitalization Cost ($)	Additional Psychotherapy Cost ($)	Initial Cost (treatment phase) ($)	Days Subsequently Hospitalized (20–44 months)	Later Hospitalization Cost ($)	Total Treatment Cost ($)
Control								
Raw	12	113.5	7,945	—	7,945	99.8	6,986	14,931
Corrected	12	146.4	10,248	—	10,248	99.8	6,986	17,234
Experimental								
Raw	21	78.4	5,488	892	6,380	56.4	3,948	10,328
Corrected	21	71.8	5,026	892	5,918	56.4	3,948	9,866

445

therapists were experienced or inexperienced or a psychologist or psychiatrist, the average cost for providing psychotherapy was $892 per patient. This increases the per patient cost of treatment for the experimental group to $6,380 for the uncorrected data and $5,918 for the corrected data, savings of $1,565 and $4,330, respectively, during the initial treatment period (20 months). This still represents a 20 percent savings for the uncorrected data and a 42.3 percent savings for the corrected data.

Direct cost of treatment does not simply end when the patient is discharged. The frequency and duration of further hospitalizations are related to the quantity and quality of earlier treatment. Table 16 also presents the hospitalization data for the two groups during the 24 months following the end of the treatment phase of the project. The difference between the groups is clear and striking. The patients not receiving psychotherapy were hospitalized almost twice as much in the follow-up period as patients receiving psychotherapy. When the cost of this further hospitalization is added, the total cost of treatment for the comparison group averages $14,931 uncorrected, and $17,234 corrected, as contrasted with $10,328 uncorrected, and $9,866 corrected, for the experimental group. This is a savings of $4,603 (30.8 percent) and $7,368 (42.8 percent), respectively, per patient. This cost saving occurs along with the human and social benefit of greater clinical improvement and more human way of life! When viewed from a longer term perspective, the total treatment cost comparisons therefore increase radically. Such a perspective has always been the justification for psychotherapy, although systematic data have rarely been available.

There are some more detailed issues that might be worth raising. First, in our project, the patients were paid expense money ($5/session) so that they could afford to come to their outpatient psychotherapy sessions (to defray costs of transportation, baby-sitters, etc.). Many patients, of course, refused reimbursement as totally unnecessary or periodically unnecessary, but for some patients reimbursement was essential to the continuation of their treatment. The additional cost was nominal, averaging less than $100 per experimental patient. (This was one of a number of measures taken to deal with the specific problems and resistances of the economically poor patient in psychotherapy.)

The costs of training and supervision of the inexperienced therapists comprise still another category of expense. These costs include the time for which the inexperienced therapist was paid while in supervision and seminars, and the costs of the experienced consultant while supervising or teaching. Time spent in individual supervision with a truly experienced supervisor is better used than time spent in clinical seminars; it is more important to learn the specifics of how to produce good treatment than it is to learn how to talk generally about what one hopes to accomplish with a patient. A ratio of four supervision sessions to one seminar is reasonable; supervision in a group setting can be valuable and economical.

In our project, the average "cost of training" per experimental patient treated by inexperienced therapist was $1,325. This figure is artifically high because only a small part of the trainee therapist's work week was spent doing psychotherapy for the project. If it were a major part of their work load, as it would be if such treatment were routine, the training cost would, at most, be approximately $450/patient. Moreover, the project "training costs" are those incurred by very inexperienced therapists and with highly qualified supervisors who provide intensive supervision. These expenses represent costs in the first 2 years of training. With each year of training, the cost of training should decrease until another experienced and highly qualified professional results. We believe that even an experienced therapist with as much as 5 years of experience should continue to receive supervision because psychotherapy, particularly with schizophrenic patients, is a complex and exhausting endeavor in which support, encouragement, and the fine tuning of one's understanding and skills are critical.

Table 17 shows the treatment and hospitalization costs per patient of using experienced versus inexperienced therapists. Surprisingly enough, total treatment costs of using experienced therapists at private practice rates are less than the costs of using inexperienced therapists, even without including training costs! Savings, using experienced therapists over medication alone, are $10,052 (51.8 percent) to $8,932 (67.3 percent) per patient.

Even with the addition of $450 per patient training cost to data for those patients treated by inexperienced therapists, we find

TABLE 17.

Average Treatment Plus Training Data for Controls and for Patients Treated by Experienced and Inexperienced Therapists

Group	n	Days Hospitalized (0–20 months)	Initial Hospitalization Cost ($)	Additional Psychotherapy Cost ($)	Initial Cost (treatment phase) ($)	Days Subsequently Hospitalized (20–44 months)	Later Hospitalization Cost ($)	Total Treatment Costs ($)	Training Costs ($)	Treatment Cost plus Training ($)
Controls										
Raw	12	113.5	7,945	—	7,945	99.8	6,986	14,931	—	14,931
Corrected	12	146.4	10,248	—	10,248	99.8	6,986	17,234	—	17,234
Treated by experienced therapists										
Raw	7	37.4	2,618	1,827	4,445	6.2	434	4,879	—	4,879
Corrected	7	86.3	6,041	1,827	7,868	6.2	434	8,302	—	8,302
Treated by inexperienced therapists										
Raw	14	98.8	6,916	425	7,341	81.7	5,719	13,060	450	13,510
Corrected	14	64.5	4,515	425	4,940	81.7	5,719	10,659	450	11,109

that the total costs including training are slightly less than the "medication alone" control group for the raw hospitalization data, saving only $1,421 per patient (9.5 percent). For the corrected data, a savings of $6,125 per patient, or 35.5 percent, is found for this comparison.

In evaluating these figures, one must realize that while it is economically advantageous to use already trained and experienced therapists, if they are available, obviously it is a social good to train therapists. Otherwise, there would soon be no experienced therapists.

It may be worthwhile to detail further the cost effectiveness by profession, a comparison we find repugnant because the real differences are not associated with professional degree, but with relevance of training and experience; however, we feel that these data need to be presented because of the political ramifications of statements made about competency and effectiveness, without reference to data, suggesting that a particular degree, without relevant training, provides competence.

Psychologists tend to cost less, everything else being approximately equal. Experienced psychiatrist therapists of the caliber of those used in the project could be hired for $35 per hour, and experienced psychologist therapists for $25 per hour in 1970. Trainees (residents in psychiatry and graduate students in clinical psychology) could be hired for $8 per hour and $6 per hour, respectively.

Table 18 presents the cost comparison of psychologists and psychiatrists. Using the corrected data, total costs of treatment were $17,234 per patient for the medicated control group, $12,221 for those receiving psychotherapy from a psychiatrist, and $7,813 for those receiving psychotherapy from a psychologist. Thus, the direct treatment cost of psychotherapy as compared to medication is 29 percent less when given by psychiatrists and 55 percent less when given by psychologists. The cost savings of psychotherapy by psychologists as compared to psychiatrists is $4,408 per patient, or 36 percent less. (The raw data comparisons are equally striking when comparing the professions: a 17 percent savings gained when using psychiatrists as psychotherapists and a 33 percent savings gained when using psychologists.)

TABLE 18.

Length of Hospitalization and Treatment Costs for Controls and for the Psychologist- and Psychiatrist-treated Groups

Group	n	Days Hospitalized (0-20 months)	Initial Hospitalization Cost ($)	Additional Psychotherapy Cost ($)	Initial Cost (treatment phase) ($)	Days Subsequently Hospitalized (20-40 months)	Later Hospitalization Cost ($)	Total Treatment Cost ($)	Training Cost ($)	Treatment Cost plus Training ($)
Controls										
Raw	12	113.5	7,945	—	7,945	99.8	6,986	14,931	—	14,931
Corrected	12	146.4	10,248	—	10,248	99.8	6,986	17,234	—	17,234
Psychologists (pooled)										
Raw	9	118.4	8,288	863	9,151	7.2	504	9,655	300	9,955
Corrected	9	87.8	6,146	863	7,009	7.2	504	7,513	300	7,813
Psychiatrists (pooled)										
Raw	12	62.9	4,403	1,190	5,593	93.5	6,545	12,138	300	12,438
Corrected	12	59.8	4,186	1,190	5,376	93.5	6,545	11,921	300	12,221

Our calculations are based on psychologists who received salaries and fees approximately 25 percent below those of psychiatrists. This was standard practice between 1965 and 1970; however, psychologists and psychiatrists now tend to receive equal private practice rates (although psychiatrists still tend to receive higher salaries at public clinics). If we increase the $25 per hour paid our senior psychologist to $35 per hour (parity with the senior psychiatrist) and increase the psychology intern's salary to $8 (parity with psychiatric residents at that time), the total costs over the 44 months for patients seen by psychologists becomes $8,140 per person, which is still $4,081 or 33 percent less than treatment provided by psychiatrists, when the corrected data are used. Thus, the added savings obtained by using psychologists as psychotherapists is *not* a result of the differential salaries.

Thus, the savings are considerably greater when psychologists provide the psychotherapy. But more importantly, there is the same or better treatment outcome. Table 19 reports data on improvement in the schizophrenic thought disorder by psychologist provider versus psychiatrist provider. As previously stated, the thought disorder is the most central symptom in schizophrenia (Bleuler 1950; Lidz 1973). Patients treated by psychologists showed greater improvement in the schizophrenic thought disorder than the patients of psychiatrists or the medication-only group.

If these figures seem surprising, the apparent discrepancy with other published data disappears if the detailed information in

TABLE 19.

Comparison of Improvement in Patient Ability To Think Logically for Controls and for the Psychologist- and Psychiatrist-treated Groups

Group	n	Test Errors[a]
Controls	12	17.5
Psychologist-treated (pooled)	9	11.0
Psychiatrist-treated (pooled)	12	14.7

[a]Data are for test (Drasgow-Feldman Visual-Verbal) errors at end of treatment phase (corrected for initial performance). Lower values indicate greater improvement.

Table 18 is examined. If only the short-term data (i.e., up to 20 months) are considered, the patients treated by psychiatrists in our project cost less than those treated by psychologists. Psychiatrists produced an early discharge of patients by a greater reliance on medication (continuing adjunctive medication was prescribed to 10 of their 12 patients), whereas psychologists tended to concentrate on producing fundamental changes in the thought disorder of patients (continuing adjunctive medication was prescribed to only 2 of 9 patients). Only two of the psychology trainees were in the group using adjunctive medication; only two psychiatric residents were in the group not using adjunctive medication. While in the study the difference in profession thus parallels the difference in reliance on medication, a similar parallel occurs in general.

It is nonetheless noteworthy that the patients treated by psychologists via psychotherapy were only hospitalized an average of 7.2 days in the 2-year follow-up, as compared to 93.5 days for patients of psychiatrist psychotherapists (and 99.8 days for the medicated control group).

A note of caution about all of the findings of the project is warranted. We cannot repeat too often that the real differences in the fields of psychiatry and psychology have to do with *relevant* training, experience, and motivation. We have talked of the effectiveness of experienced therapists/supervisors and the importance of the development of such professionals. But all psychologists and psychiatrists called "experienced" are not the same. They do not have the same training, education, experience, interests, or motivation. These matters are critical to the kind of treatment employed, its effectiveness, and the cost of treatment.

Our finding that psychotherapy is effective with schizophrenic patients would generalize only to therapists interested in understanding the total human condition, including seemingly bizarre behavior and so-called irrational thoughts. They must be trained in psychodynamics. (This, of course, does not mean an artifically "blank" therapist discussing esoteric issues abstractly, no matter how sophisticated.) The therapist must be comfortable with his own feelings and fantasies, and must have experience specifically with schizophrenic patients. Equally important is experience with and knowledge of people of the socioeconomic class and ethnic group of the patient. Thus, by *relevant*, we mean all of the above, that is, training, experience, and knowledge about (a) psychotherapy, (b) schizophrenic patients, and (c) the specific socioeconomic class and/or ethnic group.

To repeat, these results would generalize only if the experienced therapists are well motivated and relevantly trained, and if the inexperienced therapists are also well motivated and receiving relevant supervision; however, the implications of the findings of the Michigan State Psychotherapy Project are simple and ought not to be startling. Psychotherapy produces significantly greater patient change than medication, and is particularly effective in changing the thought disorder. Moreover, in the long run, psychotherapy costs less than treatment by medication. In addition, it is a good thing for the therapist to be experienced and to believe in the treatment he or she practices.

Issues in Psychotherapy Research with Schizophrenic Patients

The question of the relative effectiveness of psychotherapy, medication, and combined medication and psychotherapy as treatments for schizophrenic patients is a difficult and important matter about which clinical observation alone has not proved decisive. As previously described, six controlled studies have been undertaken. Unfortunately, their results conflict. Since no study is without flaw, and since there are many specifications of relevant conditions which may vary (e.g., type of psychotherapy, situation in which the treatment is carried out, training and motivation of therapists, types of medication, dosage level, patient population, criteria of improvement), it is useful to specify the differing conditions under which differing results have been obtained.

It is particularly relevant to compare the California study with ours because their patients are more nearly comparable than the others, and their implications for clinical treatment seem exactly opposite to those drawn from our study. The Pennsylvania and Wisconsin studies successively served to clarify the problems involved in this research area, but drew no strong conclusions about treatment. The Massachusetts study (Grinspoon, Ewalt, and Shader 1972) and the Illinois study (Paul and Lentz 1977) worked with a markedly different population, chronic and chronically hospitalized patients.

The California study has been presented as a conclusive one. Their book (which included no follow-up data) was nonetheless described in the preface as "the definitive study" which would "never" have to be repeated. They concluded that medication was the treatment of choice, from both a cost and clinical perspective, and that psychotherapy made no appreciable difference. Our findings suggest a contrary conclusion.

STRENGTHS AND WEAKNESSES OF THE CALIFORNIA AND MICHIGAN STATE STUDIES

Some of the strengths of their study were the large number of subjects, the study of five treatment modalities, and the attempted control for the personality of the therapist. Some of the weaknesses were the lack of attention to relevant experience of the therapist, the apparent lack of attention to *relevant* training for the therapists, gross discontinuity (termination) of the psychotherapy at discharge from the hospital, inconsistent timing of evaluations, contaminated criteria of outcome, and idiosyncratic data analyses (including, among other things, procedures which eliminated the sickest patients from consideration).

Some of the strengths of our study are the careful attention to relevant training and experience of the therapists, carefully "blind" evaluations, evaluations at regular chronological intervals, and no deletion of patients for being too sick. Some of the weaknesses are the small sample size, discontinuity of patient-doctor relationship in "drug alone" treatment, and a number of uncontrollable external circumstances, such as the hospital staff bias against psychotherapy and for medication, and the Detroit "riot" near the hospital during the middle of the project, which made Black patients feel guilty about getting help from white therapists. The latter circumstances are important biases, but ones which worked in the direction of minimizing the effects of psychotherapy.

It has been objected (May and Tuma 1970a, 1970b; Tuma and May 1975) that the evaluations on our study were not blind, that the techniques of data analysis were inappropriate, that the experience of nonmedical therapists cannot be considered experience, that arbitrary scores were assigned to untestable patients at the various outcome evaluations, and that patients were included who should have been deleted because of organic impairments and/or utilization of medication.

None of these objections are factually correct.

They have also objected that there were not a large number of cases in the study, nor were there a large number of therapists, that the experienced therapists supervised the inexperienced therapists, that the assignment of patients to therapists was not random (although assignment to treatment groups was random), and that these findings conflict with other studies.

These objections are facts.

The number of cases and the number of therapists had to be small so that we could be sure that the patients really were appropriate, and that the therapists were practicing psychoanalytic therapy. Any number of observations of the wrong patients treated haphazardly would be of little scientific value. That there were only two experienced therapists, who also were the supervisors, was necessary for us to be sure that the experienced therapists really had something to teach and were known to their professional colleagues to be clinically effective. The assignment of patients to each treatment group was rigorously randomized, but within the psychotherapy groups it was not random. The first two cases in each group had to be assigned to the experienced therapists so that the student therapists could observe the treatment of these cases and discuss them as part of their training. Cases were assigned on the basis of the therapists' schedules after that; however, selection of cases was made on the same basis throughout the project by people who did not know to which treatment group the subjects would be assigned, let alone which therapists.

That these findings conflict with those of other studies in the literature is understandable inasmuch as there are some aspects of this project that are unusual, although they ought not to be. First of all, the therapists wanted to practice psychotherapy with schizophrenic patients; there were no reluctant therapists. The student therapists wanted to work with their particular supervisors and viewed them as people from whom they thought they could learn. The experienced therapists (who were also the supervisors) had over 10 years experience, not only in working with schizophrenic patients, but also in working with poor people and Black people (80 percent of the patients were Black). The same therapist worked with the patient on an inpatient and outpatient basis. Any understanding of psychotherapy which takes the concept of transference seriously would utilize such a procedure.

It may be worth noting that other studies have not shown psychotherapy to be effective with schizophrenic patients because either: (1) they used unwilling therapists (and therapy is not likely to be effective if the therapist does not want to do it), (2) they used supervisors who had little experience or interest in doing psychotherapy with schizophrenic patients, and it is axiomatic that people cannot teach what they do not know, (3) they had therapists inexperienced in doing psychotherapy with schizophrenia, and people do not generally do well that which they have never done before, (4) they used therapists who were not familiar with patients of the socioeconomic class or of the ethnic subgroup of the patients, (5) they have examined the patients on the day of termination of psychotherapy, discharge, and other irregular intervals, (6) they have not measured the thought disorder with any degree of care, (7) they base their conclusions on ward behavior, not real world functioning, (8) they did not do long-term follow-up of the patients, or (9) they have done all of these. Under such conditions of poor "quality control" of psychotherapy and inappropriate evaluation, psychotherapy is not effective.

PSYCHOTHERAPY QUALITY CONTROL

Evident in the above paragraph is our concern about the general lack of attention to quality control of the psychotherapy provided in psychotherapy research projects, and particularly in research on the psychotherapy of schizophrenic patients. In every reasonably rigorous study on the effectiveness of psychotherapy with schizophrenic patients that we have reviewed, in each study where psychotherapy has been reported as unhelpful, quality control of *relevant* training, experience, and motivation has not been maintained. For example, the Massachusetts study (Grinspoon, Ewalt, and Shader 1972) appears to have very rigorous controls. It does have rigorous controls for the medication versus no medication comparison, but not very comparable controls for the psychotherapy versus no psychotherapy comparison. Moreover, the therapists were not working in their usual way (e.g., frequency of session) or with economic and ethnic subgroups with which they were therapeutically familiar. "Experienced" therapists referred to experience doing some kind of psychoanalytic treatment, not experience in working with resistant schizophrenic patients. One-third of the "senior experienced" therapists found themselves "for the first time in their life in a long-term therapy relationship with a resistant patient" (Grinspoon et al. 1972, p. 259). The therapists were *not* paid for their time. It is reported that "half of these therapists felt this to be no problem." Presumably, the other half did.

The California project and the Michigan State project differed considerably in the attention paid to the control of the quality of the psychotherapy being provided. How different the concept of relevant training and experience was on the two projects, is reflected by the fact that there were no psychologists as therapists in the California project (in a hospital where Dr. May helped set policy), and that in two previous critiques (May and Tuma 1970a; May 1974), they emphasize the value of the experience of treating "physical (and emotional) disorders in medical school and during internship," while we would consider experience even in treating neurotic patients by psychotherapy only partially relevant. Nowhere do they emphasize the importance of understanding sociocultural factors as they influence therapeutic technique with schizophrenic patients.

It is of interest that in both the California and Massachusetts studies, only psychiatrists are used as therapists, and in both studies psychotherapy was not effective. A mystique concerning the medical degree and its value seems to obscure the need for specifically relevant training. The phrase "fully trained psychiatrist" is used to describe someone who has "never treated a resistant patient" in continuing psychotherapy. This use of language is not objectionable, unless it is taken to imply competence at skills never acquired. It is interesting to note that the Wisconsin project, the Illinois project, and the Michigan State project use psychologists (as well as psychiatrists) as therapists and find psychotherapy potent. This may reflect, not some equally mysterious mystique about the PhD., but an underlying variable—a concern with the processes called psychotherapy, and a belief that whatever the process, it can be and must be learned and cannot be assumed simply by professional affiliation.

Let us consider some of the specific details of the psychotherapy provided on the California project and on the Michigan State project:

1. Experience of therapists. The Michigan State project used both experienced and inexperienced therapists. The experienced therapists had over 10 years of relevant experience in doing psychotherapy with schizophrenic patients, and in doing psychotherapy with lower-class and ethnic groups similar to the project patient population. The California project used only inexperienced "medical" therapists who had "very, very little experience with psychotherapy of schizophrenia" (Wexler 1975).

2. Experience of supervisors. The Michigan State project utilized two relevantly experienced and relevantly trained supervisors with over 10 years experience with patients of the socioeconomic and ethnic subgroup of schizophrenic patients. Not only were they experienced in doing psychotherapy with schizophrenic patients, they were experienced at working in the way the project required, that is, working with difficult patients without medication or with adjunctive medication. Even this difference raises differential problems, and like all problems in psychotherapy, one cannot teach appropriate techniques to others unless one has first learned it oneself. The California project used supervisors who were "distinguished" psychoanalysts, but whose training and experiences with schizophrenic patients was highly variable, and in some cases essentially nonexistent. They were experts in this area by designation, not by training or experience.

3. Knowledge of patient population. Knowledge of the characteristics and consequent specific resistances of people of a given socioeconomic, ethnic, and subcultural background is at least as important as knowledge of the specific psychopathology being treated. The two supervisors in the Michigan State project were better acquainted with poor and with Black patients than are most psychotherapists. It is not clear how familiar the supervisors of psychotherapy in the California project were with patients of the socioeconomic and subcultural background of the patients, even

though these patients were not so low in the socioeconomic hierarchy as were our patients.

4. Training of inexperienced therapists. We believe that learning a complex skill is difficult. In the early phases of the Michigan
State project, careful attention was paid to training. In addition to
didactic reading material, the inexperienced therapists observed,
and later discussed, the psychotherapy of the experienced therapist
working with schizophrenic patients. The initial sessions of the
inexperienced therapist were also observed and discussed by the
supervisors and other trainees. In the later phases of the project,
conventional supervision sessions were held. It is unclear what
special attention was given to the kind and amount of psychotherapy training in the California project. Apparently it consisted of
supervisory hours on project patients in addition to whatever
training was usual in the residency; however, Wexler (1975) noted
that there was tremendous variation in the quality, frequency, and
intensity of the supervision. Training and supervision of the therapists was not a closely attended to matter in the California project.

5. Motivation of therapists. In the Michigan State project, the
inexperienced therapists were truly volunteers. The trainees
wanted to learn to practice psychotherapy with schizophrenic
patients, and chose their supervisors as someone whose training
they valued. Trainees were paid for the extra difficulty and time
invested in learning psychotherapy with schizophrenic patients and
treating the project patients. In the California project, all therapists
were required, as part of their residency, to practice five kinds of
therapy. Participation was required, and no special recompense was
given for the extra work and effort involved. It was a well-intended
but confounding "control" to have each therapist practice each
treatment. The intent was to control for the personality of the
therapist, but it ignored the roles of motivation, interest, and
needed skills. Certain treatments such as ECT or drugs require little
or no personal involvement with the patient and are usually
reported by psychiatric residents as feeling continuous with their
previous medical training. Psychotherapy and psychosocial treatments raise entirely new issues and perspectives which require
considerable new learning and a complex personal involvement with
patients that seems discontinuous with previous training. These
differences provoke anxiety, and schizophrenic patients in par-

ticular provoke anxiety in their supposed therapists. The frank discussion (Grinspoon et al. 1972) of countertransference reactions to schizophrenic patients by "senior staff members" (who by our standards were to a large extent really inexperienced therapists with this kind of patient) illustrated how demanding this work really is. For the psychiatric resident to face this work without his old friend, medication, is to make him feel naked in the face of the enemy. An experienced and kind supervisor can be helpful in facing such situations.

As in most studies which report that psychotherapy adds little to the treatment of schizophrenic patients, there are major questions about the quality of the psychotherapy provided. One must wonder whether any psychotherapy was provided in the California project.

The California project has little to say about the effectiveness of psychotherapy, with or without medication. It does answer the question: "Is psychotherapy provided by inappropriately trained but medically qualified psychiatric residents of much use?" The answer is "no."

The Michigan State Project asks the question: "Is psychotherapy provided by appropriately trained professionals (psychiatrists *and* psychologists) useful?" The answer is "yes." Both experienced and inexperienced psychiatrists and psychologists produced improvement in their patients not achieved through routine "medication only" treatment.

The fact that the trainees in the Michigan State Psychotherapy Project really did learn to do psychotherapy effectively, as evidenced by the actual progress of their patients during the project, clearly indicates that psychotherapy with schizophrenic patients is a skill that is both teachable and learnable. If society does not choose to train psychotherapists, it will not be because they would not be effective.

RESEARCH DESIGN ISSUES

Both the California project and the Michigan State project were conducted in the real world, and faced obstacles which contaminated their design and findings. There are decisions about research design that must be made. They are generally made with an eye toward what the questions to be answered are. No one design is perfect, and there are advantages and disadvantages to all options. The major differences between the two projects concerned the number of cases studied, selection of patients, nature of evaluations, timing of evaluations, handling of untestable subjects, blindness of evaluations, continuity of treatment, and statistical procedures.

Patient population and selection. In both the California project and the Michigan State project, the patients were drawn from a public hospital and on clinical examination were considered clearly schizophrenic. Nonetheless, there were striking differences between the patients selected in the two projects in demographic characteristics as well as severity of pathology. The California project managed to select in an "unbiased" manner an unusual set of patients. The "average" California patient was high school educated, with above average IQ, employed predominantly as a skilled laborer (or as a housewife). In other words, the patients were at least lower-middle class. By contrast, the "average" patient of the Michigan State project was a high school dropout, with below average IQ, and employed as an unskilled laborer (or receiving public assistance). In other words, the patients were lower class, poor, and predominantly Black.

The sociologic data have been unequivocal that the typical schizophrenic population is predominantly poor and lower class. For example, Hollingshead and Redlich (1958) reported schizophrenic patients as twleve times more frequent among people from the lowest socioeconomic class (on a five-class basis) than in the highest. Aside from the proportion being Black, which will vary with geographic and urban location, the demographic characteristics of the patients of the Michigan State project were consistent with those reported of schizophrenic patients treated at public hospitals in the United States, while the patients of the California project seem to have been, at least inadvertently, subject to some kind of economic screening. This may be the result of the California project intentionally choosing as a treatment population of the "middle third" in severity (i.e., neither the very sick nor the relatively well). It is not clear why this should exclude the poor so effectively.

An additional screening on the basis of severity of symptoms occurs in the California project, even though it is never described as such. The data were analyzed only in terms of patients who took both the pretest and post-test, thus excluding the sicker patients. It is a practically easier, but hardly comprehensive, procedure of investigation that leads to conclusions applicable only to those patients well enough and cooperative enough to take elaborate testing before treatment. No such limitation makes sense if we are talking about the treatment of schizophrenia. The Michigan State sample was biased toward the severest cases, since these were the cases where the diagnosis was the most clear-cut.

Number of cases. The California project had a large sample. There were 228 patients, or some subset depending on which comparison or publication cited. The Michigan State project had a modest sample. There was a total of 36 original patients, one of whom died within the first month of treatment. A large sample permits subtle differences to be statistically significant. A small sample permits only striking differences to be statistically significant.

It was possible to do more careful data-gathering on the patients, including carefully detailed and more rigorously blind outcome evaluations, and to obtain greater quality control of psychotherapy with a small sample. Since many of the characteristics of the patient population became clear only after repeated follow-ups, less careful work, as is unfortunately necessary with a large sample, would be more misleading. Accuracy of inference is obviously affected not only by the number of cases, but even more by any systematic (planned or unintentional) bias in selecting these cases.

Randomization. Both studies attempted randomization. In the Michigan State project, suitable patients were selected in sets of three, and randomly assigned to the three groups. Patient selection and assignment was done in 4 months in the same manner with the same criteria by research personnel not involved in treatment or supervision. In the California project, assignment to treatment groups was also random, but not assignment to therapist. Patients were selected over a 2-year time span.

Assignment between experienced and inexperienced therapists, and among inexperienced therapists, on the Michigan State project was on a rotation basis, because of training demands and the schedules and commitment of the inexperienced therapists. Supervisors had no role in the selection of their patients. Any differences in patient characteristics reflect possible week-to-week fluctuation in admissions (although they were well within the bounds to be expected from random variation). All therapists treated whatever patients were assigned to them. In the California project, a disqualifying condition for the assignment of a psychotherapy case was assignment to a resident in his first 6 months. Seventeen percent of the psychotherapy cases were randomly assigned to such disqualified residents and had to be reassigned.

Continuity of treatment. Both studies have problems with the continuity of treatment. The California project interrupted psychotherapy on day of discharge from the hospital, and did not routinely provide follow-up psychotherapy with either the same or different therapists. Medication, however, was maintained after discharge. The Michigan State project maintained continuity of psychotherapy, and even of psychotherapists, up to one year of hospitalization or up to 20 months of total treatment. The same psychotherapist had the patient both as an inpatient and as an outpatient; however, there was a discontinuity of treatment setting (but not treatment) for the medication-only patients.

This represents a real difference in the two studies, undoubtedly reflecting differences in the values and interests of the investigators. In the California project, careful attention was paid to maintaining continuity of medication, but not of psychotherapy. Undoubtedly, this reflects a genuine concern that the drug treatment be given under optimal conditions. In the Michigan State study, continuity of psychotherapy was maintained, but not as much attention to continuity of prescriber within drug treatment. Drug treatment was maintained, but the transfer of hospital (if prolonged hospitalization was necessary) meant that a new psychiatrist was in charge of medication, even if the hospital was in other ways better equipped. Being more centrally concerned with quality control of the psychotherapy, the Michigan investigators took account of the fact that psychotherapy is a relationship in which transference factors are an essential therapeutic tool, and any interference with these factors is a disturbance of the therapeutic process. The relationship is undoubtedly a factor in all medical treatment, including the drug treatment of schizophrenia (Shapiro 1971), but it is not emphasized in the literature, or in clinical discussion by competent medication-oriented psychiatrists. It is not generally believed that changing the prescriber while maintaining the medication and dosage interferes with treatment. Therefore, such stringent care was not undertaken, although it would have been a nice control to have maintained.

Drug dosage. Both studies permitted psychiatrists to adjust medication and dosage level for each patient individually, in terms of their judgment of the optimal dosage for the patient at that time. Neither study held medication at a fixed arbitrary level, but allowed it to vary in accordance with good clinical practice.

In the California project, medication was reported in terms of average total dosage. For the medication-alone group, it was: males, 4.02 g trifluoperazine (Stelazine), females, 3.19 g. For the medication and psychotherapy group, it was: males, 3.71 g, females, 2.2 g. The maximum daily dosages ranged from 20 to 120 mg for the medication-alone group, and they ranged from 4 to 120 mg for the psychotherapy with medication group.

In the Michigan State project, dosage levels typically were approximately 400 mg of chlorpromazine (Thorazine) daily, varying at different times from a low of 100 mg to a high of 1,400 mg daily. It would be inappropriate to label the psychotherapy without medication as contaminated by drug usage. Although three patients in that group did receive medication briefly, two were deleted for other research reasons, as described earlier, and deleting the third "contaminated" patient would increase the apparent effectiveness of psychotherapy.

The medication-alone group in the Michigan State project and the medication-alone group in the California project were hospitalized the same length of time. This would suggest comparability of the medication and of the clinical judgment of the medication-oriented psychiatrists in charge of such treatment. If anything, the comparison between the use of medication in the two projects would favor the clinical effectiveness of the prescribing psychiatrists in the Michigan State project, since these patients had a worse prognosis. But the real difference between the two projects is that this level of clinical effectiveness represents the best group in the California project, and the least benefited group in the Michigan State project.

Untestable patients. In any investigation of schizophrenic patients, there will be some patients who cannot be tested. This is particularly the case before treatment begins. We are suspicious of any research data on schizophrenic patients that does not report such difficulties.

The way this problem is dealt with influences the conclusions that can be drawn. There are four options for dealing with this: (1) replace untestable patients with testable ones; (2) exclude from data analysis those untestable patients; (3) medicate to whatever point is necessary for testing; (4) use "untestable" as a score on the pretesting. We have already described a theoretically meaningful way of quantifying this latter option, with built-in statistical checks on its appropriateness.

Before choosing any of these options, it is assumed that one will use experienced, benign examiners who will go to considerable trouble and are effective in getting cooperation from very resistant patients. Certainly that was the procedure on the Michigan State project. It was possible to test patients who were refusing to talk to their therapists and the ward staff. You cannot get such cooperation if you use inexperienced examiners or experienced examiners who are inexperienced in testing schizophrenic patients. Nonetheless, there will be some patients who are untestable.

The California project excluded the most severely disturbed one-third of their acute patients routinely. Despite this, they had patients who were untestable, even in the middle range of patients. They excluded from data analysis patients who refused pretreatment testing. Obviously, they also had to exclude any patient who refused post-testing. Their procedures were simple and straightforward, but they introduced systematic bias.

The Michigan State project handled the problem of *initially* untestable patients using the fourth option. Theoretically determined initial scores were assigned, and checked for appropriateness (with respect to determining regressions), so that no patient need be excluded from data analysis simply for being initially untestable. Obviously, if patients were untestable at later evaluations, they could not be included in the data analyses for that particular test. All patients took all intellectual tests at the end of treatment, which reflects two things: the care and perseverance of the evaluation and research staff, and that patients were, in all groups, less sick at the end of the project than at the beginning.

This illustrates a very basic difference in the approaches of the two projects. In the California project, larger numbers of subjects were depended upon to make generalization possible, but systematic biases were not considered. In the Michigan State project, the number of cases was small, but careful attention was paid to quality control of evaluations as well as of treatments. It was strongly felt that no study of treatment with schizophrenic patients should exclude patients because they are too sick.

Timing of evaluations. The California project and Michigan State project differed in the timing of evaluations. Of course, both projects tested patients before treatment, although with somewhat different success. The California project used a variable interval post-treatment evaluation schedule determined by the discharge of the patient from the hospital. The Michigan State project utilized a fixed interval outcome evaluation schedule, evaluating the patients 6, 12, and 20 months after they had begun treatment, whether or not they were continuing or resisting treatment. After all, continuation of treatment is itself a treatment effect, which may represent either health or sickness.

The California study, insofar as it draws conclusions from evaluations, which it tends not to, draws them from evaluations made on the day of discharge. This is another bias against the psychotherapy group, since this was also the day of termination of psychotherapy in that project, and the day of termination of psychotherapy is well known to be a time of crisis, particularly if the psychotherapy was meaningful.

The California project is really conceptualized and hence designated as a study of in-hospital treatment of schizophrenic patients, as if a mental hospital were comparable to a surgical ward where processes not continuous with life occur. That project reflects a mystique about the mental hospital that implies a special potency independent of the treatment process.

The Michigan State project sees the hospital as an adjunctive facility where the same therapeutic processes do or do not occur as could occur in other settings. The hospital setting has advantages and disadvantages, and these can be specified. Indeed, in private practice, other settings are commonly used to provide support, protection, supervision, or availability to treatment. Medication is not more or less effective in the hospital, nor is psychotherapy. The Michigan State project was a study of the treatment of schizophrenic patients in its complete sense, that is, both inpatient and outpatient, and it was evaluated as such.

Nature of evaluations. There were differences in the nature of the outcome evaluations on the two projects. First, the Michigan State project made extraordinary efforts to locate and get cooperation with the evaluation, lest a systematic bias be introduced. Second, the specific measures used to measure the thought disorder differed in their sensitivity. The Michigan State project included a number of intellectual tests known to reflect psychopathologic impairment, including one specifically designed and validated as measuring schizophrenic thought disorders (the VVT). The California project used fewer and more general measures, relying primarily on ward adjustment ratings, or disguised ward adjustment, such as the Menninger Health-Sickness rating scale. In fact, the measures used in the California project were all considered by the Michigan State project but rejected because the literature on their validity was discouraging, or because they were too diffuse and insensitive to disturbances that were specifically schizophrenic.

Blindness of evaluations. The California project and Michigan State project differed in terms of the "blindness" of the evaluations. The California project used primarily criteria which are likely to be "contaminated" by knowledge of the patient's treatment and the value system of the evaluators, e.g., discharge, ward behavior, and therapist reports. The "independent" team of psychoanalysts making clinical ratings relied heavily on narrative accounts of the patient that were prepared by personnel (nurses, therapists, and social workers) fully cognizant of the treatment the patient had received, in addition to their own interviews. It is not clear whether the psychologic tests were given and evaluated "blindly." The issue of blindness on the California project is particularly relevant, given May's description of the iron-handed authority he had over all hospital personnel.

In the Michigan State project, particular care was taken to ensure the "blindness" of the clinical ratings. The psychiatrist who conducted the clinical status interviews and the psychologists administering the Rorschach and TAT were not informed to which treatment group the patient belonged. Of course, a good clinical status interview is not likely to leave the interviewer "blind"; these interviews were recorded on tape, and references to treatment deleted from the tapes before being rated blindly with regards to clinical status by independent judges, as described earlier. Separate independent raters also blindly rated the Rorschach and TAT. Discharge was not entirely blind, but it was determined by ward chiefs not involved in the research, and probably biased against the project. Follow-up rehospitalization data were entirely blind.

Statistical methods. Both studies used analyses of variance and covariance. The California project chose to report the majority of their findings in terms of analysis of variance, since they report covariates to be basically nonsignificant. The Michigan State project chose to report its findings in terms of analysis of covariance and analysis of variance when covariates were not relevant.

The California project's use of statistics, however, is more creative than convincing. Many of their procedures are questionable for regression effects, and for possible biased selection of subsets of the data. Comparisons are made for subsets of as few as two-thirds of the cases, since the sicker patients who would not take some tests either pretreatment or post-treatment are excluded from analysis. It must be remembered the project was already using a restrictive range of the "middle third" of severity. In addition, the procedure of "winsorizing," deleting the patients (on whom they have data) who are doing best and those who are doing the worst in each group, leads to ignoring 20 cases in his data when winsorizing once, and 40 cases when winsorizing twice.

The particular subset of patients used by the California project varies almost with each test of significance. It would be necessary for the analyses to be rigorous to check each time that the distributions of the samples *actually used* are within the limits of random variation on relevant background characteristics. There is no evidence such tests of significance were routinely carried out.

Moreover, when they utilize analyses of covariance, it is in an unusual way (Forsythe et al. 1973). Regression coefficients are determined only from 44 "control" patients, which means that fewer coefficients will be found to be statistically significant than if the total sample were used. In addition, a new "stopping rule" was devised for this study which justified stopping earlier, i.e., taking into account fewer covariates than more conventional statistical procedures, even if the total sample had been used. Thus, the procedures must result in the conclusion that fewer background characteristics need be taken into account, and that taking these into account is less important and makes less difference than more traditional statistical procedures. Given that even in a rigorously randomized design some differences in background characteristics and prognoses must occur by chance, their statistical analyses seem intended not to discover these differences or take them into account. It would be interesting to see if more conventional regression analyses would change their findings in any major way.

The Michigan State project used analysis of covariance. This allowed for correction for possibly relevant background variables in our study, after a multiple regression procedure determined which of the many possibly relevant background variables need to be taken into account. May and Tuma's objection to our procedures do not impress us with their statistical sophistication. In recent years, the severe limitations of covariance analysis (Campbell 1970) have become clear; however, our data meet these most recent strigent standards. Matching, difference scores, and analysis of variance (as used in the California project) are subject to more serious errors and regression effects as Campbell, among others, has made clear. Moreover, the F-test, as used in the Michigan State project, is not invalidated by minor violations and certain known kinds of major violations of normality assumptions, particularly where the small sample size will permit only large effects to be significant. Analysis of covariance was used because it was most appropriate for that situation, that is, most sensitive and least biased. Interestingly enough, analysis of variance yields essentially the same results with the data of the Michigan State project, except for one comparison between the Supervisor B and B trainees on one variable.

Conclusion

No study is perfect. Moreover, no two studies are identical. It would be inappropriate simply to discard *apparently* conflicting data. A more fruitful approach is to examine carefully the contrasting conditions that give rise to these seemingly contradictory results. It is our contention that careful scrutiny of the current research does not reveal "gross inadequacies" in some, and perfection in others, but differing conditions under which meaningfully different results have occurred, which are consistent not only with each other, but with clinical experience.

The California and the Michigan State projects differed in the questions they were attempting to answer and differed in how they attempted to gather data to answer those questions. The California study was aimed at evaluating specifically in-hospital treatment provided by untrained residents. The Michigan State project was concerned with the total course of treatment in and out of the hospital, provided by relevantly trained professionals. It was as much an assessment of the effectiveness of training as it was of the effectiveness of treatment. The projects differed, therefore, in terms of the quality control of the therapy provided. In addition, they differed in terms of the quality control of the outcome evaluations. In both cases, the Michigan State Psychotherapy Project was more attentive to these issues.

The current data suggest the following: medication seems more helpful for schizophrenic patients than no treatment at all; psychotherapy for schizophrenic patients by "average" inexperienced (but medically qualified) therapists is not of much help. If careful quality control of what it is that is called psychotherapy is maintained, psychotherapy is helpful for schizophrenic patients.

We would urge all future researchers to strive for the greatest rigor possible, consistent with being sure the phenomenon being studied is the one intended, namely, that "psychotherapy" is psychotherapy, and the "experience" and "training" are relevant experience and training. As Gendlin has stated (Gendlin 1973), "just because two people are talking in a room and one is called a doctor and the other labelled a patient, it does not mean that any psychotherapy is occurring."

References

Abraham, K. (1953). A complicated ceremonial found in neurotic women. *Selected Papers on Psychoanalysis, Vol. I,* pp. 157–163. New York: Basic Books.

Adler, A. (1946). Melancholia and paranoia (1914). *The Practice and Theory of Individual Psychology,* pp. 246–262. London: Kegan, Paul, Trench, Trubner, Ltd.

—— (1968). Nervous insomnia (1914); Individual psychological conclusions on sleep disturbances (1919). *The Practice and Theory of Individual Psychology.* pp. 163–183. Totowa, N.J.: Littlefield, Adams.

Adler, K. A. (1961). Depression in the light of individual psychology. *Journal of Individual Psychology* 17:56–67.

Aichorn, A. (1935). *Wayward Youth.* New York: Viking.

Alexander, F., and French, T. M. (1946). *Psychoanalytic Therapy.* New York: Ronald Press.

Alexander, V. K. (1956). A case study of a multiple personality. *Journal of Abnormal and Social Psychology* 52:272–276.

Allport, G. W. (1954). *The Nature of Prejudice.* Reading, Mass.: Addison-Wesley.

American Psychological Association (1947). Recommended graduate training program in clinical psychology. *American Psychologist* 2:539–558.

Arieti, S. (1955). *Interpretation of Schizophrenia*. New York: Brunner/ Mazel.

—— (1974). *Interpretation of Schizophrenia*. (2nd ed.) New York: Basic Books.

Arlow, J. A., and Brenner, C. (1964). *Psychoanalytic Concepts and the Structural Theory*. New York: International Universities Press.

Atwood, G. (1972). Note on a relationship between suicidal intentions and the depressive mood. *Psychotherapy: Theory, Research, and Practice* 9:284–285.

Avery, D., and Winokur, G. (1976). Mortality in depressed patients treated with electro-convulsive therapy and antidepressants. *Archives of General Psychiatry* 33:1029–1037.

Beckett, P. G. S., Robinson, D. B., Frazier, S. H., Steinhilber, R. M., Duncan, G. M., Estes, H. R., Litin, E. M., Gratton, R. T., Lorton, W. L., Williams, G. E., and Johnson, A. M. (1956). The significance of exogenous traumata in the genesis of schizophrenia. *Psychiatry* 19:137–142.

Bellak, L. (1948). *Dementia Praecox*. New York: Grune and Stratton.

—— (1954). *The TAT and CAT in Clinical Use*. New York: Grune and Stratton.

—— (1958). *Schizophrenia*. Plainfield, N.J.: Logos.

——, and Loeb, L. (1969). *The Schizophrenic Syndrome*. New York: Grune and Stratton.

—— (1979). *Disorders of the Schizophrenic Syndrome*. New York: Basic Books.

Bergler, E. (1946). Problems of suicide. *Psychiatric Quarterly Supplement* 20:261–275.

Berke, J. H. (1979). *I Haven't Had To Go Mad Here*. Harmondsworth, Middlesex, England: Penguin.

Bettelheim, B. (1950). *Love Is Not Enough*. New York: Free Press.

—— (1955). *Truants from Life*. New York: Free Press.

—— (1956). Schizophrenia as a reaction to extreme situations. *American Journal of Orthopsychiatry* 26:507–518.

—— (1967). *The Empty Fortress*. New York: Free Press.

Bettelheim, S., and Hartmann, H. (1951). Parapraxes in Korsakow psychoses. In *The Organization and Pathology of Thought*. ed. D. Rappaport. New York: Columbia University Press.

Bleuler, E. (1911). *Dementia Praecox, or the Group of the Schizophrenias*. English translation, 1950. New York: International Universities Press.

Bleuler, M. (1971). Some results of research in schizophrenia. In *The Schizophrenic Syndrome: An Annual Review. Vol. I.* ed. R. Cancro, pp. 3–16. New York: Brunner/Mazel.

Bockoven, J. S. (1972). *Moral Treatment in Community Mental Health.* New York: Springer.

Bonaparte, M. (1953). *Female Sexuality.* New York: International Universities Press.

Bookhammer, R. S., Myers, R. W., Schober, C. C., and Piotorowski, A. Z. (1966). A 15-year clinical follow-up study of schizophrenics treated by Rosen's "direct analysis" compared with controls. *American Journal of Psychiatry* 123:602–604.

Borofsky, G. L., VandenBos, G. R., and Karon, B. P. (1970). Changes in the "Pathogenesis" of Schizophrenic Patients Resulting from Psychoanalytic Treatment. Paper presented at the Society for Psychotherapy Research, Chicago, June.

Boyd, D. A. (1942). Mental disorders associated with childbearing. *American Journal of Obstetrics and Gynecology* 43:148–163, 335–349.

Braginsky, B., Braginsky, D., and Ring, K. (1969). *Methods of Madness: The Mental Hospital as a Last Resort.* New York: Holt, Rinehart, and Winston.

Breggin, P. R. (1979). *Electro-shock: Its Brain-disabling Effects.* New York: Springer.

Brody, M. W. (1959). *Observations on "Direct Analysis."* New York: Vantage Press.

Burlingham, D. (1952). *Twins.* New York: International Universities Press.

Campbell, D. T. (1970). Experimental and Quasi-experimental Designs for Psychotherapy Research. Address presented at the Society for Psychotherapy Research, Chicago, June.

Cancro, R. (1968). Thought disorder and schizophrenia. *Diseases of the Nervous System* 29:846–849.

—— (1969). Clinical prediction of outcome in schizophrenia. *Comprehensive Psychiatry* 10:349–354.

Carter, R. E. (1966). The Measurement of Emotional Health Through the Use of Estavan's Modified Paired Comparison Technique. MA dissertation, Michigan State University.

Cerletti, U. (1950). Old and new information about electroshock. *American Journal of Psychiatry* 107:87–94.

Ciompi, L. (1980). Catamnesic long-term study on the course of life and aging of schizophrenics. *Schizophrenia Bulletin* 6:606–617.

Clark, R. A., and Sensibar, M. R. (1955). The relationship between symbolic and manifest projections of sexuality with some incidental correlates. *Journal of Abnormal and Social Psychology* 50:327–334.

Davidson, G. M. (1936). Concerning schizophrenic and manic-depressive psychosis associated with pregnancy and childbirth. *American Journal of Psychiatry.* 92:1331–1346.

Denny, M. R., and Ratner, S. C. (1970). *Comparative Psychology.* Homewood, Ill.: Dorsey.

Doane, J. A., West, K. L., Goldstein, M. J., Rodnick, E. H., and Jones, J. E. (1980). Parental affective style and communication deviance as predictors of subsequent schizophrenia spectrum disorders in vulnerable adolescents. Department of Psychology, UCLA, Los Angeles, CA.

Duff, R. S., and Hollingshead, A. B. (1968). *Sickness and Society.* New York: Harper and Row.

Dunham, H. W. (1965). Community and schizophrenia: an epidemiological analysis. *Lafayette Clinic Monographs in Psychiatry.* Detroit: Wayne State University Press.

Dunnett, C. W. (1955). A multiple comparison procedure for comparing several treatments with a control. *Journal of the American Statistical Association* 50:1096–1122.

Edwards, A. L. (1954). Experiments: their planning and execution. In *Handbook of Social Psychology.* ed. G. Lindzey. Reading, Mass.: Addison-Wesley.

Eissler, K. R. (1952). Remarks on the psychoanalysis of schizophrenics. In *Psychotherapy with Schizophrenics.* eds. E. Brody and F. C. Redlich. New York: International Universities Press.

Ekstein, R. (1971). *The Challenge: Despair and Hope in the Conquest of Inner Space.* New York: Brunner/Mazel.

Ellis, A. (1959). New light on masturbation. In *Sex Without Guilt.* pp. 19–29. New York: Hillman.

Erikson, E. H. (1963). *Childhood and Society.* 2d ed. New York: Norton.

Evans, A. L. (1976). Personality Characteristics of Child-abusing Mothers. Unpublished PhD dissertation, Michigan State University.

Fairbairn, R. W. D. (1954). *An Object-Relations Theory or Personality: Psychoanalytic Studies of the Personality.* New York: Basic Books.

Farber, L. H., and Fisher, C. (1943). An experimental approach to dream psychology through the use of hypnosis. *Psychoanalytic Quarterly* 12:202–216.

Farberow, N. L., Shneidman, F. S., and Leonard, C. V. (1961). Suicide among schizophrenic mental hospital patients. In *The Cry for Help*. ed. N. L. Farberow and E. S. Shneidman. pp. 78–109. New York: Mc-Graw-Hill.

Federn, P. (1952). *Ego Psychology and the Psychoses*. New York: Basic Books.

Feinsilver, D. B., and Gunderson, J. G. (1975). Psychotherapy for schizophrenics: is it indicated? In *Psychotherapy of Schizophrenia*. ed. J. G. Gunderson and L. R. Mosher. pp. 403–430. New York: Aronson.

Feldman, M. J., and Drasgow, J. (1951). A visual-verbal test for schizophrenia. *Psychiatric Quarterly Supplement* 25:55–64.

Fenichel, O. (1939). *Problems of Psychoanalytic Technique*. Albany, N.Y.: Psychoanalytic Quarterly.

—— (1945). *The Psychoanalytic Theory of Neurosis*. New York: Norton.

Ferenczi, S. (1950a). Introjection and transference. In *Sex in Psychoanalysis*. pp. 35–93. New York: Brunner/Mazel.

—— (1950b). On obscene words. In *Sex in Psychoanalysis*. pp. 132–153. New York: Brunner/Mazel.

—— (1950c). The ontogenesis of symbols. In *Sex in Psychoanalysis, Selected Papers. Vol. I*. pp. 276–281. New York: Basic Books.

—— (1953). To whom does one relate one's dream? In *Further Contributions to the Theory and Technique of Psychoanalysis*. p. 349. New York: Basic Books.

Forsythe, A. B., Engleman, L., Jennrich, R., and May, P. R. A. (1973). A stopping rule for variable selection in multiple regression. *Journal of the American Statistical Association* 68:75–77.

Fraiberg, S., Adelson, E., Shapiro, V. (1975). Ghosts in the nursery. *Journal of Child Psychology* 14:387–421.

French, T. H. (1954). The integrative process in dreams. In *The Integration of Behavior. Vol. 2*. Chicago: University of Chicago Press.

Freud, S. (1892). A case of successful treatment by hypnotism. *Complete Psychological Works. Vol. 1*. pp. 115–130. London: Hogarth, 1966.

—— (1900). *The Interpretation of Dreams*. New York: Macmillan, 1950.

—— (1911). Psychoanalytic notes upon an autobiographical account of a case of paranoia (dementia paranoides). *Collected Papers. Vol. 3*. pp. 316–357. London: Hogarth and the Institute for Psychoanalysis, 1950.

—— (1915). A case of paranoia counter to psychoanalytic theory. *Complete Psychological Works. Vol. 14*. pp. 262–300. London: Hogarth, 1957.

—— (1916). *A General Introduction to Psychoanalysis.* New York: Liveright, 1935.

—— (1931). Female sexuality. *Collected Papers. Vol. 5.* p. 253. London: Hogarth and the Institute for Psychoanalysis, 1950.

—— (1933). *New Introductory Lectures on Psychoanalysis.* New York: Norton.

—— (1937). Analysis terminable and interminable. *Collected Papers. Vol. V.* pp. 316–357. London: Hogarth and the Institute for Psycho-analysis, 1950.

Friedberg, J. (1975). *Shock Treatment Is Not Good for Your Brain.* San Francisco: Glide Publications.

Friedlander, K. (1940). On the "longing to die." *International Journal of Psycho-Analysis* 21:416–426.

Fromm, E. (1951). *The Forgotten Language.* New York: Rinehart.

Fromm-Reichmann, F. (1947). Transference problems in schizophrenia. In *Contemporary Psychopathology.* ed. S. S. Tomkins. pp. 371–380. Cambridge, Mass.: Harvard University Press.

—— (1950). *Principles of Intensive Psychotherapy.* Chicago: University of Chicago Press.

Gendlin, E. T. (1967). Therapeutic procedures in dealing with schizo-phrenics. In *The Therapeutic Relationship and Its Impact.* ed. C. R. Rogers, E. T. Gendlin, D. J. Kiesler, and C. B. Truax. Madison, Wisc.: University of Wisconsin Press.

—— (1973). Discussion of "Psychotherapy Is Effective With Schizo-phrenics." Symposium, American Psychological Association Con-vention, Montreal, August 28.

——, and Rogers, C. R. (1967). The design of the research. In *The Therapeutic Relationship and Its Impact: A Study of Psychotherapy with Schizophrenics.* ed. C. R. Rogers, E. T. Gendlin, D. J. Kiesler, and C. B. Truax. Chapter 2. pp. 23–28. Madison, Wisc.: University of Wisconsin Press.

Gilman, T. T., Marcose, F. L., and Moore, A. U. (1950). Animal hypnosis: a study in the induction of tonic immobility in animals. *Journal of Comparative and Physiological Psychology* 43:99–111.

Giovacchini, P. L. (1979). *Treatment of Primitive Mental States.* New York: Aronson.

Goldstein, A. P. (1962). *Therapist-Patient Expectancies in Psychotherapy.* New York: Pergamon Press.

Goldstein, K. (1954). The Psychology of Schizophrenia. Lecture, Prince-ton University.

Goldstein, M. J., et al. (1975). Long lasting phenothiazines and social therapy in community treatment of acute schizophrenics. *Psychopharmacology Bulletin* 11:37–38.

Grace, W. J., and Graham, D. T. (1952). Relationship of specific attitudes and emotions to certain bodily states. *Psychosomatic Medicine* 14: 243–251.

Greenblatt, M. (1977). Efficacy of ECT in affective and schizophrenic illness. *American Journal of Psychiatry* 134:1001–1005.

Grier, W. H., and Cobbs, P. M. (1968). *Black Rage.* New York: Bantam Books.

Grinker, K. R., and Spiegel, J. P. (1965). *Men Under Stress.* New York: McGraw-Hill.

Grinspoon, L., Ewalt, J. R., and Shader, R. I. (1972). *Schizophrenia, Pharmacotherapy, and Psychotherapy.* Baltimore: Williams and Wilkins.

Guilford, J. P. (1954). *Psychometric Methods.* New York: McGraw-Hill.

Gulliksen, H., and Tukey, J. W. (1957). Reliability for the Law of Comparative Judgment. Technical report. Princeton: Princeton University Press.

Gunderson, J. G. (1977). Drugs and psychosocial treatment of schizophrenia revisited. *Journal of Continuing Education in Psychiatry* 38: 25–40.

———, Mosher, L. R. eds. (1975). *Psychotherapy of Schizophrenia.* New York: Aronson.

Guntrip, H. (1969). *Schizoid Phenomena, Object Relations, and the Self.* New York: International Universities Press.

Hall, C. S. (1953a). A cognitive theory of dream symbols. *Journal of General Psychology* 48:169–186.

——— (1953b). *The Meaning of Dreams.* New York: Harper and Row.

Hartmann, H. (1964). *Essays on Ego-Psychology.* New York: International University Press.

Hauri, P. (1977). *The Sleep Disturbances* Kalamazoo, Mich.: Upjohn.

Hebb, D. O. (1951). The role of neurological ideas in psychology. *Journal of Personality* 20:39–55.

Hendrick, I. (1940). Suicide as wish-fulfillment. *Psychiatric Quarterly* 14:30–42.

Heston, L. (1966). Psychiatric disorders in foster home reared children of schizophrenic mothers. *British Journal of Psychiatry* 112:819–825.

——— (1970). The genesis of schizophrenia and schizoid disease. *Science* 167:249–256.

Hollingshead, A. B., and Redlich, F. C. (1958). *Social Class and Mental Illness*. New York: Wiley.

Horwitz, L. (1974). *Clinical Prediction in Psychotherapy*. New York: Aronson.

Huxley, A. (1954). *The Doors of Perception*. New York: Harper and Row.

Institute of Medicine (1979). *Sleeping Pills, Insomnia, and Medical Practice*. Washington, D.C.: National Academy of Sciences.

Jacobi, J. (1949). *The Psychology of Jung*. New Haven: Yale University Press.

—— (1955). The Symbolism of Numbers. Unpublished lectures delivered at the C. G. Jung Institute, Zurich, January 28 and February 4, as part of her course, "Pictures from the Unconscious." (Notes transcribed and made available to the author through the courtesy of Dr. I. E. Alexander of Princeton University.)

Jensen, V. W., and Petty, T. A. (1958). The fantasy of being rescued in suicide. *Psychoanalytic Quarterly* 27:327–339.

Jones, E. (1951). On "dying together" with special reference to Heinrich von Kleist's suicide. In *Essays in Applied Psychoanalysis. Vol. I.* pp. 9–15. London: Hogarth.

Jones, M. (1953). *The Therapeutic Community*. New York: Basic Books.

Jung, C. G. (1915). *The Theory of Psychoanalysis*. New York: Nervous and Mental Disease Publishing Co.

—— (1920). *Collected Papers on Analytical Psychology*. London: Bailliere, Tindall, and Cox.

—— (1953). *Psychology and Alchemy*. New York: Pantheon.

—— (1954). *The Practice of Psychotherapy*. New York: Pantheon.

—— (1956). *Mysterium Coniunctionis*. Zurich: Rascher.

Kallman, K. J. (1938). *The Genetics of Schizophrenia*. Locust Valley, N.Y.: Augustin.

Karon, B. P. (1958). Some clinical notes on the significance of the number four. *Psychiatric Quarterly* 32:281–288.

—— (1960). A clinical note on the significance of an "oral" trauma. *Journal of Abnormal and Social Psychology* 61:480–481.

—— (1963). The resolution of acute schizophrenic reaction: a contribution to the development of non-classical psychotherapeutic techniques. *Psychotherapy: Theory, Research and Practice* 1:27–43.

—— (1964a). A note on the treatment of age as a variable in regression equations. *American Statistician* 18:27–28.

—— (1964b). Suicidal tendency as the wish to hurt someone else, and resulting treatment technique. *Journal of Individual Psychology* 20: 206–212.

—— (1968). Problems of validities. In *Projective Techniques in Personality Assessment*. ed. A. I. Rabin. pp. 85–111. New York: Springer.

—— (1975). *Black Scars*. New York: Springer.

——, and O'Grady, P. (1969). Intellectual test changes in schizophrenic patients in the first six months of treatment. *Psychotherapy: Theory, Research, and Practice* 6:88–96.

——, and O'Grady, P. (1970). Quantified judgments of mental health from the Rorschach, TAT, and clinical status interview by means of a scaling technique. *Journal of Consulting and Clinical Psychology* 34:229–235.

——, and Rosberg, J. (1958a). Study of the mother-child relationship in a case of paranoid schizophrenia. *American Journal of Psychotherapy* 12:522–533.

——, and Rosberg, J. (1958b). The homosexual urges in schizophrenia. *Psychoanalysis and Psychoanalytic Review* 45:50–56.

——, and Saunders, D. R. (1958). Some implications of the Eysenck-Prell study of "The inheritance of neuroticism:" a critique. *Journal of Mental Science* 104:350–358.

——, and VandenBos, G. R. (1970). Experience, medication, and the effetiveness of the psychotherapy with schizophrenics: a note on Drs. May and Tuma's conclusions. *British Journal of Psychiatry* 116:427–428.

——, and VandenBos, G. R. (1972). The consequence of psychotherapy for schizophrenic patients. *Psychotherapy: Theory, Research, and Practice* 9:111–120.

——, and VandenBos, G. R. (1975). Treatment costs of psychotherapy versus medication for schizophrenics. *Professional Psychology* 6: 293–298.

——, and VandenBos, G. R. (1977). Psychotherapeutic technique and the economically poor patient. *Psychotherapy: Theory, Research, and Practice* 14:169–180.

——, and VandenBos, G. R. (1978). Psychotherapy with schizophrenics requires relevant training. *Schizophrenia Bulletin* 4:480–483.

Kernberg, O. (1975). *Borderline Conditions and Pathological Narcissism*. New York: Aronson.

—— (1976). *Object Relations Theory and Clinical Psychoanalysis*. New York: Aronson.

Kety, S. (1959a). Biochemical theories of schizophrenia. Part I. *Science* 129:1528–1532.

—— (1959b). Biochemical theories of schizophrenia. Part II. *Science* 129:1590–1596.

Kiev, A. (1968). *Curanderismo*. New York: Free Press.

Kirk, A. R. (1976). Socio-psychological Factors in Attempted Suicide Among Urban Black Males. PhD dissertation, Michigan State University, Department of Psychology.

Klein, M. (1948). *Contributions to Psychoanalysis, 1931–1945*. London: Hogarth.

Klerman, G. L., Sharaf, M. R., Holzman, M., and Levinson, D. J. (1960). Sociopsychological characteristics of resident psychiatrists and their use of drug therapy. *American Journal of Psychiatry* 117:111–117.

Kohut, H. (1971). *The Analysis of the Self*. New York: International Universities Press.

—— (1977). *The Restoration of the Self*. New York: International Universities Press.

Krystal, H. (1975). Affect tolerance. In *Annual of Psychoanalysis. Vol. 3.* ed. J. Frosch and N. Ross. New York: International Universities Press.

Levy, D. M. (1943). *Maternal Overprotection*. New York: Columbia University Press.

Liberson, W. T. (1948). Prolonged hypnotic states with local signs induced in guinea pigs. *Science* 108:40–41.

Lidz, T. (1973). *The Origin and Treatment of Schizophrenic Disorders*. New York: Basic Books.

—— (1977). Reply to Kety, et al. *Schizophrenia Bulletin* 3:522–526.

Luborsky, L. (1962). The patient's personality and psychotherapeutic change. In *Research in Psychotherapy. Vol. 2.* ed. H. Strupp and L. Luborsky. Washington, D.C.: American Psychological Association.

—— (1977). Curative factors in psychoanalytic and psychodynamic psychotherapy. In *Psychiatry: Areas of Promise and Advancement.* ed. J. P. Brady, J. Mendels, M. Orne, and W. Rieger. New York: Spectrum.

Magaro, P. A. (1976). The cultural context of madness and its treatment. In *The Construction of Madness.* ed. P. A. Magaro. Elmsford, N.Y.: Pergamon.

Mahler, M. S., Pine, F., and Bergman, A. (1975). *The Psychological Birth of the Human Infant*. London: Hutchinson.

Malan, D. H. (1963). *A Study of Brief Psychotherapy*. London: Tavistock.

—— (1976a). *Toward the Validation of Dynamic Psychotherapy*. New York: Plenum.

—— (1976b). *Frontiers of Brief Psychotherapy*. New York: Plenum.

——, Bacal, H. A., Heath, E. S., and Balfour, F. H. (1968). A study of psychodynamic changes in untreated neurotic patients: I. Improvements that are questionable on dynamic criteria. *British Journal of Psychiatry* 114:525-555.

——, Bacal, H. A., Heath, E. S., and Balfour, F. H. (1975). Psychodynamic changes in untreated patients: II. Apparently genuine improvements. *Archives of General Psychiatry* 32:110-126.

Mann, J. (1973). *Time-limited Psychotherapy*. Cambridge, Mass.: Harvard University Press.

May, P. R. A. (1968). *Treatment of Schizophrenia: A Comparative Study of Five Treatment Methods*. New York: Science House.

—— (1974). Psychotherapy research in schizophrenia: another view of present reality. *Schizophrenia Bulletin* 126-132.

—— (1975). Schizophrenia: evaluation of treatment methods. In *Comprehensive Textbook of Psychiatry*. ed. B. M. Freeman, et al. pp. 923-938. Baltimore: Williams and Wilkins.

——, and Tuma, H. H. (1970). Methodological problems in psychotherapy research: observations of the Karon-VandenBos study of psychotherapy and drugs in schizophrenia. *British Journal of Psychiatry* 117:569-650.

——, Tuma, H. H., and Dixon, W. J. (1976). Schizophrenia: a follow-up study of results of treatment: I. Design and other problems. *Archives of General Psychiatry* 33:474-478.

——, Tuma, H. H., Yale, C., Potepan, R., and Dixon, W. J. (1976). Schizophrenia: a follow-up study of results of treatment. *Archives of General Psychiatry* 33:481-486.

McAdams, M. T., Linder, R. L., Lerner, S. E., and Burns, R. S., ed. (1980). *Phencyclidine Abuse Manual*. Los Angeles: University of California, Extension, Los Angeles.

McKie, R. R. (1971). A Clinical Study: Relationship of Anger and Fear to Aggression in Murderers and in Non-violent Offenders. PhD dissertation, Michigan State University, Department of Counseling, Personnel Services, and Educational Psychology.

Meduna, L. J., and Friedman, E. (1939). The convulsive-irritative therapy of psychosis. *Journal of the American Medical Association* 112:501–509.

Melnick, B., and Hurley, J. R. (1969). Distinctive personality attributes of child-abusing mothers. *Journal of Consulting Clinical Psychology* 33:746–749.

Meltzoff, J., and Kornreich, M. (1970). *Research in Psychotherapy.* New York: Atherton.

Menninger, K., Mayman, M., and Pruyser, P. (1963). *The Vital Balance: The Life Process in Mental Health and Illness.* New York: Viking.

Menninger, R. A. (1957). Psychological factors in the choice of medicine as a profession. *Bulletin of the Menninger Clinic* 21:51–58.

Merriam, K. A. (1976). The experience of schizophrenia. In *The Construction of Madness.* ed. P. Magaro. pp. 3–19. Elmsford, N.Y.: Pergamon.

Meyer, R. G., and Karon, B. P. (1967). The schizophrenogenic mother concept and the TAT. *Psychiatry* 30:173–179.

Michel-Hutmacher, R. (1955). Das Körperinnere in der Vorstellung der Kinder. *Schweizerische Zeitschrift fuer Psychologie und ihre Anwendungen* 14:1–26.

Miner, J. B. (1957). *Intelligence in the United States.* New York: Springer.

Mitchell, K. M. (1968). An analysis of the schizophrenic mother concept by means of the TAT. *Journal of Abnormal Psychology* 73:571–574.

—— (1969). Concept of "pathogenesis" in parents of schizophrenic and normal children. *Journal of Abnormal Psychology* 74:423–424.

—— (1970). The Concept of "Pathogenesis" Among Parents of Schizophrenic, Delinquent, and Normal Children. Unpublished manuscript, University of Arkansas.

Mosher, L. R. (1975a). Evaluation of psychosocial treatments. In *Psychotherapy of Schizophrenia.* ed. J. G. Gunderson and L. R. Mosher. pp. 253–268. New York: Aronson.

—— (1975b). Psychotherapy research. In *Psychotherapy of Schizophrenia.* ed. J. G. Gunderson and L. R. Mosher. pp. 243–252. New York: Aronson.

Moss, L. M., and Hamilton, D. M. (1956). The psychotherapy of the suicidal patient. *American Journal of Psychiatry* 112:814–820.

Mosteller, C. F. (1951). Remarks on the method of paired comparisons: I. The least squares solution assuming equal standard deviations and equal correlations. *Psychometrika* 16:3–9.

Neill, A. S. (1960). *Summerhill: A Radical Approach to Child Rearing.* New York: Hart.

Nichols, N. (1970). The Relationship Between Degree of Maternal Pathogenicity and Severity of Ego Impairment in Schizophrenic Offspring. Unpublished PhD dissertation, University of Michigan.

Niederland, W. G. (1959a). Schreber: father and son. *Psychoanalytic Quarterly* 11:151–169.

—— (1959b). The "miracled-up" world of Schreber's childhood. In *Psychoanalytic Study of the Child*. pp. 383–413. New York: International Universities Press.

—— (1972). The Schreber case sixty years later. *International Journal of Psychiatry* 10:79–84.

Nolan, E. G. (1960). Uniqueness in Monozygotic Twins. PhD thesis, Princeton University, Psychology. *Dissertation Abstracts* 21:247.

Pasquarelli, B. (1952). Psychotic reactions to pregnancy. In *Manic-Depressive Psychosis and Allied Conditions*. ed. L. Bellak. New York: Grune and Stratton.

Paul, G. L., and Lentz, R. J. (1977). *Psychosocial Treatment of Chronic Mental Patients: Milieu vs. Social Learning Programs*. Cambridge, Mass.: Harvard University Press.

Perry, J. W. (1961). Image, complex, and transference in schizophrenia. In *Psychotherapy of the Psychoses*. ed. A. Burton. New York: Basic Books.

Porteus, R. G. (1959). *The Maze Test and Clinical Psychology*. Palo Alto, Calif.: Pacific Books.

Potash, H. (1964). Schizophrenic Interaction and the Double Bind. PhD thesis, Michigan State University, Department of Psychology.

Prouty, G. F. (1976). Pre-therapy: a method of treating pre-expressive retarded and psychotic patients. *Psychotherapy: Theory, Research, and Practice* 13:290–294.

Rabin, A. I., and King, G. F. (1958). Psychological studies. In *Schizophrenia: A Review of the Syndrome*. ed. L. Bellak. Plainfield, N.J.: Logos.

Rapaport, D. (1967). *The Collected Papers of David Rapaport*. New York: Basic Books.

Rappaport, M., et al. (1980). Schizophrenics for whom phenothiazines may be contra-indicated or unnecessary. In *Controversy and Psychiatry*. ed H.K.H. Brody and P. Brady. Philadelphia: Saunders.

Ratner, S. C. (1967). Comparative aspects of Hypnosis. In *Handbook of Clinical and Experimental Hypnosis*. ed. J. E. Gordon. New York: Macmillan.

—— (1975). Animals' defenses: fighting in predator-prey relations. In

Nonverbal Communication of Aggression. ed. Pliner, Krames, and Alloway. New York: Plenum.

——, and Thompson, W. R. (1960). Immobility reactions of domestic fowls as a function of age and prior experience. *Animal Behavior* 8:186–191.

Robins, E., Gassner, S., Kayes, J., Willmaan, R. H., and Murphy, G. E. (1959). The communication of suicidal intent. *American Journal of Psychiatry* 115:724–733.

Rogers, C. R. (1942). *Counseling and Psychotherapy.* Boston: Houghton-Mifflin.

—— (1951). *Client-centered Therapy.* Boston: Houghton-Mifflin.

—— (1961). *On Becoming a Person.* Boston: Houghton-Mifflin.

——, Gendlin, E. T., Kiesler, D. J., and Truax, C. B. (1967). *The Therapeutic Relationship and Its Impact: A Study of Psychotherapy with Schizophrenics.* Madison, Wisc.: University of Wisconsin Press.

Rogler, L. H., and Hollingshead, A. B. (1965). *Trapped: Families and Schizophrenia.* New York: Wiley.

Rosberg, J., and Karon, B. P. (1958). The oedipus complex in an apparently deteriorated case of schizophrenia. *Journal of Abnormal and Social Psychology* 57:221–225.

——, and Karon, B. P. (1959). A direct analytic contribution to the understanding of post-partum psychoses. *Psychiatric Quarterly* 33:296–304.

Rosen, J. N. (1953). *Direct Analysis.* New York: Grune and Stratton.

Rosenfeld, H. A. (1965). *Psychotic States: A Psychoanalytic Approach.* New York: International Universities Press.

Rosenthal, D., and Kety, S. ed. (1968). *The Transmission of Schizophrenia.* Elmsford, N.Y.: Pergamon.

Sakel, M. (1938). The nature and origin of the hypoglycemic treatment of psychoses. *American Journal of Psychiatry* 94(supp.):24–40.

Sanua, V. (1969). Sociocultural aspects. In *The Schizophrenic Syndrome.* ed. L. Bellak and L. Loeb. pp. 256–310. New York: Grune and Stratton.

Schatzman, M. (1973). *Soul Murder: Persecution in the Family.* New York: Random House.

Scheflen, A. E. (1961). *A Psychotherapy of Schizophrenia: Direct Analysis.* Springfield, Ill.: Thomas.

Schilder, P. (1935). *The Image and Appearance of the Human Body.* London: Kegan Paul.

Schmideberg, M. (1948). A note on suicide. *Psychoanalytic Review* 35: 181–183.

Searles, H. F. (1965). *Collected Papers on Schizophrenia and Related Subjects.* New York: International Universities Press.

Sechehaye, M. A. (1951). *Symbolic Realization.* New York: International Universities Press.

Segal, H. (1950). Some aspects of the analysis of a schizophrenic. *International Journal of Psychoanalysis* 31:268–278.

———— (1977). *Klein.* Glasgow, Scotland: Williams Collins.

Seidenberg, R., and Harris, L. (1949). Prenatal symptoms in postpartum psychotic reactions. *Psychiatric Quarterly* 23:715–719.

Shapiro, A. K. (1971). Placebo effects in medicine, psychotherapy, and psychoanalysis. In *Handbook of Psychotherapy and Behavior Change.* ed. A. Bergin and S. Garfield. New York: Wiley.

Siassi, I. (1974). Psychotherapy with women and men of lower classes. In *Women in Therapy.* ed. V. Franks, and V. Burtle. New York: Brunner/Mazel.

Siegel, M. (1976). Confidentiality. *Clinical Psychologist* 30:1–23.

Silverberg, W. V. (1952). *Childhood Experience and Personal Destiny.* New York: Springer.

Singer, M., and Wynne, L. (1965a). Thought disorder and family relations of schizophrenics: III. Methodology using projective techniques. *Archives of General Psychiatry* 12:187–200.

————, Wynne, L. (1965b). Thought disorder and family relations of schizophrenics: IV. Results and implications. *Archives of General Psychiatry* 12:201–212.

————, Wynne, L. (1966). Principles for scoring communication defects and deviances in parents of schizophrenics: Rorschach and TAT scoring manuals. *Psychiatry* 29:260–288.

Spitz, R. (1965). *The First Year of Life.* New York: International Universities Press.

Srole, L., Langner, T. S., Michael, S. T., Kirkpatrick, P., Opler, M. K., and Rennie, T. A. (1978). *Mental Health in the Metropolis.* ed. L. Srole and A. K. Fischer. New York: New York University Press.

Stoller, R. J. (1968). *Sex and Gender.* New York: Aronson.

Sullivan, H. S. (1953). *The Interpersonal Theory of Psychiatry.* New York: Norton.

———— (1962). *Schizophrenia as a Human Process.* New York: Norton.

Toch, H. (1975). *Men in Crisis.* Chicago: Aldine.

Tomkins, S. S. (1947). *The Thematic Apperception Test.* New York: Grune and Stratton.

—— (1962). *Affect, Imagery, and Consciousness. Vol. I.* New York: Springer.

—— (1963). *Affect, Imagery, and Consciousness. Vol. II.* New York: Springer.

Tuma, A. H., and May, P. R. A. (1975). Psychotherapy, drugs, and therapist experience in the treatment of schizophrenia: a critique of the Michigan state project. *Psychotherapy: Theory, Research, and Practice* 12:138–142.

VandenBos, G. R., and Karon, B. P. (1971). Pathogenesis: a new therapist dimension related to therapeutic effectiveness. *Journal of Personality Assessment* 35:252–260.

Vaughn, C. E., and Leff, J. P. (1976). The influence of family and social factors on the course of psychiatric illness. *British Journal of Psychiatry* 129:125–137.

Vernon, P. E. (1936). The matching method applied to investigations of personality. *Psychological Bulletin* 33:149–177.

Volkan, V. D. (1976). *Primitive Internalized Object Relations.* New York: International Universities Press.

Walton, H. J. (1958). Suicidal behavior in depressive illness: a study of etiological factors in suicide. *Journal of Mental Science* 104:884.

Wender, P. H. (1969). The role of genetics in the etiology of the schizophrenics. *American Journal of Orthopsychiatry* 39:447–458.

——, Rosenthal, D., and Kety, S. S. (1975). Distorted picture. *Contemporary Psychology* 20:986–987.

——, Rosenthal, D., and Kety, S. S. (1976). Wender et al. reply. *Contemporary Psychology* 21:74–75.

——, Rosenthal, D., Zahn, T., and Kety, S. (1971). The psychiatric adjustment of the adopting parents of schizophrenics. *American Journal of Psychiatry* 127:1013–1018.

Wessman, A. E., and Ricks, D. F. (1966). *Mood and Personality.* New York: Holt, Rinehart and Winston.

Wexler, M. (1951). The structural problem in schizophrenia. In *Psychotherapy with Schizophrenics.* ed. E. B. Brody and F. C. Redlich. pp. 179–201. New York: International Universities Press.

—— (1975). Comment on the five treatment comparative study. In *Psychotherapy of Schizophrenia.* ed. J. G. Gunderson and L. R. Mosher. New York: Aronson.

Whiting, J. W. M., and Child, I. L. (1953). *Child Training and Personality: A Cross-Cultural Study*. New Haven: Yale University Press.

Will, O. A. (1961). Process, psychotherapy, and schizophrenia. In *Psychotherapy of the Psychoses*. ed. A. Burton. New York: Basic Books.

Williams, R. and Karacan, I. ed. (1978). *Sleep Disturbances: Diagnoses and Treatment*. New York: John Wiley and Sons.

Wowkanech, N. K. (1973). Changes in Affect Expressed on the TAT by Schizophrenics Before and After Psychotherapy. MA thesis, Michigan State University.

Wyatt, R. J., Termini, B. A., and Davis, J. (1971). Biochemical and sleep studies of schizophrenia: I. Biochemical studies. *Schizophrenia Bulletin* 4:10–44.

Wynne, L. and Singer, M. (1963a). Thought disorder and family relations of schizophrenics. I: A research strategy. *Archives of General Psychiatry* 9:191–198.

————, Singer, M. (1963b). Thought disorder and family relations of schizophrenics. II: A classification of forms of thinking. *Archives of General Psychiatry*. 9:199–206.

Yi-Chuang, L. (1962). Contradictory parental expectations in schizophrenia: dependence and responsibility. *AMA Archives of General Psychiatry* 6:219–234.

Index